Medieval Academy Reprints for Teaching 2

Medieval Academy Reprints for Teaching

Translations and
Introduction by
R.K. Gordon

THE STORY OF TROILUS

AS TOLD BY

BENÔIT DE SAINTE-MAURE

GIOVANNI BOCCACCIO

GEOFFREY CHAUCER

ROBERT HENRYSON

Published by University of Toronto Press
Toronto Buffalo London
in association with the Medieval Academy of America

First published by J.M. Dent and Sons Ltd in 1934
This edition reprinted from the 1964 Dutton paperback edition by arrange-
ment with J.M. Dent & Sons Ltd

Canadian Cataloguing in Publication Data

Main entry under title:

The Story of Troilus as told by Benoît de Sainte-
Maure, Giovanni Boccaccio, Geoffrey Chaucer,
Robert Henryson

(Mediaeval Academy reprints for teaching; 2)
Reprint of the 1964 ed. published by Dutton.
Contents: Le roman de Troie / Benoît de Sainte-Maure
– Il Filostrato / G. Boccaccio – Troilus and
Criseyde / G. Chaucer – The testament of Cresseid /
R. Henryson – Glossary.
ISBN 0-8020-6368-3

1. Troilus – Legends. I. Gordon, Robert K., 1887–
1973. II. Mediaeval Academy of America. III. Series.

PN57.T84S76 1978   808.81'9'351   C79-003432-8

TO
J. P. G.

PREFACE

In translating the *Filostrato* I was kindly helped in some passages by Mrs. E. K. Broadus. The rendering of the poem by Messrs. Griffin and Myrick has been in my hands frequently and profitably.

By the kind permission of the Oxford University Press, the text of Chaucer and Henryson used here is that of Professor Skeat.

R. K. G.

CONTENTS

INTRODUCTION

HIGH on iron pillars in Chaucer's House of Fame stand those who bear up the story of Troy: Homer, Dares, Dictys, Lollius, Guido, Geoffrey of Monmouth, and Virgil. But among these historians there is not entire harmony and good feeling:

> Oon seyde, Omere made lyes,
> Feyninge in his poetryes,
> And was to Grekes favorable;
> Therfor held he hit but fable.

There were three objections to Homer: he represented the gods fighting with men, he was thought to be unfair to the Trojans (the ancestors, so it was believed, of the peoples of western Europe), and he had been born too late to be an eye-witness of the events he described. Medieval readers thought a more reliable account of what had taken place at Troy was to be found in two small books of Latin prose: *De Excidio Trojae Historia* by Dares Phrygius, who gave the Trojan side, and *Ephemeris Belli Trojani* by Dictys Cretensis, who spoke for the Greeks.

Dares is prefaced by a letter purporting to be written by Cornelius Nepos to his uncle Sallust. In it the writer declares that he came upon the book in Athens, and translated it faithfully into Latin. He adds that Dares lived in Troy during the siege,[1] and wrote from first-hand knowledge. The book, though it consists of only forty-four very short chapters, begins with Jason's expedition and goes on to the fall of Troy. Dictys also is provided with a romantic prefatory letter from Lucius Septimius to Quintus Aradius. It tells us that, when Dictys died in Crete, his book (written in Phoenician characters) was placed in a casket and buried with him. In the reign of Nero an earthquake broke open the tomb and exposed the casket to view. Found by some shepherds, it was brought to Nero. By his orders it was transcribed into Greek letters and then placed in a library. The Greek was then rendered into Latin by Septimius. In the book itself Dictys tells us

[1] There is a Dares in Homer in the fifth book of the Iliad.

that he was with the Greeks at the siege of Troy, and that he supplemented what he saw for himself by questioning Ulysses and others. He includes in his story an account of the fortunes of the Greek leaders after the destruction of Troy.

In their present form these books are not very old; the Latin of Dares probably belongs to the sixth century A.D., that of Dictys to the fourth century A.D. But behind the romantic statements in the prefaces there probably lies some truth. Our short, disjointed Dares is very likely an abridgment of a fuller Latin text, now lost. That fuller text may, in its turn, be the descendant of a Greek version. There is also good evidence that our Dictys is a translation of a Greek original.

Of the two books, Dares was the more popular. In a list of notable figures on the Trojan side he includes: 'Troilum magnum, pulcherrimum, pro aetate valentem, fortem, cupidum virtutis'; and in the following chapter (xiii), in a similar catalogue of Greeks, we find: 'Diomedem fortem, quadratum, corpore honesto, vultu austero, in bello acerrimum, clamosum, cerebro calido, inpatientem, audacem,' and 'Briseidam formosam, non alta statura, candidam, capillo flavo et molli, superciliis junctis, oculis venustis, corpore aequali, blandam, affabilem, verecundam, animo simplici, piam.'

These are three of the chief persons of our story. Some of their qualities, so baldly listed here, still persist nearly a thousand years later in Chaucer's portraits. His Diomede

> Was in his nedes prest and corageous;
> With sterne voys and mighty limes square,
> Hardy, testif, strong, and chevalrous
> Of dedes lyk his fader Tideus,
> And som men seyn he was of tunge large.

And his Criseyde, like Briseida, is of middling height and has joined brows. In 'capillo flavo et molli' lies the germ of Chaucer's line:

> The mighty tresses of hir sonnish heres.[1]

But in our Dares, however it may have been in a lost longer

---

[1] Chaucer refers to Dares more than once, but there is no proof that he drew upon him directly for any of his material. Indeed, it is likely that by Dares he means a poem written at the end of the twelfth century by Joseph of Exeter. It is an elaborated version of Dares and appears to have passed under the name of Dares Phrygius. From it Chaucer took some details for the portraits of Diomede, Criseyde, and Troilus in Book V, lines 799–840.

version, these three persons are not linked by any story. That came six centuries later (*c.* 1160) in Benoît de Sainte-Maure's *Roman de Troie*. This long poem—over thirty thousand lines—is based, Benoît tells us, chiefly on Dares and in a less degree on Dictys. Did Benoît have before him an earlier and longer version of Dares, and, if so, did that version contain the love-story of Troilus and Briseida? We do not know. But, whether Benoît invented the tale or not, his is the earliest form of the story that has come down to us. True, it makes a very small part of the *Roman de Troie*. Nor is it told as a continuous unbroken episode. It consists of several passages, thrust apart by the intrusion of other matters, especially by descriptions of battle. And not only is the story half buried under the mass of 'Troyane gestes,' it is also left half told. It does not begin till the lovers are about to be separated. Their happiness before fortune's wheel had cast them down is implied but not described; and the sorrows of Troilus before he won his lady are not even implied.

Among the historians of the Trojan war mentioned by Chaucer is Guido de Columpnis or de Columna. He was a judge at Messina in Sicily from 1257 to 1280. In 1287 he completed his *Historia Trojana,* an account of the Trojan war in Latin prose. Though he frequently cites Dares and Dictys as his sources and makes no mention of Benoît, it has been clearly proved that his main reliance was on the French poem. Wishing to be regarded as a serious historian, he probably considered it more dignified and impressive to refer to authorities older than Benoît and not written in the vernacular. Guido's history, though heavy and moralizing in tone as compared with Benoît, was accepted as the standard work on the subject. One of its English descendants is Lydgate's *Troy-book*.

Out of Benoît and Guido came Boccaccio's *Il Filostrato.*[1] Sad and lonely in Naples because of the absence of his lady, Maria d'Aquino, the young Boccaccio thought, as Chaucer's Troilus did:

> O blisful lord Cupyde,
> Whanne I the proces have in my memorie,
> How thou me hast werreyed on every syde,
> Men mighte a book make of it, lyk a storie.

Turning over in his mind old tales of parted and unhappy

---

[1] 'The One Prostrated by Love.'

lovers, he found none better suited to help him express his own grief than the story of Troilus.   In his hands it ceased to be a mere episode in a vast Troy-book.   It now had a poem to itself.   Boccaccio completed the story by describing the love of Troilus and Criseida[1] before their parting.   He is the first

> The double sorwe of Troilus to tellen,
> That was the king Priamus sone of Troye,
> In lovinge, how his aventures fellen
> Fro wo to wele, and after out of joye.

Into the old story Boccaccio put his own longings and sorrows.   Troilus is the central figure, and Troilus is Boccaccio.   In Benoît we hear almost nothing of the grief of Troilus after he has lost his mistress.   It was left for Boccaccio to show how Troilus

> mounted the Troyan walls
> And sigh'd his soul toward the Grecian tents,
> Where Cressid lay that night.

It is Boccaccio that we have also to thank for Pandarus. He is usually with one of the lovers, and his presence enables Boccaccio to make a fuller use of dialogue than he could otherwise have done.   The language of the Italian poem owes very little to Guido or Benoit.   It is likely, however, that in shaping his story Boccaccio took hints from some scenes in Guido and Benoit besides those relating to Troilus and Briseida. When, for example, Boccaccio described how Troilus first saw his lady in the temple, he doubtless remembered the passage in his sources where Achilles sees Polyxena at a religious festival.   But we must also believe that he did not forget that he himself had first seen Maria d'Aquino in the church of San Lorenzo at Naples.   Reading and personal experience both helped to make the poem what it is.

About fifty years later the story was retold by Chaucer in a poem almost half as long again as the *Filostrato*.   But the poem is not only longer; it is also deeper.   The *Filostrato* is the work of a young poet; *Troilus and Criseyde* is the work of a man of middle age and of wide knowledge of both men and

---

[1] In Boccaccio the heroine's name is no longer Briseida, but Criseida. In the Iliad we have Briseis, daughter of Brises, and Chryseis, daughter of Chryses.   The accusative forms are Briseida and Chryseida.   Boccaccio's heroine differs from Benoît's in another respect.   She is a widow.   Boccaccio apparently thought a widow the ideal mistress, as being more free than a married woman and more experienced than a girl.

books. The tone is no longer lyrical and personal. Chaucer does not identify himself with Troilus. He writes of the sorrows and joys of the servants of love, but he is not one of them. He allows himself a smile at the extravagances of 'these loveres.' Comedy and romance live side by side in the poem, and neither injures the other. If the English poem has less intensity and concentration than the Italian it has greater variety and complexity.

Chaucer's imagination has left none of the three chief persons in the story unchanged. Troilus is the least altered, but even he is different. In the scene in the temple, Boccaccio's hero not only mocks at the sufferings of men in love, but he is also cynical about women. Chaucer's hero holds love folly because of its perplexities and sorrows, but he speaks no evil of women.

Pandarus and Criseyde are really new characters. In the Italian poem Pandarus is a Trojan youth, another Troilus. In Chaucer he is Criseyde's uncle, not her cousin, no longer very young, devoted to the lovers but looking at life with different eyes. He mocks at himself as at one who always hops behind in the dance of love. With him comedy and homely speech come into the poem. His talk makes up nearly a quarter of the whole work. It is one of the triumphs of the poem that Chaucer gives us the raciness of prose dialogue without sacrificing the easy flowing music of his verse.

> Quod Pandarus, 'ma dame, god yow see,
> With al your book and al the companye!'
> 'Ey, uncle myn, welcome y-wis,' quod she,
> And up she roos, and by the hond in hye
> She took him faste, and seyde, 'this night thrye,
> To goode mote it turne, of yow I mette!'
> And with that word she doun on bench him sette.

Pandarus is a born manager and delights in his own skill. In the scene at the house of Deiphebus everybody acts as he wishes, and yet nobody

> But God and Pandare wiste al what this mente.

All through the first four books of the poem he is ready with advice to Troilus and Criseyde. He knows what they should do, and he makes them do it. He abounds in energy and resource. It is only when Criseyde's falseness is clear beyond doubt that he is at a loss.

> He nought a word ayein to him answerde;
> For sory of his frendes sorwe he is,
> And shamed, for his nece hath doon a-mis;
> And stant, astoned of these causes tweye,
> As stille as stoon; a word ne coude he seye.

The English Criseyde is far more complex and elusive than the Italian heroine. She is slowly won to love; she yields ground gradually and reluctantly. By deft touches Chaucer refines away the eager sensuality of Boccaccio's character. He adds scenes to the story to show the stages of her surrender. Just after Pandarus has pleaded for his friend, Troilus, returning from a successful sally against the Greeks, rides up the praising street, and

> Criseyda gan al his chere aspyen,
> And leet so softe it in hir herte sinke
> That to hir-self she seyde, 'who yaf me drinke?'

Soon afterwards she listens, in the soft evening light, to the tender song of Antigone in praise of love. And

> every word which that she of hir herde
> She gan to prenten in hir herte faste;
> And ay gan love hir lasse for to agaste
> Than it dide erst, and sinken in hir herte,
> That she wex somwhat able to converte.

And when her women have brought her to her bed and all is quiet, she lies in the stillness with her thoughts. Then

> A nightingale, upon a cedre grene,
> Under the chambre-wal ther as she lay,
> Ful loude sang ayein the mone shene,
> Paraunter, in his briddes wyse, a lay
> Of love, that made hir herte fresh and gay.

And when sleep comes it brings to her the dream of the white eagle who tears out her heart, replacing it with his own. And she feels no pain or fear.

But the depth and sincerity of character that Chaucer gives her make a difficulty. It is not easy to believe that she who called upon

> Simoys, that as an arwe clere
> Thorough Troye rennest ay downward to the see,

to turn back to its source if she should prove false is 'slydinge of corage,' and that, after a short time in the Greek camp, both Troilus and Troy

> Shal knotteles through-out hir herte slyde.

Chaucer puts the responsibility for her conduct on his authorities. He finds it written thus 'in the stories' and cannot alter it; but, he adds,

> if I mighte excuse hir any wyse,
> For she so sory was for hir untrouthe,
> Y-wis, I wolde excuse hir yet for routhe.

Chaucer frequently assures us that he is following his author closely, and twice he gives his name as Lollius. He also tells us that he is translating the story out of Latin. Lollius is mentioned in the *Hous of Fame* as one of the writers on the Trojan war. No medieval reference to him outside of Chaucer has been discovered, and no such writer on Troy is known to us. Probably he never existed. Chaucer's belief in him may have been due to a passage in one of Horace's *Epistles*:

> Troiani belli scriptorem, Maxime Lolli,
> Dum tu declamas Romae, Praeneste relegi.

If this passage came under Chaucer's eyes with one or two slight changes in text, he might easily have read it as a reference to 'Lollius, greatest of writers on the Trojan war.' But this, of course, does not explain why he gives to Lollius the credit due to Boccaccio. He may have wished, as Guido did, to claim the authority of an old Latin writer for his story. But it is hard not to believe that Chaucer's humour is at work when, in some of his most original scenes, he professes the most humble reliance on his source.

William Thynne in his edition of Chaucer (1532) included Robert Henryson's *Testament of Cresseid*, and the poem came to be thought of as a sort of continuation of Chaucer's story. Henryson, one of Chaucer's Scottish disciples, is supposed to have died about 1500. How long before 1500 he wrote the *Testament* we do not know. He tells us how Cresseid, turned off by Diomede, goes to her father's house. Angrily she denounces Venus and Cupid, and the outraged gods punish her with leprosy. The scenes in the lazar-house are of a harsh and powerful realism. When Henryson brings Troilus and Cresseid face to face, he rises to the height of his theme.

After Henryson the story of Troilus was degraded by ballad-makers and others. Criseyde's sad prophecy was fulfilled:

> Allas, of me, unto the worldes ende,
> Shal neither been y-writen nor y-songe
> No good word, for thise bokes wol me shende,
> O rolled shall I been on many a tonge!
> Through-out the world my belle shal be ronge;
> And wommen most wol hate me of alle,
> Allas, that swich a cas me sholde falle!

By the time of Shakespeare, Criseyde had become a mere wanton, and Shakespeare in his play left her such.

BENOÎT DE SAINTE-MAURE:
LE ROMAN DE TROIE

LE ROMAN DE TROIE

. . . Homer, who was a wondrous clerk and wise and learned,
wrote of the destruction, of the great siege, and of the cause
whereby Troy was laid waste, so that it was nevermore the
abode of men. But his book does not tell the truth, for we know
well, beyond any doubt, that he was born a hundred years after
the great hosts met in battle. No wonder if he errs since he
never was there and saw nothing thereof. When he had made
his book and brought it to Athens, there was accordingly
exceeding great debate. They wished to condemn him because
he had made the gods fight with mortal men. That was
accounted folly and wondrous folly in him that he made the gods
fight like human beings against the Trojans, and likewise made
the goddesses fight with the people. And, when they read his
book, many rejected it for that reason. But Homer had such
great fame and wrought so much afterwards, as I find, that his
book was accepted and held in reverence.

A great time afterwards, when Rome had already long
endured, in the time of the worthy Sallust, who was esteemed
so powerful, rich, and nobly born, and a wondrous clerk and
learned, this Sallust, I read, had a very wise nephew. He was
called Cornelius and was learned and trained in letters. He
was much praised; he had a school at Athens. One day he was
looking in a cupboard to find some books of magic. He turned
over so many that among others he found the history that Dares
had written, made, and told in the Greek tongue. This Dares
of whom you hear now was fostered and born in Troy. He
dwelt there, and did not leave till the army had departed.
Many a deed of valour he did himself both in assault and in
battle. He was a wondrous clerk and learned in the seven arts.
Wherefore he saw that the matter was so great that neither
before nor since has there been a greater; thus he was minded
to preserve the memory of these deeds. He wrote the history
of them in Greek. Each day he wrote it thus, as he beheld it
with his eyes. Everything they did in the day, either in battle
or combat, that night this Dares wrote it all, as I tell you.
Never on any account would he refrain from saying and setting

3

forth the truth. Therefore, though he was of the Trojans, he did not on that account show more favour to his own people than he did to the Greeks. He wrote the truth of the story. For a long time his book was lost, so that it was not found or seen. But Cornelius discovered it at Athens and translated it. By his wit and skill he turned it from Greek into Latin. We must believe him and hold his story true far rather than him who was born a hundred years or more later, who knew nothing, indeed, except by hearsay.

This story is not hackneyed and is nowhere to be found. It had not yet been related till Benoit de Sainte-Maure came upon it and made it and told it and wrote the words with his own hand, so fashioned and wrought, so set down, so arranged, that none of them, greater or less, is out of place. I shall begin the story here, I shall follow the Latin closely, I shall put in nothing but as I find it written. Nor do I say or add any good word, even had I the skill, but I shall follow my matter.

I shall tell you then and in few words with what deeds the whole book will deal and of what I wish to treat. . . . And how the worthy Lord Achilles went to Delphos for the reply of the oracle, where he saw visions; and how Calchas departed thence with him . . . how Calchas, the seer and most wise augur, craved and asked for his daughter, whose name was Briseida, whom Troilus had loved; and how Priam gave her up. . . . Afterwards you may hear further how the worthy daughter of Calchas went out from Troy in the sight of all, the lament she made at parting, and how then Diomede in the Grecian army entreated her to love him. Straightway afterwards I shall describe to you how she was angry with her father for his treachery to the Trojans, whom he had forsaken, and for his folly; you will hear too his answers and his words. . . . Then I shall tell you the true love and the distress and grief that the son of Tydeus felt for Troilus's lady. . . . Afterwards the book tells how the grievous and deadly strife began again, in which a thousand good warriors died, and in which the noble and worthy Troilus surpassed all on both sides; how he wounded Diomede through the body with a mighty stroke, and also how he reviled him because of his lady Briseida. Very harsh were the reproaches, and they were told and repeated in many places. Then you will hear how the daughter of Calchas repented that she was false in love and that she was faithless and untrue and treacherous. . . . Afterwards you will hear how he (Troilus) cried out against the daughter of Calchas, who loved his worst and mortal foe; he spoke great evil of maidens. . . . Then you may hear what marvels he (Achilles) did at a later time, how in the nineteenth battle he slew Troilus with his hand, his men greatly aiding him. . . .

Diomede was very powerful, large and square of limb, and very tall. His look was exceeding cruel; he made many a false promise. He was very bold, and very quarrelsome, and very cunning in fight; he was very overbearing and arrogant, and greatly was he dreaded. Very hard was it to find one who was willing to stand against him. Nobody could control him; he was a very evil man to serve. But many times he underwent many torments and many combats because of love. . . .

Briseida was graceful; she was not small, but yet not very tall. She was more beautiful and more fair and more white than a lily or than snow on the branch; but her brows were joined, which a little misbecame her. She had very beautiful eyes and was very charming in speech. She was very pleasant in manner and sober in bearing. Greatly was she loved, and greatly did she love; but her heart was not constant. And she was also very shamefaced, modest and kindly and full of pity. . . .

Troilus was wondrous beautiful; he had a laughing cheer, ruddy face, a clear open look, and broad brow. He had a true knightly appearance. He had fair hair, very charming and naturally shining, eyes bright and full of gaiety; none ever had beauty like theirs. Whenever he was in good humour his look was so gentle that it was a pleasure to behold him; but I tell you truly that towards his enemies he bore another aspect and look. He had a high nose, well shaped; his frame was well fitted to bear arms. He had a well-made mouth and beautiful teeth, whiter than ivory or silver; a square chin, a long and straight neck, which suited well the wearing of armour; shoulders very finely made, gradually sloping; breast sturdy beneath the hauberk; well made hands and fine arms; he was well shaped in the waist; his garments sat well upon him; he was powerful in the hips; he was a wondrous fair knight. He had straight legs, arched feet, his limbs fairly fashioned in every part; and he had a very wide stance, and was also of very fine stature. He was tall, but bore himself well. I do not think there is now a man of such worth throughout the length of the world who so loves joy and delight, or who says so little to give displeasure to others, or who has so rich a nature, or who so desires fame and honourable exploits. He was not insolent or haughty, but light of heart and gay and amorous. Well was he loved, and well did he love, and endured many great trials. He was not old, but still a young man, the fairest of the youths of Troy and the most worthy, except his brother Hector, who was in truth leader of the army and supreme among the warriors: Dares declares this plainly to us. He was the flower of chivalry, and in that Troilus was quite worthy of his brother; his brother was excellent in valour, in courtesy, and in generosity. . . .

You may hear how on that very day Calchas, famed for his magic lore, had come thither. He was the son of Testor, a Trojan. Calchas had great wisdom; he brought gifts to Apollo; he came to beg the god for mercy on those of Troy, to learn what they should do and how they should bear themselves. The king and the people of the country had sent Calchas there to offer their gifts on the altar and to hear the god's answer, and to learn what they were to suffer from the people who were coming against them. The answer of the god was as follows: 'Take heed,' it said, 'that in the morning thou go straight to the fleet of the Grecian host. Thou shalt go with them to Troy; thou art wise; thou shalt instruct their people. They will have great need of thy wisdom. Let them not go away till they have taken Troy and avenged themselves on the people. Thus shall it come to pass, for such is my will.'

Calchas and Achilles, who had never seen one another, met in the temple. Then they talked much together; they revealed their secrets to one another; they had wondrous joy together. Achilles took him away and lodged him at his house; he laboured much to serve him and to do all his pleasure. They took an oath to be true companions. So far did matters proceed with them that they journeyed to Athens. Achilles told the barons what the oracle had said to him. He declared and related to them all the promise that had been made to them: 'They shall have victory: let them know that clearly; henceforth they shall have no fear.' Never was such joy heard as the men of the fleet made. Calchas told and set forth the truth point by point, how the Trojans had sent him to the god, to whom they had offered gifts—'to hear and to know what Apollo would in truth say as to what would befall them, and whether they would be able to resist you who were about to come thither. They chose me there and sent me and laid the mission upon me.

I had come thither in their name; greatly did I desire to aid them. I had done all I could; I was within the god's temple; I laid the gifts I had brought from Troy upon the altar. I had made sacrifice to him in the manner and fashion in which I knew it should be made. I do not wish to make a long tale of it to you, but the divine voice said this to me: that I should come to Athens on the seashore to declare this to you, to tell you and to warn you that you should never depart or have peace with the Trojans till Troy was destroyed and the people killed and vanquished. . . .'

The Greeks had been very glad before and full of joy, but now Calchas cheered and heartened them much more. They received him with great delight and with great rejoicing. . . .

Then came Diomede with seven score knights and more, and on the other side Troilus had not less but more. They dashed forward on their horses; then they dealt each other blows on their coloured shields and on their helmets painted with flowers. The hauberks, white and of double strength, were broken against the steel. Lances passed through bodies; souls and bodies were parted there. They so hewed at one another on the great helmets that they were cloven even to the teeth: thus they strove together. Diomede and Troilus unhorsed each other. The fighting between them was stern and hard, for each was exceeding valiant. If they did not splinter their lances, yet they never fought with them again. Diomede was the first to remount. So wrathful and so ashamed was he that he smote Troilus on the helmet, so that he beat down the rim. The one was on foot, the other on horseback. They were not equally matched. Diomede attacked him fiercely, and struck and smote him in many places; and Troilus drew his steel blade and struck his horse dead. He clove it down to the breast. And Diomede, who had a valiant heart, was not daunted or dismayed; nor did he spare Troilus. They dealt one another great blows and strokes. The swords rang on the helmets; they beat them down on the hauberks. The marks showed on the armour, so did they slash each other on the head. Very grievous was the strife and without quarter and without mercy; and then the crowd parted them. Had it continued, the combat would have had a fatal ending. When the two barons were remounted, there was great fighting between their men. Many a knight was wounded and struck down from his horse. Diomede, I can truly say, was none the worse off that day. If he lost his own horse, he made a very good exchange, for he took away that of Troilus. . . .

Calchas, the wise and courteous, had a daughter of high worth, beautiful and courteous and well-taught; great was her fame; she was called Briseida. Calchas had told Agamemnon and the other kings and Telamon that they should demand her from Priam. 'He wished not henceforth that she should dwell longer with them, for fortune, he knew, was very hostile to them. Thus he did not wish her to perish with them; he wished her to leave and to be with him in the camp.'

This request was well urged; many speeches were made. The Trojans blamed Calchas; they said that he was baser than a dog. 'Of all dishonoured and vile men he is the most miserable, he who was rich and mighty among us. Then he deserted us and went to you.'

King Priam swore and declared that, if he had him in his power, he would make him suffer an ignoble death, that is, to be broken and torn to pieces by horses. 'If it were not that the maiden is noble, and worthy and wise and beautiful, she should be burned and torn to pieces because of him.'

I wish not to be tedious. King Priam granted her to them. 'She may go; let her depart; for he hates nothing,' he tells them, 'so much as the old man, the traitor; he wishes that nothing belonging to him should be or remain in the city.' . . .

Whoever had joy or gladness, Troilus suffered affliction and grief. That was for the daughter of Calchas, for he loved her deeply. He had set his whole heart on her; so mightily was he possessed by his love that he thought only of her. She had given herself to him, both her body and her love. Most men knew of that.

When it was told her, so that she knew it to be true, that she was to be forced and constrained to go to the camp and that she could no longer stay in Troy, she had great grief and distress. Tears came from her eyes, sighs from her heart. 'Alas,' she said, 'what a fate is mine when the city where I was born forsakes me thus! Even to a servant of lowest rank it would have been a great shame. I know no king, or duke, or count who now honours or befriends me. Henceforth now tears will wet my face every day without respite. Ah, Troilus, what trust I put in you, my fair sweet love! Never henceforth in your life will anybody love you more than I. King Priam has done very ill to send me away from his city. Please God, I shall not live till break of day. I will seek and crave for death.'

At night Troilus, who was overwhelmed by grief, went to her. There was no comfort; each of them wept tenderly, for well they knew that on the morrow they would be far asunder; no longer would they have chance or occasion to enjoy their love. While yet they might, they kissed one another continually. But the grief that touched their hearts made tears drop from their eyes upon their lips. Between them was neither anger nor pride, difference nor disagreement. Those who brought this upon them made them suffer great grief and sadness; to those may God nevermore grant joy. He who parts sweet lovers must atone for the evil deed, as the Greeks did, who afterwards paid grievously for it. Troilus had hated them before this; afterwards he showed and proved to them that they had done a thing to him that he long remembered. Never could they prevent him from making them pay dearly.

They were together for the night, but for them it lasted a very short while. Very painful was the parting; they uttered laments and sighs. And on the morrow, when it was clear day, the damsel made ready. She caused her loved possessions to be gathered together; her clothes and garments to be packed up. She arrayed and adorned her body with the most precious raiment she had. She had a tunic of silk broidered with gold, with rich and skilful work upon it, furred with ermine, so long that it swept the ground. Very splendid and charming it was, and so well did it become her body that nothing in the world, had she worn it, would have suited her better than that. . . . When she had fairly arrayed her body, she took leave of many people, who were very sad because of her. The maidens and the queen felt great pity for the damsel, and Lady Helen wept much. And that courteous lady parted from them with tears and outcries, for sorely was her heart afflicted. Nobody looked upon her without pity.

They brought out a palfrey for her. Never, I think, did damsel ride better. Some of the king's sons bore her company; more than three went out with her. Troilus, who loved her greatly and beyond measure, took her rein. But now he will suffer loss; henceforth he is forsaken. Wherefore every one sighed and lamented. But if the damsel herself is afflicted, she will in time be at peace again; she will soon have forgotten her grief and changed her feelings, so that those of Troy will be of small account to her. If to-day she has sorrow, she will have joy again, as great as any that ever was. Soon she will have changed her love; soon she will be comforted once more. . . .

The damsel thought she would die when she had to leave him whom she so loved and held dear; nor did she ever cease praying him to forget her not, for while she lived henceforth she would not love another. She would always keep her love for him; never should another have it, nor should any one have joy of her.

'Fair lady,' he said, 'I pray you now, if ever you did love me, let it appear at this time. I wish not that our love should lessen; on my side, I tell you plainly, it will diminish no whit. My heart will always be true; I will never change for another.'

Each uttered vows to the other before they parted. They had now ridden so far that they were out of the city. They delivered her to those appointed, who very gladly received her. Diomede came to meet them, King Telamon, King Ulysses, King Ajax, Menestheus, he who was lord and duke of Athens, and fully sixty knights, of whom the poorest was a rich count. The damsel wept sorely; nothing availed to comfort her. Great was her grief because of Troilus, who thus was parted from his love. In him was no joy or laughter; he turned away very sad and troubled. And the son of Tydeus, who was to suffer great pain ere he won her or merely kissed her, led her away.

'Fair lady,' he said, 'with good right does he esteem himself highly who possesses your love. I should like to have your heart and to hold you as my own, and I pledge myself to be yours while I live. Although it is very soon, and although we are so near the camp, and though I see you afflicted, troubled and fearful and distressed, I entreat you of your great mercy to receive me wholly as your knight and lover. I must needs suffer great pain till it please you to grant that. But much I doubt and fear your heart is hostile towards me and those in front of us. I know that you will always be inclined to the people who have fostered you: one must not blame you for that. But often have I heard it said that people who had never seen each other or become acquainted and known to each other had great love between them; very often does that come to pass. Fair lady,' said Diomede, 'I have never had aught to do with love. I have had no mistress, nor have I been a lover. Now I feel that love draws me toward you. No wonder that he is caught who looks upon your great beauty. Be assured then in very truth that on you I shall set my dear hope. I never look to have great joy till I am wholly sure of having your love, and till I have the delight of holding you in my arms and kissing

you, your eyes and your mouth and your face. Sweet lady, let
not anything I crave of you or say to you cause you displeasure,
and hold it not a villainy. You will be begged and entreated
to love, I know, in many ways. In this place are all the men of
high worth in the world, and the richest and fairest and best;
and they will ask you for your love. But know this, fair lady—
I speak truly unto you—that if you take me for your lover you
shall have naught but honour there. He who wins your love
must be of high repute and great name. Fair lady, if I offer
myself to you, refuse not my devotion. Take this heart and
this love and accept me for your knight. Henceforth I will
ever be a loyal and honourable lover to you all the days of my
life. Many a damsel have I seen, and known many a lady, but
never have I prayed any to love me thus. You are the first;
you shall also be the last. If I fail with you, I swear by God
that I will never labour to win another. I will not do it—I know
that truly—and if I may have your love, I will keep it and do
no wrong. You shall find nothing to blame in me that will
ever cause you displeasure. I will submit to very sore pain if
by my embraces and kisses I can relieve you of the heavy sighs
and bitter weeping with which I see you burdened and weighed
down. So shall I bring you such comfort that you will be
joyous. I give myself up to your service; great joy will be mine,
if it is your will. Henceforth I am devoted to you. God grant
me success, and may you not reject me. For he who loves and
entreats one who hates him loses all his labour.'

Briseida was wise and worthy; she answered him in few
words. 'My lord,' she said, 'at this time it is not well or reasonable or right for me to promise to love you, for you might always
account me light and senseless. You have told me your pleasure,
and I have listened and given you good hearing. But I have
not known you well enough to grant you my love so soon. Most
men go much astray in their conduct; many a damsel is deceived
by those who are faithless, lying, and false. They betray loyal
hearts. That is a very sad thing to see, when we must needs
put our faith in love. For one who laughs there are six who
weep; I wish not to go from bad to worse. He who has as
much distress and anxiety and as much grief and trouble in his
heart as I have, is very little concerned with love or happiness
or joy. My good friends, whom I knew and loved, are abandoned
and left in that place whither I think I shall never return, and
in which I was held in high honour. There is no wealth or
goodly thing that I had not at will; now I am put away from all.

Therefore I hold myself less dear. No wonder is it if I am afflicted. Nor is it at all fitting, so please you, for a damsel of my station to accept love imprudently in the camp. If she has any wisdom in her, she must keep herself free from reproach. Even those who act most warily, secretly in their chambers, cannot keep people from talking of them. I shall now be in a multitude and crowd; I shall be alone, without other ladies. I should not like to do aught that men could blame. I will not do it; I have no mind thereto. But I esteem you of noble lineage and in my opinion worthy, discreet, and well-taught. I wish not to make you believe anything that is not wholly trustworthy and true. There is no damsel under heaven so rich, or of so high repute, or so fair, if she is willing to love anybody, who could reject you. Under other circumstances I would not refuse you, but at present I have neither inclination nor desire to love you or any other. Thus you may be very sure, if I were willing to give myself to love, I would hold none more dear than you. But I have no thought or wish that way, and may God give me none such.'

Diomede was wise and worthy. He understood clearly at the first words that she was not very cruel. He spoke thus to her about his feelings: 'Fair lady, know this for a truth: I will set my hope upon you, I will love you with true love, I will obey your commands if you will but have pity on me as your lover. Since Love wills that I give myself to you, I neither resist nor deny him. Ever henceforth will I serve him at his will and pleasure. He will reward me with you; I seek no other gift from him. And if I had no expectation of that, I should not serve him with good heart. Henceforth I will be among his followers; and, if I but kiss your mouth, none in the Trojan host will be richer than I.'

Diomede would have said much more, but they were near the tents. He could not speak further to her before they had to part. A hundred times he craved mercy from her, that she should take him for her lover. He took one of her gloves from her, without anybody knowing or perceiving. Much he rejoiced at that, and did not note at all that she was in any degree angered thereby. Then Calchas, who had come out to meet them, arrived. Warmly he welcomed her and she him; and often they kissed each other. They embraced many times; Calchas wept in pity. The old man talked with his daughter and very often kissed and fondled her.

'My lord,' she said, 'tell me how this is. This is wondrous

strange conduct I behold in you, who have so acted as ever henceforth to bear a reproach, who help your foes that they may destroy your friends and the land where you were born, and who have exchanged your great inheritance, your riches, your wealth, and your honours for poverty and exile. How will you, who have aided such a work, ever have a light heart again? What has become of your clear intelligence, so lofty and noble? Where has it gone? You are very bitterly reproached, and so indeed you must be. They had exalted you above all, above lord and bishop and father and chief. Most shameful is this business. A man should rather dread shame than flee from or avoid death. Every man, we know, must die—that lot is common to all—and, if he can die honourably, his body is blessed and his soul goes to great bliss. But he who is dishonoured in this world will be held very vile in the next. Horrible hell and darkness is prepared for him, and most rightly. My lord, my heart is greatly troubled that Pluto and Proserpine and the other infernal gods have such hatred towards you. They have brought this evil, this shame, this injury upon you. What had you in your heart that you returned not to the city and came not back to us? Why were you so cruel as to come here among our mortal foes to do us harm and contrive our loss? You had better have gone to dwell in one of those isles of the sea till this siege was ended. Lord Apollo acted very ill if he gave you such answer and commanded you to do this. Cursed now be that prophecy, that gift, and that fate that brings such dire shame upon you. He who forfeits honour in this world must think meanly of himself.'

Then she began to weep, and so distressed was her heart she spoke no further at all.

Calchas replied to the damsel. 'Daughter,' he said, 'I wished not this fate should be mine. I knew well that I should be sorely blamed; but I could not deny or refuse the gods. I could not oppose their will; everything might have gone ill with me. I had to do the thing and to come here, as soon as Apollo commanded. Never did I do anything so against my will. I should not be dishonoured therefor, for had it been according to my wish this business would have gone all otherwise. Nobody knows the grief my heart suffers night and day. But were I so senseless as to wish to go against the will of the gods or to oppose them in aught, I am sure that they would take such vengeance that ever to me it would be grievous, painful, deadly, and perilous. Above all, I am sure and I know that I shall see the Trojans dead and destroyed; hence it is better for us to escape elsewhere than to perish with them in the city. They will be killed, conquered, and captured, for thus have the gods ordained it. This cannot last much longer. Every hour have I thought of how to bring you here to me; I have been concerned about nothing else. Now that I have you, all is well with me. No longer shall I be distressed and afflicted.'

There was much gazing at the damsel; the Greeks praised her greatly to one another. 'She is very beautiful,' they all said. Diomede bore her company till she alighted at the pavilion. . . . When the damsel reached the tent, where her guide aided her to dismount—and often he changed colour on her account—he took leave of her with difficulty.

But the high princes and lords came to look upon her and to ask her news. Courteously and briefly and wisely she gave answer to all. They welcomed and honoured her much, and they all comforted her greatly. She was happier now than she had expected, for often she beheld things that gave her pleasure. Before she sees the fourth evening she shall have neither wish nor desire to return to the city. Fickle and infirm, her feelings were very soon changed; very weak and inconstant was her heart. Dearly did those of loyal heart pay for that; often they suffered pain and evil on that account. . . .

Diomede joined battle with Troilus because of the damsel. He unhorsed him and took the steed by the bridle. He called a young squire of his and handed it over to him. 'Go at once,' he said, 'quickly to the tent of Calchas of Troy and say to his fair-haired daughter that I send her this steed. I have won it from a knight who strives greatly to gain her favour. And tell her that I beg her not to resent my words and that in her is all my life.'

He alighted in front of the tent, then entered the pavilion, of which the pegs and all the poles and the knobs and the eagles were of fine gold and which was exceeding beautiful. The son of Cariz de Pierre Lee saluted the damsel on behalf of his liege lord.

'Lady,' he said, 'he sends you this precious horse as a token of his love. Be assured he does not forget you. He won it but now, as I can report to you, from Troilus, who is so wont to find favour with you. He cast him down on the sand. He made such a charge—I beheld him with my own eyes—and was so exceeding fierce, that a hundred were all overthrown, of whom the strongest is now pale and wan. He sends you word that for you he suffers and that he is wholly yours.'

The damsel took the horse by the little gold ring. 'Tell thy lord from me,' she said, 'that his love injures me in this. For, if any one seeks to please me by doing my will and meeting my wishes, and if any one is well disposed towards me, in so far as he craves my favour and loves and cherishes me, he must not damage or harm him. Well I know, if he loves me at all, that he would treat my people better; he must spare them all. But, if there is any one to tell me, I shall hear indeed before the fourth day that he (Troilus) will have taken vengeance for this horse with his sword; its loss will be well redeemed. It is not wrong to seize property in payment of a debt, for under heaven there is not such a knight. I think indeed that he will follow his prey; little will he care who sees him. He who thinks to defend it against him may pay for it dearly. Go back, return to the battle. Greet thy lord thus from me, and say to him thus, that I should do wrong if I hated him since he loves me. I give him no love that will profit him.'

The squire departed from her. He returned to the great and deadly battle where so many warriors, so many counts, so many rich barons met death. . . .

But Diomede's horse sank right down under him. It fell beneath him sorely stricken. Before he rose to his feet again, Polydamas had given the steed to a squire of his; he made a present of it to Troilus. Five hundred saw the encounter and were greatly moved to envy thereby. And the women, who held him dear, pointed him out to one another. Much did they speak together and uttered very many words in praise of him. When Troilus saw the horse, he was very pleased with such a rich gift. Within his heart he said and declared that he would do knightly deeds on it, so that his love should hear him spoken of. And so he did. . . .

Whoever had rest, repose, or weal, the son of Tydeus had none of these. He suffered such anxiety from love that sleep came not to him in his bed; he could not sleep, he did not close his eye; he was at rest neither night nor day. Often he thought, often he sighed. Often he had joy, often distress; often he was afflicted, often he was pleased. So hardly did love treat him that his colour changed and altered, and many times he broke into a sweat that had no heat for him and that he felt not.

Such often are the darts of love; often it shows in the face of him whom it holds in its sway. Very grievous indeed are its assaults; it makes one suffer deadly torments. He who is in the power of true love has no rest at all.

Thus was it with Diomede, who henceforth had neither joy nor peace. He had great fear; he was not certain that h should ever possess her. His hope of joy was in the daughter of Calchas the Trojan; he feared that never should he lie with her under the coverlet by night or day. Much would he suffer to attain that; all his thoughts turned thereto. If she granted him not this, he was dead and beyond hope of recovery. Many times he went to see her, but she was very prudent. Well she knew by his sighs that he was wholly subject to her. Wherefore she was three times as stern. . . . Diomede, who loved so strongly that he could not suffer or endure more, was forced to make entreaties. Often he went to her to crave mercy; often he told her that because of his love he could not be at rest night or day; he could not eat or sleep; thinking and tears and sighing made him grow pale and distressed. It was most humiliating to beg her favour. . . . Often he forgot what he most desired to say. Long he bore this torment before he could by any effort win delight or joy from her.

One day he had gone to entreat her when she was looking at the horse that had belonged to her lover. It has been fully told and related how he made a present of it to her. He was in great distress and sadness. He thought to be avenged on her before the game was done. Had the damsel dared do it and had she not feared shame and reproach, she would gladly have sent it back to him. But it might soon have been the worse for her; she was very much hated in the camp. When she saw him, she taunted him thus. 'My lord,' she said, 'too great generosity impoverishes a man and lessens his worth and does him injury; most men suffer want therefrom. You would not have been so needy the other day, at the great battle, when he who so hates you took your precious horse from you and gave it not back, if you had then had this steed. It would, I think, have been serviceable to you. You parted with it too soon. I fear you had need of it. Had I known your lack, you could at once have had it again. It is good to give to one from whom the gift can be reclaimed; the Trojans are wise in that. He who thinks to disinherit them and cast them out of their country undertakes no easy task. Their knights and warriors are valiant. My lord,' she said, 'I will lend you the horse; I can do naught else. You would not be able to find its equal. Since you have lost your own, it is very well for you to have this. I lend it to you. But they are strong in pursuit; if you are not careful, they will regain it. Be sure they will make a great effort to accomplish that. He who is in possession of yours is not cowardly or timid; it could not be in worthier hands.'

'Lady,' he said, 'it is not to be denied that he is very valiant in a great battle or in tournament; but it is not to be wondered at if a knight loses his steed. He who will strive in arms and endure great combats wins and loses many times. I am not in great need or trouble on that account. I have plenty of horses. But, if you entrust it to me, I shall keep it with all my power. I shall be in very sore straits before I let it go from me. More than three lives shall pay for it. Henceforth I see and feel sure and know that the great pain I suffer for you, whereby my heart endures strain and stress and knows no joy or relief, or bliss or comfort or solace; and that the waiting I undergo, will turn wholly to gladness for me. So long will I beseech you till you have mercy on me. This I wait for; this I crave; this I long for; this I desire. Then will my sighs have an end. All my joy will be fulfilled as soon as I possess you. This rests with you to decide, sweet love; may your succour not be late in coming! Grievous were it for me if your mind should not change. If I had no hope of you, I think I should never again bear or hold shield or lance. It would be better for me to be dead than to live on. My life would be too burdensome. My love, turn your heart towards me. You are so beautiful and worthy and wise that I cannot, fair creature, think of aught but you. Now it shall be as you wish and as you command. I can do no otherwise, but to you I give and surrender myself.'

The damsel was well pleased, and she rejoiced much and was glad that he was in her power. To take the place of his pennant she gave him the right sleeve off her arm of new and fresh silk. He who felt the pangs of love for her was glad. . . . Henceforth Troilus may know that it will be useless for him to wait for her any longer. Her love towards him is destroyed; and in time to come that was dearly paid for. . . .

Diomede with his followers and Troilus with the Phrygians assembled first of all. These two divisions moved against each other, and they filled a large part of the field. The horses showed great fear. From far off men heard the trampling and the earth trembling under them. They couched their lances as they came.

They struck each other in the middle of the shields and on the hauberks of fine mail. The lances broke and flew in splinters and cast knights from their saddles. In the great striking and clashing many were of necessity overthrown who rose not again. Those who escaped the lances drew brands of sharp steel; many necks were smitten there; seven hundred had their sides gashed. So many were dead and sorely wounded that the whole field was strewn with them. Diomede was much enraged when he saw his men die thus, and the Trojans bear themselves in this fashion. He urged his horse towards Troilus. His whole ebony lance, on which was the silken sleeve, passed through the shield, on which was figured a lion. He made him feel it at his side. The other failed not in his turn to strike; he forced away the shield from his body and deeply pierced the hauberk, so that the blood flowed from his body. But he had not received a mortal wound nor one that did him great hurt through stroke of sword or lance. They were eager to begin the fight with bright sharp brands of steel, so that their heads should bleed before they parted. But Menelaus came there with more than four thousand men. . . .

With no truce made or demanded or asked for between them, the fifteenth battle began before the week was over. It was wondrous great and marvellous. Many counts and kings died there, and chiefs and dukes of high repute. Well did the Trojans avenge themselves; they bore themselves valiantly, and dearly sold the victory the Greeks hoped to gain. Two thousand were silenced by death, and they lay pale and cold on the field. Be assured they were grievously stricken. Diomede was sore wounded there through the body by a mighty thrust from a great and well-held lance, so that the silken pennant remained in his side. He was borne off the field for dead. It was Troilus who fought with him, in the sight of a thousand knights and more. And thus he spoke to him scornfully: 'Go now and bide with the woman, with the daughter of old Calchas, who, they say, does not hate you. For her love I had spared you, if I had thought of it in a less evil hour. And yet her short-lived faith, her falseness and her wrong-doing and her betrayal of me have brought all this upon you. Her sins and her false love for me have done you hurt. By you I send her word that now we two are parted. If you have been to her what I used to be, there will be plenty more accepted lovers before the siege is ended; you will have to keep good watch.

You may have her wholly to yourself now, but she has not yet made an end, since she finds pleasure in the trade of love. For, if there are so many that somewhat please her, the very innkeepers will have her favours. It will be wise for her to take thought from whom she may draw profit.'

These taunts were clearly heard. Neither Trojans nor Greeks forgot them; nor was there a day in all the month that they were not reported in a hundred places. They were cried and uttered loudly in that place where Diomede lay wounded. . . .

When Diomede was wounded and the daughter of Calchas knew it, he comforted himself as best he could; but he could not so hide his feelings that no laments and tears and sighs came from him. He showed clearly that he loved her in his heart more than any other living person. Never till that day had he given much sign of loving her, but he could not conceal it then. Great was his grief and distress. He did not let her visit him in his tent for fear men would speak of it. Henceforth all his thought was set on her; henceforth he loved her; henceforth he was possessed by desire for her; but he feared greatly to lose her.

His wound was very grievous; the Grecian host was greatly dismayed thereat, and she wept for it with her sweet eyes. And often she went to see him, though old Calchas reproached her and threatened and forbade her to do so. One could see that from this time she was wholly inclined towards him: her love, her heart, and her thought. Well she knew that she was acting very shamefully. Very wrongly and disloyally she thus left Troilus; she did great evil—she felt that—and deeply did she wrong him who was so beautiful, rich, and worthy, and who vanquished them all in deeds of arms.

To herself she thought and said: 'Henceforth no good will be written of me, nor any good song sung. No such fortune or happiness will be mine henceforth. Evil and senseless was my thought, I deem, when I betrayed my lover, for he deserved it not at my hands. I have not done as I should; my heart should have been so set and fixed on him that I should have listened to no other. I was false and inconstant and mad when I gave heed to words; he who wishes to keep himself loyal must never listen to words; by words the wise and the most cunning are deceived. From this time forth those who love me not will not lack things to say of me; the Trojan women will talk of me. I have done shame most horrible to damsels and rich maidens. My treachery and my ill deeds will always be told to them.

Needs must that be grievous unto me, and so it is. Very changeable and faithless is my heart; for I had the best lover to whom ever a maiden might give her love. Those whom he loved I should have loved, and those who would seek his harm I should have hated and avoided. How wise I am appears in this: that to him whom he most hates I have against reason and right granted my true love. From this time forth I shall be greatly scorned for that. And what avails it to repent? That can never be amended. To Diomede then I will be true, for he is very worthy and a good warrior. Never can I return to Troy nor leave him. Too fully already have I set my heart upon him; because of that I did that which I have done. And it had not been thus were I still in the city. My heart would never have thought of wavering or changing, but in this place I was without counsel and without a friend and without a loyal champion. Thus I had need of hope to relieve me of affliction and distress. Long could I wait and lament and suffer and endure even to death had I comfort from there. I had been dead ere now had I not taken mercy on myself. Though I have wrought folly, I have won the game. I shall have joy and gladness, even as my heart was in great sorrow. He will be able to speak ill of me who was slow to bring me comfort. One need not grieve or torment oneself because of the vulgar crowd. If all the world is happy and my heart sad and troubled, it profits me nothing. But much my heart grieves and bleeds that I have been faithless, for nobody who has set his love where his heart is not at rest, but troubled and full of fear and regret, can act honestly. Often I am content; often I am distressed; often it is well with me, and greatly do I wish it to be so; often my eyes are filled again with tears; thus in truth is it now. God be gracious unto Troilus! Now that I cannot have him, nor he me, I give and surrender myself to Diomede. Dearly should I like to have this boon—that I should not remember what I have done in the past. Sorely does that trouble me. My conscience reproaches me, which greatly torments my heart. But I must turn all my heart and mind to Diomede from this time forth, willingly or unwillingly, since he looks to me for love, so that he may be happy and joyous therein, and I with him, since things are thus. Now I find my heart resolved and ready to do his pleasure. From now on he will find no more pride in me. I have so fed him with false hopes in my speech that now I will do his will and his pleasure and his wishes. God grant I have joy and weal therein!' . . .

Afterwards he (Troilus) complained with great bitterness of his
lady, who had left him and given her love to his enemy. He
called ladies faithless and maidens false. He said it was an
evil thing to put your trust in them, for there were very few of
them who were faithful in love and free from fickleness and
disloyalty. 'Whoever jests thereof, I do not. The daughter
of Calchas has played me false.'

Often now she heard herself spoken of; the damsels made
great mock of her. They hated her deeply and wished her
much ill; they loved her not as they had been wont to do. She
had done shame to them all. That would always be a reproach
unto her. . . .

So long had the battle lasted that midday was already well
past. At that moment came Troilus with a very great force;
no longer did he tarry. Three thousand followed at his back.
Then were there no Greeks so bold as not to give way at once.
Then horses were spurred; there men were pursued and beaten
down; cries and shouts were heard there; the elephants made
such a noise that one would not have heard thunder there. So
many men were overthrown there that the Greeks were all put
to flight and discomfited. If these fled, there were plenty to
pursue. In truth they lost many men on the field. They
were already hard by the tents when the followers of Achilles
sallied forth. There were two thousand of them in one troop,
and not three of them without strong shields and mail. Without any delay they went against their enemies, lances couched,
shields on their arms. And the Trojans received them well
on the points of their burnished blades, so sternly that the charge
of all the knights came to an end. They had no desire or eagerness, to tell you the truth, to go farther.

To help the Myrmidons the Greeks at once attacked again.
There was such fighting there, such slaughter and such turmoil,
that nobody could describe it. The Myrmidons were resolved
not to forget their lord's wish. They sought Troilus amid the
press; they attacked only his squadron. Then they assailed
each other and dealt each other blows with lances and naked
swords. Heads were cloven there, and fists and feet and arms
cut off; dread was the struggle there. Troilus was very furious
when he saw gathered about him those who were seeking his
death. He drew his sword of keen steel; then he attacked them,
then he dealt them wounds. He had no fear lest they should
all take vengeance. He went against them where the press was

thickest. He whom he struck was done for. Never did any one, so Dares tells us, see a man make such slaughter or such massacre. Great streams of blood ran there. He had wholly routed them, killed, wounded, and stricken them; he had put them to flight, when his horse was killed. It was struck with two swords; it could no longer stand. It stretched itself on the ground, and Troilus fell on it. He had no companion or comrade with him. Before he could get up, Achilles had come upon him. Alas, how many sword-blows there were upon him now! And Achilles contrived to get his head bare of armour. To them he had offered a great resistance, a hard fight; but what does that avail? It is of no service or help to him, for the base Achilles cut off his head before he could receive any aid. He wrought great cruelty and felony. May he pay dearly therefor, even if he should repent. He fastened the body of the warrior to the tail of his horse. Then he dragged it after him, so that those in the battle beheld it.

GIOVANNI BOCCACCIO
IL FILOSTRATO

IL FILOSTRATO

MANY times before now, most noble lady, it has chanced that I, who almost from my boyhood even to this present have been a servant of love, finding myself in his court among noble men and fair ladies, who were there likewise, heard this question discussed and debated: A young man ardently loves a lady, but fortune grants him no happiness with her except that he may sometimes see her, or sometimes speak of her, or meditate sweetly upon her. Which then of these three things gives the most delight? And it never happened that each of these three things failed to be defended by many with earnestness and keen arguments, this being upheld by one and that by another. And since this question seemed closely related to my dealings with love, which had been more ardent than happy, I remember that I, deluded by false seeming, often mingling with the debaters, urged and maintained that to be able to think sometimes of the loved person was a greater delight by far than either of the other two could afford; declaring, among other arguments which I put forward, that it is no small part of the lover's bliss to be able, according to the thinker's desire, to have mastery of the beloved person, and to make her, according to his fancy, kind and loving, though that should last no longer than the thought. For it could not happen thus with seeing nor with speaking. O foolish judgment, O ignorant verdict, O vain argument, how far from the truth were you! To me in my misery bitter experience makes that clear now. O sweetest hope of my troubled mind and sole comfort of my stricken heart, I shall feel no shame in laying open to you how mightily truth made her way into my clouded thoughts, truth, against whom in childish error I had taken up arms. And to what person, able to lighten somewhat the penance laid upon me—whether by love or fortune I know not—for my false opinion, to what person could I tell it but to you?

Therefore, O fairest lady, I declare it to be true, that after you departed from the delightful city of Naples in the sweetest season of the year and went to Sannio, and thus suddenly took from my eyes, which yearn for your heavenly beauty more than for aught else, that which your presence should have made me prize aright, but which I did not, the loss of you made me quickly know its value. And your absence has so saddened my soul beyond measure that I can clearly understand how great was the joy, but little perceived by me at the time, which came to me from the sight of your gracious beauty. But I shrink not from telling, nor am I minded to leave unsaid, what happened to me after your departure, though it is set forth more fully elsewhere than here. Thus will this truth appear more manifest, and a very great error will be refuted.

I say, therefore—and so may God soon restore to my eyes, by the sight of your fair face, the peace which they have lost —that, when I learned that you had departed hence and gone to a place where no honourable reason for seeing you could ever bring me, my eyes, through which the most gentle light of your love entered my mind, have, beyond what my words can make believed, bathed my face and filled my sad breast many times with so many and such bitter tears, that not only has it been a wondrous thing how so much moisture has come to my face and breast from my eyes, but also they would perforce have stirred pity not in you alone, whom I believe to be as kind-hearted as you are noble, but in him who was my enemy and had a breast of iron. Nor has this happened only when the memory of having lost your gladdening presence has saddened my eyes, but whatever has appeared before them has been a source of greater misery to them. Alas, how often, to save themselves suffering, have they of their own accord avoided looking at the temple, the balconies, the public squares, and the other places, where once, full of longing and desire, they sought to see and sometimes did see your countenance; and in their grief they have forced my heart to utter that verse of Jeremiah: 'How doth the city sit solitary that was full of people, she that was great among the nations.' In truth, I will not say that all things sadden them equally, but I declare that only in one quarter do they find lessening of their grief, when they gaze towards those places, those mountains, that part of the heavens, among which and beneath which I firmly believe that you are. And thus every breeze, every gentle wind which comes thence I receive upon my face, as if beyond any doubt it has touched yours. And yet this solace endures not very long; but as we sometimes see flames playing upon things covered with oil, so upon my stricken heart plays this comfort, but takes flight on a sudden when the thought comes upon me that I cannot see you, though my desire to do so is kindled beyond measure.

What shall I say of the sighs which in the past delightful love and sweet hope were wont to draw, burning, from my breast? In truth I have nothing to say of them except that, multiplied by the manifold increase of my most great anguish, they are thus violently driven out through my mouth a thousand times each hour.   And likewise my voice, which ere now was sometimes stirred, by some secret joy which came from your pure beauty, to amorous songs and to speech full of eager love, has been heard ever since calling upon your gentle name, and upon love for favour, and upon death to end my woes; and the greatest lamentations could have been heard by anybody who had been at hand.

Such a life, then, I lead far from you, and ever the better do I understand how great was the welfare and the joy and the delight that came from your eyes, though in days gone by I recked too little of it.   And though tears and sighs allow me time to speak of your worth, and now also of your grace, your gentle manners and womanly pride, and your bearing surpassing others in beauty, which I have ever before my mind's eye in its fullness; and though I say not that my soul receives no pleasure from such speaking or thinking, yet this pleasure comes mingled with a most fervent desire which inflames all my other desires into so great a longing to see you that I can hardly govern them within me and keep them from drawing me, in the face of all seemly honour and sober counsel, to where you are dwelling.   But yet, swayed by the wish to care for your honour rather than my own salvation, I hold them in check; and having no other remedy and feeling the way to seeing you again to be closed against me for the reason I have given, I fall once more to weeping.   Ah, woe is me, how cruel and pitiless is fortune to me in my joys, ever a stern mistress and chastiser of my faults!   Now, poor wretch that I am, I know.   Now I feel, now I see most clearly, how much more good, how much more pleasure, how much more sweetness was in the true light of your eyes when turned towards mine than in the false flattery of my thoughts.   So then, O radiant light of my mind, fortune, by robbing me of the sight of you in your loveliness, has scattered the mist of error which I used to uphold.   But in truth it needed not so bitter a medicine to purge my ignorance; a lighter chastisement would have set me again in the right road.   So of what avail now is my strength against that of fortune? It cannot resist, however much I may use reason. However it fall out, I have at any rate by your departure come to such a pass as my writing has already declared to you; and with this most grievous trouble of mine I have come to be certain of that which before in my ignorance I argued against. But now I must come to that goal, for the sake of which I have continued writing thus far. And I declare that, beholding myself fallen into such great and sharp adversity by your going away, I first thought of keeping my anguish wholly within my sad breast, lest it might chance, if revealed, to be the cause of much greater. And adhering strongly to this purpose brought me very close to desperate death, and indeed, had it come, it would beyond any question have been dear to me then. But, later, moved by some secret hope that it might yet be my fortune at some time to see you again, and to turn my eyes again to their first happiness, there was born in me, not only fear of death, but desire of long life, however wretched I should be in it while I did not see you. And knowing very clearly that, if I kept the grief I felt wholly hidden in my breast, as I had purposed, it was impossible but that at some time, out of the thousand times when it came upon me in its fullness, exceeding all measure, it should so triumph over my strength, already very much weakened, that death would certainly follow, and therefore I should see you no more. Governed by more sober counsel, I changed my purpose, and determined to give it outlet from my sad breast in some fitting lamentation, so that I might live and be able, moreover, to see you again, and by living to remain longer in your service. And such a thought no sooner came to my mind than, along with it, I straightway perceived the means to my end. And in that circumstance, as if I were inspired by a mysterious divine power, I found the surest augury of future happiness. And the way was this: that, in the person of somebody stricken with love as I was and am, I should tell my sufferings in song. And so with zealous care I fell to turning over old stories in my mind to find one which I could fitly use as a cloak for the secret grief of my love. Nor did another come to my mind more suited to meet my need than the valiant young Troilus, son of Priam, most noble King of Troy. For inasmuch as his life, if any faith may be put in old stories, was saddened by love and by his lady being far from him after Criseida, so dearly loved, was restored to her father Calchas, my life after your going hence has been much like unto it. And therefore in his person and his fortunes I found most happily a frame for my idea; and afterwards, in light rhyme and in my Florentine idiom, in a very moving style, I set down his sorrows and my own as well. And putting my sorrows into song, now at this time and now at that, I have found a great relief, as at the outset was my expectation. It is true that I have given in like style a part of his happy life before his most bitter griefs, and I set this down, not because I wish anybody to think that I can boast a like happiness, for fortune never so far favoured me, nor can I bring myself to hope for it, nor in any way hold the belief that it will come to pass. But I wrote it for this reason, that when one has beheld happiness one understands much better how great and of what nature is misery which afterwards befalls. And yet this happiness is like my fortunes, in so far as I drew no less pleasure from your eyes than Troilus found in the happy love which fortune granted him with Criseida.

Therefore, worthy lady, I have put these rhymes together in the form of a little book as an enduring memorial, for those who will look upon it in time to come, both of your worth, with which in the person of another they are in many parts adorned, and of my sadness; and when they were set down, I did not think it a seemly thing that they should come into the hands of any other person before yours, for you have been the true and only begetter of them. And thus, though it is a most slight gift to such a noble lady as you are, yet because the affection which I, who send it, feel is very great and full of pure devotion, I venture to send them, trusting that they will be received by you, not through my merit, but through your kindness and courtesy. And if you chance to read them, as often as you find Troilus weeping and lamenting the departure of Criseida, you will be able to understand and know my very words, tears, sighs, and agonies; and whenever you find portrayed the beauty of Criseida, her manners, and any other excellent quality in a woman, you can understand that it is spoken of you. Of the other matters, of which there are many in addition to these, none, as I said before, has reference to me; nor is given here on my account, but because the story of the noble young lover demands it. And if you are as wise as I deem you to be, you will thus be able to understand from these things how great and of what sort my desires are, what is their goal, and what beyond all else they crave, or if they deserve any pity. Now I know not if these rhymes will so prevail as to touch your chaste mind with compassion as you read them, but I pray Love to give them this power. And, if this comes to pass, I beg you as humbly as I can that you take thought touching your return, so that my life, which is hanging by a most slender thread and barely sustained by hope, may at sight of you be happily restored to its former surety. And if this, perchance, cannot come about as soon as I should desire, at least with some sigh or kindly prayer intercede with Love for me that He may give some peace to my troubles and solace my hapless life. My long discourse craves to be ended, and therefore, to bring it to a close, I pray him who has put my life and my death in your hands to kindle in your heart that desire which alone can bring about my salvation.

CANTO I

Some are wont to invoke the favour of Jove in their pious beginnings; others call upon the strength of Apollo. It was my way to pray to the muses of Parnassus when I had need, but of late love has made me change my old and fixed custom since I have been enamoured of thee, my lady. Thou, lady, art the clear and beauteous light by whom I live wisely in the dark world; thou art the north star which I follow that I may come to port. O anchor of safety, thou art she who is all my welfare and my comfort. Thou art my Jove, thou art my Apollo, thou art my muse; this I have proved and this I know.

And now that I desire, by reason of thy going hence, more grievous to me than death and more painful, to describe what was the sorrowing life of Troilus after amorous Criseida had gone from Troy, and how, ere that, she had been gracious unto him, it is fitting I should come to thee for grace, if I am to be able to achieve my task. Thus, O fair lady, to whom I have been and always shall be faithful and subject, O beautiful light of those fair eyes in which love has set all my joy, O single hope of him who loves thee more than himself with perfect love, guide thou my hand, govern my wit in the work I am now to write. Thy image is fixed so strongly in my sad breast that thou hast greater sway there than I myself. Drive forth from it my despairing voice in such guise that my grief will show itself in another's sorrow, and make it so sweet that he who hears it may be stirred to pity. Thine be the honour, if these words win aught of praise, and mine the toil.

And, you who are lovers, I pray you hearken to what my lamenting verse will say; and, if it chance that in your hearts any spirit of pity should awaken, I pray you entreat Love for my sake, through whom I live far from the sweetest pleasure that any creature ever held dear.

Round about Troy were the Grecian kings, mighty in arms; and each, according to his strength, showed himself bold, proud, valorous, and gallant; and they beleaguered it ever more closely from day to day with their troops, in one common resolve to avenge the outrage and rape wrought by Paris upon Queen Helen.

At that time Calchas, whose high learning had already won

mastery of every secret of great Apollo, wishing to know the truth about the future, as to which should prevail—the long endurance of the Trojans or the great boldness of the Greeks— perceived and saw the Trojans slain after long war and the land laid waste. And thus, foreseeing and wise, he resolved to depart secretly; and having chosen place and time for flight, he set forth towards the Grecian host. And he saw many coming thence to meet him, and they received him with glad faces, hoping for excellent and good counsel from him in every chance and danger.

Great stir was there when it was known far and wide through the whole city that Calchas had fled thence; and men spoke of it in divers ways, but all as an evil thing. And they said that he had sinned and had acted foully as a traitor; and the greater part of the people were scarcely kept from going to set fire to his house.

In such hard case Calchas had left a daughter of his, a widow, called Criseida, who was so fair and so like an angel to look upon that she seemed not a mortal thing, and to my judgment as prudent, wise, modest, and well-bred as any lady born in Troy.

And she hearing the harsh clamour roused by her father's flight, sorely afflicted to find herself amid such a threatening outcry, in sad garments and shedding tears, threw herself on her knees at Hector's feet, and with very pitiful voice and look, excusing herself and accusing her father, made an end of her speech by craving mercy. Hector was by nature easily moved to pity; and thus, seeing the sore weeping of her who was fairer than any other creature, comforted her somewhat with gentle speech, saying: 'Let thy father, who has done us such wrong, go forth—and evil be his fortune—and do thou bide with us in Troy as long as it pleases thee, safe and happy, without harm. Surely thou shalt ever have from all of us the favour and honour thou mayest wish for, as if Calchas were here. May the gods give him fit reward!'

For this she thanked him warmly and would have spoken further, but he suffered her not. And so she rose and returned to her house and lived there in quietness. There did she dwell while she was in Troy with such household as became her dignity to maintain, wondrously modest in her ways and life; nor did she need to take care of son or daughter, for it had never been her fortune to have a child. And she was loved and honoured by all who knew her.

Between the Trojans and Greeks things went for the most part as they do in war. At times the Trojans sallied forth from their city valiantly against the Greeks; and many times, if the story says truly, the Greeks went with great daring, pillaging on every side, burning and consuming castles and towns. And, though the Trojans were sore pressed by their enemies, the Greeks, it did not come to pass, therefore, that the sacrifices to the gods were ever neglected; but the wonted rites were observed in every temple. But in all things they showed greater and more solemn honour to Pallas than to any other, and held her in higher esteem.

And so when the fair season had come that reclothes the meadows with herbs and flowers, and when all creatures feel gladness and show forth their love in divers acts, the Trojan elders went to make ready the wonted honours to the fateful Palladium, at which festival both ladies and knights alike were present, and all gladly. And among them was the daughter of Calchas, Criseida, arrayed in black; and, even as the rose surpasses the violet in beauty, so was she fairer than any other lady; and she alone more than any other gladdened the great festival, standing in the temple nigh the door, stately in beauty, gracious and discreet.

Troilus went about, as young men are wont to do, glancing now here and now there in the great temple, and took his stand with his companions now in this place and now in that, and fell to praising now this lady and now that and likewise to slighting them, as a man who found no more pleasure in one than in another and who rejoiced to be free. Moreover, from time to time, as he walked about in this manner, when he saw any one gazing fixedly at any lady and sighing, he pointed him out to his companions with a laugh, saying: 'That sad fellow has put fetters upon his freedom, so much did it trouble him, and has placed it in that lady's hands. Note well how little his brooding profits him. Why give love to any woman? For even as the leaf flutters in the wind, so in one day, fully a thousand times, do their hearts change, nor do they think of the pain any lover feels for them, nor do any of them know what they desire. Oh, happy is he who is not caught by their delights and can hold himself aloof. I have found before now by my own great folly what this cursed fire is. And if I were to say that love did no show me courtesy and give me joy and gladness, I should surely lie; but all the good taken together was little or nothing when put beside my torments and sad sighs when my mind was set on love. Now I have escaped, thanks to him who took more pity on me than I did on myself, I mean Jove, the true God, from whom ever comes mercy; and I live in peace. And although I find pleasure in watching others, I keep myself from the wayward course and laugh gladly at those in the toils; I know not whether to call them lovers or fools.'

O blindness of worldly minds! How often do things fall out not at all as we planned! Troilus goes now mocking the frailties and troubled loves of other people without a thought of what Heaven is hastening to bring upon him. For love pierced him more deeply than any other ere he left the temple.

Thus then, while Troilus went up and down, jeering now at one and now at another and often looking now on this lady and now on that, it befell by chance that his roving eye pierced through the company to where charming Criseida stood, clad in black, under a white veil, apart from the other ladies at this most solemn festival. She was tall, and all her limbs were in keeping with her height; her face was adorned with heavenly beauty, and in her look there showed forth womanly pride. And with her arm she had taken the mantle from before her face; and she had made room for herself by moving the crowd a little aside. And as she drew again into herself, that act of hers, somewhat disdainful as if she said, 'None may stand here,' gave pleasure to Troilus; and he fell to looking more closely upon her face, which more than any other seemed to him worthy of high praise, and he had the greatest delight in gazing fixedly between this man and that at her shining eyes and her countenance of heavenly beauty.

And he, who a little before had been so wise in blaming others, was not aware that Love with his darts had his dwelling in the beams of those fair eyes; nor did he remember the scornful words he had spoken in front of his servants, nor did he perceive the arrow that flew to his heart until in truth it stung him.

Finding greater pleasure in this lady in the black mantle than in all others, Troilus, without saying what cause held him there so long, secretly gazed upon her he so desired; and revealing naught to any one, he gazed as long as the rites in honour of Pallas lasted. Then with his companions he went forth from the temple. And he did not go forth such as he had been when he entered, unfettered and free of care; but he came out heavy-thoughted and more stricken with love than he knew. And he kept his desire closely hidden lest the scornful words he had spoken of others a little before should be turned against him, if perchance the longing into which he had fallen should come to be known.

After Criseida had left the noble temple, Troilus returned to his palace with his companions and remained with them there a long time making merry. The better to hide the wound that love had made, he uttered many jibes at those who loved. Then, feigning that other business pressed upon him, he gave leave to each to go where he would. And when everybody had gone, he went all alone to his room, where he sat down, sighing, at the foot of his bed. And he began to recall the pleasure he had had in the morning at the sight of Criseida, telling over the true beauties of her face and praising each in turn. Much did he praise her movements and her stature; and from her manners and bearing he esteemed her a lady of most noble spirit and counted it great good fortune for himself to love such a lady. And much greater yet would it be if by long devotion he might bring it about that he should be loved by her nearly as much as he loved her, or at the least not be refused as her servant.

Imagining that neither travail nor sighing for such a lady could be ill spent and that his desire, were it ever known by any, would be greatly praised, and hence his suffering, if discovered, less blamed, the light-hearted youth debated with himself, all unaware of his coming woe. Wherefore, bent on pursuing this love, he took purpose to act discreetly, deciding first to hide the desire born in his amorous mind from every friend and servant, unless forced to reveal it. And lastly he thought that love when made known to many bore as its fruit trouble and not joy.

And besides these matters he turned his thoughts to many others: how he should make his love known and how he should draw the lady to him. And then, full of high hopes and light of heart, he fell to singing and was wholly resolved to love none but Criseida, for he held as worthless any other lady he might see or whom he had ever found pleasing.

And at such times he spoke to Love with piteous voice: 'O lord, thine henceforth is the soul that once was mine; and this to me is pleasing, since thou hast given me one to serve whom I know not whether I should call a woman or a goddess; and never was there so fair a lady arrayed in black, under a white veil as she seems to me. Thou standest in her eyes, true lord, as in a place worthy of thy might. Therefore, if my service pleases thee at all, I pray thee to win from them the saving of my soul, which lies prostrate beneath thy feet; so did the keen arrows wound it that thou didst shoot against it when thou didst show me her fair face.'

The glowing fires of love spared not the royal blood nor recked aught of the power or greatness of soul that was in Troilus, nor of his bodily strength or valour; but, as fire is kindled in fit fuel, dry or half dry, so in the new lover did all his limbs burn. By his thoughts from day to day and by his delight in them he now made so much the more dry tinder within his proud heart; and he fancied he should draw kindly water from her fair eyes to quench his cruel burning. Wherefore he slyly sought to look often upon them, nor was he aware that by them was the fire kindled the more. And whether he went here or there, whether he was walking or sitting, alone or with his friends according to his pleasure, drinking or eating, by night and day and in every place, he was ever thinking of Criseida; and he said that her high worth and delicate features set her above Polyxena in every beauty and also above Helen.

Nor did an hour of the day go by when he said not to himself a thousand times: 'O clear light that wakens love in my heart, O fair Criseida, would to God that thy noble nature, which robs my face of its hue, would move thee to rue somewhat upon me. None other but thee can make me light of heart, thou only art she who can give me aid.'

All thought of the great war and of his own weal fled from him; and in his breast he hearkened only to what spoke of the high worth of his lady. And, his mind thus fraught, he was eager only to heal the wounds of love, and to that task he had given all his study, and in it found his pleasure.

The sharp battles and the stern encounters in which Hector and his other brothers, followed by the Trojans, took part moved him little or not at all from thoughts of love, although often they saw him ahead of others in the most dangerous onsets, performing marvels in arms. So said they who stood and watched him. But it was not hatred of the Greeks which urged him to this, nor desire for victory to free Troy, which he saw hard pressed by siege; but it was the longing for glory, in order that he might the better please, which wrought all this. And through love, if the story speaks truth, he became so fierce and mighty in arms that the Greeks dreaded him like death.

Already had love robbed him of his sleep, and turned him from his meat and so weighed down his thoughts that the paleness in his face gave true sign of his trouble, although for the most part he hid it with feigned laughter and innocent speech.

And whoever saw him thought this had come to pass by the strain of the war upon him.

And it is not very clear to us whether Criseida, by reason of the cloak he threw over his conduct, was not aware of this, or whether she feigned not to know; but this is very plain and manifest, that she seemed no whit touched by Troilus and the love he bore her and remained unpitying as if she were not loved. And therefore Troilus felt such grief as may not be told, fearing at times that Criseida was moved by some other love, and thus held him of little worth and would not receive him into her service. And he pondered a thousand ways by which he might, in all honour, make her aware of his burning desire.

And thus, when occasion offered, he fell to complaining of love, saying to himself: 'Troilus, now art thou caught, who wert wont to jape at others. None was ever so consumed as thou art through not knowing how to guard thyself from love. Now art thou taken in the snare, a thing thou didst blame in so many others and could not ward off from thyself. What will be said of thee by other lovers, if this love of thine should be known? One and all they will jape at thee, saying among themselves: "Lo, there is he, the man of wisdom, who used to mock at our sighs and amorous plaints; now he has come to the same pass as ourselves; praised be Love who has brought him to such a plight." What will be said of thee among the noble kings and lords, if this be heard of? Well may they say in their displeasure: "See how this man has lost his senses, who in these sad times of stress has but now been trapped by love. And when he should be stout-hearted in the war, his thoughts are spent on love."

'And now, O woeful Troilus, since it has been thy fate to love, would thou hadst become thrall to one who felt even a little love whence thou mightest draw solace. But she for whom thou weepest feels no more than a stone, and remains as cold as ice hardening under a clear sky, and I am consumed like snow in the fire. And now would that I were come even to the port to which my sad state is thus leading me. To me that would be a solace and great comfort, for by death I should be quit of all torment. For, if my woe, as yet unknown to any, be discovered, my life will be filled with a thousand insults every day, and above all others I shall be called a fool.

'Ah, Love, come to my aid! And thou, for whom I weep, captive as man never was before, ah, Have a little pity on him who loves thee much more than his own life! Turn now, I pray thee, thy fair face towards him, and be moved by Love, who makes me suffer these torments for thy sake. Ah, refuse not to grant me this grace.

'If thou dost this, lady, I shall renew my life like a flower in a fresh meadow in spring. Nor will it then be a weariness to me to wait, or to see thee disdainful or proud. And, if this is grievous to thee, ah, cruel one, do thou at least cry to me, who am ready to do thy every pleasure: "Kill thyself"; and indeed I will do it, thinking to please thee by that act.'

Then he spoke many other words, wept and sighed and called her name, as he is wont to do who loves overmuch and finds no mercy for his moans. And all his words were vain and were carried away by the winds, and none of them came to her; and thus each day his torment increased a hundredfold.

CANTO II

While matters stood thus with him, one day when Troilus was alone and heavy-thoughted in his chamber, there came unexpectedly in upon him a Trojan youth of high lineage and very bold spirit. And he, seeing him lying stretched upon his bed and shedding tears, cried: 'What is this, dear friend? Have these times of stress now vanquished thee thus?'

'Pandarus,' said Troilus, 'what chance has brought thee here to see me die? If our friendship has any power, may it please thee to go hence, for I know that to see me die would be more grievous to thee than aught else; and longer life is not for me, so is my strength overcome and taken from me. And believe not that the siege of Troy, or toil of arms, or any fear has brought this trouble upon me; that is the least of my cares when set beside the others. Something else constrains me even to wish that I may die, and therefore it is that I grieve at my ill-fortune. And let it not distress thee, my friend, that I am silent and tell it not to thee, for that is for the best.'

Then did pity grow in Pandarus, and the desire to know this matter. Wherefore he spoke further: 'If our friendship is, as of old, a pleasure to thee, reveal to me what is the cruel fortune that makes thee so desire death; for it is not the act of a friend to keep aught hidden from his friend. I wish to share this pain with thee, if I can give no solace to thy hurt; for it is right to have all things in common with a friend, both woe and pleasure; and I think thou knowest well if I have loved thee through fair and foul, and if I would perform any great service for thee, whatever the undertaking may be.'

Then Troilus uttered a great sigh and said: 'Pandarus, since indeed thou desirest to know my torment, I shall tell thee shortly that which is my undoing; not because I expect through thee to end my longing or to find peace, but only to satisfy thy earnest entreaty, which I know not how to deny. Love, against whom he who defends himself is soonest caught and strives in vain, so kindles my heart with fond delight that I have set every other pleasure far from me; and this does me such hurt, as thou canst see, that a thousand times my hand has barely held itself back from taking my life. Let it suffice thee, my dear friend, to know my griefs, which nevermore shall be laid open; and I pray thee, in God's name, if thou art at all loyal to the love between us, reveal not this desire to others lest great harm follow. Thou dost know what thou didst wish to know; go and leave me here to combat my distress.'

'Oh,' said Pandarus, 'how couldst thou keep such a great passion hidden from me? For I would have given thee counsel and aid, and would have found some way to win thee peace.'

And Troilus said to him: 'How should I have had this from thee, whom I have ever seen unhappy through love, and thou knowest not how to help thyself? How then dost thou think thou canst succour me?'

Pandarus said: 'Troilus, I know thou sayest truth, but many times it chances that he who knows not how to guard himself from poison keeps others safe by good counsel. And ere now the blind man has been seen to walk where the man who sees well goes not without stumbling; and though a man take not good counsel, he may give it in another's danger. I have loved unluckily, and unhappily for me I still love; and this comes about because I have, like thee, loved another in secret. It will be as God wills at the last. The love I have ever borne thee I bear and shall bear thee, nor shall there ever be any who will learn what thou mayest say to me.

'Wherefore, my friend, put thy trust in me and tell me who makes thy life so grievous and hard; and fear not lest I blame thee for loving, for sages of old declared in their wise discourses that love could not be taken from the heart unless it freed itself through long lapse of time. Leave thy anguish, leave thy sighs, and lessen thy grief by speech. Do thus and thy torments will pass, and greatly too does ardour slacken when he who loves sees companions with like desires. And I, as thou knowest, love against my will, nor can I do away nor add to my grief.

'It may be that she who torments thee is such that I shall be able to achieve thy pleasure, and I would satisfy thy desire, if I could, more than ever I did my own; thou shalt see. Let me know who it is for whom thou hast this grief. Rise up; do not lie there; consider that thou canst talk with me as with thyself.'

Thus Troilus remained for a space undecided, and after heaving a grievous sigh, and with a hot flush spread over his face through shame, answered: 'Dear friend, a most fit reason has kept me from laying my love open and clear before thee, for she that has brought me to this pass is thy kinswoman.' And he spoke no word more.

And he fell back on the bed prostrate, weeping bitterly and hiding his face. And to him Pandarus said: 'Dear friend, too little faith has planted such distrust in thy breast. Come, cease the wretched outcry thou makest, if thou wouldst not slay me; if she thou lovest were my sister, thou shouldst have thy pleasure of her, were it in my power. Rise up, tell me, say who she is, tell me at once, that I, who have no other wish, may see a way to comfort thee. Is she a lady who is in my house? Ah, tell me at once, for, if it is she I think, I do not believe that the sixth day will pass before I draw thee from so wretched a plight.'

To this Troilus made no answer, but shrouded his face more each moment. And yet, hearing what Pandarus promised, he began to hope somewhat more, and wished to speak and then checked himself, such shame did he feel at opening the matter to him. But, Pandarus urging him, he turned towards him weeping, and uttered these words: 'My Pandarus, I would I were already dead when I think to what love has driven me; and, if I could keep it hidden without wronging thee, I should not have ceased feigning. But I can do so no longer; and, if thou art as wise as thou art wont to be, thou canst see that love has not ordained that man should love by law, and that he should turn from her on whom his desire is fixed. Others, as thou knowest, love their sisters, and sisters their brothers, and sometimes daughters their fathers and fathers-in-law their daughters-in-law; and at times it is even wont to happen that stepmothers love their stepsons. Love for thy cousin has taken me, which grieves me sorely. I mean Criseida.' And when he had said this, he fell back upon his bed, face downwards, weeping.

When Pandarus heard her named, he spoke thus, laughing: 'My friend, I pray thee in God's name be not distressed; love could not have set thy desire in a better place, for she in truth is worthy of it, if I know aught of manners, or of greatness of soul, or high worth, or beauty. No lady was ever of higher worth, none more gay and more ready of speech, none more pleasing or more gracious, none of greater soul, among all who have ever lived. Nor is there anything so high that she would not attempt it as readily as any king, nor would she lack courage to achieve it, if she but had the power.

'Only one quality my cousin has, besides those I have spoken of, that tells somewhat against thee, that she is virtuous above all other ladies and is more scornful of the things of love. But, if naught else stands in our way, doubt not that with my flattering words I shall find a means to deal with this that will meet thy needs. Have patience to endure and hold in check thy hot desire. Well canst thou see that love has set thee in a place befitting thy worth; stand fast then in thy purpose. And be of good cheer as to thy happiness, which I believe will soon come, if thou drive it not away with thy weeping. Thou art worthy of her and she of thee, and in this matter I shall use all my wits.

'Do not believe, Troilus, that I see not clearly that such loves become not a well-reputed lady, or that I am not aware of what will befall me and her and hers if such a thing should ever come to be spoken of by the world, that, by our folly, she who used to be the seat of honour has become a shameful creature through love. But, as long as desire is not reckless in act and everything likewise is kept secret, it seems to me fair to hold that every lover may obey his deep yearning, if he is discreet in deed and in outward show and brings no shame on those to whom shame and their honour are things of moment.

'In truth I believe that every lady leads an amorous life in her wishes, and that naught but fear of shame holds her back; and, if full contentment can be given to such desire without loss of honour, he who takes her not is a fool, and not overmuch, I think, does the penalty grieve her. My cousin is a widow and desirous; and if she were to deny it, I should not believe her.

'Wherefore, knowing thee to be wise and prudent, I can please both of you and give equal solace to each. But you must keep it secret, and it shall be as though it were not. And I should do wrong if I did not all I could in thy service; and do thou be wise in keeping such acts hidden from others.'

So happy in mind was Troilus as he hearkened to Pandarus that it seemed to him he was already almost set free from all his torment, and more hotly was his love kindled. But after he had been silent for a space, he turned to Pandarus and said to him: 'I believe what thou sayest of her, but by reason of that the task seems the harder to my eyes.

'But how will the yearning I feel within me grow less? for I have never seen her take note of my love. If thou shouldst tell her of it, she would not believe thee. Then, fearing thee, she will blame this passion and thou wilt achieve naught. And if she had it in her heart, yet in order to show herself virtuous unto thee she will not listen. And besides this, Pandarus, I should not wish thee to think that I desired of such a lady anything to hurt her fair name; but all I wish is that she find it pleasing that I should love her. This would be a crowning favour unto me if I should gain it. Seek this, and I ask no more of thee.' And he lowered his eyes, somewhat abashed.

And to him Pandarus replied, laughing: 'What thou sayest does no harm. Leave me alone to act, for I can kindle the flames of love and have store of fit speeches. And ere this I have been able to bring harder tasks to happy issue in the face of strange difficulties. Mine shall be all this toil, and let the sweet fruit be thine.'

Quickly did Troilus leap to the ground from his bed, embracing and kissing him, protesting that to win the war against the Greeks would be to him a triumph of no account compared with this desire that presses him so hard: 'My Pandarus, I trust myself to thee, thou wise one, thou friend; thou knowest all that is needed to end my struggle.'

Pandarus, eager to serve the youth whom he greatly loved, left him to go where he pleased and made his way to where Criseida abode. And she, seeing him coming to her, stood up and greeted him from afar, and Pandarus her. And, taking her by the hand, he led her with him into an apartment.

There after laughter and soft words, merry jests, and very kind speeches, as are common at times between kinsfolk, he paused a space as one who wishes to come to his goal with new arguments if he can, and began to look earnestly and fixedly at her fair face.

Criseida, seeing this, said with a smile: 'Didst thou never see me before, cousin, that thou thus starest at me?'

To whom Pandarus replied: 'Thou knowest that I have seen thee and purpose still to do so; but thou seemest to me beautiful beyond thy wont, and to my mind thou hast more to praise God for than any other fair lady.'

Criseida said: 'What means this? Why more now than in the past?'

And Pandarus replied to her gaily and quickly: 'Because thy face is the luckiest that ever lady had in this world, if I am not mistaken. I have heard it pleases a goodly man so beyond measure that it is his undoing.'

Criseida reddened a little in shame when she heard what Pandarus said, and looked like a morning rose. Then she uttered these words to Pandarus: 'Make not a mock of me, for I should rejoice at any good fortune that befell thee; he whom I pleased must have little to do, for this has never before happened to me since I was born.'

Then said Pandarus: 'Let us leave jesting; tell me, hast thou noted him?'

And she replied to him: 'Not one man more than another, or may I die. It is true that from time to time I see someone pass here who always gazes at my door, nor do I know if he is seeking to see me or musing of other things.'

Then said Pandarus: 'Who is he?'

And Criseida said to him: 'Truly I know him not, nor can I tell you more of him.'

And Pandarus, seeing that she spoke not of Troilus but of another, made answer quickly to her: 'He whom thou hast wounded is a man known to all.'

'Who is it, then,' said Criseida, 'who so delights to see me?'

To whom then Pandarus: 'Since He who set bounds to the world made the first man, I do not think He ever set a soul in any other more perfect than his, who loves thee so much that it could never be told. He is of noble soul and most honourable in speech and eager for honour; in his natural judgment wise beyond other men, nor is any man greater in knowledge; valiant and bold and of open countenance. I could not tell all his worth. Ah, how happy is thy beauty when such a man prizes it above another!

'Well is the gem set in the ring, if thou art wise as thou art fair. If thou become his, as he has become thine, well will the star be joined with the sun; nor was ever youth so well joined to maid as thou wilt be to him, if thou wilt be wise. Blessed wilt thou be if thou see the matter aright. Once and once only does fortune come to every creature in the world, if he know how to take it. He who lets it slip when it comes, let him cry out against himself for his calamity and blame not others. Thy lovely face of fairest beauty has brought it to thee; now be wise in using it. Leave weeping to me, who, born in evil hour, have found favour with neither God, the world, nor fortune.'

'Art thou but trying me, or dost thou speak in earnest,' said Criseida, 'or hast thou left thy senses? Who should have his pleasure of me unless he first became my husband? But tell me, who is this, is he a stranger or a citizen that is so stricken by me? Tell me if thou wilt—if it is right to tell me—and do not for no reason thus cry out: "Ah me!"'

Pandarus said: 'He is indeed a citizen, nor one of the least, and my great friend. And from his breast—it may be by the power of fate—have I drawn forth what I have made known to thee. He lives unhappy and wretched in his sorrow, so does the beauty of thy face consume him; and that thou mayest know who loves thee, Troilus is he who desires thee so greatly.'

Then Criseida stood still and looked at Pandarus; and her colour became that of the morning sky when it grows pale; and she scarce kept back the tears that gathered to her eyes ready to fall. Then, as her lost boldness came back to her, murmuring at first a little to herself, with a sigh she spoke thus to Pandarus: 'I thought, Pandarus, that, if I had ever fallen into such folly as to desire Troilus, thou wouldst not only have chided but also have beaten me. For thou art a man who shouldst seek my honour. O God, help me! What will others do when thou dost set thy wit to make me follow the way of love?

'Well do I know that Troilus is a great man and of high worth, and any great lady should be pleased with him; but since my husband was taken from me my desire has always been far from love, and my heart is still sad over his grievous death; and as long as I live his parting will dwell in my memory.

'And if anybody should come to have my love, in truth I should give it to him, if only I believed it would do him pleasure. But, as thou must plainly know, such desires as he now has are common things and last four days or six and then lightly pass. For, as thought changes, so does love.

'Wherefore let me lead the life that fortune has shaped for me. He will easily find a lady to love who will please him, both humble and gentle. It befits me to remain virtuous. Ah, Pandarus, in God's name, let not this answer seem grievous unto thee, and find comfort for him in new pleasures and other pastimes.'

Pandarus felt himself slighted when he heard the damsel's speech, and had got up as if to leave. Then he stopped and turned again to her, saying: 'I have praised one to thee, Criseida, whom I would commend to my own sister, or to my daughter, or to my wife if I had one, or may God not grant me happiness. For I feel that Troilus is of greater worth than thy love would be; and yesterday I saw him in such a plight by reason of this love that I felt deep pity. It may be thou dost not believe this and therefore it touches thee not. Well do I know that thou wouldst be forced to pity him if thou knewest what I do of his passion. Ah, for love of me, have mercy upon him! I do not believe that there is in the world a more secret or faithful man than he, and he is loyal beyond any other; nor does he desire or see aught but thee. And, though thou art dressed in mourning weeds, thou art still young, and it is allowed thee to love. Lose no time; forget not that old age or death will take away thy beauty.'

'Alas,' said Criseida, 'thou sayest truly. Thus do the years carry us away little by little; and most do die ere they tread the path of love to the end. But now leave thinking of this and tell me if I can yet have the solace and sport of love, and in what manner thou didst first take note of Troilus.'

Then Pandarus smiled and answered: 'I will tell thee what thou wishest to know. The day before yesterday, when matters were quiet because of the truce made then, Troilus was urgent that I should go with him for sport through the shady woods. When we had sat down there, he fell to talking with me of love and then to singing of it to himself. I was not nigh him, but hearing him murmur, took heed of him; and from what I can remember he complained to Love of his torment, saying: "My lord, now in my face and in my sighs does that show forth that I feel within my heart by reason of that charming beauty that has caught me with its loveliness. There art thou, where fixed in my heart is the image that more than aught else delights me. And there dost thou see my soul filled with heavy thoughts, vanquished by thy brightness, which holds it encompassed and bound; and ever, dear lord, it calls out for that sweet peace that only the fair and beauteous eyes of that lady can give it. Then, in God's name, if thou wishest not my death, make this fair creature aware of my love, and by prayers to her win me that joy that is wont to give peace to thy subjects. Ah, my lord, doom me not to die. Ah, in God's name, see how my tortured soul cries aloud day and night, such fear it has lest she slay it. Dost thou fear, my lord, to light thy flames beneath her dark robe? No glory of thine will be greater than this. Pierce her breast with that desire that dwells within mine and torments me. Ah, faithful lord, do that, I pray thee, so that her sweet sighs may through thy working bring comfort to my longings."

'And, when he had said this, with a deep sigh he lowered his head, saying I know not what. Then he fell silent as if weeping. When I saw this, there came upon me a suspicion of what the matter was; and I resolved, when time should better suit, to ask him some day with a laugh the meaning and reason of his song. But a time did not offer itself for this till to-day, when I found him all alone. When I entered his chamber, thinking he might be there, he was on his bed. And, seeing me, he turned away, at which I began to suspect somewhat; and, drawing nearer, I found he was weeping bitterly and sorely lamenting. I comforted him as best I could, and with subtle art and many a ruse I drew his trouble from him, pledging first my faith that I should never tell it to any man. This devotion of his moved me, and for his sake I am come to thee, and I have told thee shortly what he craves in every point.

'What wilt thou do? Wilt thou remain disdainful, and wilt thou let him, who in his love for thee has no care of himself, come to such a cruel death, to a wretched fate or evil fortune? Wilt thou allow such a man to perish because of his love for thee? If thou wert dear to him, not only for thy fair face and for thy eyes, thou mightest even yet deliver him from bitter death.'

Then said Criseida: 'From afar thou didst discern the secret of his breast, though he held it with a firm hand when thou didst find him weeping upon his bed. And so may God make him happy and untroubled and me also, for what thou hast said has stirred pity within me. I am not cruel, as it seems to thee, nor so empty of pity.'

She paused awhile; then after a deep sigh—for already was she stricken by love—spoke further: 'Ah, I see whither thy eager pity makes thee tend, and I will do what thou wishest, since by that I must needs please thee, and he is worthy of it. Let it be enough that I see him. But to escape shame and perchance worse, I pray him to be discreet, and to do naught that may be a reproach either to me or himself.'

'My sister,' said Pandarus then, 'thou speakest well, and I will entreat him to do so. In truth he will not fail—I know him to be of such good bearing and so wise—unless it happen by evil chance, which God forbid. And such reward will I contrive for thee that it will be a pleasure unto thee. God be with thee, and do thy duty.'

When Pandarus had departed, fair Criseida withdrew alone into her chamber, pondering in her heart each little word of Pandarus and the news he had brought, and in what manner it had been spoken. And joyously she debates and speaks to herself, and as she does so she often sighs and calls Troilus to mind more than she is wont to do.

'I am young, beautiful, charming and gay, a widow, rich, noble and beloved, without children and with a care-free life; why should I not give myself to love? If perhaps virtue forbids this to me, yet I shall be careful and shall keep my desire so secret that it will not be known that I have ever had love in my heart.

'Each day my youth slips from me; must I lose it so miserably? I know no lady in this land without a lover; and most, as I know and see, are in love, and am I to lose my time for naught? And to do as others do is no sin and can be blamed by none. Who will desire me if I grow old? In truth, nobody; and to regret then is only to increase my sorrows. It avails naught to repent afterwards or to say sadly: "Why didst thou not love?" It is well, therefore, to provide for oneself in good season. He who loves me is handsome, noble, wise, and prudent, and fresher in beauty than a lily in the garden; of royal blood and highest worth; and Pandarus, thy cousin, does highly praise him. What, then, art thou to do? Why not receive him within thy heart as he has thee? Why not give him thy love? Dost thou not hear how pitiful is his lament? Oh, what delight wilt thou have with him if thou lovest him as he loves thee!

'And now is not a time to take a husband; and even were it, to keep one's freedom is by far the wiser choice. Love that comes from such a friendship is always more welcome to lovers; and let beauty be as great as thou wilt, it is soon stale to husbands, for they are ever lusting after some new thing. Water got by stealth is a far sweeter thing than wine possessed in abundance: so the hidden joy of love quite surpasses that of holding a husband ever in one's arms. Therefore welcome eagerly thy sweet lover, whose coming has assuredly been ordained for thee by God, and satisfy his hot desire.'

For a while she was silent; then her thoughts changed. 'Ah, wretched creature,' she said, 'what art thou about to do? Dost thou not know how miserable a life it is with a lover when desire fails? for always one must needs be whelmed in laments and sighs and in grieving. And to these is added jealousy, which is far worse than wretched death.

'As for this man who now loves thee, he is of far higher condition than thou art. This amorous eagerness will pass away, and he will always treat thee ill and leave thee sorrowful, dishonoured, and perplexed. Take heed what thou doest; when wisdom comes too late, it never has been, never is, and never will be of any worth.

'But, even supposing that this love will last for long, how canst thou know that it will stay concealed? It is indeed vain to trust to fortune and well to know how little human counsel can avail. If the matter is openly revealed, thou mayest count thy fair name that till now has been so good as for ever lost. Therefore leave such loves to those who find pleasure in them.' And after she had said this, she fell to sighing deeply, nor was she able now to drive out from her chaste breast the fair face of Troilus. Wherefore she turned to her first thought, now blaming it and now praising; and thus wavering she long remained.

Pandarus, who had parted well pleased from Criseida, had turned aside to nowhere else but had gone straight to Troilus; and before he had reached his side he began to speak: 'Comfort thee, brother, for I think I have achieved much of thy great desire.' And sitting down, he told him swiftly, without pause, how matters had gone.

As little flowers that droop and close in the chill of night all open out and stand straight upon their stalks when the sun brightens, so was it with Troilus's weary spirit; and casting up his eyes, he spoke as one set free: 'Praised be thy peerless worth, fair Venus, and that of Cupid, thy son.'

Then he embraced Pandarus fully a thousand times and kissed him as often, so happy that he could not have been more so had a thousand Troys been given him. And very slowly he went with Pandarus alone to look upon the beauty of Criseida, eagerly watching to perceive if any change of bearing had been wrought in her by what Pandarus had spoken.

She was standing at one of her windows, and it may be that she was expecting what came to pass. She showed herself neither haughty nor scornful towards Troilus when he stared at her, but with modesty she looked steadily at him over her right shoulder. And Troilus went his way rejoicing, giving thanks to Pandarus and to God.

And that coldness that had held Criseida uncertain which path to choose fled away as she praised his manners, his pleasant bearing and his courtesy; and so suddenly was she taken that she desired him beyond any other good, and grieved much over the time she had lost when she had not known his love.

Troilus sings and is wondrous gay, jousts, is open-handed, and joyously bestows gifts; and often he renews and changes his dress, loving more fervently every hour. And to him it is a delight, and not a burden, to follow love, to gaze discreetly at Criseida, who, no less discreet, showed herself at times charming and gay. But, as we see every day, the more wood the greater the fire, so, when hope grows, love too very often increases. And hence Troilus felt high desire prick him more mightily than before in his stricken heart; and thus sighs and torments came upon him again, stronger than at first.

And at times Troilus lamented bitterly to Pandarus thereof, saying: 'Wretched am I, for Criseida has so reft me of life with her fair eyes that I am minded to die through the strong desire that overwhelms my heart and there burns and consumes me. Alas, what shall I do, I who should rest satisfied with merely her great courtesy? She looks at me and suffers me to gaze modestly at her. This should be enough for my raging desires; but my eager appetite would fain have I know not what more; so unruly are the passions that rouse it that he who has not felt them would not believe how this flame, increasing hour by hour, torments me.

'What then shall I do? I know not what to do save to call upon thee, fair Criseida; thou alone canst help me, thou peerless lady, thou art she who alone canst quench my fire, O sweet light and little flame of my heart. Could I have one winter's night with thee, I would bide in hell afterwards for one hundred and fifty.

'What shall I do, Pandarus? Hast thou naught to say? Thou seest me burn in this fire and seemest no whit moved by my sighs that consume me. Aid me, I pray thee dearly, tell me what to do, counsel me a little, for if I have no help from thee or her, I have run into the snares of death.'

Then said Pandarus: 'I understand clearly, and I hear all thou dost say; nor have I ever made false pretence to aid thee in thy sufferings, nor ever shall. And I am ready always to do for thee not only what is fitting, but all things and need no urging by force or entreaty. Lay open to me thy warm desire.

'I know that in all things thou seest six times more than I do; yet, were I in thy place, I should set forth to her in writing by my hand all my suffering; and besides this, I should, appealing to God, love, and her courtesy, entreat her to take pity upon me; and, when thou hast written this, I will bear it to her without delay. And, furthermore, I will entreat her to the best of my power to have mercy on thee. What she will answer thou wilt see, and even now my mind surely believes that her reply will please thee; and therefore write and set down all thy loyalty, all thy suffering, and then thy desire. Let there be nothing kept back.'

This counsel pleased Troilus greatly, but he answered like a timid lover: 'Alas, Pandarus, thou wilt see—for ladies, as we perceive, are shamefaced—that Criseida for shame will refuse with scornful words the writing thou wilt bear, and we shall have made our state beyond measure worse than before.'

To this Pandarus said: 'If it pleases thee, do what I say, and then leave me to act. For if love befriend me, I think to bring thee an answer written with her own hand. And if that pleases thee not, thou mayest remain timid and sad. If thou wilt still cling to thy torment, it will not be for me to make thee happy.'

Then said Troilus: 'Let thy will be done. I shall go and write; and I entreat Love by his courtesy that he may bring the writing, the letter, and the venture to a happy issue.'

And he went thence to his room, and forthwith, like a wise man, wrote a letter to his most dear lady, and thus he said: 'How can he who lies in anguish, in sore grieving, and in hard plight, as I do because of thee, lady, give greeting to any? In truth it should not be asked of him; and so I follow not the common use of others; and for this reason alone thou wilt receive from me here no wishes for thy well-being, for there is none in me unless thou give it me.

'I must do what Love wills, Love who has ere now emboldened baser men than me; and he constrains me to write the words as thou wilt see, and demands obedience of me as is his wont. Wherefore, if aught in this is amiss, do thou blame him and pardon me, I pray thee, O my sweet hope.

'Thy lofty beauty and the splendour of thy fair eyes and graceful manners, thy dear modesty and womanly worth, thy ways and actions more excellent than those of others, have in my mind so fixed him as lord and thee as lady that no chance save death would be strong enough to wrench them out.

'And whatever I do, the fair image of thee ever brings a thought to my heart that drives out everything that speaks of aught but thee, although in truth my soul, now become the handmaiden of thy high worth, in which alone I set my hope, longs for none but thee. And thy name is ever in my mouth, and strikes my heart with ever stronger desire.

'From these things, lady, is born a fire that consumes my soul day and night without allowing me to find a place of rest. My eyes weep, and my breast sighs, and I feel myself wasted away little by little by this flame that lies within me. Wherefore to thy high worth alone must I turn if I wish to be saved. Only thou canst soothe these grievous pains to sweet peace when thou wishest; only thou, O lady mine, canst turn these bitter afflictions to true calm; only thou by the exercise of pity canst take from me the torment that so destroys me; only thou, as my lady, canst fulfil the desire of my heart. Therefore, if ever through perfect faith, if ever through great love, if through desire to serve well at all times and under all conditions, good or bad, any one did merit grace, grant that I be such a one, my dear lady; grant this to me who come to thee as to her who is cause of all my sighs.

'Well I know that what I crave has not been earned by my service; but thou alone who hast wounded my heart, thou and none other, canst make me worthy of a greater thing when thou wishest; O thou longed-for bliss of my heart, lay down the high disdain of thy great soul, and, noble as thou art in thy deeds, be gracious unto me. I am sure now that thou wilt be full of pity as thou art fair, and that thou, wisely gay and gracious, wishing not that I should die in misery through greatly loving thee, O lady of delight, wilt yet turn my sore anguish into sweet joy. I pray thee, if my prayer avails aught, by that love to which now, it may be, thou art less indifferent. Although I am but a small gift and have little power and far less worth, I am, in all truth, wholly thine. If I speak not worthily, yet thou art wise, and thy understanding will be better than my speech; and likewise I hope that thou wilt act towards me better and more generously than I deserve. May love dispose thy heart thereto.

'There were many other things I had to say, but I shall not utter them lest they be a trouble unto thee; and, so to make an end, I pray Love, the sweet lord, that, as he has made thee the source of my delight, so he may be equally pleased to set thy desire upon me, so that as I am thine, thou shalt some day become mine and never be taken from me.'

And thus, when he had written all these things on a paper, he folded it properly, and on his cheeks all wet with tears bathed the gem and afterwards sealed it and put it in Pandarus's hand, but first kissed it a hundred times and more, saying: 'O my letter, happy shalt thou be, for thou shalt come into the hand of that lady.'

Pandarus, taking the devout letter, went to Criseida, and she, seeing him come, left the company in which she was, and went part of the way to meet him full of fear and desire; and she was as an eastern pearl to look upon. From afar they exchanged greeting, and then took each other by the hand.

Then said Criseida: 'What matter brings thee here now? Hast thou new tidings?'

And to her Pandarus straightway said: 'Lady, I have tidings good and of fair aspect for thee, but they are not so for somebody else, as may appear to thee in this unhappy letter from him who seems to be dying because of thee, so little concern hast thou for him. Take it and look carefully upon it, and any answer will make him light of heart.'

Criseida stood timidly and took it not; and her gentle look did somewhat change, and then she said softly: 'My Pandarus, do thou have some regard for me and not only for the youth, so may love bring thee to a state of peace. Consider whether that which thou askest now is seemly—judge thyself thereof—and think whether I do well to take the letter and whether thy request is very honourable, and whether it is good to do a deed, in itself wanton, to lessen the sufferings of another. Ah, my Pandarus, leave it not with me; carry it back, for the love of God.'

Somewhat troubled by this, Pandarus said: 'A wondrous thing is this to think of—that each woman, when others are by to see, should appear coy and angry about what is most desired by ladies. I have spoken to thee so much of this, thou shouldst not now be over-nice with me. I pray thee, do not deny me this now.'

Criseida smiled as she heard him, and took the letter and put it in her bosom. Then she said to him: 'When I find time I shall read it as best I can. If in this I do ill, my reason is that I can do no less than please thee. May God look down from heaven and have regard to my lack of cunning.'

Pandarus departed after he had given it to her; and she, greatly desiring to see what it might say, having found an excuse, left her companions sitting where they were. She went to her room, unfolded it, read and re-read it with pleasure, and clearly did she see that Troilus was far more hotly in love than showed in his bearing. And this was welcome to her, because she felt herself pierced to the very heart. And therefore she had been heavily afflicted, though outwardly it showed not at all. And when she had well noted each written word, she praised and thanked Love for that, saying to herself: 'I must find time and place to quench this fire. For if I let it grow to too fierce a flame, it might chance that the hidden desire would be seen in my pale face, and that to me would be no small misfortune. And for myself I purpose not to die nor to cause the death of any one when I can joyously drive away my own and another's trouble. In sooth, I am not minded to be as I have been till now. If Pandarus come again for the answer, I shall give him a pleasing and welcome one, even were the price higher than I must pay. Nor shall Troilus ever again be able to call me empty of pity. Would that I were now in his sweet arms, held closely face to face.'

Pandarus, who had been often urged by Troilus, returned to Criseida, and smiling said: 'What thinkest thou of my friend's writing?'

Straightway she grew red and said naught but 'God knows that.' And Pandarus made answer to her: 'Hast thou answered?' And she mockingly said to him: 'So soon?'

'If ever,' said Pandarus, 'I am to be able to act for thee, let it be done now.'

And she to him: 'I know now how to do it well.'

'Ah,' said Pandarus, 'strive to please him, and love is wont to teach well; I have so great desire to comfort him that thou wouldst not believe it though I pledged my faith. Only thy answer could do that.'

'And I will do it since it so pleases thee, but God grant the thing go well!'

'Ah, so it will,' said Pandarus, 'for he is worthy, and this more than aught else will give him delight.'

Then he went his way, and she in a corner of her room to which others were rarely wont to come sat down to write after this manner: 'To thee, discreet and mighty friend, whose love for me does greatly blind thee; to thee as a man enslaved beyond measure by me, Criseida sends greeting, if she can count her honour safe, and then humbly commends herself to thy high worth, eager to please thee if no harm come to my virtue or chastity.

'From him who loves thee with so perfect a love that he cares no longer for my honour or my good name, I have received papers filled with thy writing. Therein I have read of thy sad life, not without grief, or may I not have the happiness I crave. And, tear-stained though they were, yet have I read them closely. And carefully thinking of all things, and pondering thy suffering and thy request, thy faithfulness, and thy hope, I see not how I can very fittingly meet thy demand, wishing as I do to give my whole care to what is most to be desired in the world, which is to live and die with a fair name.

'Although it would be a good thing to pleasure thee were the world what it ought to be, yet since it is what it is, we must perforce accept it. To do aught else might bring dread sufferings upon us. The pity that moved me for thee I must needs, despite myself, put away; and little will be the solace thou gettest from me.

'But so great is the worth I feel in thee, that I know thou wilt see clearly what befits me and wilt be content with this answer I give thee, and wilt set bounds to thy sore torment, which grieves my heart and gives me great distress. In sooth, were it not unseemly, gladly should I do what would please thee.

'As thou canst see, the writing and art of this letter are of small account, and I would fain it brought thee more pleasure. But as yet thy wishes cannot find fulfilment. It may be that some day doing will take the place of good will. And, if it seem well to thee, check somewhat thy sorrow that I have not answered all thou hast said.

'I say naught of the declarations thou dost make, for I am sure thou wouldst perform all things. And in truth, though I am of little worth, I do protest more than a thousand times that thou canst have me for thine if the cruel fire consume me not, which forsooth thou wouldst not wish. I say no more, save to pray God to satisfy thy desire and mine.'

And, when she had spoken in this fashion, she folded the letter and sealed it and gave it to Pandarus, who, forthwith seeking the youth Troilus, came to him with it and presented it to him with the highest delight. And he, having taken it, speedily read what was written there; and, sighing, he felt a change wrought in his heart by the words.

But yet in the end, as he carefully repeated all that she had written, he said to himself: 'If I understand her, love binds her; but like one who is guilty she still seeks to hide herself under a shield. But, if love give me strength to endure, she will not long be able to keep herself from coming to quite other speech.'

And Pandarus, to whom he told all, thought the same. Wherefore Troilus is lighter of heart than was his wont and lays aside for a little his sad grief. And he hopes that soon the hour must come when his torment shall bear fruit; and this he craves, and for this he calls aloud day and night, as one who desires naught else. From day to day his longing grew, and, although hope helped him to endure, yet was he heavy at heart, and it must be believed that his distress was great. And thus it may be supposed that in his strong desire he often wrote letters; and answers to these came to him, now frequently and now rarely, and sometimes they were joyous and sometimes cruel.

And thus he often complained of love and of fortune, whom he held to be his foe, and many times he said to himself: 'Alas, if love's nettle pricked her a little more, even as it pierces and hurts me, then would my life, bare of solace, soon come to the happy haven; but ere I come there I shall be dead.'

Pandarus, who saw the flames kindled in the breast of him he loved, was often unstinting in his entreaties to Criseida, and told her everything that he had clearly noted touching Troilus. And she, listening gladly, said: 'I can do naught else. I am doing for him what thou didst order me, my dear brother.'

'This is not enough,' replied Pandarus, 'I wish you to comfort him and speak to him.'

And Criseida made answer to him: 'I am not minded ever to do this for him, for I am by no means willing to yield him the crown of my virtue. I shall ever love him as a brother because of his great goodness and his virtue.'

Pandarus answered: 'The priests praise this crown in those whom they cannot rob of it; and each of them discourses like a saint; and then they steal upon as many of you as they can in your sleep. Nobody will ever know of Troilus. He is now in great torment and finds his only good in the hope of thy favour. He who can do good and does it not acts very ill, and to waste time is more displeasing to a man the wiser he is.'

Criseida said: 'I know that he is so worthy as to have regard for my honour, and that he is so honourable as to ask of me only seemly things. And by my hope of salvation I swear to thee that, save in the thing thou askest, I am his a thousand times more than I am my own, so does his courtesy charm me.'

'If he charms thee, what more dost thou seek? Ah, leave this coyness. Dost thou mean him to die of love? Thou wilt be able to count thy beauty dear indeed if thou slayest such a man. Ah, tell me when thou wishest him to come to thee, for to him that is a greater prize than heaven holds, and tell me how and where. Be not anxious to conquer all thy scruples.'

'Alas, to what hast thou brought me, my Pandarus, and what dost thou wish me to do? Thou hast broken and destroyed my virtue. I dare not look thee in the face. Ah, wretched me, when shall I regain it? The blood grows cold about my heart when I think of what thou dost ask; and thou art unconcerned, and dost look on the matter with untroubled eyes. Would I had died the day I gave ear to thee here in my room. Thou didst plant a desire in my heart that I scarce think will ever leave it, and that will bring upon me the loss of honour—ah, wretched me!—and infinite woes. I can do no more. Since it is thy pleasure, I am ready to fulfil thy wish.

'But, if any entreaty find favour in thy eyes, I pray thee, my sweet and dear brother, that every deed and word of ours be kept secret. Thou canst see well what might follow if such love should come to light. Ah, speak thereof to him and make him understand; and, when the time comes, I will do what his pleasure craves.'

Pandarus answered: 'Guard thy own lips, for neither he on his part nor I shall ever say aught.'

'Now,' she said, 'thou dost hold me very foolish when thou seest me all trembling with fear lest it be known. But as the honour and shame that shall be ours touch thee as well as me, I shall leave the matter in peace, and thou wilt do henceforth as thou wilt.'

Pandarus said: 'Doubt not of that, for we shall be very cautious therein. When wilt thou that he come to speak to thee? Let us now bring this matter to a head, for what must needs be done is far better done quickly; and love is much better hidden after the deed, when you have agreed together what you are to do.'

'Thou knowest,' said Criseida, 'that in this house are women and other people with me, of whom some are to go to the approaching festival; and then shall I be with him. Let not this delay be grievous unto him; I shall talk to thee of the manner of his coming then. Only take heed that he be discreet, and that he know how to hide the feelings of his heart.'

CANTO III

O shining light, whose ray has guided me thus far on my flight through Love's domain, now must thy gleam with doubled brightness guide my wit and make it such that I may show forth every part of the fairness of Love's sweet sway, of which Troilus had come to be worthy.

And to that kingdom does he come who loyally, with wisdom and virtue, can endure the passion of love in all its might; very seldom can any one come there by other ways. Therefore, O fair lady, refuse not my high desire; graciously grant that which I ask, and I shall not cease to sing thy praises.

Although Troilus was still in great torment, yet he seemed in good estate, thinking only of how he might please Criseida, and remembering that she replied humbly to his letters when she wrote, and moreover that, whenever he saw her, she looked upon him so sweetly that it seemed to him he felt the highest delight.

Pandarus, as I said before, had parted from the lady, his thoughts in accord with hers; and joyful in mind and look he sought Troilus, whom he had left on his setting out, torn between happy hope and sad laments. And he went searching for him here and there until he found him in a temple deep in thought.

And as soon as he had come to him, he drew him aside and began to speak to him: 'My friend, when of late I saw thee languish so grievously from love, that pressed so hard upon me that my heart for thy sake took on itself a great part of thy torment; and, to give thee comfort, I have never rested till I have found thy solace. For thee have I become a go-between; for thee have I cast my honour to the ground; for thee have I corrupted my sister's pure breast and planted thy love in her heart; nor will it be long ere thou see her with more delight than my tongue can tell thee, when thou wilt have fair Criseida in thy arms.

'But, as God knows, who sees all things, and as thou knowest, too, no hope of gain, but only the faith I bear thee as a friend has led me to this and brought me to act in such a way that thou shouldst win thy reward. Wherefore I pray thee, if the longed-for boon is not snatched from thee by cruel fortune, act as befits a wise man. Thou knowest that among the people she is of holy repute, nor has aught but what is all good ever been said of her by any; now it has come to pass that thou hast it in thy hands, and canst rob her of it if thou dost what is not fitting, though this cannot happen without great shame to me, who am at once her kinsman and her adviser.

'Wherefore I pray thee as earnestly as I can that this business be kept secret between us. From Criseida's heart I have taken every feeling of shame, and every thought opposed to thee, and have so worked upon her by speaking of thy true love that she loves thee, and is ready to do what it pleases thee to command. And to bring this to pass naught is lacking but fit occasion; and, when thou hast that, I will put thee in her arms to take thy delight there; but, in God's name, see to it that such act is not spoken of, and that by no chance it escape from thy breast. Nor, my dear friend, let it displease thee if many times I beg this of thee; thou seest that my entreaty is indeed honourable.'

Who could tell all the gladness that the soul of Troilus felt when he heard Pandarus? The more he spoke, the more did his sorrow lessen. The sighs of which he had such store left him, and the wretched pain went away; and his tearful face, now full of hope, became joyous. And just as the newly-come spring suddenly reclothes with leaves and blossoms the little trees, which had stood bare in the harsh season, and makes them beautiful, and reclothes the meadows and hills and every riverside with grass and fair new flowers, so did Troilus, swiftly full of new joy, laugh with happy countenance.

And after a little sigh, looking Pandarus in the face, he said: 'Dear friend, thou must remember both how and when thou didst find me weeping in the bitterness I was wont to have in my loving, and how I changed not when thy words would fain have discovered what was the cause of my suffering. And thou knowest how stubbornly I kept myself from revealing it to thee, who art my one dear friend; and because of that there was no peril in saying it, though it was not a modest act. Think now, then, how I could ever bring myself to that, I who in telling it to thee tremble with fear lest some other should hear. May God keep such ill fortune far from us. But none the less I swear to thee by that God who has equal sway over heaven and earth, and as I hope to come not into the hands of cruel Agamemnon, that, if my life were eternal, as it is mortal, thou mayest rest secure that to the utmost of my power this secret shall not escape me, and in all my acts shall be upheld the honour of that lady who has wounded my heart. How much thou hast said and done for me I know well and clearly see, nor could I ever repay thee by any act, for thou, I may say, hast drawn me out of hell and worse to heaven. But for the sake of our friendship, I beseech thee no longer lay that foul name upon thyself when thou comest to help a friend in need. Leave that to the wretched misers whom gold leads to such service. Thou hast done it to save me from the bitter griefs in which I was and from the cruel strife which I had with thoughts that preyed upon me and troubled every sweet memory—as a friend should do when he sees a friend in torment. And that thou mayest know what great good will I bear thee I have my sister Polyxena, prized above others for her beauty, and also there is with her that fairest Helen, who is my kinswoman—open thy heart if either is pleasing unto thee—then leave it to me to work with whichever it be.

'But now that thou hast done so much, far more than I should have asked of thee, fulfil my desire when thou hast opportunity. To thee I turn, and from thee alone do I look for my high pleasure and my comfort, my joy and weal and solace and delight; nor shall I do aught but as thou shalt say. When my delight is won, thou wilt find thy pleasure therein.'

Pandarus was pleased with Troilus, and each busied himself with his own matters. But, though to Troilus each day seemed a hundred till he could hold that lady in his arms, yet did he endure, and with lofty argument hold in check, the violence of his desire, giving the night to thoughts of love and the day to toil, with his followers, in the service of Mars.

And thus the time desired by the two lovers came. Wherefore Criseida called Pandarus to her and told him all her design. But Pandarus lamented concerning Troilus, for that the day before he had gone some distance away with certain men on matters of moment touching the war, though he was expected to come back at any time. He told her this, and the hearing of it was a great grief to her. But, notwithstanding this, Pandarus, as a devoted friend, forthwith sent a speedy servant to fetch him. And he, taking no rest, in short space reached Troilus, who, hearing why he had come, with light heart made ready to return.

And when he came to Pandarus, he learned from him all that he was to do. Wherefore with great impatience he awaited the night, which seemed to him to flee away; and then in silence, with Pandarus alone, he took his way to where Criseida watched for him in loneliness and fear. The night was dark and cloudy as Troilus wished; and, as he went, he carefully scanned everything that he thought might thwart by little or much his amorous desire and cause him grievous torment. And alone by a secret way he entered the house, which was already silent.

And in a certain place, remote and dark, he waited, as was enjoined upon him, for the lady; nor was the tarrying for her hard and burdensome to him, nor the not seeing plainly where he was. But undaunted and full of trust he often said to himself: 'The courteous lady will soon come, and I shall be more glad than if I alone were lord of the world.'

Criseida had clearly heard him come, for, as had been arranged, she had coughed, so that he might hear; and in order that it might not be wearisome for him she often spoke in a loud voice; and speedily she dispatched all her people to sleep, saying that she was so drowsy that she could no longer remain awake. When everybody had gone to sleep and the whole house was left quiet, Criseida quickly came to where Troilus was in the secret place. And he, hearing her come, stood up, and with glad face went to meet her, waiting in silence, ready to do whatever she might command.

The lady had a lighted torch in her hand, and all alone she came down the stairs and beheld Troilus eagerly awaiting her. And she greeted him, and then said, as fairly as she could: 'My lord if I have offended thee by keeping thy royal splendour captive in such a place, I pray thee, in God's name, to pardon me, my sweet love.'

And to her Troilus said: 'Fair lady, sole hope and bliss of my mind, ever before me has been the star of thy lovely face in its splendour and brightness, and this little place has been more dear to me in sooth than my palace; it needs not to ask pardon for this.'

Then he embraced her, and they kissed each other on the mouth. They left not that place ere they had embraced each other a thousand times with sweet gladness and keen delight. And as many times more did they kiss one another, burning as they did with equal fire and holding one another very dear. But when they made an end of these greetings, they mounted the stairs and entered the chamber.

It would take long to describe the joyousness, and it would be impossible to tell the delight they had together when they came thither. And they disrobed and went to bed; and there the lady, who had still kept her last garment, said to him playfully: 'O mirror mine, the newly married are shamefaced on the first night.'

And to her Troilus said: 'My soul, I pray thee that I may have thee naked in my arms as my heart desires.'

And then she: 'See how I rid myself of it'; and, casting off her shift, she quickly threw herself into his arms. And each with fervour held the other close, and they did feel the utmost sweetness of love.

O sweet and much desired night, what wert thou to the two happy lovers! I could not portray it had I the skill of all the poets bestowed upon me. Let him who has ever had a guerdon of love such as was theirs think of it, and he will know in part what was their bliss.

And all night they left not one another's arms; and, clinging thus together, they thought they were taken one from the other, or that it was not true that they were in each other's arms, as indeed they were; but they thought they dreamed that they embraced, and often one asked the other: 'Do I hold thee in my arms, or do I dream, or art thou thyself?'

And with such desire did they gaze upon one another that neither turned away his eyes; and one said to the other: 'O my love, can it be that I am with thee?'

'Yes, dear heart,' did the other often make answer, 'thanks be to God.'

And many times they held each other very close and exchanged sweet kisses.

Often Troilus kissed the fair amorous eyes of Criseida, saying: 'You plant such fiery darts of love in my heart that I am all aflame; you seized upon me, and I sought not escape by flight, as does he who is in doubt. You hold me and always will hold me, O my beautiful eyes, in love's net.'

Then he kissed them and kissed them yet again; and Criseida also kissed his. After that he kissed her whole face and her breast; and no hour passed without a thousand sighs, not those grievous ones that make men pale, but sighs of devout love that showed what affection lay in their breasts; and afterwards their delight was renewed.

Ah, let the wretched misers think of this, who blame him who is in love and who has not wholly given himself, as they do, to gaining wealth in some way; and let them consider whether, holding it very dearly as they do, it ever offered such delight as is offered in a single moment to him who has been happy in his love. They will say yes, but they will lie; and with laughter and gibes they will call this love a painful madness; and they see not that in a single hour they will lose themselves and their wealth without having known in their lives what joy is. God make them unhappy and give their possessions to lovers.

Happy in each other, the two lovers began to speak together, and to tell, one to the other, of past laments and agonies and sighs; and all this speech they often broke with ardent kissing; and, banishing past distress from their thoughts, they took delightful pleasure together. No talk was there of sleep, but they desired to keep eager vigil lest any of the night be lost. They could not weary of one another, however much they did and said which they thought belonged to the act of love. And they let not the hours run fruitless past, but turned each one to profit that night.

But when, near day, they heard the cocks crow because of the rising dawn, the desire to be in one another's arms was kindled again; and they complained of the hour that must divide them and put them in new torment that neither had yet known, by parting them when they were now more than ever burning with love.

And when Criseida heard them crowing, she said sadly: 'O my love, now must thou rise if indeed we wish to hide our desire; but I would embrace thee a little, my love, before thou risest, that I may feel less pain at thy going hence. Ah, embrace me, my sweet life.'

Troilus embraced her, almost weeping, and pressing her close, kissed her, cursing the day that came to part them so quickly. Then he said to her: 'To leave thee grieves me exceedingly. How can I ever go from thee, since thou, O lady, dost bestow on me the bliss I feel? I know not how it is I still live when I think that I must needs leave thee against my will, and that already I have been banished from life and over me death has great power. Nor know I how or when I shall come again. O Fortune, why dost thou exile me from such pleasure, which more than aught else enchants me, and why dost thou rob me of solace and peace? Ah, what shall I do if at the very outset the longing to return here presses so hard upon me, poor wretch that I am, that my life cannot bear it? Ah, pitiless day, why comest thou so soon to divide us? When will thy light sink, so that I may see thee make us happy again? Alas, I know not.'

And then, turning to Criseida, he kissed her face in its fresh beauty, saying: 'If I thought, O fair lady mine, that I should ever dwell in thy mind, as I hold thee in mine, that would be more precious to me than the kingdom of Troy, and I should endure this parting, although I yield to it against my will; and I should hope to come again, when time and place are set, to quench as now our fire.'

Criseida replied to him with a sigh, while she held him close in her arms: 'My soul, if I remember aright, I heard it said long since that Love is a greedy spirit, and when he grasps anything he holds it so tightly and firmly clasped in his clutches that by no counsel can it be set free. Through thee he has so caught me, my dear bliss, that if I wished to be again what I was before, think not that I could do so. Morning and evening thou art ever fixed in my mind; and, if I thought that I were so in thine, I should hold myself more blessed than I could ask. Wherefore distrust not my love, for never have I had such feeling for another; and, if thou dost eagerly desire to return here, I desire it far more than thou; nor when the chance is given me wilt thou be before me in coming hither again. Heart of my body, I give myself to thee.' And when she had said this, she kissed him with a sigh.

Troilus rose against his will after he had kissed her a hundred times. But, seeing what needs must be, he fully dressed himself; and then, after many words, he said: 'I do thy will, I go hence. Let not thy promises fail me; and I commend thee to God and leave my spirit with thee.'

She had no voice wherewith to answer, such pain oppressed her at his going. But Troilus with a swift step took his way towards his palace; and he felt clearly that love tormented him far more than it had done in his earlier desires; so much had he found Criseida to surpass what he had before conceived of her.

When Troilus had returned to the royal palace, he quietly went to bed to win some ease by sleeping if he might; but sleep could not enter his breast, such unrest did new thoughts cause him when he recalled past delight and considered how much more precious was fair Criseida than he had believed. And he kept turning over in his mind every act of hers and her wise speech; and often also he would repeat her pleasant and sweet jesting. And ever he felt love for her greater by far than he had before imagined; and with such thoughts he was kindled to greater love and knew it not.

Likewise did Criseida, speaking of Troilus in her heart. And rejoicing to have such a lover she offered boundless thanks to love; and to her it seemed full a thousand years ere her dear lover should come again to her, and she should hold him in her arms and kiss him often as she had done on the night just gone.

In the morning Pandarus had come to Troilus, who had risen, and he greeted him; and Troilus returned his greeting and eagerly threw his arms round his neck: 'My Pandarus, welcome art thou!' And lovingly he kissed him on the brow. 'As surely as I do live, my friend, thou hast raised me from hell to paradise. If I should die a thousand times a day for thee, I could never bring to pass a tiny part of what I know well thou dost deserve. Thou hast set me in joy after bitter grief.' And again he kissed him, and then he said: 'My sweet bliss, how glad thou makest me! When shall I again embrace thee? The sun, which sees the whole world, does not look upon so fair and pleasing a lady, if my words deserve belief, so gracious, fair, and charming as is she by whose kindness more than by aught else I truly live in gladness. Praised be love, who made me hers, and praised also be thy good service. And verily thou hast not given me a thing of small worth; nor hast thou given me to a person of little worth. My life shall be ever pledged to thee, and it shall be always at thy pleasure; thou hast raised it from death to life.'

And here he fell silent, in greater happiness than ever. Pandarus heard him and paused a space and then replied to his words thus gaily: 'If I have done anything that is pleasing to thee, my fair sweet friend, I am glad; and it is to me a great delight. But yet more than ever do I remind thee to set a check on thy amorous desire and to be discreet, so that, now that thou hast banished torment by enchanting joy, thou fall not again to distress by unrestrained speech.'

'I will act so as to please thee,' replied Troilus to his dear friend. Then in highest joy he told him the happy things that had befallen him, and spoke further: 'I tell thee indeed that never was I in the snares of love as now I am, and far more than erstwhile burns within me now the fire that I have drawn from the eyes and face of Criseida. I burn more than ever, but this new fire that I feel is of a different sort from that before; and now this sport of love refreshes me, for in my heart I am ever thinking of the beauty that doth cause it. But it is true that it makes my desire somewhat more eager than before to come again to her loving arms and to kiss her delicate face.'

The youth could not have his fill of talk with Pandarus touching the gladness he had felt and the delight and the bliss that had crowned his sufferings, and the perfect love he bore unto Criseida, in whom alone he had set his hope. And every other concern of his and every strong desire was forgotten.

After a short time Troilus' happy fortune yielded him opportunity for his love. And when night had fallen he went forth alone from his palace and saw no star in the sky. He went secretly by the way he had gone before to his delight, and waited noiseless and hidden in the wonted spot.

As Criseida had come before, so now did she come in fit time, and did all things as before. And after each had given the other happy and gracious greeting as much as seemed fit to them, in great gladness, hand in hand, they entered the chamber, and without delay they lay down together.

When Criseida had Troilus in her arms, she began to speak thus joyously: 'What lady has been or ever could be who could know such bliss as I do now? Ah, who would fear to go forthwith to death, if so it had to be, to win only a little of such great bliss?'

Then he began: 'My sweet love, I know not what to say, nor could I ever utter the sweetness and the burning desire thou hast set in my breast; and there I would fain have thee always, even as I have thy image. Nor would I crave aught else of Jove, if he would grant me this, than that I should ever be as I am now. I do not believe that he can ever slacken this fire, as I once believed he would when we had been often together; but I saw not clearly. Like a blacksmith thou hast cast water on the flame, so that it burns more than before, and so it is that I never loved thee as I love thee now, for day and night I desire and long for thee.'

Thus did Troilus speak to her as they held each other in close embrace. And in their playfulness they used all those words that are wont to be said by one lover to another in such delights, kissing each other on the mouth, the eyes, and the breast, giving one another the caresses that had been unspoken in their letters.

But cruel day drew near and made itself known by clear signs, which each of them railed against in anger; for to them it seemed to come much earlier than it was wont; and this in sooth was grievous to them both. But since there was no help both rose forthwith. They parted, one from the other, in their wonted way, after many sighs; and they laid plans to satisfy those desires again at no distant time; so that by being with each other they might abate the torments of their love and spend their joyous youth, while it lasted, in this happiness.

Troilus was content and passed his time in song and merriment. The high beauty and charming countenances of all ladies save his Criseida he counted as naught; and he believed that all other men lived in sad affliction compared with himself, so greatly did his happy fortune give him delight and pleasure.

Sometimes he took Pandarus by the hand, and with him went into a garden, and first of all fell into talk of Criseida, of her worth and courtesy. Then, far from all sadness, he began gaily to sing with him in such fashion as is here set down without any change.

'O light eternal, whose untroubled radiance makes beautiful the third heaven, whence are poured down pleasure, desire, pity, and love, friend of the sun and daughter of Jove, gracious mistress of every gentle heart, undoubted source of the strength that moves me to sweet sighs of bliss, ever may thy might be praised.

'Heaven, earth, sea, and hell each feels thy power, O clear light; and, if I discern the truth, plants, seeds, and grass likewise. Birds, beasts, fish in the sweet season feel thy eternal vapour, and men and gods; nor without thee can any creature in the world be of worth and endure.

'O fair goddess, thou first didst move Jove gladly to achieve those great works through which all things live and have their being; and thou dost often make him merciful to the wretched deeds of us mortals; and dost turn the chastisement that we deserve into glad and pleasant rejoicings. And thou didst send him down hither in a thousand forms, when thou didst crave from him now one thing, now another.

'Fierce Mars, thou dost render benign and humble to thy will, and thou dost drive out all wrath. Thou dost banish vileness and dost fill him who sighs for thee, O goddess, with lofty pride. Thou dost make each deserving of and fit for high power according to his desires. Thou makest each one who is at all kindled with thy flame courteous and of good bearing.

'Thou, fair goddess, dost hold in unity houses and cities, kingdoms and provinces, and all the world; thou art the true cause of friendships and of their dear fruit. Thou alone knowest the hidden qualities of things, by which thou dost contrive such harmony as to cause wonder in him who knows not how to see thy power aright.

'Thou, O goddess, dost lay thy law upon the world and it is upheld thereby; nor is any one an enemy to thy son who repents not of it if he persists. And I, who once did speak against him, now as is fitting do confess myself so deeply in love that I could never say how much.

'And, if it chances that any one blames me, little care I, for he knows not what he says. Let mighty Hercules defend me in this, who could not guard himself from love, and therefore does every wise man praise him. And he who does not wish to be guilty of falsehood will never say that that ill becomes me which ere now was fitting for Hercules.

'And thus I love, and among the great effects wrought by thee this gives me most pleasure and delight. This do I pursue and, if my mind sees clearly, all delights are brought to fullness and perfection therein more than in aught else. Beside this all else sinks in esteem; this makes me follow that lady who, beyond all others, is of sovereign worth.

'This prompts me now to rejoice and will ever do so, if only I lack not wisdom. This prompts me, O goddess, to praise thy clear and mighty ray so greatly; and I give thanks that no arms defended me from thy bright face, in which I beheld thy virtue revealed and thy power shining clear.

'And I bless the time, the year, the month, and the day, the hour, and the moment when that lady, modest, fair, charming, and courteous, first appeared to my eyes; and I bless thy son, who through his power kindled me by her virtue and who has made me a true servant unto her, putting my peace in her eyes.

'And I bless the fervent sighs that for her I have sent forth from my breast; and I bless the laments and the torments that perfect love has caused me to suffer; and I bless the eager desires caused by her countenance, fairer than all else, because with these I have won a lady so lofty and so gracious.

'But above all I bless God, who gave such a dear lady to the world, and who, besides, in this dark world shed such light in my understanding that my desire was kindled for her rather than for any other; and for this no man could render fitting thanks.

'If a hundred tongues were in my mouth and each one spoke, and if I had the lore of all poets in my breast, I could not utter her true virtues, her noble gentleness and bountiful courtesy. Wherefore I earnestly pray that she who has the power may grant her long to be mine and make me grateful therefor.

'For thou, O goddess, art she who can do this if thou but wilt, and greatly do I crave this of thee. Who then will be able to call himself happier if thou turnest all the time that fate is to grant me to my pleasure and to hers? Ah, do it, O goddess,

now that I have found shelter in thy arms, which I had left,
nor knowing thy true virtue.

'Let him who will pursue dominion and riches, arms, horses,
wild beasts, dogs, birds, the studies of Pallas, and the valorous
deeds of Mars, for I wish to spend all my time in gazing upon the
fair eyes of my lady and her true beauties; and these, as I gaze,
exalt me above Jove, so full is my heart of love.

'I cannot pay thee the thanks due to thee from me, O fair
eternal light, and therefore it is better to be silent than not to
render them fully. But, nevertheless, wilt thou not come to
my aid? Prolong, keep secret, correct, and govern my ardour
and that of her to whom I have given myself, and grant that
she shall never be another's.'

He was ever foremost in fight in the adventures that befell
in their war. For he sallied forth from the town against the
Greeks, so valiant and so strong and so proud that all feared
him, if the story speaks truly. And this spirit, so exalted
above the common level, was bestowed upon him by love, whose
loyal servant he was.

In times of truce he went fowling with falcons, gerfalcons,
and eagles; and sometimes he went hunting with dogs, and pursued bears, boars, and great lions; he disdained all the small
animals. And, at the times when he saw Criseida, a new
countenance and beauty came upon him as on a falcon when it
casts off its hood. His talk was all of love or gentle usages,
and he was full of courtesy. He took great delight in honouring
the valiant, and likewise in driving cowards far from him.
It pleased him also to see youths deck themselves with fair
comeliness; and he deemed all who loved not to be lost, whatever their estate. And, though he was of royal blood, and if
he wished could have had great power, he showed himself
gracious to all alike, although at times some man deserved it
not. Thus did love, which can do all things, decree that he
should please others by his deeds. Pride, envy, and avarice
he held in scorn and was humble towards everybody.

But, thanks to envious fortune, which allows nothing in this
world to remain stable, this happiness lasted but a short space.
By a new turn of her wheel, as commonly chances, she showed
him her wrathful face and, turning all things upside down,
bereft him of the sweets of Criseida's love, and changed his
glad love into sad grief.

CANTO IV

While the Greeks held the city beleaguered and closely besieged, Hector, in whose hands lay all the conduct of the war, made choice of his friends and of other Trojans also, and bravely with his chosen men he sallied forth against the Greeks on the great plains, as he had often done before with varying fortunes in the fight. The Greeks came to meet him, and they spent all that day in stern battle. But at last the struggle went ill with the Trojans, and thus they all had to flee with loss and travail, and many perished grievously and sadly; and many noble kings and other great barons went thence as prisoners. And among them was Antenor the Magnificent, Polydamas his son, and Menestheus, Xanthippus, Sarpedon, Polymnestor, Polites also and the Trojan Ripheus, and many more whom Hector's prowess could not rescue in the flight, so that there was great and bitter lament in Troy, and the foreshadowing, so it seemed, of far heavier calamity.

Priam craved a truce, and it was granted him; and they began then to talk together touching the exchange of prisoners and the giving of gold for the surplus. And, when Calchas heard this, he came among the Greeks with changed face and loud lament, and indeed by his hoarse shouting gained some hearing from them.

'My lords,' began Calchas, 'I was a Trojan as you all know; and, if you remember well, I am he who first gave hope to your enterprise and declared that you would gain the destined goal, that is, victory in your struggle, and that by you Troy would be beaten down and burned.

'What ways and means to follow to this end you know, for I have showed them unto you; and, in order that all your wishes might come to complete fulfilment in the time foretold, I put not my trust in any messenger, nor in any book open or sealed, but came to you, as you see, to give you counsel and aid in this. And, wishing to do this, I was forced to depart craftily and very secretly, without winning anybody's consent, and this I did. As soon as bright day had turned to dark I went forth alone and noiselessly came here; and naught did I bring with me, but abandoned all that I had.

'Of that in truth I reck little or nothing except for a young daughter, whom I left there. Alas, cruel and heartless father that I was, would that I had brought this lonely girl to safety here! But fear and haste suffered it not. This makes me grieve for what I have left in Troy; this robs me of gaiety and gladness. Nor as yet have I seen a fitting season when I might ask to regain her; therefore have I held my peace. But now a time has come when I may have her if I can win this favour from you. And, if she cannot now be had, I shall lose all hope of ever seeing her again; and henceforth I shall heedlessly let my life pass away, caring no more to live than to die.

'With you here are noble Trojan barons and many others, whom you exchange with your enemies for your prisoners. Grant me but one of them, and by rendering him up I may have my daughter. In the name of God, great sirs, give this happiness to a wretched old man, who is empty and bare of all other solace. And be not swayed by desire to have gold for the prisoners, for I swear to you in God's name that all the power of the Trojans, and all their riches, is surely in your hands; and, if I mistake not, soon will fail the prowess of him who bars the way to the desire of all of you, and this will come to pass by violent death.'

And as the aged priest was speaking thus, humble in words and look, he was ever wetting his cheeks with tears, and tears moistened all his hoary beard and hard breast. Nor did his prayers fail to move pity, for, when he made an end of speaking, the Greeks all shouted loudly: 'Let Antenor be given unto him.'

Thus it was done; and Calchas was content and laid the carrying out of the matter upon the envoys. And they spoke of his desire to King Priam and to his sons and to the lords who were there also. And thus the business was debated, and brief answer given to the ambassadors: if they should yield up the persons asked for, theirs should be given to them.

Troilus was present when the Greeks made their demand, and hearing Criseida asked for, on a sudden he felt himself pierced clean through the heart, and so keen a pain that he thought he should die there where he sat. But with difficulty he held in check, as was fitting, his love and sorrow. And, filled with anguish and cruel fear, he waited for what the answer should be, debating with no ordinary concern what he should do if so great a disaster should come upon him, and if he should hear it declared among his brothers that Criseida should be given up to Calchas, and wondering how he might wholly thwart that.

Love made him ready loyally to oppose the whole matter, but

against that on the other side spoke reason, and made that high undertaking very doubtful for fear that Criseida, dreading shame, should be angered thereby. And thus stood the timid youth between two choices, torn between desire of this and that. While he stood in such uncertainty, many things were debated among the barons as to what must needs be done as things now stood; and, as has been said, full answers were given to those who awaited a reply—that surrender should be made of Criseida, who had never been kept from going.

Even as the lily in the fields that has been injured by the plough droops and fades in too hot a sun, and its fair colour is sicklied o'er, so, at the words delivered unto the Greeks after the Trojans had taken counsel together, did Troilus under such a weight of loss and peril fall in a faint, stricken by mighty grief.

And Priam took him in his arms, and so did Hector and his brothers, fearing greatly as to what had befallen him. And all endeavoured to comfort him, and like skilled men they strove to revive his lifeless powers, now rubbing his wrists and now many times bathing his face; but little as yet did their efforts avail. He lay among his brothers, stretched out and prostrate, and kept still a spark of life. And his face was pale and without colour, and he was all livid and seemed more a dead than a living thing, bearing such marks of suffering that he made all weep; so dire was the thunderbolt that struck him down when he heard of Criseida being given up.

But his sad spirit, after wandering long ere it returned, came softly back; and he, all confused like one newly awakened, suddenly rose to his feet, and, before any one should ask him what he had felt, pretending to be concerned with other matters, he parted from them.

And he made his way towards his palace, without listening and turning to anybody, and sighing and cast down as he was, wishing the company of nobody, went into his room and said he wished to rest. And thus everybody, friends and servants, however dear, went out, but first they closed the windows.

In what follows, now, O fair lady, I care not greatly whether I am aided by thee, because (unless frail memory lies) my wit will be able of itself to describe well the heavy grief by which it is weighed down by thy going hence and needs no help from thee, who art the cause of such bitter pain.

Till now I have sung with glad heart of the bliss Troilus felt in love, though it was mingled with sighs. Now must I turn from happiness to sorrow. Wherefore if thou dost not hearken unto me, I care not, for thy heart must needs change and arouse in thee pity for me, whose life more than any other is heavy-laden.

But yet, if it reach thy ears, I pray thee, for the love I bear thee, have some regard to my woes, and by thy return restore me the comfort that thou didst rob me of by thy going hence. And if thou wishest not to find me dead, come back quickly, for little is the life that thy departure has left me.

When Troilus was thus left alone in his closed and dark chamber safe from the intrusion of any man, and having no fear of being overheard, he fell to uttering the grief with which the sudden disaster had loaded his sad breast in such a way that he seemed not a man but a furious animal. Not otherwise does the bull go leaping now here, now there, after it has received the mortal stroke, and roaring in misery shows what pain has come upon it, than did Troilus, flinging himself down and wildly striking his head against the wall, and his face with his hands, his breast and aching arms with his fists. His sad eyes, pitying his heart, wept sorely and seemed two fountains that cast out abundant water. The deep sobs he uttered in his weeping and his fruitless words robbed him of his strength; and ever in his strange speech he begged for naught but death, and cursed and made mock both of the gods and himself.

After his great frenzy had abated and his weeping had by lapse of time grown milder, Troilus, consumed by burning sorrow, cast himself for a while upon his bed, and yet not at all did he cease, even for a little, to weep sorely and to sigh so heavily that his head and breast scarce endured the great agony to which he gave himself up.

A little while after he began to say to himself in his weeping: 'O wretched fortune, what have I done unto thee that thou dost so oppose all I desire? Hast thou no longer any concern save my anguish? Why so soon hast thou turned thy darkened face towards me, who ere now loved thee far more than any other god, as thou, cruel one, dost know?

'If my life, carefree and joyous, was displeasing unto thee, why didst thou not humble the pride of haughty Ilium? Why didst thou not take my father from me? Why not Hector, on whose valour rests all our hope in these times of stress? Why didst thou not carry off Polyxena, and why not Paris and Helen too?

'If only Criseida had been left to me, I should care for no other great loss, nor should I utter plaint. But thy shafts are ever loosed against those things that give us most joy. To show more plain the might of thy fickleness thou takest away all my comfort. Ah, would that thou hadst slain me first!

'Alas, love, sweet and charming lord, who knowest what lies in my soul, how will it fare with my sorrowful life if I lose this happiness, this peace of mine? Ah, gentle love, true lord, who ere now didst solace my mind, what shall I do if I am reft of her to whom by thy will I have wholly given myself? I shall weep and shall stay where I am, ever grieving while life remains in this tormented body of mine. O wretched and distraught soul, why fleest thou not from the most hapless body alive? O downcast soul, leave my body and follow Criseida. Why dost thou not? Why dost thou not vanish away?

'O sad eyes, whose sole comfort was in beholding our Criseida, what will you do henceforth? Ever will you remain in sad affliction now that she is parted from you; and your strength will be destroyed, overthrown, and vanquished by your weeping. In vain henceforth will you gaze on other virtuous ladies if she by whom you lived is taken from you.

'O my Criseida, O sweet delight of the sad heart that calls upon thee, who now will give comfort to my torments? Who will give peace to my eager longing? Alas, if thou goest away, he who loves thee more than himself must needs die in his misery. And I shall die not having deserved that. Let the blame rest on the pitiless gods.

'Ah, that this going hence of thine had been so far delayed that by long use I, poor wretch, had learned to endure! I mean not that I should not have resisted letting thee go with all my might; but if, in spite of that, I had seen this come to pass, thy departure would have been easy for me to bear, which now seems so grievous unto me.

'O old man of evil life, O crazed old man, what madness moved thee, or what disdain, to go unto the Greeks since thou art a Trojan? Thou wert honoured in all our kingdom, no native or stranger more than thou. O wicked counsel, O breast stuffed with treacheries, deceits, and malice, would that I had thee, as I should like, in Troy! Would thou hadst died the day thou didst go hence, would thou hadst died at the feet of the Greeks when thou didst first open thy mouth to demand her who makes me burn with love! Ah, what ill hap for me that thou camest into the world! Thou art cause of the grief that afflicts me. Would that Menelaus had planted in thy heart the spear that pierced Protesilaus! If thou wert dead, I should surely live, for there would be none to seek Criseida; if thou wert dead,

I should not be desolate, and Criseida would not go from me; if thou wert dead—most clearly do I see it—that which troubles me would not so press upon me. Thus is thy life the wretched cause of my death and of my grievous fate.'

A thousand sighs hotter than fire went forth from his amorous breast mingled with plaints and words of grief, all crowding each other; and so did these lamentings overmaster him that the youth's strength was all spent, and thus he fell asleep; but he slept little ere he waked once more. And, sighing, he got upon his feet, went to the door, which he had locked, and opened it; and to a special servant of his he said: 'Haste thee, call Pandarus forthwith and make him come to me.' And then, full of grief, he went to the darkness of his room, deeply sighing and sorely burdened.

Pandarus came, and he had already heard what the Grecian ambassadors asked; and, besides, how the lords had agreed to yield up Criseida. And with his face full of dismay thereat, his thoughts busy with Troilus's sorrows, he entered the dark and quiet room, and knew not whether to utter sad or cheerful words.

Troilus, as soon as he had seen him, ran to embrace him, weeping so violently that no man could fitly describe it. And when sad Pandarus saw this, he fell to weeping, so did he grieve for him. And in such fashion, doing naught but utter loud laments, did they remain for a space, without speaking at all.

But after Troilus had mastered himself, he first began to Pandarus: 'I am dead; my happiness is turned to sorrow. Ah, wretched sorrow, envious fortune robs me of my sweet comfort and, along with it, my solace and disport. Hast thou yet heard how Criseida has been taken by the Greeks?'

Pandarus, who wept no less, made answer: 'Yes, would that it were not the truth! Woe is me, for I thought not that this time, so sweet and unalloyed, would end so soon; and I could not see that anything could harm thy perfect happiness, except noising it abroad. Now I see how worthless were all my thoughts. But why dost thou inflict such anguish on thyself? Why such grief and such torment? Thou hast had what thou didst long for; with that alone thou shouldst be content. Leave these and other woes to me, for I have ever loved, and never have I had a glance from her for whom I perish and who alone could give me peace. And besides that, this city is full of beautiful and charming ladies; and, if my wish for thy happiness deserves to be trusted, there is none of them, the fairest thou wilt, who will not be pleased to show thee mercy, if thou wilt suffer the pangs of love for her. Therefore, if we lose this lady, we shall find plenty of others. And, as I have often heard it said before, the new love always drives out the old; new pleasure will take the present suffering from thee, if thou dost what I say. Therefore be not inclined to die for this lady, nor to be an enemy to thyself. Dost thou think to regain her by weeping? Or to keep her from going away?'

When Troilus heard Pandarus, he fell to weeping more violently, and afterwards he said: 'I pray God to send me death ere I commit such a crime. Though the other ladies are beautiful, charming, and wise—and I grant thee that—none of them was ever like her to whom I have given myself, and I am wholly hers. From her fair eyes flew the sparks that kindled in me the fire of love; these, passing through my eyes in thousands, gently brought love with them into my heart. And love felt them there and was pleased; and there they first lighted the flame whose strong heat has been the source of all that is of worth in me.

'So mighty is that flame I could never quench it, even if I so desired, which I do not. And, even were it greater, I should not grieve, if only Criseida remained with us. For it is her going hence and not love that makes the impassioned heart feel pain; and there is no other lady—let this cause displeasure to none— who can rival her in aught. How then could love or comfort offered me by any one turn my desire to another lady? Enough of anguish have I to bear in my heart, but I would allow much more to enter there, even unto the bitterest woes, before I would set my heart upon another lady. May love, God, and all this world prevent that!

'Only death and the grave can part me from my steadfast love. Whatever shall befall me because of that, these shall lead my soul and with it my love down to hell to the final agony. There together shall they weep for Criseida whose I shall ever be wherever I am, if love is not forgotten in death.

'Therefore, in God's name, Pandarus, cease to talk of this, that another lady should come into my heart, where I cherish Criseida in her modest garb as a sure token of the joys that have been mine, however grievous now her going hence—of which there is talk among us, for we see that she is not yet taken away—is to the mind that broods on its own sorrow.

'Thou speakest in downright fashion, as if thou arguest that to lose is less pain than never to have had. If this is in thy mind,

Pandarus, it is plain folly. For that which cruel fortune brings upon him who has been happy surpasses all other grief, and he who says otherwise is far from the truth.

'But tell me, if thou carest for my love, since it seems to thee so light a matter to change in love as but now thou didst declare to me, why hast thou not altered thy course? Why dost thou endure such suffering in thy hapless love? Why hast thou not pursued another lady, who would have given peace unto thy life? If thou, who art used to hard treatment from love, hast been unable to change to another, how can I, who lived in joy and gladness with love, drive it from me as thou urgest! Why do I see bitter misfortune overwhelm me now? I am bound in another fashion that thy mind conceives not. Believe me, Pandarus, believe me, that when love, by offering the highest delight, lays hold on any mind, it can never be driven forth; but it may grow weak in course of time, if grief, or death, or poverty, or not seeing the beloved person is not the cause thereof, as has happened ere now to many a one.

'What then shall I do, poor wretch that I am, if I lose Criseida in this way? For Antenor is exchanged for her. How much better were death to me, or never to have been born! Alas, what shall I do? Despair is in my heart. Ah, death, come to me who crave for thee; ah, come, leave me not to suffer in my love.

'O death, thou wilt be as sweet to me as life is to him who lives in gladness. Already thy dread countenance repels me not; come therefore and end my pain. Ah, tarry not, for this fire has already made every vein burn so hotly that I shall welcome thy chill stroke. Ah, come now, for in truth my heart longs for thee. In God's name, kill me; let me not live in this world till I see my heart pass out from my body. Ah, do it, death; I pray thee, in God's name. Far more grievous to me than dying will that be. Grant my desire in this. Thou slayest so many against their will that thou mayest well do me this grace.'

Thus did Troilus weep and lament; and Pandarus did likewise, and yet he often offered comfort as lovingly as he could. But such comfort availed naught; nay rather did his dolorous weeping grow ever greater and his torment, so ill was he pleased therewith.

And to him Pandarus said: 'Dear friend, if my arguments please thee not, and if her going hence is as grievous to thee as it seems, why dost thou not seek a remedy to save thy life, in so far as thou canst, and carry her off? Paris went to Greece and brought away Helen, the flower of all other ladies. And wilt thou, in thy own Troy, not be so bold as to carry off a lady whom thou lovest? If thou wilt have faith in me, thou wilt do this. Drive grief away, drive away, banish thy anguish and grievous woes; wipe the sad tears from thy face, and show forth now thy great spirit and so act that Criseida shall be ours.'

Troilus then replied to Pandarus: 'I see well, my friend, that thou usest all thy wit to lift my bitter sorrows from me. I have thought of what thou speakest of, and have pondered many other things also, although I weep and surrender myself wholly to the grief that is greater than all my strength, so heavy has been its mighty stroke.

'And yet I have never been able in my ardent love to leave the path of duty; nay, rather, taking thought thereof, I have seen that these times allow no such wildness. But if all our men had come back here, and Antenor, too, I should reck naught of breaking faith. Rather would I do it whatever might betide. If I carry her off by violence, I fear then to harm her honour and her good name, nor do I know certainly that she would be pleased thereat; and yet I know that she loves me greatly. Wherefore my heart dares not shape a resolution, for on the one hand it longs for this, and on the other it fears to displease her, for I should not wish to have her against her will.

'I had also thought of asking my father, in his graciousness, to grant her unto me. Then I think that this would be to accuse her and to make known what has passed between us. And, besides, I have no hope that he would give her—and so fail to fulfil his promise—and he would declare her of lower rank than me, to whom he wishes to give a lady of royal blood.

'And thus I weep and bide here, worn out in the perplexity of love, and know not what to do. For, even if love is mighty, I feel its great strength to be lacking in me; and on every side hope flees away, and there are more and more things to cause me torment. Would I had died on the day when first I was kindled by such desire.'

Then said Pandarus: 'Thou wilt do as thou pleasest, but, if I were so hotly in love as it is clear thou art, however heavy this burden, and, if I had the power thou hast, I would, unless prevented by force, do my utmost to carry her off, no matter who might be displeased. Love does not consider things so scrupulously as it seems thou dost, when the impassioned mind burns as needs it must. And, if love so fiercely preys upon thee, follow its urging and manfully combat this raging torment and be willing rather to be somewhat blamed than to die wretchedly in sad lamenting.

'The lady thou hast to carry off is not opposed to thy wishes, but she is one who will be pleased with what thou wilt do. And if too much evil should result therefrom, or too much blame of thee, thou hast the means to mend that forthwith—that is, to bring her back. Fortune helps him who is bold and spurns the coward.

'And, even if this thing please her not, in short time thou wilt win peace again. Not that I think she would be angered, such delight has she in the love thou bearest her. That her good name should be lessened is, to tell the truth, of less account and less disturbing. Let her make shift without it as Helen does, as long as she fulfil all thy desire.

'Therefore take courage, be daring. Love cares for neither promise nor faith. Show some spirit now, make some effort on thy own behalf. I shall be with thee whenever danger befalls so far as my power allows me. Dare but to act. The gods must needs aid us afterwards.'

Troilus listened very closely to what Pandarus said and answered: 'I am content. But, were my flames kindled a thousandfold more, and were my torment greater than it is, I would not for my own pleasure do harm to that gentle lady; rather would I die first. Therefore I wish first to know her feelings.'

'And so let us go hence and stay no longer here. Wash thy face, and let us return to court and mask our grief with a smile. As yet people are aware of naught, but by remaining here we make all who know it to marvel. Now do thou so act as not to fail in keeping well thy secret, and I will contrive that thou shalt speak with Criseida this evening.'

Most speedy rumour, which relates false and true equally, had flown throughout all Troy on swiftest wings and with fluent speech had told what and of what sort was the message brought by the Greeks, and that Criseida had been given by the king to the Greeks in exchange for Antenor.

And when Criseida, who cared no longer now for her father, heard this news, she said to herself: 'Alas, my poor heart!' And greatly did that distress her, for she had turned her desire to Troilus, whom she loved more than aught else. And, fearing lest what she heard said might be true, she dared not ask questions.

But, as we see it happens that one lady goes to visit another, if she likes her, when something has come to pass, so did many ladies, all full of piteous joy, come to spend the day with Criseida; and they began to tell her the matter from beginning to end, how she had been surrendered and on what terms.

One said: 'In truth I am right glad that thou art returning to thy father and art to be with him.'

Another said: 'She will be able to arrange the peace for us and contrive it with him who, as you know by report, can give effect to any decision he wishes.'

This and much other women's talk she heard as though she were not there, without answering, deeming it of no account. And her fair face could not hide the high and noble thoughts of love wakened in her by the news she had heard. Her body was there, and her mind was elsewhere, seeking Troilus she knew not in what place. And these ladies, who thought to bring her solace by their presence, talking much among themselves, troubled her greatly, for in her mind she felt a passion wholly different from what was apparent to those who were there. And very often she hastened their leave-taking, though with womanly courtesy, such longing had she to be left to herself.

She could not help uttering some sighs or letting fall a little tear at times. These were signs of the suffering that pressed upon her heart; but those fools who sat about her believed that the damsel did this because of her grief at having to leave them, who were wont to be her companions. And each wished to comfort her for what caused her no sorrow; many words they spoke to console her for having to part from them. And this was as if they had scratched her heels when her head itched. For she had no thought of them but only of Troilus, whom she was leaving.

But after much empty prating such as most women do, they took their leave and departed. And she, overmastered and hard-driven by bitter grief, slowly entered her room, weeping softly, and seeking no help from anybody's counsel in her great trouble, she made lamentation such as was never made before. In her grief she threw herself upon her bed, weeping more violently than can be said. And often she beat her white breast, calling upon death to slay her, now that by cruel fate she was forced to forsake her delight. And pulling at her fair hair, she tore it out, and a thousand times each hour she begged for death.

She said: 'Alas, hapless wretch that I am in my sorrow, whither am I bound? Ah, unhappy that I am, born in an evil hour, where am I leaving thee, my sweet love? Ah, that I had been stifled at birth or had never seen thee, my sweet desire, now that fortune so cruelly takes me from thee and thee from me!

'What shall I do, when I, my life filled with sadness, shall no longer be able to see thee? What shall I do sundered from thee, O Troilus? Truly I think I shall never more eat or drink; and, if my distraught soul does not of itself leave my body, I will drive it forth with all my might by starving myself, because I see that my fortune will go steadily from bad to worse.

'Now in truth I shall be widowed, since I must needs part from thee, heart of my body; and garments black shall be a true sign of my sufferings. Alas, poor creature that I am, what heavy thought the parting breeds in me! Alas, Troilus, how can I endure to see myself severed from thee? How can I live lacking my heart? In truth it will stay here with our love, and to lament with thee our grievous parting, which we must needs go through as a reward for such true love. Alas, Troilus, wilt thou bear now to see me leave thee, without setting thyself by love or by might to keep me?

'I shall go away, and I know not if ever I shall see thee again, my sweet love; but thou, who so lovest me, what wilt thou do? Alas, wilt thou have the strength to bear such grief? Verily, I shall not endure it, for woes too heavy will break my heart. Alas, might it but come quickly, for then I should be quit of this heavy anguish.

'O my father, base and disloyal to thy country, woe worth the hour that so evil a thought entered thy breast as to wish to join the Greeks and leave the Trojans! Would to God thou wert lifeless in the depths of hell, thou base dotard, who, in the last years of thy life, hast wrought such treachery.

'Ah, hapless, sad, and desolate am I, who must suffer the penalty for thy sin, I, who deserved not such a life of sorrow because of any fault of my own. O heavenly truth, O kindly light, how dost thou allow things to be thus ordered, that one should sin and another weep as I do, who have not sinned and who am undone by grief?'

Who could ever tell fully what Criseida uttered in her weeping? In sooth not I, for my words are less than the truth, so wild and terrible was her distress. But, while she was making such laments, Pandarus came, to whom entrance was never forbidden, and went into the room where she made her pitiful outcry. And he looked at her on her bed, sunk in sobs, in weeping, and in sighs, and saw all her breast and her face bathed in tears and her eyes yearning to shed tears, and giving plain proof, by her disorder, of her bitter griefs. And when she beheld him, she hid her face in shame between her arms.

'That was an evil hour,' began Pandarus, 'when I left my bed; for it seems to me that wherever I go to-day I see all around me grief, torments, laments, agonies, and other woes, sighs, distress, and bitter sorrow. O Jove, what wilt thou do? I believe thou sheddest tears from heaven, so little favour do our deeds find with thee.

'But thou, my unhappy sister, what dost thou purpose to do? Dost thou think to resist the fates? Why destroy thy fair countenance by such cruel and wild lamentings? Rise up and turn to me and speak, lift up thy face and dry thy sad eyes a little and hearken to what I say, for I am sent to thee by thy sweet friend.'

Then Criseida turned and uttered such a cry as could not be described. And she gazed at Pandarus, saying: 'Ah, wretched me! What does my love desire? I must needs part from him in tears, for so does cruel fortune decree. Does he wish for sighs or tears, or what does he crave? I have enough if he send for them.'

Her countenance had the look of one who is being borne to the tomb; and her face of heavenly beauty appeared all disfigured. Her loveliness and charming smile had fled away and forsaken it; and round her eyes a purple circle told plainly of her suffering.

And, when he saw this, Pandarus, who had wept long that day with Troilus, could not hold back tears of sorrow but began to weep likewise in grief with her, leaving unuttered what he had purposed to say. But, after they had thus mourned together for a while, Pandarus was the first to check his lament; and he said: 'Lady, I think thou hast heard, but am not certain thereof, how thou art asked for by thy father, and how already the decision has been made by the king to give thee up. And so thou must go hence this week if I have heard truly. And how grievous a thing this is to Troilus can scarce be told, for he in his sorrow has no wish but for death. And he and I to-day have shed such store of tears that I marvel whence they have come. Now at last by my counsel he has somewhat checked his weeping, and it seems he longs to be with thee. Wherefore at his desire I have come to tell thee this before thou goest hence, so that together you may a little ease your hearts.'

'Great is my grief,' said Criseida, 'as of one who loves him more than she loves herself. But his suffering affects me more than my own when I hear that because of me he longs for death. If ever a heart should break through keen sorrow, mine will break now; now does cruel fortune glut herself upon my losses; now do I know her sly deceits. Grievous to me, God knows, is the going hence; but more grievous is it to see Troilus sore afflicted and so much beyond my endurance that, by my faith, I shall straightway die; and I shall die hopeless of aid when I see my Troilus thus stricken. Bid him come when he will; this will be my greatest comfort in my agony.'

When she had said this, she fell prone again, then with her face upon her arms began once more to weep. And to her Pandarus said: 'Alas, poor wretch, what wilt thou do now? Wilt thou not find some solace in the thought that the hour is so nigh when he who so loves thee will be in thy arms? Rise up, check thy wildness, that he find thee not in such disorder. If he knew thou didst thus, he would slay himself, nor would any be able to hinder him. And, if I thought that thou wouldst stay thus, he should not, believe me, set foot here if I could prevent it, for I know that that would work him harm. Therefore rise up, be calm, that thou mayest lighten and not add to his trouble.'

'Go,' said Criseida, 'I promise thee, my Pandarus, I will try to do thus. When thou art gone, I will straightway rise from my bed, and I will keep my suffering and the loss of my delight all pent within my heart. Only have him come, and come in his wonted way, for he will find the door open as of old.'

Pandarus found Troilus heavy-thoughted and so downcast in look that he was stricken with pity for him, and said unto him: 'Art thou now so low-spirited as thou appearest, valorous youth? Thy love has not yet left thee. Why then art thou so melancholy that thy eyes already look dead in thy head? Thou didst live long without her; does not thy heart give thee strength still to live? Wert thou born into the world only for her? Show thyself a man, and pluck up thy heart a little, drive these sorrows from thee and these moans, in some measure at least. I have made no stay in any place save here with thee since I spoke to her and was long with her. And, from what I see, thou sufferest not half as much distress as the lady; and so hot are her sighs, and so does this departure sadden her that her troubles are twenty-fold greater than thine. Therefore calm thyself somewhat, so that at least thou mayest know in this sorry pass how dear thou art to her.

'I have but now arranged with her that thou shouldst go to her and be with her this night, and thou wilt lay before her in the fairest manner thou canst what thou hast already planned. Thou wilt soon find what will be wholly pleasing to her; perchance you will find ways greatly to lighten your sorrows.'

And Troilus answered him with a sigh: 'Thou sayest well, and thus will I do.' And many other things he said, but, when it seemed time that he should go, Pandarus left him to his thoughts. And he went forth and it seemed to him a thousand years till he was in the arms of his dear love, whom afterwards fortune cruelly took from him.

When the time had come, Criseida came to him with a kindled torch as she was wont and folded him in her arms; and he, weighed down with heavy sorrow, took her in his; and both, though silent, could not hide their stricken hearts, but, clinging to each other and speaking no word, they began to weep violently. And each held the other closely embraced, all bathed in tears. And though they wished to speak, they could not, so did their agonized laments and sobs and sighs prevent them; and yet they often kissed and drank each other's falling tears and took no heed that they were unnaturally bitter.

But, when their spirits, worn out by the travail of weeping and sighs, had been calmed by the easing of their sad torments, Criseida, lifting towards Troilus her eyes filled with the sadness of sharp desires, said with faltering voice: 'O my lord, who takes me from thee, and whither shall I go?'

Then she fell in a faint, her face upon his breast; and her strength left her, by such mighty grief was her heart constrained, and her spirit struggled to take wing. And Troilus gazed upon her countenance and called upon her and saw no sign that she heard him. And her eyes had grown veiled as she fell, and from this he thought that she was dead.

And Troilus, beholding this, stricken with double grief, laid her down, often kissing her tearful face, seeking if he might see in her any sign of life. And sadly he felt her all over, and amid his weeping he said that it seemed to him she had left this so comfortless life. She was cold and without any feeling for aught that Troilus could see, and this seemed to him plain proof that she had ended her days. Wherefore, after lamenting a great while, he, before doing aught else, dried her face and laid her body in order, as men are wont to do with the dead.

And, when he had done this, with resolute mind he drew his sword from the sheath, wholly determined to lay hold on death so that his spirit might follow his lady's in so sad a fate and bide with her in hell, since cruel fortune and ill-starred love drove him forth from this life.

But first, kindled with high disdain, he said: 'O cruel Jove, and thou, pitiless fortune, behold I go the way you wish. You have taken from me my Criseida, whom I thought you would rob me of by other sleight than this. And where she now is I know not, but I see her body here most foully slain by you. And I will quit the world and follow her with my spirit since that is your will. It may be in that other world I shall win better fortune with her, and find peace for my sighing, if there is loving there as I once heard there is. Since you wish not to see me live, at the least put my soul with her.

'And thou, O city, which I leave still at war, and thou, Priam, and you, my dear brothers, God be with you, for I am going beneath the ground following after the fair eyes of Criseida; and thou for whom I am so sore oppressed by grief and who pluckest the soul from my body . . .' He meant Criseida. And now he stood ready to die, the sword at his breast.

And then, reviving from her faint, she heaved forth a most deep sigh and called upon Troilus. And to her he said: 'My sweet love, dost thou still live?' And, shedding tears, he took her again in his arms and as best he could lightened her suffering with his words and gave her comfort. And the distraught soul came back again to the heart whence it had taken flight.

And, being for a while all wildered, she was silent, and then, seeing the sword, she began: 'Why was that drawn forth from its sheath?' And, weeping, Troilus told her what his intent had been. Whereat she said: 'What is this that I hear? So then, if I had lain thus a little longer, thou wouldst have slain thyself in this place. Ah, woe is me! What hast thou told me? Never would I have remained alive when thou wert gone, but I would have pierced my sad breast. Now have we great cause to praise God. Go we now to bed; there we shall talk of our woes. If I may judge by the wasted torch, a great part of the night is already gone.'

As their close embraces had been at other times, so were they now; but these had more of the bitterness of tears than the others had had of sweetness. And forthwith there began again between them sweet and sad discourse.

And Criseida began: 'Sweet friend, listen most heedfully to what I say. When first I heard the sad news of the treachery of my base father—so may God watch over thy fair face for me —never did woman feel such great trouble as I felt then; for I care nothing for gold, city, or palace, but only for staying ever with thee in joy and pleasure and thou with me. And I was minded to give up all hope, for I thought I should never see thee again. But since thou hast seen my soul take flight and once more return, I feel certain thoughts pass through my mind, which perchance may aid us. And I wish these to be laid open to thee ere we grieve further, for perhaps we may still hope for good.

'Thou seest that my father demands me, but I would not obey him by going hence were I not constrained by the king, whose faith, as thou must know, cannot be broken. And so I must needs go with Diomede, who has been the framer of these harsh covenants, whenever he returns. Would to God he might never come back in these cruel times!

'Thou knowest that all my kinsfolk are here except my father, and all my possessions remain here yet. And, if I remember aright, there is ever talk between you and the Greeks of peace to end this dread war; and, if his wife is given back to Menelaus, I believe you will obtain it, and I know that already you have nearly brought it to pass. If you achieve that, I shall return here, for I have nowhere else to go; and if perchance you fail in that, I shall find opportunity to come here in time of truce, and thou knowest it is common to allow women to pass thus; and my kinsfolk will be glad to see me here and will invite me. Then we can have pleasure, though the waiting for it is a sore distress. But he who wishes joy to come to him later in fuller measure must be ready to bear hardship. I know indeed that, even while we are in Troy, we must at times pass many days with bitter pangs without seeing each other.

'And besides this, whether peace comes or not, a greater hope of returning springs in me. My father has now this desire, and perhaps imagines that by reason of his evil-doing I cannot bide here without fear of violence or without blame falling upon me. But, when he knows that I am honoured here, he will not be concerned about my return.

'And to what end should he keep me among the Greeks, who, as thou seest, are ever in arms? And, if he keeps me not there, I see not where else he could send me. And I think he would not do so if he could, because he would not wish to trust me to the Greeks. It is fitting therefore to send me here again, and I see nobody to hinder that.

'He is, as thou knowest, old and miserly; and he has possessions here, which, if he sets store by them, may make him heed what I shall tell him and make him send me back here in the best way he can. For I shall show him how I can find a remedy for aught that may befall; and in his greed he will rejoice in my return.'

Troilus listened closely to the lady, and her speech swayed his mind. And it seemed to him that what she declared downrightly to be thus must be near the truth. But yet, because he loved her much, he was slow to put faith in it. But at the last, searching his own mind as one eager to be persuaded, he brought himself to believe it.

Wherefore part of their heavy grief went from them, and hope returned. And then, their minds being less troubled, they began again the sport of love. And as the bird fluttering from leaf to leaf in the new season takes delight in his song, so did they, talking to one another of many things.

But the heart of Troilus could not forget that she must needs go thence, and he began to speak after this manner: 'O my Criseida, far more beloved than any other goddess and more to be honoured by me, who but now would have slain myself supposing thee dead, what will my life be, thinkest thou, if thou returnest not soon? Count this as certain as death, that I would kill myself if thou shouldst tarry one moment too long in thy return here. Nor do I see well yet how I shall make shift without grievous and bitter languishing, knowing that thou art elsewhere. And a new doubt is born in me, that Calchas will keep thee and that thy words will not be fulfilled.

'I know not whether peace will ever be made. Whether it comes or not, I scarce believe he will ever wish to come here again, for he would not think that he could bide here free from the ill-fame of his great wrongdoing. If we are not minded to deceive ourselves in this, and if he demands thee with such urgency, I can hardly have faith that he will send thee back.

'And he will give thee a husband from among the Greeks, and he will point out to thee that, when thou art besieged, thou art in danger of coming to a sorry plight. He will flatter thee and cause thee to be honoured by the Greeks. And, as I hear, he is held in reverence there and his power highly prized; and thus it is that I fear anxiously thou wilt never return to Troy. And this is more grievous to my thoughts than I can tell thee,

O fair loved one; and thou alone hast in thy hands the key of my life and death, and canst at will make my life wretched or blissful, O thou bright star, by whom I steer my course to the happy haven. If thou forsakest me, forget not that I shall die.

'Therefore, in God's name, let us find ways and means, if they can be found, to prevent thy departure; let us go to some other country; let us care not if the king's promises be unfulfilled, as long as we can escape harm at his hands; and far from here are peoples who will gladly welcome us and who, moreover, will ever look upon us as persons of high rank. Therefore let us flee hence in secret and go there together, thou and I; and what span of life we have left in the world, heart of my body, let us spend it together in delight. I would fain have this, and this I long for, if it seems well to thee; and this is safer, and every other plan appears to me difficult.'

Criseida, sighing, answered him: 'My dear love and joy of my heart, all those things and even more might come about after the manner thou hast said; but I swear unto thee, by those darts of love that have pierced my breast because of thee, that neither commands, flattering speeches, nor a husband shall ever turn my desire from thee.

'But what thou hast said touching our flight is not, as I deem, prudent counsel. In these dire times it behoves thee to take thought and to have regard for thyself and thy people. For, if we flee, as thou hast said, thou mightest see three evil things spring from that. One would come from broken faith, which brings more ill than some believe. And that would be a danger to thy people, for, if for the sake of a woman thou didst leave them without thy aid and counsel, they would inspire in others fear of betrayal. And, if my wit errs not, you would be much blamed therefor, nor would the truth ever be believed by anybody who had seen only this.

'And, if any time asks for faith or loyalty, it seems to be a time of war; for nobody has enough strength to stand for long alone. Many join together hoping that what they venture for others will be ventured for them. For, if they rely upon themselves and their wealth, their trust therein will fail them.

'On the other hand, what thinkest thou might be said among the people touching thy flight? They would not say that love with his keen darts had brought thee to such a step, but fear and baseness. Therefore yield not to such thoughts if ever they should find way into thy heart, if thy repute, which speaks so clearly of thy valour, is at all dear to thee.

'Consider, moreover, with what infamy my fair name and my chastity, now held in highest esteem, would be stained, nay, wholly destroyed and ruined for me; nor would they ever be redeemed by any plea or by any power I could wield, whatever I might do, if I should live a hundred thousand years.

'And besides this, I wish thee to take heed of what comes to pass in almost all matters. There is nothing so vile that, if guarded well, comes not to be desired with painful longing, and the more thou dost burn to possess it, the sooner does loathing enter thy heart if thou art given full power to look upon it and, besides, to keep it. Our love, which gives thee such pleasure, does so because thou must needs act warily and but seldom come to this delight. But, if thou hadst me at thy will, the glowing torch that now kindles thee and likewise me, would soon be quenched. For, if we wish our love to last, as now we do, it must ever be enjoyed by stealth.

'Wherefore take comfort and, by turning thy back upon her, vanquish fortune and weary her out. No man in whom she found a bold heart would ever be slave to her; let us follow his course. Meanwhile contrive some journey for thyself and forget thy sighs therein, for on the tenth day, without fail, I shall come again hither.'

Then said Troilus: 'If thou wilt be here within ten days, I am content. But meanwhile by whom will my sad woes be at all relieved? Even now, as thou knowest, I cannot pass an hour without great torment if I see thee not; how shall I be able to pass the ten days ere thou returnest?

'Ah, in God's name, find some way of staying. Ah, go not, if thou seest any means of escaping it. If I understand aright what I hear from thee, I know thee to be of keen wit. And, if thou lovest me, thou dost plainly see that I am wasted away even with the thought that thou art going hence. Thou canst think what my life will be afterwards if thou dost depart.'

'Alas!' said Criseida, 'thou slayest me and dost bring greater melancholy upon me than thou thinkest, and I see thou trustest not in my promise as much as I believed. Ah, my sweet love, why hast thou so little faith? Why dost thou cast away thy self-mastery? Who would believe that a mighty man of arms cannot endure ten days' waiting?

'I believe that it is far better to decide as I have said unto thee. Sweet my lord, be content with that; and receive this into thy heart for a truth—that when I depart from thy sweet presence my very soul does weep, perhaps more than thou believest or thinkest. Well do I feel it through all my senses.

'Sometimes, my soul, to spend time in waiting is a means to gain time. Because I am restored to my father, I am not snatched from thee, as thou declarest. And let not thy heart think that I have so little wit as not to find ways and means of returning to thee, whom I more desire than my life. Far too much do I love thee.

'And I pray thee, if my prayer avails aught, both by the great love thou bearest me and by that I bear thee, which is no less great, that thou find comfort in this journey. If thou didst know what great distress I feel at beholding thy tears and the deep sighs that come from thee, it would trouble thee and thou wouldst grieve at uttering so many.

'I hope to live for thee in joy and gladness, and to return speedily and to find a way to thy delight and mine. Let me see thee in such spirit before I go hence, that I may not have more sorrow than what a too fiery love has planted in my mind. Do this, I pray thee, sweet one in whom I trust.

'And I pray thee, while I am far away, let not thyself be caught by delight in any lady or by strange desire. For, if I heard that, thou must know for a truth that I would slay myself as one distraught, grieving for thee beyond reason. Wouldst thou forsake me for another, thou, who knowest I love thee more than ever woman loved man?'

To these last words Troilus answered with a sigh: 'If I wished to do what now thou dost speak of and suspect, I cannot see how I ever could. Love for thee has so caught me I cannot see how I should go on living. This love I bear thee, and the reason thereof I shall unfold to thee, and in few words. Beauty, which commonly snares other men, drove me not to love thee; gentle breeding, which is wont to wake the desire of men of high birth, drew me not to love thee; nor yet adornments, nor wealth made me feel love for thee in my heart, though with all these thou art more richly graced than ever was amorous lady. But thy proud and noble bearing, thy high worth and courtly speech, thy manners more courteous than those of other ladies, and thy charming womanly scorn, by which every vulgar appetite and deed appeared vile in thy eyes—these filled my mind with love for thee. Such art thou to me, O sovereign lady mine. Nor can the years, nor fickle fortune, take these things away, and therefore with more anguish and with greater sorrows do I live in the desire of ever possessing thee. Ah, wretched being that I am, what can offset my loss if thou, my sweet love, goest away? In truth, nothing except eternal death. That alone will put an end to my woes.'

After they had talked much and shed tears together, the dawn now being at hand, they made an end, and each held the other in close embrace. But, when the cocks had long crowed, after fully a thousand kisses, both rose up, each expressing faith in the other, and thus in tears they parted.

CANTO V

That same day Diomede came, purposing to give Antenor to the Trojans. Wherefore Priam yielded Criseida to him, and she was so burdened with sighs, lamentations, and grief that whoever saw her was troubled. There also was her lover in such sadness that nobody had ever seen a man in such plight. True it is that by mighty effort he wondrously hid within his sad breast the great struggle he had against sighs and tears; and in his cheer little or nothing showed, although he longed to be in solitude, and there to weep and lament and find ease by unburdening his heart.

Oh, how many thoughts came to his proud mind when he saw Criseida yielded up to her father! His whole body trembling with anger and wrath, he raged within himself and said in a low voice: 'O miserable wretch, what more do I wait for? Is it not better to die once than to live and languish forever in grief? Why do I not break these dealings by force of arms? Why do I not slay Diomede here? Why do I not cut down the old man who has brought these things to pass? Why do I not defy all my brothers? Would that they were now all destroyed! Why not put Troy to weeping and doleful outcry? Why not steal away Criseida now and heal my sorrow? Who will forbid it if indeed I am resolved to do so? Why not address myself to the Greeks to see if they would give Criseida unto me? Alas, why do I tarry longer? Why not run thither at once and make them give her to me?' But fear lest Criseida might be slain in such a struggle made him forsake such a bold and daring plan.

And when Criseida saw that, however sad she was, she must needs depart with the appointed company, she mounted her horse, and began to say to herself in angry scorn: 'Ah, cruel Jove and malicious fortune, whither do you bear me against my will? Why does my grief give you such delight? Harsh and pitiless, you snatch me from the happiness that was closest to my heart; and perchance you think you would be humiliated by any sacrifice or honour offered by me, but you are deceived. I shall not cease from uttering complaints in abuse of you and to your dishonour until I come again to see once more the fair face of Troilus.'

Afterwards she turned disdainfully towards Diomede and said: 'Let us go now; we have shown ourselves enough to this people. Now they may hope for a remedy for their woes if they scan carefully the honourable exchange thou hast made in giving up a king so mighty and so feared for a woman.' And, when she had said this, she put spurs to her horse, saying naught but farewell to her retainers. And clearly did the king and his barons perceive the lady's scorn. Forth she went and heeded not leave-takings or speeches and looking at nobody. And she departed from Troy, and she was destined nevermore to return thither and to abide with Troilus.

As an act of courtesy, Troilus, with hawk on hand, and with many companions, mounted his horse and accompanied her till she was clear outside the walls, and fain would he have done so even to her dwelling-place, but it would have been too undisguised a thing, and would too have been deemed an act of small wisdom.

And now Antenor, restored by the Greeks, had come among them, and the Trojan youths had received him with great rejoicing and with honour. And though this return was very painful to the heart of Troilus, Criseida having been given up, yet he received him with fair countenance and made him ride ahead with Pandarus.

And now, when it came to taking leave of one another, he and Criseida tarried for a space and gazed into one another's eyes, nor could the lady check her tears. And then they took each other by the right hand; and Troilus then drew so close to her that she could hear him when he spoke softly, and said: 'Return, cause me not to die.'

And, adding nothing further, he turned his steed, his face all flushed; and to Diomede he said naught. And Diomede alone noted this behaviour and saw clearly the love betwixt the two; and in his thoughts he found several reasons in proof thereof; and while he whispered of this to himself, he was secretly allured by her.

Her father received her with great joy, although such love was a burden unto her. She remained silent and shy, wholly consumed with bitter grief and in sorry plight, yet faithful to Troilus in her heart, though she was soon to change and forsake him for a new lover.

Troilus returned to Troy in sadder anguish than ever was man before; and with a stern and lowering face he paused not till he reached his palace. Dismounting there, far heavierthoughted than he had ever been before, he allowed none to speak a word to him, but went alone into his chamber.

There he gave free utterance to the grief he had held in check and called upon death to come. And he wept for his bliss that seemed to him to be lost; and so loudly did he cry out that it may be he was heard by those who passed through the court. And he spent the whole day in such lamenting that neither servant nor friend beheld him.

If the day was passed in grief, the night, now come with its darkness, did not lessen it; nay, his weeping and great sorrow were redoubled. So did his loss overmaster him. He cursed the day he was born and the gods and goddesses and nature, and his father and all who had spoken in favour of the giving up of Criseida.

Moreover, he abused himself that he had let her depart thus and that he had not acted upon the plan he had made for attempting to flee with her, and bitterly did he repent and was ready to die of sorrow thereat; or that at least he had not asked for her, for perhaps she would have been granted unto him.

And turning now this way and now that and finding no comfort in his bed, he said to himself at such times, weeping the while: 'What a night is this! When I think on the night that is past, it was at this time, if I mistake not the hour, that I kissed the white breast, the mouth and the eyes and the fair face of my lady and often embraced her. She kissed me, and, as we talked, we made merry together gaily and joyously. Now I am alone, weary and weeping, doubtful if ever such a happy night is destined to come again; now I hold the pillow in my embrace and feel my burning love grow greater, and my hope less because of the grief that conquers it.

'What shall I do, hapless wretch that I am? Shall I bide my time, if indeed I have the power to do so? But, if my mind is so saddened at her going hence, how may I hope for strength to continue thus? For one who loves well, as I do, there can be no rest, for the night has been even as the day that went before it.'

Neither Pandarus nor any other person had been able to go to him that day; and thus, when morning had come, he had him quickly summoned, so that he might a little ease his troubled heart by talking to him of Criseida. Pandarus came thither, and clearly did he perceive what Troilus had done that night and also what he wished for.

'O my Pandarus,' said Troilus, hoarse from crying aloud and

long weeping, 'what shall I do when the fire of love does so lay hold on all my being that I cannot rest either much or little? What shall I do in my woe, now that fortune has so turned against me that I have lost my sweet friend? I think I shall never see her more; would that I had fallen dead when I let her go from me yesterday! O sweet bliss, O my dear delight, O fair lady, to whom I did give myself! O my sweet soul! O sole joy of these sad eyes, now changed to streams, ah, dost thou not see that I am dying and dost thou not bring me help?

'Who now looks upon thee, sweet soul, in thy beauty? Who sits by thee, heart of my body? Who listens to thee now, who talks with thee? Alas, not I, most hapless of all men! Tell me, what doest thou? Dost thou think of me at all now, or hast thou forgotten me because of thy old father, who now holds thee? It is because of this that I live in such grievous pain.

'Such words as thou hearest from me now, Pandarus, I have uttered all night, nor has this torment of love allowed me to sleep; or if any slumber has come to break my suffering, it is of no avail because while I sleep I dream of fleeing away or of being alone in dread places or in the hands of fierce enemies. And it does so trouble me to look upon these things, and such dread is in my heart, that it were better for me to bide awake and to grieve. And oftentimes trembling comes upon me, which shakes and startles me, and makes it seem as I were falling downwards from a height. I am roused from sleep and call loudly upon love and likewise upon Criseida, praying now for mercy and now for death.

'To such a pass, as thou hearest, have I, poor wretch, come, and I bemoan my lot and our parting more than I should ever have believed possible. Alas, I confess that I cannot help hoping still for solace and that the fair lady will return and bring it back to me; but my heart, which loves her, denies me this and is ever calling out for her.'

After he had spoken and discoursed in such fashion for a great while, Pandarus, sorrowing over such heavy and grievous distress, said: 'Ah, Troilus, if this sadness is to be soothed and ended, tell me, dost thou not believe that others besides thee have sometimes felt the affliction of love, or have been forced to part? Some of these others are, in truth, as deep in love as thou art—by Pallas I swear it to thee. And besides there are those, I feel sure, who are more luckless than thou; and yet they have not yielded themselves up, as thou hast, to live in such despair. But they strive to lighten their grief with hope when it weighs too heavily.

'Thou shouldst do likewise. Thou sayest that she has promised thee to return here by the tenth day. That is not such a long absence but what thou shouldst be able to wait without being glum and languishing like a witless fellow. How couldst thou bear the affliction if she had to go hence for a year? Banish dreams and fears; cast them to the winds, for that is what they are. From melancholy they come, and they make thee see what thou fearest. God alone knows the truth of what shall be; and dreams and auguries, to which foolish people give heed, are not worth a mite and tell little or nothing of the future.

'Therefore, in God's name, relent towards thyself, lay aside this raging grief. Do me this favour, grant me this boon. Rise up; let thy thoughts be not so downcast, and speak to me cheerily of the past, and set thy noble mind on the future. For what is gone will very soon come again. Therefore be of good hope and take comfort.

'This city is large and full of delight, and now is a time of truce, as thou knowest; let us go to some pleasant place far from here, and there shalt thou stay with one of these kings, and with him while away thy troubled life till the time is past that has been set by the fair lady who has wounded thy heart.

'Ah, do so, I pray thee. Rise up. To give way to grief, as thou dost, is an unmanly act, and so too is it to lie prostrate. And, if men knew of thy behaviour so witless and strange, thou wouldst be abashed; and they would say that like a coward thou didst weep at these harsh times and not from love, or that thou didst make pretence of being sickly.'

'Alas, he who suffers great loss weeps much, nor can he who has not experienced that know what is that bliss that I have let go. Wherefore I ought not to be blamed if forever I did naught but weep; but, my friend, since thou hast entreated me, I shall take comfort as best I can in order to serve thee and to give thee pleasure.

'May God soon send the tenth day, so that I may be once more light of heart, as I was when it was proposed to give her up. Never in the sweet springtime was rose so fair as I am ready to become when I shall look upon the fresh face of that lady on her return to Troy who is the cause of my torment and unrest.

'But where can we go to make merry, as thou dost propose? Should we go to Sarpedon, how can I tarry there when always

I shall have in my mind the question whether perchance she might not for some reason return before the day set. For if this should come to pass, I should not wish to be absent for all the world is worth and for all it can offer.'

'Ah,' replied Pandarus, 'if she returns, I shall have someone come for me forthwith, and I shall put a man here for this and nothing else, so that we shall know clearly, for now verily none wishes it more than I do. Therefore thou wilt not on this ground give up the plan. Let us go to the place thou spokest of but now.'

The two companions started out on the road, and after about four miles they arrived where Sarpedon was; and he, learning this, went gladly to meet Troilus and gave him cordial welcome. They, though wearied by much sighing, yet joyously made merry with the mighty baron. He, as one who in all things was nobler of heart than any other man, did each of them wondrous honour, now with hunts, now with the gracious charm of fair ladies of high worth, with songs and music, and always with magnificent splendour of banquets, so many and of such sort that their equal had never been given in Troy.

But what mattered all these things to faithful Troilus, whose heart was not set thereon? His thoughts were elsewhere, in that place whither the yearning in his mind often carried them. And always in his mind's eye he saw Criseida, who was as his god; and he imagined now one thing, now another, and often sighed for her and love. Every other lady, whatever her worth and beauty, was displeasing to his sight; every pleasure, every sweet song was tedious to him while he beheld not her in whose hands love had placed the key of his unhappy life. And he was happy only in so far as he could think of her and leave all other matters.

And neither evening nor morning passed that he called not on her with sighs: 'O fair light, O morning star!' Then, as if she were at hand to listen, a thousand times and more he called her 'thorn-rose' and begged her to greet him; but ever he had to make an end too soon. The embrace ended in sighing.

No hour of the day passed that he uttered not her name a thousand times; ever her name was on his lips; and in his heart and mind he pictured her fair face and courtly words. The letters she had sent him he turned over fully a hundred times a day, such pleasure did he find in looking upon them again.

And they had not tarried there for three days when Troilus said to Pandarus: 'What more is there for us to do here? Does any duty bind us to live and die here? Are we to wait till we are sent packing? To tell the truth, I would fain go hence. Ah, in God's name, let us go; we have been long enough with Sarpedon and have been made welcome.'

Then Pandarus: 'Did we come here now to fetch fire, or is the tenth day come? Ah, be calm yet for a little, for to go now would seem a slight. Where wilt thou go, and in what place wilt thou stay with more content? Ah, let us tarry two days more; then we shall go; and, if thou wishest, we shall return home.'

Although Troilus against his will remained, yet he persisted in his former thoughts, nor did what Pandarus said to him bear any fruit. But after the fifth day they took their leave, though it displeased Sarpedon, and returned to their own houses, Troilus saying on the way: 'O God! Shall I find my love come again?'

But Pandarus, as one who was fully aware of all Calchas intended, spoke otherwise to himself: 'This longing of thine, so fiery and eager, will have a chance to cool, if what I heard even while she was here does not mislead me; and I believe the tenth day and month and year will pass ere thou see her again.'

When they had returned home, they went together into a chamber and sat down and talked much of Criseida. And Troilus ceased not to utter burning sighs. But after a space they rose up, and Troilus said: ' Let us go and at least see her house, since we can do naught else.'

And, when he had said this, he took his Pandarus by the hand, and forced himself to smile. And he descended from the palace, and to the others who were with him he made pretence of different reasons to hide the wounds he felt from love; but when his eyes fell upon the closed house of Criseida, he felt new anguish. And it seemed to him his heart would be broken when he saw the door shut and the windows. And so did the newborn passion work upon him that he knew not whether he stood or went; and his face, all distorted, would have plainly betrayed him to anybody who had given him a fleeting glance.

Then, distraught by his new suffering, he spoke with Pandarus as best he could, and said: 'Alas! What a place filled with light and joy wert thou when thou didst contain that beauty who held all my peace of mind in her eyes; now, lacking her, thou art left in darkness; nor do I know if ever thou art destined to possess her again.'

Thence he goes riding through Troy, and each place came

back to his mind. And as he went he spoke about them to himself: 'There did I see her laugh gaily; there did I see her looking towards me; there did she give me gracious greeting; there did she make merry, and there stand in thought; there did I see her take pity on my sighs. There did she stand when with her fair and beauteous eyes she made me bondsman unto love; there did she stand when she kindled my heart with a burning sigh; there did she stand when in her womanly goodness she vouchsafed to do me pleasure; there I did see her proud, and there my gracious lady showed herself humble unto me.'

Then, as he thought of this, he spoke further: 'O love, long hast thou shown thy power in me, if I am willing now to reveal the truth about myself and if indeed my memory brings back to me what is true. Wherever I go or stay, if I discern clearly, I note fully a thousand signs of thy conquest by which in triumph thou hast prevailed over me, who formerly made mock of every lover. O mighty and most dreadful lord, well hast thou avenged the slight put upon thee. But now that my soul has given itself wholly to thy service, as thou canst clearly see, let it not die in misery, restore it to its former joy. Use thy force upon Criseida as thou dost upon me, so that she return and put an end to my woes.'

At times he went to the gate by which his lady had departed: 'From here went forth she who is my comfort; from here went forth my sweet life; as far as that place did I bear her company, and there did I part from her, and there in sorrow did I touch her hand.' Thus he spoke to himself, shedding tears at the memory of each thing.

'Hence didst thou depart, O heart of my body; when wilt thou return from there, my dear love and my sweet desire? In sooth, I know not, but these ten days will be more than a thousand years. Ah, shall I ever see thee come again to give me joy with thy charming ways as thou didst promise? Ah, will that ever be? Ah, would it were now!'

And it seemed to him that his face was pale beyond its wont, and therefore it came into his mind that at times men pointed at him, as if they said: 'Why has Troilus grown so downcast and so distraught?' There were none who pointed him out, but he who knows the truth is suspicious.

And thus he found pleasure in setting forth in verses who was the cause of his grief. When he was worn out by sorrow, he uttered sighs and found some respite, as it were, from his trouble. While he waited in these dark days, he went about singing in a low voice and lightening his heart o'erburdened with love, in this fashion: 'The sweet sight and the beautiful gentle glance of the fairest eyes ever seen, now lost to me, make my life seem such a burden that I am ever uttering groans. And now to such a pass have I been brought that in place of the light and easy sighs I was wont to give I long for death because thou art gone, so sorely am I afflicted.

'Alas, love, why didst thou not smite me at the outset, so that I should have died? Why, alas, didst thou not send forth from me the burdened spirit within me? For now I see myself cast down from my high station to the depths. There is no solace to my grief, O love, save death, now that I find myself severed from those fair eyes in which ere now I did behold thee.

'When, in courteous greeting, I turn my eyes somewhat towards a fair lady, so destroyed is all my mastery over myself that I cannot check my lament. So do the wounds of love bring to my mind my lady, from sight of whom, ah wretched me, I am so distant that gladly would I die, if love allowed.

'Since my fate is so cruel that everything that meets my eyes brings me more sadness, let thy hand, O love, close them, for the love of God, now that I can no longer see my dear one. Let me leave my flesh, O love, for, when life is conquered by death, it should be a joyous thing to die, and thou knowest well whither the soul must go. It will go to those fair arms where fortune did cast my body. Dost thou not see, O love, that already my face is marked with the hue of death? Thou dost behold the anguish that drives out my soul. Draw it forth and bear it to the bosom I most love, where it looks to find peace, for now it finds pleasure in naught else.'

When he had uttered these words in his song, he fell again to sighing as before. By day in his walk and by night in his bed he thought ever of his Criseida. Nor did he take delight in aught else, and often did he count the days that had passed, thinking that he should never reach ten, by which time Criseida was to come again from the Greeks. The days seemed long to him, and the nights more lasting than they were wont to be. He measured from the first streaks of dawn even till the stars showed forth, and he said: 'The sun has fallen into new errors, nor do his steeds run as once they did.' Of the night he spoke in the same way, and counted the hours one by one.

The old moon was already horned when Criseida departed, and he had seen it in the morning when he left her house. Wherefore often he said to himself: 'When this becomes new-horned, as it looked when our lady went away, then will my love have come hither again.'

He gazed at the Greeks encamped before Troy; and whereas before when he beheld them he was wont to be stirred to wrath, so now he looked upon them with delight; and the air that he felt breathe upon his face he was wont to think of as sighs sent from Criseida. And often he said: 'In that place or in that is my sweet lady.'

In such fashion and in many other ways he passed the time, uttering sighs; and with him always was Pandarus, who often upheld him with comfort, and as best he could sought to engage him in light and joyous speech, ever giving him good hope of his beautiful and worthy love.

CANTO VI

On the other side, upon the seashore, with few women, among armed men, was Criseida. And she, far from her sweet love, spent her nights in bitter tears—for by day she must needs hold them in check—and thus her fresh and delicate cheeks had grown pale and thin. She wept, speaking softly to herself of the joy she had once known with Troilus; and she would picture to herself all that had passed between them, and would bring to mind all their words, whenever she had time and power to do so. And thus seeing herself far from him she shed bitter tears. Nor would any man have been so hard of heart, if he had heard her sad plaint, as to keep himself from weeping with her. So bitterly did she weep, when a moment of time was allowed her, that it cannot be fully told. And what pressed more hardly upon her than aught else was that she had none to sorrow with her.

She looked upon the walls of Troy, and the palaces, the towers, and the fortresses; and to herself she said: 'Alas, what joy, what happiness, and what delights had I there once! And now here in dreary sadness I waste my beauty that was held so dear. Alas, my Troilus, what art thou doing now? Does anything still bring me to thy mind?

'Ah, hapless creature that I am! Would now that I had believed thee, and that together we two had gone wherever and to whatever realm it had pleased thee. For then I should not have known these griefs, nor have lost so many precious days. Afterwards, at some time, we should have gone back; and who would have spoken ill of me then, if I had gone with such a man as he?

'Ah, hapless creature that I am! For I see too late that my wisdom is now an enemy unto me. I fled the bad and pursued the worse, and thus my heart is bare of joy; and in vain I call on death to comfort me, since I cannot see thee, O sweet friend, and fear to see thee never again. May the Greeks soon be as desolate as I am.

'I shall do all I can to flee hence, if in no other way I am allowed to come and rejoin thee as I promised. Let the smoke go where it will, and let my act draw upon me what consequence it may. For, rather than die of grief, I am willing that he who wishes may talk and raise a cry touching this.'

But soon a new lover turned her aside from so high and great a purpose. Diomede used every argument he could to make his way into her heart. Nor in course of time did he fail in his endeavour, and in brief space he drove out Troilus and Troy and every thought she had of him, whether false or true. Not four days had she been there since the bitter parting when an honourable reason for coming to her was found by Diomede; and he discovered her sighing and alone, and as if wholly changed since the day he had first ridden with her and brought her thither from Troy. And this to him seemed a great marvel.

And at first sight of her he said to himself: 'My labour, I believe, is all in vain; this lady, as I see, is sad through love of another, heavy-thoughted and of constant mind. It would ask a master's art for me to drive out the first that I myself might find entrance. Alas, what ill-fortune was it for me that I went to Troy and brought her here!'

But being a man who ventured much and had a bold heart, he determined that, even in truth should he die for it, he would lay open to her the grievous injuries that love had made him suffer for her sake since her coming thither, and how he had first been kindled by love for her. And, sitting down, he gradually turned the talk whither he wished. And first he fell to speaking of the stern war between them and the Trojans, and asked her what she thought of it and whether she deemed their plans senseless or vain. From this he came to ask whether the manners of the Greeks seemed strange to her; nor did he long delay asking her why Calchas was slow to give her in marriage.

Criseida, whose heart was still constant to her sweet love in Troy, noted not his cunning, but answered Diomede as love prompted her; and often she pierced his heart with bitter grief, and sometimes gave him glad hope of what he craved.

And, emboldened as he talked with her, he began to speak thus: 'Fair lady, if I have viewed aright that face of heavenly beauty that is more pleasing unto me than any I have ever seen, I seem to behold it changed by harsh grief since the day we left Troy and, as you know, came here. Nor know I what may be the reason, unless it be love, which, if you are wise, you will cast away and hearken unto reason; for it were well for you to do as I say. The Trojans, one may say, are held in prison by us, as you see. For we are resolved not to go hence till we have brought the place low with sword or fire. Think not that any one therein will ever receive mercy from us; nor is there anybody, either of those living in the world or dead in hell, who has wrought other folly or who shall do so, to whom the punishment we shall deal out to Paris for his deed, if we are able, will not be a most clear warning. And were there twelve Hectors, as there is but one, and sixty brothers, we shall, if Calchas deceives us not here by tricks and falsehoods, win, and that soon, the longed-for triumph over them all, however many they be. And their death, which will come apace, will show clearly that our hope is not false.

'And do not think that Calchas would have asked so earnestly to have you again, if he had not foreseen what I say. I had much talk with him touching this matter before he did so, and considered every side of it. And thus to remove you from such danger he took counsel to demand you back. And I encouraged him, hearing of your wondrous virtues and other qualities; and learning that Antenor was to be given for you I offered myself as an ambassador; and he laid upon me that task, knowing very well my good faith. Nor were the goings and comings a labour to me, thanks to seeing you, speaking to you, coming to know you, and hearing you. Wherefore I am minded to say to you: O lady fair and beloved, give up the deluding love of the Trojans; drive forth from your mind this sorry hope that makes you sigh in vain now, and call back the bright beauty that gives more pleasure to him who notes it than any other. For Troy has now come to such a pass that all hopes that men have there are lost. And, even should it stand for ever, the king and his sons and those who dwell there are barbarous and graceless and of little worth when set beside the Greeks, who can take the lead of all other nations in noble customs and fair bearing. You are now among courtly men, whereas you were among senseless brutes. And believe not that among the Greeks there is not love far nobler and more perfect than among the Trojans; and your high worth and great beauty and your face, so heavenly fair, will find here a full worthy lover, if it please you to accept him. And if it were not unpleasing to you, I would more gladly be he forthwith than be king of the Greeks.'

And, when he had said this, his face grew red as fire, and his tongue faltered somewhat. He bent his glance to the ground, turning his eyes a little from her. But then, moved by sudden thought, he began again, more fluent of speech than before, and with swift words spoke further: 'Let it not be a grief to you:

I am of as gentle birth as any man in Troy. If my father Tydeus had lived—he died fighting at Thebes—I had been king of Calydon and Argos, as even yet I purpose to be; nor should I have come as a stranger into my kingdom, but well known, of ancient family and highly esteemed; and, if it may be believed, offspring of a god, so that among the Greeks I am not of least account. Therefore I pray you, if my prayer avails aught, to banish all melancholy and to receive me as your servant, if in your eyes I seem worthy and such a one as befits your sovereignty. I shall be such a one as your modesty and the noble beauty that I behold in you more than in any other require, if you will also cherish Diomede.'

Criseida listened and shyly made answer in few and halting words, as his speech asked of her. But when she heard these last words, she said to herself that he was greatly daring; and she looked askance at him with scorn, such hold had Troilus yet upon her; and thus she spoke in a low voice: 'Ah, Diomede, I love that land where I was bred and fostered; and this war is as grievous to me as may be, and fain would I see her set free. And if cruel fate shuts me out from her, this is a great cause of distress to me. But I pray that fair guerdon be given thee for all trouble that has come upon thee for my sake.

'Well do I know that the Greeks are of high worth and courteous, as thou sayest; but the noble virtue of the Trojans is not therefore less. Their qualities have appeared in the exploits of Hector; nor do I think it wisdom to slight others because of quarrels or for any other reason, and afterwards to exalt oneself above them.

'I have not known love since he died to whom as my husband and lord I loyally gave it; nor have I ever cared thus for any Greek or Trojan, nor have I desire to care for any, nor ever shall. That thou art come of royal blood I fully believe and have indeed heard that. And this raises great wonder in me, that thou canst set thy heart on a woman of small account and humble rank as I am. The fair Helen would become thee. I am burdened with trouble and am not minded to welcome such tidings. I say not, therefore, that it grieves me in sooth to be loved by thee.

'The times are harsh, and you are in arms. Let the victory that thou dost look for come; then shall I know much better what to do. It may be that pleasures will delight me more than they do now, and thou mayest speak to me again; and perchance thy words will be dearer to me than they are now.

A man must heed time and season when he wishes to win others.'

This last speech was very pleasing to Diomede; and he thought that beyond question he might still hope for favour, which indeed he won later, to his delight. And he replied to her: 'O lady, I pledge you my faith as fully as I can that I am at your command and shall always be ready.' And he spoke no further, and after this he went his way.

He was tall and fair of person, young, fresh, and very pleasing, and mighty and proud, it is said, and as ready of speech as ever any Greek was; and by nature he was inclined to love. And when he had gone Criseida in her sorrows fell to thinking of these things, in doubt whether to approach or flee from him.

These matters cooled her eager thoughts, which had been set only on returning; they worked upon her whole mind, which had been inclined towards Troilus, and checked her desire. And new hope did somewhat put to flight her heavy grief; and, swayed by these reasons as she was, it came to pass that she fulfilled not her promise to Troilus.

CANTO VII

Troilus, as has been said before, passed the time longing for the appointed day, which indeed came after he had waited long. Wherefore, under show of having other business in hand, he went alone towards the gate, talking much about this matter with Pandarus. And, as they went, they looked towards the camp to see whether they might spy anybody coming towards Troy. And each person, alone or accompanied, whom they saw coming towards them, they took to be Criseida, until he was so close to them as to be clearly recognized. And thus they lingered till past noon, often deceived, as the event proved, by their readiness to believe.

Troilus said: 'As far as I can see, she would not now come before dinner. She will find it much harder than she would wish to free herself from her old father. What counsel hast thou to offer me? I believe indeed that she would have come if she had been able, and if she had not stayed to dine with him.'

Pandarus said: 'I believe thou sayest the truth. Therefore let us go, and afterwards we shall come again.' Troilus assented, and in the end thus they did. And it was long ere they returned; but, as it proved, their hope played them false, and they found it a thing of naught. For this fair lady came not, and by now the ninth hour was far gone.

Troilus said: 'It may be that her father has prevented her and wishes her to stay till evening, and therefore her return will be delayed. Let us now take our station outside, so that her entrance be not hindered, for often these warders are wont to hold in talk whoever comes, and do not single out those whom they should.'

Twilight came, and then evening came; and many persons had misled Troilus. And he had remained, ever gazing towards the camp, and he had looked at all those who came from the shore to Troy, and he had asked some for tidings and had gained nothing of what he sought.

Wherefore he turned to Pandarus, saying: 'This lady has done wisely, if I understand her ways aright. She wishes to come secretly; therefore she waits for night, and I commend her. She does not wish to give the people occasion to wonder or to say, "Has she who was asked for in exchange for Antenor come back so soon?" Therefore, my Pandarus, I pray thee for the love of God let not the waiting be burdensome to thee. We have naught else to do now; let it not grieve thee to grant my desire. And, if I err not, I think I see her. Ah, look yonder, seest thou what I do?'

'No,' said Pandarus, 'if my eyes are open, what thou pointest at seems to me a cart.'

'Alas, thou sayest truth,' said Troilus. 'And thus it is because I am so eager that what I wish should straightway come to pass.'

The sun's light had already died, and some stars showed in the sky, when Troilus said: 'I know not what sweet thought comforts me in my longing; be assured she will come to-night.'

Pandarus laughed, but silently, at what Troilus said, and knew clearly the reason that prompted him to say it. And in order not to make him more sorrowful than he was he feigned to believe him and said: 'This poor youth looks for a wind from Mongibello.'

The waiting was for naught, and the warders made a great noise above the gate, calling upon citizens and strangers to enter unless they wished to remain without, also the country folk and their beasts. But Troilus tarried more than two hours. At last, when all the sky was bright with stars, he returned within with Pandarus.

And, although in his heart he had often beguiled the time, now with this hope and now with that, yet among these many hopes love prompted him to trust in that which had least of folly in it. Wherefore, once again he spoke to Pandarus, saying: 'We are foolish to have expected her this day. She told me she would stay ten days with her father and bide there no whit longer, and then she would return to Troy. The end of the time is this very day. Therefore she ought to come to-morrow, if we count aright; and we have waited here the livelong day, so forgetful has desire made us. We must needs, Pandarus, come again early to-morrow morning.'

And thus they did. But little did it avail to look up and down, for already she had turned her thoughts elsewhere; so that, after standing long at gaze, as they had done the day before, they went in again when night had fallen. But to Troilus that was exceeding bitter. And the glad hope that had been his had now scarce anything to fasten on. Wherefore he grieved much within himself and began to lament greatly touching her and love; nor did it seem to him that for any reason she should have so delayed to come again after promising faithfully to return. But, sighing, Troilus awaited the third and the fourth and the fifth and the sixth day after the tenth day, which had already passed; and he hoped for and yet despaired of her return. And after these days he was granted a yet longer spell of hope, and all in vain. Still she returned not, and meanwhile Troilus wasted away.

The tears and sighs that had been checked by the comforting words of Pandarus came again unsummoned and gave outlet to his burning desires; and those that had been held back by hope came from him, now that he knew himself beguiled, increased full twenty-fold by his sufferings and more violent than before. And all his old yearnings came upon him again; and, besides, there was the betrayal that it seemed to him he had suffered, and the angry spirit of jealousy, a heavier sorrow than any other and unrelieved, as they who have felt it know. And thus day and night he wept as much as he himself and his eyes could endure to weep. He scarcely ate and drank, so full of anguish was his sad breast; and moreover he could not sleep unless worn out by sighing. And he held his life and himself in utter scorn, and he shunned pleasure as he would fire, and likewise, as far as he could, he kept himself from all merriment and all company. And his look so changed that he seemed rather a wild beast than a man; nor would anybody have recognized him, so pale and haggard was his face. All the strength of his body had gone from him, and there was scarce force enough in his limbs to sustain him; nor would he take any solace that anybody proffered him.

Priam, who saw him so cast down, called to him once, saying: 'My son, what has come upon thee? What thing is this that so grieves thee? Thou dost not seem the same, thou art pale. What makes thee to live thus wretchedly? Tell me, my son. Thou dost barely stand on thy feet, and if I see aright, thou art very faint.'

Hector said the same to him, and Paris and his other brothers and sisters, and asked whence this great grief had come to him and from what ill-tidings. And to them all he said that he felt pain in his heart, but what it was none could learn at all from him by their questions.

One day, filled with sadness by reason of her broken faith, Troilus had laid him down to sleep, and in a dream he saw the dire offence of her who caused his sorrow. For it seemed to him he heard a great and horrible crashing within a shady wood. And when he lifted his head he thought he saw a great boar plunging through. And then afterwards he thought he beheld Criseida beneath its feet, and with its tusk it drew forth her heart. And, so it seemed to him, Criseida heeded not so sore a hurt, but took as it were delight in what the animal did. And this caused him such distress that it broke his troubled sleep. When he was awake, he fell to thinking of what he had seen in his dream. And it seemed to him he understood clearly what his vision meant, and quickly he bade Pandarus be called. And when he had come, Troilus, weeping, began: 'My Pandarus, my life no longer finds favour with God. Thy Criseida, alas, has played me false, she, in whom more than in any other I put my trust. She has given her love to another, and that is far more grievous unto me than death. The gods have revealed it to me in a dream,' and thereupon he told him all the dream.

Then he fell to telling him what this dream meant, and thus he said: 'This boar that I have seen is Diomede; for his grand-father killed the boar of Calydon, if we may believe our fore-fathers, and ever since, as it appears, his descendants have borne the boar as a crest. Alas, it is a bitter and true dream. He must have won her heart, that is, her love, with his speaking. He has her, as thou too mayest plainly see. Ah, hapless is my life. He alone prevents her return. If it were not for that, she could easily have come again, nor would her old father or any other cause have kept her back. And thus, believing in her, I have been deceived and made a mock of while in vain I awaited her coming.

'Alas, Criseida, what cunning wit, what new delight, what tempting beauty, what anger at me, what just disdain, what fault of mine, or what cruel whim has so wrought as to turn thy proud heart to another? Alas, constancy! Alas, promises! Alas, faith and loyalty! Who has cast you out from her I love? Alas, why did I ever let thee go? Why did I put faith in thy cruel counsel? Why did I not take thee away with me as, alas, I desired? Why did I not break the pledges that had been given, as my heart prompted me when I saw thee yielded up? Then wouldst thou not be faithless and false, nor I desolate. I believed thee and firmly trusted that thy faith was pure, and that thy words were truth most sure and more clear than is the light of the sun unto men. But thou didst speak with double meaning and slyness, as is clear now from thy light ways; for not only hast thou not come back to me, but thou hast set thy love on another man.

'What shall I do, Pandarus? I feel a flame fiercely kindled anew in my mind, so that there is room for naught else in my thoughts. Fain would I lay hold on death with my hands, for in such a life there would be no longer any joy. Now that fortune has brought me to so evil a plight, to die will be a pleasure, whereas to live would be a burden and distress.'

And when he had said this, he ran to a sharp knife that hung in the room and would have stabbed himself in the breast with it, had he not been checked by Pandarus, who seized the hapless youth, after seeing him voice his despair in words usual at such times, with sighs and shedding of tears.

Troilus cried: 'Ah, my dear friend, in God's name I pray thee, hold me not. Bent as I am on this thing, let me follow my cruel desire. Hold me not, unless thou wish to learn what manner of death it is to which I hasten. Free me, Pandarus, for, if thou dost not, I shall strike thee and then slay myself. Let me remove from the world the saddest body alive; let me by dying give pleasure to our faithless lady, whom I shall not cease to follow amid the dark shadows in the realm of pain; let me slay myself, for a life of languor is worse than death.' And, so speaking, he struggled to gain the knife, which the other kept from him.

Pandarus still strove with him, holding him tightly, and had it not been that Troilus was weak, Pandarus's strength would have been overcome, so did Troilus, possessed by rage, shake him. Yet at the last Pandarus put the knife beyond his reach; and, weeping, he forced him against his will to sit down with him.

And after bitter tears he turned, full of pity, towards him with these words: 'Troilus, I have ever believed thee so devoted to me that, if I had ventured for my sake or another's to ask thee to slay thyself, thou wouldst have done it forthwith as bravely as I would for thee in any situation. And yet at my entreaties thou hast not willingly refrained from a foul and hateful death; and had I not now been stronger than thou, I should have seen thee die here. I looked not to see thee fail in the pledges thou hast given me, yet even now thou canst make amends for this, if thou dost heed and profit by what I say.

'As far as I can see, thou hast imagined that Criseida belongs to Diomede. And, if I have grasped well what thou hast said, naught save the dream makes thee believe this. And thou dost lay hold on this fancy because of the animal that wounds with its tusks; and, unwilling to give it further thought first, thou dost wish to end sad tears with death. I have told thee before that it was folly to set too great store by dreams. There never has been, nor is there, nor ever will be, a man who can with certainty interpret well what fancy in differing guises may show to others in their sleep; and ere now many have believed one thing, when another, opposite and wholly different, has come to pass. So might it come about with this. It may be that, whereas thou dost take the animal to be hostile to thy love, it is favourable unto thee and will not, as thou thinkest, do thee any harm. Dost thou deem it an honourable act for any man—let alone one of royal blood, as thou art—to slay himself with his own hands, or to make such outcry because of love? Thou shouldst have set about this matter all otherwise than thou didst. It had been well first craftily to discover if it were true—as thou couldst have done—and if thou hadst found it false or partly so, then shouldst thou have risen above faith in dreams and their falsity, which bring evil upon thee. If thou shouldst find it true that thou hast been forsaken by Criseida for another, thou shouldst not deliberately set all thy thoughts on death. For I know not any by whom it has not always been condemned. But it were a good thing to resolve on mocking her as she has mocked thee. And, even if tormenting thoughts thrust thee on to die in order to lessen thy anguish, thou shouldst not have made the choice thou didst. For there was another way to win thy desire. And indeed thy low thoughts should not have hidden it from thee; for in front of the threshold of Troy's gate are the Greeks, and they will slay thee and crave no pardon. We shall go then together in arms against the Greeks when thou wishest to die. There shall we, like well-famed youths, fight against them, and slaying them we shall manfully die, not unavenged. Nor in sooth shall I forbid thee to seek death at their hands, if I but perceive that a just cause moves thee to desire death in such a venture.'

Troilus, who was still trembling in fierce rage, listened to him as well as he could in his grief. After hearing him for a long time he wept as one still sorrow-stricken. He turned to Pandarus, who was waiting to see if he had abandoned his mad purpose, and, weeping, thus he spoke, ever breaking his words with sighs. 'Be assured of this, Pandarus, that in all I can do I am wholly devoted to thee. It will not be burdensome to me to live and to die to please thee; and, if but now, possessed by frenzy, I was untouched by sage counsel when thou didst set upon me for my own good, thou in thy excellence must not marvel thereat. My sudden belief in my sad dream led me into that error; now, with my anger abated, I see clearly my great mistake and my mad desire. But, if thou dost perceive by what test I can find the truth of this suspicion, tell me, I pray thee for God's sake, for I am bewildered, and by myself I see it not.'

And Pandarus said to him: 'In my opinion thou shouldst test her by writing; because, if she cares not for thee, I think we shall have no answer from her; and, if we have, we can clearly see from the written words whether thou art still to hope for her return or whether she has given her love to another man. Thou hast not once written to her since she left, nor she to thee; and the cause of her tarrying might be such that thou wouldst say that she had been right in staying; and it might be such that thou wouldst blame lack of resolution rather than any other fault. Write to her therefore, for if thou dost it well, what thou art seeking will be made clear to thee.'

Troilus was already ill-pleased with himself; therefore he believed him willingly. And, having gone aside, he ordered that writing materials be given him forthwith, and it was done. And having pondered somewhat on what he was to write, he began calmly and wrote to his lady straightway and said thus: 'Fair lady, to whom love gave me and to whom he still binds me and ever while I live will bind me with pure faith, forasmuch as thou by going hence didst leave my soul here distraught by greater suffering than any one believes, it commends itself to thy great excellence and can send thee no other greeting. Though thou hast become all but a Greek, thou wilt surely receive my letter, for so enduring a love as holds and as has held us joined in friendship is not soon forgotten; and I pray it may last forever. Therefore take it and read it even to the end.

'If thy servant may in any case complain of his lord, it may be I should have cause to complain of thee, when I think of the faith I put in thy devout affection and many promises and the swearing to all the gods that thou wouldst return by the tenth day. And now forty days are passed, and yet thou hast not come. But, since what is thy pleasure must be mine also, I dare not protest; but, as humbly as I can, burning more than ever with love, I write my thoughts to thee. And likewise I tell thee of my ardent desire and also of the life I have led, being eager to know what thy life has been since thou wert exchanged and sent among the Greeks.

'It seems to me, if I mistake not the course of thy thoughts, that thy father's flatteries have prevailed with thee, or that new love has made its way into thy mind, or—rare though it is to see a dotard turn free-handed—that the grasping Calchas has become gracious. In our last bitter weeping together thy schemes led me to expect something wholly different. Then thou hast lingered so long beyond the time we agreed on, for according to thy promises thou wert to come again so soon. If it were because of the first or third reason, thou wouldst have made this clear to me, since thou knowest that I oppose not and did not oppose what thou didst wish, and that I should have borne it patiently, even though it had been very grievous unto me. But much I fear that a new love is the cause of thy long tarrying; and, if it were so, it would be a sorer woe to me than any I have yet known. And, if my devotion has deserved this, thou shouldst not now have a chance to learn of it. By reason of this I live wretchedly in such fear that it takes from me delight and hope.

'This fear drives me to utter cruel cries when I would fain be at rest; this fear alone holds sway within my thoughts, and I know not what to do. This fear, alas, is slaying me; nor know I how to guard myself against it, nor have I any longer the power. This fear has brought me to such straits that I am of service neither to Venus nor to Mars.

'Since thy going hence my sad eyes have never ceased to weep; since then I have been able neither to eat nor drink, neither to rest nor sleep, but have ever uttered groans. And what men could have heard most often on my lips was the constant utterance of thy name and the calling upon thee and love for succour—this alone, I think, kept me from death. Thou mayest now perceive clearly what I should do, were I indeed certain of what I suspect. In sooth I think I should slay myself if I heard thou hadst so betrayed me. And to what end should I live on here if I had lost my hope of thee, my loved one, to whom, living as I do in grief, I look for my only solace?

'Sweet songs and genial gatherings, birds and dogs and pleasant walks, fair ladies, temples and great feasts, which in the past I was wont to seek out—now I shun them all, and they are hateful to me whenever I fall to thinking that now thou, my sweet love and sovereign hope, dost linger far from here. The bright flowers and the fresh grass, which paint the meadows with a thousand colours, cannot delight my soul, sore troubled, O lady, by love-longing for thee. I find joy in that part of the heavens only beneath which I think thou bidest now. I gaze thereon and say: "That now looks upon her from whom I hope for grace."

'I look upon the mountains that stand round about and upon the place that holds thee hidden from me; and, sighing, I say: "They have the chance, and care not, to behold the loveliness of her fair eyes, far from which I wear away a sorely troubled life. Would I were now one of those mountains, or that I dwelt upon one of them, so that I might see her."

'I look upon the waves making towards the sea beside which thou dost dwell now, and I say: "After they have flowed for a space, they will come where the divine light of my eyes has gone to stay and will be seen by her. Alas for my hapless life! Why can I not go in their stead and do as they do?"

'If the sun sinks, I gaze on him with envy, because it seems to me that, longing for my beloved, that is, drawn by desire for thee, he comes again to see thee more swiftly than is his wont; and after sighing I fall to hating him, and my sorrows increase. And so it is that in fear lest he take thee from me I pray night to come down speedily.

'When sometimes I hear one name the place where thou dost bide, or when sometimes I see one who comes thence, the fire in my heart, quenched by excess of grief, is kindled anew; and in my soul, bond-slave to pleasure, I seem to feel some hidden joy; and I say to myself: "Fain would I go to the place whence he comes, O my sweet love."

'But what dost thou do among armed knights, among warlike men and alarums, in tents, in the midst of sudden attacks, frightened oftentimes by the fury of clashing arms and of the raging sea, by the side of which thou now dost dwell? Ah, lady mine, is this not a dire trouble to thee, who wert wont to have such ease in Troy?

'In truth, as behoves me, I have more pity for thee than for myself. Return therefore and fulfil all thy promise ere I fall into a worse plight. I forgive thee all the hurt thou hast done me by thy delay and crave no amends save the sight of thy fair face in which is set all my heaven. Ah, I pray thee by that longing that once possessed me for thee and thee for me, and likewise by that sweet love that kindled both our hearts; and by that beauty too that thou dost own, my gentle lady; by the many sighs and pitiful lamentations that once we uttered together; by the sweet kisses and by that embrace that held us once so tightly clasped; by the great happiness and the pleasant discourse that made our delights more joyous; by that pledge too that it pleased thee to give in words of love when last we parted, since when we have come together no more.

'Turn thy thoughts to me and come again; and, if perchance thou art prevented, write and tell me who has kept thee from returning here after the ten days were over. Ah, wrong not thy sweet words; in this at least make my life happy, and tell me, my dear love, if henceforth I may ever hope to have thee. Give me but hope, and I shall wait, though it weigh upon me beyond measure. If thou dost rob me of that, I shall slay myself and end my hard life. But though the hurt is mine, let thine be the shame, for thou wilt have brought to a death so ignoble one who served thee and was guiltless of any fault.

'Forgive me if I have failed to set down my words in fit order, and, if perchance thou seest the letter I send to be all stained, for my suffering is the great cause of both, living and passing my time as I do in shedding tears; and naught that comes to pass dost check them. And so it is that these stains, so plentiful, are tears of sorrow.

'Though there is much I might still utter, I say no more save to bid thee come. Ah, do it, my love, for so thou canst, if thou but set all thy wits to the task. Woe is me, for thou wilt not know me, so changed am I by cruel sorrows. I speak no more to thee but to say, God be with thee and send thee soon to me.'

Then he gave the letter sealed to Pandarus, who sent it off. But for many days he looked in vain for an answer from her. Whence the sorrow of Troilus, too great for mortal men, abated not; and his belief in the meaning of his wild dream was strengthened, yet not so greatly that he lost hope Criseida might love him still.

From day to day his sorrow grew as hope failed him, and thus he had to lay him down in bed, for he had no strength left. But one day by mere chance, Deiphoebus, whom he greatly loved, came to see him. And Troilus, plunged in grief, noted him not and said softly: 'Ah, Criseida, make me not to die in such woe.' Then was Deiphoebus aware of what weighed upon him, and making as if he had not heard, said : 'Dear brother, why dost thou not take comfort now for thy sad heart? The glad season is at hand and shows its beauty; the meadows grow green again and adorn themselves gaily; and already the day has come when the time of truce is ended. And therefore we, in arms, shall be able as usual to make the Greeks feel our valour. Dost thou no longer wish to come armed with us, thou, who wert wont to be the first in onset and to be so dreaded by them as a fighter that thou wert accustomed to make them all flee from thee? Already has Hector ordered us to be with him to-morrow outside the moat.'

Even as a ravening lion hunting for prey rests when tired and on a sudden leaps up, tossing his mane and filled with one desire, if he perceives stag or bull or aught else he longs for, so did swift energy pour into the impassioned heart of Troilus when he heard that the doubtful strife was beginning again. And raising his head he said: 'Brother mine, I am in truth rather weak, but I have such a longing for war that with renewed strength I shall straightway rise up from this bed; and I swear unto thee, if ever I did confront the Greeks with stern and undaunted breast, I shall now fight more fiercely than before, so great a hatred do I bear unto them.'

Deiphoebus well understood the bearing of those words, and much encouraged him, and said that they would await him there, but that nevertheless he would not interfere with his comfort by tarrying longer now; and they said farewell to each other. Troilus was left with his old sorrows; Deiphoebus went quickly to his brothers and made known the whole matter to them. And they readily believed this from what they had already seen of his conduct; and in order not to make him sad they agreed together to say naught thereof and to help him. Wherefore they at once sent word to their ladies that they should all go to visit him and make merriment for him with music and singers that he might forget his troubled life.

In a short time his room was full of ladies and music and songs. On one side was Polyxena, who was of heavenly beauty; on the other side sat fair Helen; Cassandra was also there before him; Hecuba was there and Andromache, and the wives of many of his brothers and many kinsfolk were gathered there. Each as she best might gave him comfort, and one of them asked him how he felt. He answered not but gazed now at one, now at another, and in his loyal thoughts he dwelt upon the memory of his Criseida, but revealed it not save with sighing. And yet he found some pleasure both in the music and in their beauty.

Cassandra, who, as it chanced, had heard what her brother Deiphoebus had said, as if mocking him for wearing so spiritless a countenance, said: 'Brother, grievously hast thou felt, as I hear, accursed love, which shall be the ruin of us all, as we might see if we would. And yet, since thus it had to be, would that thou hadst given thy love to a noble lady, thou, who hast let thyself waste away for the daughter of a rascally priest, a man of evil life and little worth. Behold the son of an illustrious king spending his life in woe and weeping because Criseida has left him.'

Troilus was roused on hearing his sister, both because he heard her slighted whom he most loved and because his secret, though he knew not how, had reached Cassandra's ears. He thought she had learned it through the oracle of the gods. Nevertheless, fearing that it would seem true if he held his peace, he spoke.

And he began: 'Cassandra, thy eagerness to pry with thy imaginings into all secrets more than other people has ere now oftentimes brought thee sorrow; perhaps it would be wiser for thee to keep silent than to speak so wildly. Thou throwest out thy words before everybody, and I know not what thou meanest touching Criseida. Wherefore, when I see thee with too loose a tongue, I am minded to do what I have not done hitherto—to make known thy ignorance. Thou sayest that violent love for Criseida makes me pale, and thou wishest to hold that up as a great shame to me; but thine Apollo—and thou hast made a mockery of this god—has not shown thee the truth of this thing. Never did I find pleasure in such love for Criseida, and I do not believe that there is or ever has been in the world anybody so bold as to maintain this lie. And, if it were true, as thou goest about declaring, I swear by my honour that I would not let her go hence till Priam had put me to death. But I do not believe that he would have allowed that as he allowed Paris to carry off Helen, because of which we have now such dire results. Therefore check thy ready tongue. But suppose it were in truth thus, that I were in this grievous woe by reason of her; why is not Criseida in every quality worthy of any great man of whatever rank thou wilt?

'I wish not to speak of her beauty, which in every man's judgment is above that of the highest, for the fallen flower is soon faded; but consider merely her nobility, which thou dost so belittle; and let everybody here admit the truth if I speak it, and should any one deny it, let him, I pray, set forth his reasons. Wherever virtue is, there is nobility. No one of understanding will deny this; and all gentle qualities appear in her, if the result may be argued from the cause. But yet one must reach so happy a conclusion step by step, were it only to satisfy this woman, who talks so much about everybody and knows not whereof she prates. If indeed my eyes and that which others say of her deceive me not, nobody is or has ever been known more honourable than she; and, if I hear truly, she is discreet and modest beyond others, and indeed her bearing shows that; and likewise she is quiet and shy where it is fitting, which is a sign of something noble in a woman. Discretion shows in her manners and in her speech, which is most sober and wise and full of reason; and this year I saw in some degree how great was her wisdom in the excuse she offered for her father's treachery; and in her tears and the words she spoke she gave proof of her proud and most true scorn. Her ways are very frank, and therefore I think they need not be defended either by me or another. And I believe there are no knights in this land—let there be as many gallant men as you wish—whom she could not surpass in courtesy and magnificence, if she but had the power to do it. And I know this because ere now I have been where she has done such high honour to me and to others that many sitting on royal thrones would have been envious and would, like base-born men, have left and forsaken them.

'What more would you ask for in a woman now, my lady Cassandra? Royal blood? Not all those whom you see bear crown and sceptre or imperial robes are kings. Often enough have you heard it before now, a king is he who excels in virtue, not in power; and, if this lady could, dost thou not think she would queen it as well as thou? Far better than thou would she wear it, the crown I mean—dost understand? She would not be a vain woman, as thou art, who dost backbite everybody. Would God had made me worthy to have her as my lady, as gossip reports among you, for I would set the highest value on that which the lady Cassandra does belittle.

'Now begone and ill luck to you; away with you, since you cannot use fit words. Mend your foul speech and assail not the virtues of others. What new trouble and calamity is here, when a crazed woman in her vanity is set on abusing what ought to be praised and is pained if men hearken not!'

Cassandra remained silent, and fain then would she have been elsewhere. And she mingled with the ladies and spoke no further. And, when she left his presence, she went forthwith to the royal palace; nor did she ever consent to visit him again, so ill a welcome and hearing had she been given this time.

Hecuba, Helen, and the others commended what Troilus had said; and after a little while they gave him pleasant comfort with words and with merriment and with jest. And then they all went away together, each returning to her own dwelling. And afterwards they visited him many times again while he kept his bed in weakness.

Troilus, continuing thus ever in sorrow, learned how to bear it patiently; and besides, in his eager desire to show his valour against the Greeks, he quickly regained the strength he had lost by the too bitter pangs he had endured. And, besides this, Criseida had written to him and made it clear that she loved him more than ever; and she had put forth many feigned excuses for delaying so long and not returning, and had asked for still more time ere her return—which was never to take place—and he had granted it to her, hoping to see her again, but he knew not when.

And afterwards in many battles fought against the foe he showed his might in arms; and for his sighs and other bitter laments that had come to him through their contrivance he made them pay dearly beyond all reckoning, though not at so high a rate as his anger desired. But, later, death, which undoes all things, brought peace to his love and its strife.

CANTO VIII

He was, as has been said, long used to suffering; and more grievous did his state become by reason of the sorrow, too heavy ever to be told, that his father and he and his brothers felt for the death of Hector, in whose princely bravery the forts and walls and gates of Troy put their trust. And for a great while this kept him lamenting and sorrowful. But he did not, on that account, say farewell to love, though greatly bereft of hope; rather he sought by all ways and means, as lovers are wont to do, to regain, if he might, what had once been his sweet and only way of thought. And ever he excused her for not returning, believing it was not in her power. And he sent her many letters, declaring what he felt for her by night and by day, and reminding her of their happy days and of her promise to come again. Often also he sent Pandarus to her, whenever a truce or treaty was arranged, with gentle reproaches for tarrying so long. And likewise too he often purposed to go thither in the light dress of a pilgrim, but he knew not how so to disguise himself as to feel his true person sufficiently hidden; nor did he know how to devise a fit excuse to put forward if he were recognized under the concealment of such a garb. But he got nothing from her but fair words and great promises of none effect. And so he began to think that all was vanity and to suspect what was the truth of the matter—as often comes to pass when a man, leaving naught out of his reckoning, considers the facts before him—for his suspicion was not baseless.

And he was well aware that a new love was the cause of lies so many and so great; for he declared to himself that neither the flatteries of her father nor his tender embraces would so have swayed her heart. Nor was he able to see by what means he might make himself more certain touching that which his unhappy dream had revealed to him. And his faith in her love had grown greatly less; and yet, as is the common way, he who loves is full unwilling to believe anything that will add to his sufferings. But that what he had suspected of Diomede before was indeed true was proved to him not long after by a chance that stripped all excuses from him and compelled him to believe.

Troilus was still in torment, fear, and suspense by reason of his love when he heard that Deiphoebus, exulting in his booty and rejoicing greatly in his achievement, after a very long-drawn battle between the Trojans and Greeks, had returned with a richly adorned garment, reft from Diomede, who had been grievously wounded. And, while he was having it borne before him through Troy, Troilus came up and praised it highly in the presence of them all; and the better to see it he held it for a space. And while he gazed at it, his eyes glancing all over it, now here, now there, it chanced that he saw upon the breast a brooch of gold, put there perhaps for a clasp. And at once he knew it as the one he had given to Criseida when, sadly parting, he had taken leave of her on that morning after he had spent his last night with her. Thereupon he said: 'Now indeed I see that the dream is true, and my suspicion and thought.'

And when Troilus had gone his way, he sent for Pandarus. And when he had come to him, Troilus began to bewail with lamentation the love he had long had for his Criseida and plainly declared the treachery practised upon him, grieving bitterly, calling upon death as his only refuge.

And thus he began to speak, weeping as he did so: 'O my Criseida, where is thy faith, where thy love, where now thy desire, where the gift so dear that thou didst give me at thy going away? Diomede has all; and I, who loved thee more, am left weeping and desolate by thy lack of truth. From this time forth who will believe in any oath, in love, or in woman, seeing clearly thy false swearing? Alas, I know not. Nor did I ever think thou hadst a heart so harsh and cruel, that I, who loved thee more than I love myself and who, deceived by thee, still watched for thy coming, should ever be driven from thy thoughts by another man.

'And hadst thou no other jewel thou couldst give to thy new lover—to Diomede, I mean—except the one I had given thee with so many tears, to remind thee while thou wast dwelling with Calchas of me left desolate? Scorn alone made thee do it, and the desire to show most clearly thy intent. I see that thou hast cast me clean out of thy breast, while in mine I still keep the image of thy fair face, against my will, in bitter grief. Woe is me, for I was born in an evil hour. This thought slays me and robs me of any hope of joy to come, and breeds in me anguish and suffering. Wrongly hast thou driven me from thy mind, where I thought I should ever hold my station, and in my place thou hast disloyally set Diomede. But by the goddess Venus I swear to thee I will swiftly make thee grieve for it in the first battle, if it chance that I can find him and vanquish him by might. Or he will slay me and become dear to thee; but indeed I hope divine justice will have regard to my bitter grief and likewise to thy great baseness. O sovereign Jove, in whom I know reason is surely lodged, and from whom proceeds all noble virtue by which men live and move, are thy just eyes turned aside? What are thy flaming thunderbolts about? Are they idle? Or dost thou no more keep thy eyes fixed on the faults of mankind? O true light, unclouded skies, which cheer the minds of men, do away with her in whose breast are lies and deceits and betrayals, and let her never be worthy of forgiveness.

'O my Pandarus, who didst blame me so vehemently for putting faith in dreams, now thou canst see what they reveal; thy Criseida gives thee proof thereof: The gods show grace to us mortals and in different ways make clear what is hidden from us, and very often it is for our good to know it. And one of the things is this, which sometimes comes to us in our sleep. I remember to have noted it many times ere now. Would I had died then, for henceforth I look for no solace, joy, pleasure, or delight; but by thy counsel I am willing to wait, to die in arms against my enemies. May God bring Diomede face to face with me the first time I go forth to battle. Burdened by such great sorrows, I long to make him feel how my sword cuts and to slay him on the field of battle as he cries aloud; and then I care not if I am killed, as long as he dies and I find him in misery in the realm of darkness.'

Pandarus heard all in sadness, and, feeling it to be true, knew not what to say. On the one hand, love for his friend led him to remain there; on the other, shame for Criseida's wrongdoing often prompted him to depart, and he could not decide what he should do; and either to stay or to go was very grievous unto him.

At last, weeping, he spoke thus: 'I know not what to say to thee. I condemn her as strongly as I can in words like thine; and I purpose to offer no excuse for the great wrong she has done, nor ever willingly again go where she is. What I have done ere now I did for love of thee, putting aside all thought of my own honour. And if I gave thee pleasure I am very glad. With things as they stand now, I can do nothing; I am angered even as thou art. And if I saw any way of setting matters right, doubt not I should be eager to do so. May God, who can change all things, bring that to pass. With all my strength I pray him to punish her, so that she sin not again in this way.'

Great were the lamentations and the bitterness; but, for all that, fortune stayed not her course. She loved Diomede with all her heart, and Troilus wept; Diomede praised God, and Troilus, on the contrary, bewailed his lot. In the battles Troilus always played his part; and he sought for Diomede more than for other men. And many times they confronted each other face to face, with taunts bitter and harsh, and dealt each other great blows, sometimes charging each other, at other times with swords in their hands; each in his rage making the other pay dearly for his love. But fortune had not decreed that either should fall by the other's hand.

The wrath of Troilus indeed did great injury to the Greeks at different times, so great that few came against him whom he did not slay and cast from their horses, if they but waited his onset, so deadly were the blows he dealt. And, after a long space, when he had killed more than a thousand, Achilles one day unhappily slew him.

Such end had the hapless love of Troilus for Criseida, and such end had the wretched sorrow of him who never had equal; such end had the bright splendour that fitted him for a royal throne; such end had the vain hope that Troilus set on base Criseida.

O youths, in whom amorous desire springs up as your age increases, I pray you in the name of God check your eager steps towards the evil passion and see yourselves imaged in the love of Troilus, which my verse has set forth. For, if you read with right feeling, you will not easily put your trust in all women. A young woman is inconstant and desirous of many lovers, and she rates her beauty more highly than does the mirror, and has exulting pride in her youth; and the more she thinks of it the more pleasing and charming she finds it. Ever unsteady as a leaf in the wind, she cares not for virtue or reason. And many women, too, because they come of noble family and can tell over their ancestors, think that they should be preferred before others in love; and they consider courtesy a thing to be scorned and turn up their noses and carry themselves haughtily. Avoid these and deem them vile, for they are beasts, not noble ladies.

The lady of true nobility has a keener desire to be loved and finds delight in loving; she discerns and notes what is to be shunned; she rejects and chooses; she is foreseeing and forgets not her promises. Devote yourselves to these ladies, but nevertheless it is not well to choose in haste, for not all are worthy, because some, being no longer young, are less desirable.

Be cautious therefore and have compassion on Troilus and on yourself too; and it will be well with you. And in pity pray to love on his behalf that he may rest in peace in the place where he is, and may love grant you grace to love so wisely that in the end you die not for a worthless woman.

CANTO IX

Happy times are wont to make sweet verses, O sad song of mine; but in my heavy affliction love has unnaturally drawn thee forth from my sorrowful soul; and I know not how it has come about, unless it spring from some hidden virtue that has been roused and wakened in the stricken heart by the surpassing worth of our lady.

She, as I know, for often I feel it, can make me a thing of naught; and she can make me much that I am not; and hence, I think, springs the cause of thy long speaking, and I am pleased therewith. For it is rather from that than from my bitter griefs that it has come. But, whatever it may have been, we have attained the end I wished. We have reached the port we have been seeking, now among rocks, now in the open sea, driven by gentle and by stormy winds, guided over the perilous ocean by the high gleam and honoured sign of that star that sends each thought of mine quick to its proper goal, and later made itself known unto me.

Here then, I think, the anchors are to be cast and an end made of the voyage; and here with full warmth shall be offered those thanks that the grateful pilgrim must pay to him who has been our guide. And on the shore, now close at hand, we shall deck the ship of our loves with fit garlands and other honours.

Then thou, after resting a little, wilt go to the gentle lady of my thoughts. Oh, happy art thou, for thou wilt see her, which I, weary and woeful as I am, cannot do. And when thou art joyfully received by her hands, commend me humbly to her high worth, which alone can give me salvation. And in the garb, almost tear-stained, that thou wearest, I pray thee declare to her how I live under the affliction of other losses, woes, and sighs, and bitter laments, which have grieved me and still do, since the bright beams of her fair eyes have been hidden from me by her going hence, for only in their presence did I live with glad heart. If thou seest in her beautiful face any sign that she is ready to listen to thee or to sigh for my suffering, entreat her as earnestly as thou canst that she may be pleased now to return, or to order my soul to depart from me, for better is death than such life.

But take heed not to go on such a high mission without love, for it might chance thou wouldst be right ill received, and, besides, without him thou wouldst lack understanding. If thou goest with him, I think thou wilt be honoured. Go now; for I pray Apollo to lend thee such grace that she will hearken to thee and send thee again to me with a happy answer.

GEOFFREY CHAUCER
TROILUS AND CRISEYDE

TROILUS AND CRISEYDE

BOOK I

1. THE double sorwe of Troilus to tellen,
That was the king Priamus sone of Troye,
In lovinge, how his aventures fellen
Fro wo to wele, and after out of joye,
My purpos is, er that I parte fro ye.
Thesiphone, thou help me for t' endyte
Thise woful vers, that wepen as I wryte!

2. To thee clepe I, thou goddesse of torment,
Thou cruel Furie, sorwing ever in peyne;
Help me, that am the sorwful instrument
That helpeth lovers, as I can, to pleyne!
For wel sit it, the sothe for to seyne,
A woful wight to han a drery fere,
And, to a sorwful tale, a sory chere.

3. For I, that god of Loves servaunts serve,
Ne dar to Love, for myn unlyklinesse,
Preyen for speed, al sholde I therfor sterve,
So fer am I fro his help in derknesse;
But nathelees, if this may doon gladnesse
To any lover, and his cause avayle,
Have he my thank, and myn be this travayle!

4. But ye loveres, that bathen in gladnesse,
If any drope of pitee in yow be,
Remembreth yow on passed hevinesse
That ye han felt, and on the adversitee
Of othere folk, and thenketh how that ye
Han felt that Love dorste yow displese;
Or ye han wonne him with to greet an ese.

5. And preyeth for hem that ben in the cas
Of Troilus, as ye may after here,

That love hem bringe in hevene to solas,
And eek for me preyeth to god so dere,
That I have might to shewe, in som manere,
Swich peyne and wo as Loves folk endure,
In Troilus unsely aventure.

6. And biddeth eek for hem that been despeyred
In love, that never nil recovered be,
And eek for hem that falsly been apeyred
Thorugh wikked tonges, be it he or she;
Thus biddeth god, for his benignitee,
To graunte hem sone out of this world to pace,
That been despeyred out of Loves grace.

7. And biddeth eek for hem that been at ese,
That god hem graunte ay good perseveraunce,
And sende hem might hir ladies so to plese,
That it to Love be worship and plesaunce.
For so hope I my soule best avaunce,
To preye for hem that Loves servaunts be,
And wryte hir wo, and live in charitee.

8. And for to have of hem compassioun
As though I were hir owene brother dere.
Now herkeneth with a gode entencioun,
For now wol I gon streight to my matere,
In whiche ye may the double sorwes here
Of Troilus, in loving of Criseyde,
And how that she forsook him er she deyde.

_____

9. It is wel wist, how that the Grekes stronge
In armes with a thousand shippes wente
To Troye-wardes, and the citee longe
Assegeden neigh ten yeer er they stente,
And, in diverse wyse and oon ententé,
The ravisshing to wreken of Eleyne,
By Paris doon, they wroughten al hir peyne

10. Now fil it so, that in the toun ther was
Dwellinge a lord of greet auctoritee,
A gret devyn that cleped was Calkas,
That in science so expert was, that he
Knew wel that Troye sholde destroyed be,

By answere of his god, that highte thus,
Daun Phebus or Appollo Delphicus.

11. So whan this Calkas knew by calculinge,
And eek by answere of this Appollo,
That Grekes sholden swich a peple bringe,
Thorugh which that Troye moste been for-do,
He caste anoon out of the toun to go;
For wel wiste he, by sort, that Troye sholde
Destroyed been, ye, wolde who-so nolde.

12. For which, for to departen softely
Took purpos ful this forknowinge wyse,
And to the Grekes ost ful prively
He stal anoon; and they, in curteys wyse,
Him deden bothe worship and servyse,
In trust that he hath conning hem to rede
In every peril which that is to drede.

13. The noyse up roos, whan it was first aspyed,
Thorugh al the toun, and generally was spoken,
That Calkas traytor fled was, and allyed
With hem of Grece; and casten to ben wroken
On him that falsly hadde his feith broken;
And seyden, he and al his kin at ones
Ben worthy for to brennen, fel and bones.

14. Now hadde Calkas left, in this meschaunce,
Al unwist of this false and wikked dede,
His doughter, which that was in gret penaunce,
For of hir lyf she was ful sore in drede,
As she that niste what was best to rede;
For bothe a widowe was she, and allone
Of any freend, to whom she dorste hir mone.

15. Criseyde was this lady name a-right;
As to my dome, in al Troyes citee
Nas noon so fair, for passing every wight
So aungellyk was hir natyf beautee.
That lyk a thing immortal semed she,
As doth an hevenish parfit creature,
That doun were sent in scorning of nature.

16. This lady, which that al-day herde at ere
Hir fadres shame, his falsnesse and tresoun,
Wel nigh out of hir wit for sorwe and fere,
In widewes habit large of samit broun,
On knees she fil biforn Ector a-doun;
With pitous voys, and tendrely wepinge,
His mercy bad, hir-selven excusinge.

17. Now was this Ector pitous of nature,
And saw that she was sorwfully bigoon,
And that she was so fair a creature;
Of his goodnesse he gladed hir anoon,
And seyde, 'lat your fadres treson goon
Forth with mischaunce, and ye your-self, in joye,
Dwelleth with us, whyl you good list, in Troye.

18. An al th' onour that men may doon yow have,
As ferforth as your fader dwelled here,
Ye shul han, and your body shal men save,
As fer as I may enquere or here.'
And she him thonked with ful humble chere,
And ofter wolde, and it hadde ben his wille,
And took hir leve, and hoom, and held hir stille.

19. And in hir hous she abood with swich meynee
As to hir honour nede was to holde;
And whyl she was dwellinge in that citee,
Kepte hir estat, and both of yonge and olde
Ful wel beloved, and wel men of hir tolde.
But whether that she children hadde or noon,
I rede it nought; therefore I lete it goon.

20. The thinges fellen, as they doon of werre,
Betwixen hem of Troye and Grekes ofte;
For som day boughten they of Troye it derre,
And eft the Grekes founden no thing softe
The folk of Troye; and thus fortune onlofte,
And under eft, gan hem to wheelen bothe
After hir cours, ay whyl they were wrothe.

21. But how this toun com to destruccioun
Ne falleth nought to purpos me to telle;
For it were here a long digressioun

Fro my matere, and yow to longe dwelle.
But the Troyane gestes, as they felle,.
In Omer, or in Dares, or in Dyte,
Who-so that can, may rede hem as they wryte.

22. But though that Grekes hem of Troye shetten,
And hir citee bisegede al a-boute,
Hir olde usage wolde they not letten,
As for to honoure hir goddes ful devoute;
But aldermost in honour, out of doute,
They hadde a relik hight Palladion,
That was hir trist a-boven everichon.

23. And so bifel, whan comen was the tyme
Of Aperil, whan clothed is the mede
With newe grene, of lusty Ver the pryme,
And swote smellen floures whyte and rede,
In sondry wyses shewed, as I rede,
The folk of Troye his observaunces olde,
Palladiones feste for to holde.

24. And to the temple, in al hir beste wyse,
In general, ther wente many a wight,
To herknen of Palladion the servyse;
And namely, so many a lusty knight,
So many a lady fresh and mayden bright,
Ful wel arayed, bothe moste and leste,
Ye, bothe for the seson and the feste.

25. Among thise othere folk was Criseyda,
In widewes habite blak; but nathelees,
Right as our firste lettre is now an A,
In beautee first so stood she, makelees;
Hir godly looking gladede al the prees.
Nas never seyn thing to ben preysed derre,
Nor under cloude blak so bright a sterre

26. As was Criseyde, as folk seyde everichoon
That hir bihelden in hir blake wede;
And yet she stood ful lowe and stille alloon,
Bihinden othere folk, in litel brede,
And neigh the dore, ay under shames drede,
Simple of a-tyr, and debonaire of chere,
With ful assured loking and manere.

27. This Troilus, as he was wont to gyde
His yonge knightes, ladde hem up and doun
In thilke large temple on every syde,
Biholding ay the ladyes of the toun,
Now here, now there, for no devocioun
Hadde he to noon, to reven him his reste,
But gan to preyse and lakken whom him leste.

28. And in his walk ful fast he gan to wayten
If knight or squyer of his companye
Gan for to syke, or lete his eyen bayten
On any woman that he coude asype;
He wolde smyle, and holden it folye,
And seye him thus, 'god wot, she slepeth softe
For love of thee, whan thou tornest ful ofte!

29. 'I have herd told, pardieux, of your livinge,
Ye lovers, and your lewede observaunces,
And which a labour folk han in winninge
Of love, and, in the keping, which doutaunces;
And whan your preye is lost, wo and penaunces;
O verrey foles! nyce and blinde be ye;
Ther nis not oon can war by other be.'

30. And with that word he gan cast up the browe,
Ascaunces, 'lo! is this nought wysely spoken?'
At which the god of love gan loken rowe
Right for despyt, and shoop for to ben wroken;
He kidde anoon his bowe nas not broken;
For sodeynly he hit him at the fulle;
And yet as proud a pekok can he pulle.

31. 'O blinde world, O blinde entencioun!
How ofte falleth al th' effect contraire
Of surquidrye and foul presumpcioun;
For caught is proud, and caught is debonaire.
This Troilus is clomben on the staire,
And litel weneth that he moot descenden.
But al-day fayleth thing that foles wenden.

32. 'As proude Bayard ginneth for to skippe
Out of the wey, so priketh him his corn,
Til he a lash have of the longe whippe,

Than thenketh he 'though I praunce al biforn
First in the trays, ful fat and newe shorn,
Yet am I but a hors, and horses lawe
I moot endure, and with my feres drawe.'

33. So ferde it by this fers and proude knight;
Though he a worthy kinges sone were,
And wende no-thing hadde had swiche might
Ayens his wil that sholde his herte stere,
Yet with a look his herte wex a-fere,
That he, that now was most in pryde above,
Wex sodeynly most subget un-to love.

34. For thy ensample taketh of this man,
Ye wyse, proude, and worthy folkes alle,
To scornen Love, which that so sone can
The freedom of your hertes to him thralle;
For ever it was, and ever it shal bifalle,
That Love is he that alle thing may binde;
For may no man for-do the lawe of kinde.

35. That this be sooth, have preved and doth yit;
For this trowe I ye knowen, alle or some,
Men reden not that folk han gretter wit
Than they that han be most with love y-nome;
And strengest folk ben therwith overcome,
The worthiest and grettest of degree;
This was, and is, and yet men shal it see.

36. And trewelich it sit wel to be so;
For alderwysest han ther-with ben plesed;
And they that han ben aldermost in wo,
With love han been conforted most and esed;
And ofte it hath the cruel herte apesed,
And worthy folk maad worthier of name,
And causeth most to dreden vyce and shame.

37. Now sith it may not goodly be withstonde,
And is a thing so vertuous in kinde,
Refuseth not to Love for to be bonde,
Sin, as him-selven list, he may yow binde.
The yerde is bet that bowen wole and winde
Than that that brest; and therfor I yow rede
To folwen him that so wel can yow lede.

38. But for to tellen forth in special
As of this kinges sone of which I tolde,
And leten other thing collateral,
Of him thenke I my tale for to holde,
Bothe of his joye, and of his cares colde;
And al his werk, as touching this matere,
For I it gan, I wil ther-to refere.

39. With-inne the temple he wente him forth pleyinge,
This Troilus, of every wight aboute,
On this lady and now on that lokinge,
Wher-so she were of toune, or of withoute:
And up-on cas bifel, that thorugh a route
His eye perced, and so depe it wente,
Til on Criseyde it smoot, and ther it stente.

40. And sodeynly he wex ther-with astoned,
And gan hire bet biholde in thrifty wyse:
'O mercy, god!' thoughte he, 'wher hastow woned,
That art so fair and goodly to devyse?'
Ther-with his herte gan to sprede and ryse,
And softe sighed, lest men mighte him here,
And caughte a-yein his firste pleyinge chere.

41. She nas not with the leste of hir stature,
But alle hir limes so well answeringe
Weren to womanhode, that creature
Was never lasse mannish in seminge.
And eek the pure wyse of here meninge
Shewede wel, that men might in hir gesse
Honour, estat, and wommanly noblesse.

42. To Troilus right wonder wel with-alle
Gan for to lyke hir mening and hir chere,
Which somdel deynous was, for she leet falle
Hir look a lite a-side, in swich manere,
Ascaunces, 'what! may I not stonden here?'
And after that hir loking gan she lighte,
That never thoughte him seen so good a sighte.

43. And of hir look in him ther gan to quiken
So greet desir, and swich affeccioun,
That in his hertes botme gan to stiken

Of hir his fixe and depe impressioun:
And though he erst hadde poured up and doun,
He was tho glad his hornes in to shrinke;
Unnethes wiste he how to loke or winke.

44. Lo, he that leet him-selven so konninge,
And scorned hem that Loves peynes dryen,
Was ful unwar that Love hadde his dwellinge
With-inne the subtile stremes of hir yën;
That sodeynly him thoughte he felte dyen,
Right with hir look, the spirit in his herte;
Blessed be Love, that thus can folk converte!

45. She, this in blak, lykinge to Troilus,
Over alle thing he stood for to biholde;
Ne his desir, ne wherefor he stood thus,
He neither chere made, ne worde tolde;
But from a-fer, his maner for to holde,
On other thing his look som-tyme he caste,
And eft on hir, whyl that servyse laste.

46. And after this, not fulliche al awhaped,
Out of the temple al esiliche he wente,
Repentinge him that he hadde ever y-japed
Of Loves folk, lest fully the descente
Of scorn fille on him-self; but, what he mente,
Lest it were wist on any maner syde,
His wo he gan dissimulen and hyde.

47. Whan he was fro the temple thus departed,
He streyght anoon un-to his paleys torneth,
Right with hir look thurgh-shoten and thurgh-darted,
Al feyneth he in lust that he sojorneth;
And al his chere and speche also he borneth;
And ay, of Loves servants every whyle,
Him-self to wrye, at hem he gan to smyle.

48. And seyde, 'lord, so ye live al in lest,
Ye loveres! for the conningest of yow,
That serveth most ententiflich, and best,
Him tit as often harm ther-of as prow;
Your hyre is quit ayein, ye, god wot how!
Nought wel for wel, but scorn for good servyse;
In feith, your ordre is ruled in good wyse!

49. 'In noun-certeyn ben alle your observaunces,
But it a sely fewe poyntes be;
Ne no-thing asketh so grete attendaunces
As doth your lay, and that knowe alle ye;
But that is not the worste, as mote I thee;
But, tolde I yow the worste poynt, I leve,
Al seyde I sooth, ye wolden at me greve!

50. 'But tak this, that ye loveres ofte eschuwe,
Or elles doon of good entencioun,
Ful ofte thy lady wole it misconstrue,
And deme it harm in hir opinioun;
And yet if she, for other enchesoun,
Be wrooth, than shalt thou han a groyn anoon:
Lord! wel is him that may be of yow oon!'

51. But for al this, whan that he say his tyme,
He held his pees, non other bote him gayned;
For love bigan his fetheres so to lyme,
That wel unnethe un-to his folk he feyned
That othere besye nedes him destrayned;
For wo was him, that what to doon he niste,
But bad his folk to goon wher that hem liste.

52. And whan that he in chaumbre was allone,
He doun up-on his beddes feet him sette,
And first he gan to syke, and eft to grone,
And thoughte ay on hir so, with-outen lette,
That, as he sat and wook, his spirit mette
That he hir saw a temple, and al the wyse
Right of hir loke, and gan it newe avyse.

53. Thus gan he make a mirour of his minde,
In which he saugh al hoolly hir figure;
And that he wel coude in his herte finde,
It was to him a right good aventure
To love swich oon, and if he dide his cure
To serven hir, yet mighte he falle in grace,
Or elles, for oon of hir servaunts pace.

54. Imagininge that travaille nor grame
Ne mighte, for so goodly oon, be lorn
As she, ne him for his desir ne shame,

Al were it wist, but in prys and up-born
Of alle lovers wel more than biforn;
Thus argumented he in his ginninge,
Ful unavysed of his wo cominge.

55. Thus took he purpos Loves craft to suwe,
And thoughte he wolde werken prively,
First, to hyden his desir in muwe
From every wight y-born, al-outrely,
But he mighte ought recovered be therby;
Remembring him, that love to wyde y-blowe
Yelt bittre fruyt, though swete seed be sowe.

56. And over all this, yet muchel more he thoughte
What for to speke, and what to holden inne,
And what to arten hir to love he soughte,
And on a song anoon-right to biginne,
And gan loude on his sorwe for to winne;
For with good hope he gan fully assente
Criseyde for to love, and nought repente.

57. And of his song nought only the sentence,
As writ myn autour called Lollius,
But pleynly, save our tonges difference,
I dar wel sayn, in al that Troilus
Seyde in his song; lo! every word right thus
As I shal seyn; and who-so list it here,
Lo! next this vers, he may it finden here.

CANTUS TROILI

58. 'If no love is, O god, what fele I so?
And if love is, what thing and whiche is he?
If love be good, from whennes comth my wo?
If it be wikke, a wonder thinketh me,
When every torment and adversitee
That cometh of him, may to me savory thinke;
For ay thurst I, the more that I it drinke.

59. 'And if that at myn owene lust I brenne,
Fro whennes cometh my wailing and my pleynte?
If harme agree me, wher-to pleyne I thenne?

I noot, ne why unwery that I feynte.
O quike deeth, O swete harm so queynte,
How may of thee in me swich quantitee,
But if that I consente that it be?

60. 'And if that I consente, I wrongfully
Compleyne, y-wis; thus possed to and fro,
Al sterelees with-inne a boot am I
A-mid the see, by-twixen windes two,
That in contrarie stonden ever-mo.
Allas! what is this wonder maladye?
For hete of cold, for cold of hete, I dye.'

61. And to the god of Love thus seyde he
With pitous voys, 'O lord, now youres is
My spirit, which that oughte youres be.
Yow thanke I, lord, that han me brought to this;
But whether goddesse or womman, y-wis,
She be, I noot, which that ye do me serve;
But as hir man I wole ay live and sterve.

62. 'Ye stonden in hire eyen mightily,
As in a place un-to your vertu digne;
Wherefore, lord, if my servyse or I
May lyke yow, so beth to me benigne;
For myn estat royal here I resigne
In-to hir hond, and with ful humble chere
Bicome hir man, as to my lady dere.'

63. In him ne deyned sparen blood royal
The fyr of love, wher-fro god me blesse,
Ne him forbar in no degree, for al
His vertu or his excellent prowesse;
But held him as his thral lowe in distresse,
And brende him so in sondry wyse ay newe,
That sixty tyme a day he loste his hewe.

64. So muche, day by day, his owene thought,
For lust to hir, gan quiken and encrese,
That every other charge he sette at nought;
For-thy ful ofte, his hote fyr to cese,
To seen hir goodly look he gan to prese;
For ther-by to ben esed wel he wende,
And ay the neer he was, the more he brende.

65. For ay the neer the fyr, the hotter is,
This, trowe I, knoweth all this companye.
But were he fer or neer, I dar seye this,
By night or day, for wysdom or folye,
His herte, which that is his brestes yë,
Was ay on hir, that fairer was to sene
Than ever was Eleyne or Polixene.

66. Eek of the day ther passed nought an houre
That to him-self a thousand tyme he seyde,
'Good goodly, to whom serve I and laboure,
As I best can, now wolde god, Criseyde,
Ye wolden on me rewe er that I deyde!
My dere herte, allas! myn hele and hewe
And lyf is lost, but ye wole on me rewe.'

67. Alle othere dredes weren from him fledde,
Bothe of th' assege and his savacioun;
Ne in him desyr noon othere fownes bredde
But arguments to this conclusioun,
That she on him wolde han compassioun,
And he to be hir man, whyl he may dure;
Lo, here his lyf, and from the deeth his cure!

68. The sharpe shoures felle of armes preve,
That Ector or his othere bretheren diden,
Ne made him only ther-fore ones meve;
And yet was he, wher-so men wente or riden,
Founde oon the best, and lengest tyme abiden
Ther peril was, and dide eek such travayle
In armes, that to thenke it was mervayle.

69. But for non hate he to the Grekes hadde,
Ne also for the rescous of the toun,
Ne made him thus in armes for to madde,
But only, lo, for this conclusioun,
To lyken hir the bet for his renoun;
Fro day to day in armes so he spedde,
That alle the Grekes as the deeth him dredde.

70. And fro this forth tho refte him Love his sleep,
And made his mete his foo; and eek his sorwe
Can multiplye, that, who-so toke keep,

It shewed in his hewe, bothe eve and morwe;
Therfor a title he gan him for to borwe
Of other syknesse, lest of him men wende
That the hote fyr of love him brende;

71. And seyde, he hadde a fever and ferde amis;
But how it was, certayn, can I not seye,
If that his lady understood not this,
Or feyned hir she niste, oon of the tweye;
But wel I rede that, by no maner weye,
Ne semed it [as] that she of him roughte,
Nor of his peyne, or what-so-ever he thoughte.

72. But than fel to this Troylus such wo,
That he was wel neigh wood; for ay his drede
Was this, that she som wight had loved so,
That never of him she wolde have taken hede;
For whiche him thoughte he felte his herte blede.
Ne of his wo ne dorste he not biginne
To tellen it, for al this world to winne.

73. But whanne he hadde a space fro his care,
Thus to him-self ful ofte he gan to pleyne;
He sayde, 'O fool, now art thou in the snare,
That whilom japedest at Loves peyne;
Now artow hent, now gnaw thyn owene cheyne;
Thou were ay wont eche lovere reprehende
Of thing fro which thou canst thee nat defende.

74. 'What wole now every lover seyn of thee,
If this be wist, but ever in thyn absence
Laughen in scorn, and seyn, "lo, ther gooth he,
That is the man of so gret sapience,
That held us loveres leest in reverence!
Now, thonked be god, he may goon in the daunce
Of hem that Love list febly for to avaunce!

75. 'But, O thou woful Troilus, god wolde,
Sin thow most loven thurgh thy destinee,
That thow beset were on swich oon that sholde
Knowe al thy wo, al lakkede hir pitee:
But al so cold in love, towardes thee,
Thy lady is, as frost in winter mone,
And thou fordoon, as snow in fyr is sone."

76. 'God wolde I were aryved in the port
Of deeth, to which my sorwe wil me lede!
A, lord, to me it were a greet comfort;
Then were I quit of languisshing in drede.
For by myn hidde sorwe y-blowe on brede
I shal bi-japed been a thousand tyme
More than that fool of whos folye men ryme.

77. 'But now help god, and ye, swete, for whom
I pleyne, y-caught, ye, never wight so faste!
O mercy, dere herte, and help me from
The deeth, for I, whyl that my lyf may laste,
More than my-self wol love yow to my laste.
And with som freendly look gladeth me, swete,
Though never more thing ye me bi-hete!'

78. This wordes and ful manye an-other to
He spak, and called ever in his compleynte
Hir name, for to tellen hir his wo,
Til neigh that he in salte teres dreynte.
Al was for nought, she herde nought his pleynte;
And whan that he bithoughte on that folye,
A thousand fold his wo gan multiplye.

79. Bi-wayling in his chambre thus allone,
A freend of his, that called was Pandare,
Com ones in unwar, and herde him grone,
And sey his freend in swich distress and care:
'Allas!' quod he, 'who causeth al this fare?
O mercy, god! what unhap may this mene?
Han now thus sone Grekes maad yow lene?

80. 'Or hastow som remors of conscience,
And art now falle in som devocioun,
And waylest for thy sinne and thyn offence,
And hast for ferde caught attricioun?
God save hem that bi-seged han our toun,
And so can leye our jolytee on presse,
And bring our lusty folk to holinesse!'

81. These wordes seyde he for the nones alle,
That with swich thing he mighte him angry maken,
And with an angre don his sorwe falle,

As for the tyme, and his corage awaken;
But wel he wiste, as fer as tonges spaken,
Ther nas a man of gretter hardinesse
Than he, ne more desired worthinesse.

82. 'What cas,' quod Troilus, 'or what aventure
Hath gyded thee to see my languisshinge,
That am refus of every creature?
But for the love of god, at my preyinge,
Go henne a-way, for certes, my deyinge
Wol thee disese, and I mot nedes deye;
Ther-for go wey, ther is no more to seye.

83. 'But if thou wene I be thus syk for drede,
It is not so, and ther-for scorne nought;
Ther is a-nother thing I take of hede
Wel more than ought the Grekes han y-wrought,
Which cause is of my deeth, for sorwe and thought.
But though that I now telle thee it ne leste,
Be thou nought wrooth, I hyde it for the beste.'

84. This Pandare, that neigh malt for wo and routhe,
Ful often seyde, 'allas! what may this be?
Now freend,' quod he, 'if ever love or trouthe
Hath been, or is, bi-twixen thee and me,
Ne do thou never swiche a crueltee
To hyde fro thy freend so greet a care;
Wostow nought wel that it am I, Pandare?

85. 'I wole parten with thee al thy peyne,
If it be so I do thee no comfort,
As it is freendes right, sooth for to seyne,
To entreparten wo, as glad desport.
I have, and shal, for trewe or fals report,
In wrong and right y-loved thee al my lyve;
Hyd not thy wo fro me, but telle it blyve.'

86. Then gan this sorwful Troilus to syke,
And seyde him thus, 'god leve it be my beste
To telle it thee; for, sith it may thee lyke,
Yet wole I telle it, though myn herte breste;
And wel wot I thou mayst do me no reste.
But lest thow deme I truste not to thee,
Now herkne, freend, for thus it stant with me.

87. 'Love, a-yeins the which who-so defendeth
Him-selven most, him alder-lest avayleth,
With desespeir so sorwfully me offendeth,
That streyght un-to the deeth myn herte sayleth.
Ther-to desyr so brenningly me assaylleth,
That to ben slayn it were a gretter joye
To me than king of Grece been and Troye!

88. 'Suffiseth this, my fulle freend Pandare,
That I have seyd, for now wostow my wo;
And for the love of god, my colde care
So hyd it wel, I telle it never to mo;
For harmes mighte folwen, mo than two,
If it were wist; but be thou in gladnesse,
And lat me sterve, unknowe, of my distresse.

89. 'How hastow thus unkindely and longe
Hid this fro me, thou fool?' quod Pandarus;
'Paraunter thou might after swich oon longe,
That myn avys anoon may helpen us.'
'This were a wonder thing,' quod Troilus,
'Thou coudest never in love thy-selven wisse;
How devel maystow bringen me to blisse?'

90. 'Ye, Troilus, now herke,' quod Pandare,
'Though I be nyce; it happeth ofte so,
That oon that exces doth ful yvele fare
By good counseyl can kepe his freend ther-fro.
I have my-self eek seyn a blind man go
There-as he fel that coude loke wyde;
A fool may eek a wys man ofte gyde.

91. 'A whetston is no kerving instrument,
And yet it maketh sharpe kerving-tolis.
And ther thow woost that I have ought miswent,
Eschewe thou that, for swich thing to thee scole is;
Thus ofte wyse men ben war by folis.
If thou do so, thy wit is wel biwared;
By his contrarie is every thing declared.

92. 'For how might ever sweetnesse have be knowe
To him that never tasted bitternesse?
Ne no man may be inly glad, I trowe,

That never was in sorwe or som distresse;
Eek whyt by blak, by shame eek worthinesse,
Ech set by other, more for other semeth;
As men may see; and so the wyse it demeth.

93. 'Sith thus of two contraries is a lore,
I, that have in love so ofte assayed
Grevaunces, oughte conne, and wel the more
Counsayllen thee of that thou art amayed.
Eek thee ne oughte nat ben yvel apayed,
Though I desyre with thee for to bere
Thyn hevy charge; it shal the lasse dere.

94. 'I woot wel that it fareth thus by me
As to thy brother Parys an herdesse,
Which that y-cleped was Oënone,
Wroot in a compleynt of hir hevinesse:
Ye sey the lettre that she wroot, y gesse?'
'Nay, never yet, y-wis,' quod Troilus.
'Now,' quod Pandare, 'herkneth; it was thus.—

95. '"Phebus, that first fond art of medicyne,"
Quod she, "and coude in every wightes care
Remede and reed, by herbes he knew fyne,
Yet to him-self his conninge was ful bare;
For love hadde him so bounden in a snare,
Al for the doughter of the kinge Admete,
That al his craft ne coude his sorwe bete."—

96. 'Right so fare I, unhappily for me;
I love oon best, and that me smerteth sore;
And yet, paraunter, can I rede thee,
And not my-self; repreve me no more.
I have no cause, I woot wel, for to sore
As doth an hauk that listeth for to pleye,
But to thyn help yet somwhat can I seye.

97. 'And of o thing right siker maystow be,
That certayn, for to deyen in the peyne,
That I shal never-mo discoveren thee;
Ne, by my trouthe, I kepe nat restreyne
Thee fro thy love, thogh that it were Eleyne,
That is thy brotheres wyf, if ich it wiste;
Be what she be, and love hir as thee liste.

98. 'Therefore, as freend fullich in me assure,
And tel me plat what is thyn enchesoun,
And final cause of wo that ye endure;
For douteth no-thing, myn entencioun
Nis nought to yow of reprehencioun
To speke as now, for no wight may bireve
A man to love, til that him list to leve.

99. 'And witeth wel, that bothe two ben vyces,
Mistrusten alle, or elles alle leve;
But wel I woot, the mene of it no vyce is,
For for to trusten sum wight is a preve
Of trouthe, and for-thy wolde I fayn remeve
Thy wrong conceyte, and do thee som wight triste,
Thy wo to telle; and tel me, if thee liste.

100. 'The wyse seyth, "wo him that is allone,
For, and he falle, he hath noon help to ryse";
And sith thou hast a felawe, tel thy mone;
For this nis not, certeyn, the nexte wyse
To winnen love, as techen us the wyse,
To walwe and wepe as Niobe the quene,
Whos teres yet in marbel been y-sene.

101. 'Lat be thy weping and thy drerinesse,
And lat us lissen wo with other speche;
So may thy woful tyme seme lesse.
Delyte not in wo thy wo to seche,
As doon thise foles that hir sorwes eche
With sorwe, whan they han misaventure,
And listen nought to seche hem other cure.

102. 'Men seyn, "to wrecche is consolacioun
To have an-other felawe in his peyne";
That oughte wel ben our opinioun,
For, bothe thou and I, of love we pleyne;
So ful of sorwe am I, soth for to seyne,
That certeynly no more harde grace
May sitte on me, for-why there is no space.

103. 'If god wole thou art not agast of me,
Lest I wolde of thy lady thee bigyle,
Thow wost thy-self whom that I love, pardee,

As I best can, gon sithen longe whyle.
And sith thou wost I do it for no wyle,
And sith I am he that thou tristest most,
Tel me sumwhat, sin al my wo thou wost.'

104. Yet Troilus, for al this, no word seyde,
But longe he lay as stille as he ded were;
And after this with sykinge he abreyde,
And to Pandarus voys he lente his ere,
And up his eyen caste he, that in fere
Was Pandarus, lest that in frenesye
He sholde falle, or elles sone dye:

105. And cryde 'a-wake' ful wonderly and sharpe;
'What? slombrestow as in a lytargye?
Or artow lyk an asse to the harpe,
That hereth soun, whan men the strenges plye,
But in his minde of that no melodye
May sinken, him to glade, for that he
So dul is of his bestialitee?'

106. And with that Pandare of his wordes stente;
But Troilus yet him no word answerde,
For-why to telle nas not his entente
To never no man, for whom that he so ferde.
For it is seyd, 'man maketh ofte a yerde
With which the maker is him-self y-beten
In sondry maner,' as thise wyse treten,

107. And namely, in his counseyl tellinge
That toucheth love that oughte be secree;
For of him-self it wolde y-nough outspringe,
But-if that it the bet governed be.
Eek som-tyme it is craft to seme flee
Fro thing which in effect men hunte faste;
Al this gan Troilus in his herte caste.

108. But nathelees, when he had herd him crye
'Awake!' he gan to syke wonder sore,
And seyde, 'freend, though that I stille lye,
I am not deef; now pees, and cry no more;
For I have herd thy wordes and thy lore;
But suffre me my mischief to biwayle,
For thy proverbes may me nought avayle.

109. 'Nor other cure canstow noon for me.
Eek I nil not be cured, I wol deye;
What knowe I of the quene Niobe?
Lat be thyne olde ensaumples, I thee preye.'
'No,' quod tho Pandarus, 'therfore I seye,
Swich is delyt of foles to biwepe
Hir wo, but seken bote they ne kepe.

110. 'Now knowe I that ther reson in thee fayleth.
But tel me, if I wiste what she were
For whom that thee al this misaunter ayleth,
Dorstestow that I tolde hir in hir ere
Thy wo, sith thou darst not thy-self for fere,
And hir bisoughte on thee to han som routhe?'
'Why, nay,' quod he, 'by god and by my trouthe!'

111. 'What? not as bisily,' quod Pandarus,
'As though myn owene lyf lay on this nede?'
'No, certes, brother,' quod this Troilus.
'And why?'—'For that thou sholdest never spede.'
'Wostow that wel?'—'Ye, that is out of drede,'
Quod Troilus, 'for al that ever ye conne,
She nil to noon swich wrecche as I be wonne.'

112. Quod Pandarus, 'allas! what may this be,
That thou despeyred art thus causelees?
What? liveth not thy lady? *benedicite!*
How wostow so that thou art gracelees?
Swich yvel is not alwey botelees.
Why, put not impossible thus thy cure,
Sin thing to come is ofte in aventure.

113. 'I graunte wel that thou endurest wo
As sharp as doth he, Ticius, in helle,
Whos stomak foules tyren ever-mo
That highte volturis, as bokes telle.
But I may not endure that thou dwelle
In so unskilful an opinioun
That of thy wo is no curacioun.

114. 'But ones niltow, for thy coward herte,
And for thyn ire and folish wilfulnesse,
For wantrust, tellen of thy sorwes smerte,

Ne to thyn owene help do bisinesse
As muche as speke a resoun more or lesse,
But lyest as he that list of no-thing recche.
What womman coude love swich a wrecche?

115. 'What may she demen other of thy deeth,
If thou thus deye, and she not why it is,
But that for fere is yolden up thy breeth,
For Grekes han biseged us, y-wis?
Lord, which a thank than shaltow han of this!
Thus wol she seyn, and al the toun at ones,
"The wrecche is deed, the devel have his bones!"

116. 'Thou mayst allone here wepe and crye and knele;
But, love a woman that she woot it nought,
And she wol quyte that thou shalt not fele;
Unknowe, unkist, and lost that is unsought.
What! many a man hath love ful dere y-bought
Twenty winter that his lady wiste,
That never yet his lady mouth he kiste.

117. 'What? shulde he therfor fallen in despeyr,
Or be recreaunt for his owene tene,
Or sleen him-self, al be his lady fayr?
Nay, nay, but ever in oon be fresh and grene
To serve and love his dere hertes quene,
And thenke it is a guerdoun hir to serve
A thousand-fold more than he can deserve.'

118. And of that word took hede Troilus,
And thoughte anoon what folye he was inne,
And how that sooth him seyde Pandarus,
That for to sleen him-self might he not winne,
But bothe doon unmanhod and a sinne,
And of his deeth his lady nought to wyte
For of his wo, god woot, she knew ful lyte.

119. And with that thought he gan ful sore syke,
And seyde, 'allas! what is me best to do?'
To whom Pandare answerde, 'if thee lyke,
The best is that thou telle me thy wo;
And have my trouthe, but thou it finde so,
I be thy bote, or that it be ful longe,
To peces do me drawe, and sithen honge!'

120. 'Ye, so thou seyst,' quod Troilus tho, 'allas!
But, god wot, it is not the rather so;
Ful hard were it to helpen in this cas,
For wel finde I that Fortune is my fo,
Ne alle the men that ryden conne or go
May of hir cruel wheel the harm with-stonde;
For, as hir list, she pleyeth with free and bonde.'

121. Quod Pandarus, 'than blamestow Fortune
For thou art wrooth, ye, now at erst I see;
Wostow nat wel that Fortune is commune
To every maner wight in som degree?
And yet thou hast this comfort, lo, pardee!
That, as hir joyes moten over-goon,
So mote hir sorwes passen everichoon.

122. 'For if hir wheel stinte any-thing to torne,
Then cessed she Fortune anoon to be:
Now, sith hir wheel by no wey may sojorne,
What wostow if hir mutabilitee
Right as thy-selven list, wol doon by thee,
Or that she be not fer fro thyn helpinge?
Paraunter, thou hast cause for to singe!

123. 'And therfor wostow what I thee beseche?
Lat be thy wo and turning to the grounde;
For who-so list have helping of his leche,
To him bihoveth first unwrye his wounde.
To Cerberus in helle ay be I bounde,
Were it for my suster, all thy sorwe,
By my wil, she sholde al be thyn to-morwe.

124. 'Loke up, I seye, and tel me what she is
Anoon, that I may goon aboute thy nede;
Knowe ich hir ought? for my love, tel me this;
Than wolde I hopen rather for to spede.'
Tho gan the veyne of Troilus to blede,
For he was hit, and wex al reed for shame;
'A ha!' quod Pandare, 'here biginneth game!'

125. And with that word he gan him for to shake,
And seyde, 'theef, thou shalt hir name telle.'
But tho gan sely Troilus for to quake

As though men sholde han lad him in-to helle,
And seyde, 'allas! of al my wo the welle,
Than is my swete fo called Criseyde!'
And wel nigh with the word for fere he deyde.

126. And whan that Pandare herde hir name nevene,
Lord, he was glad, and seyde, 'freend so dere,
Now fare a-right, for Joves name in hevene,
Love hath biset thee wel, be of good chere;
For of good name and wysdom and manere
She hath y-nough, and eek of gentilesse;
If she be fayr, thow wost thy-self, I gesse.

127. 'Ne I never saw a more bountevous
Of hir estat, ne a gladder, ne of speche
A freendlier, ne a more gracious
For to do wel, ne lasse hadde nede to seche
What for to doon; and al this bet to eche,
In honour, to as fer as she may strecche,
A kinges herte semeth by hires a wrecche.

128. 'And for-thy loke of good comfort thou be;
For certeinly, the firste poynt is this
Of noble corage and wel ordeynè,
A man to have pees with him-self, y-wis;
So oughtest thou, for nought but good it is
To loven wel, and in a worthy place;
Thee oughte not to clepe it hap, but grace.

129. 'And also thenk, and ther-with glade thee,
That sith thy lady vertuous is al,
So folweth it that ther is som pitee
Amonges alle thise othere in general;
And for-thy see that thou, in special,
Requere nought that is ayein hir name;
For vertue streccheth not him-self to shame.

130. 'But wel is me that ever I was born,
That thou biset art in so good a place;
For by my trouthe, in love I dorste have sworn,
Thee sholde never han tid thus fayr a grace;
And wostow why? for thou were wont to chace
At Love in scorn, and for despyt him calle
"Seynt Idiot, lord of thise foles alle."

131. 'How often hastow maad thy nyce japes,
And seyd, that Loves servants everichone
Of nycetee ben verray goddes apes;
And some wolde monche hir mete alone,
Ligging a-bedde, and make hem for to grone;
And som, thou seydest, hadde a blaunche fevere,
And preydest god he sholde never kevere!

132. 'And some of hem toke on hem, for the colde,
More than y-nough, so seydestow ful ofte;
And some han feyned ofte tyme, and tolde
How that they wake, whan they slepen softe;
And thus they wolde han brought hem-self a-lofte,
And nathelees were under at the laste;
Thus seydestow, and japedest ful faste.

133. 'Yet seydestow, that, for the more part,
These loveres wolden speke in general,
And thoughten that it was a siker art,
For fayling, for to assayen over-al.
Now may I jape of thee, if that I shal!
But nathelees, though that I sholde deye,
That thou art noon of tho, that dorste I seye.

134. 'Now beet thy brest, and sey to god of Love,
"Thy grace, lord! for now I me repente
If I mis spak, for now my-self I love":
Thus sey with al thyn herte in good entente.'
Quod Troilus, 'A! lord! I me consente,
And pray to thee my japes thou foryive,
And I shal never-more whyl I live.'

135. 'Thow seyst wel,' quod Pandare, 'and now I hope
That thou the goddes wratthe hast al apesed;
And sithen thou hast wepen many a drope,
And seyd swich thing wher-with thy god is plesed,
Now wolde never god but thou were esed;
And think wel, she of whom rist al thy wo
Here-after may thy comfort been al-so.

136. 'For thilke ground, that bereth the wedes wikke,
Bereth eek thise holsom herbes, as ful ofte
Next the foule netle, rough and thikke,

The rose waxeth swote and smothe and softe;
And next the valey is the hil a-lofte;
And next the derke night the glade morwe;
And also joye is next the fyn of sorwe.

137. 'Now loke that atempre be thy brydel,
And, for the beste, ay suffre to the tyde,
Or elles al our labour is on ydel;
He hasteth wel that wysly can abyde;
Be diligent, and trewe, and ay wel hyde.
Be lusty, free, persevere in thy servyse,
And al is wel, if thou werke in this wyse.

138. 'But he that parted is in every place
Is no-wher hool, as writen clerkes wyse;
What wonder is, though swich oon have no grace?
Eek wostow how it fareth of som servyse?
As plaunte a tre or herbe, in sondry wyse,
And on the morwe pulle it up as blyve,
No wonder is, though it may never thryve.

139. 'And sith that god of love hath thee bistowed
In place digne un-to thy worthinesse,
Stond faste, for to good port hastow rowed;
And of thy-self, for any hevinesse,
Hope alwey wel; for, but-if drerinesse
Or over-haste our bothe labour shende,
I hope of this to maken a good ende.

140. 'And wostow why I am the lasse a-fered
Of this matere with my nece trete?
For this have I herd seyd of wyse y-lered,
"Was never man ne woman yet bigete
That was unapt to suffren loves hete
Celestial, or elles love of kinde";
For-thy som grace I hope in hir to finde.

141. 'And for to speke of hir in special,
Hir beautee to bithinken and hir youthe,
It sit hir nought to be celestial
As yet, though that hir liste bothe and couthe;
But trewely, it sete hir wel right nouthe
A worthy knight to loven and cheryce,
And but she do, I holde it for a vyce.

142. 'Wherfore I am, and wol be, ay redy
To peyne me to do yow this servyse;
For bothe yow to plese thus hope I
Her-afterward; for ye beth bothe wyse,
And conne it counseyl kepe in swich a wyse,
That no man shal the wyser of it be;
And so we may be gladed alle three.

143. 'And, by my trouthe, I have right now of thee
A good conceyt in my wit, as I gesse,
And what it is, I wol now that thou see.
I thenke, sith that love, of his goodnesse,
Hath thee converted out of wikkednesse,
That thou shalt be the beste post, I leve,
Of al his lay, and most his foos to-greve.

144. 'Ensample why, see now these wyse clerkes,
That erren aldermost a-yein a lawe,
And ben converted from hir wikked werkes
Thorugh grace of god, that list hem to him drawe,
Than arn they folk that han most god in awe,
And strengest-feythed been, I understonde,
And conne an errour alder-best withstonde.'

145. Whan Troilus had herd Pandare assented
To been his help in loving of Criseyde,
Wex of his wo, as who seyth, untormented,
But hotter wex his love, and thus he seyde,
With sobre chere, al-though his herte pleyde,
'Now blisful Venus helpe, er that I sterve,
Of thee, Pandare, I may som thank deserve.

146. 'But, dere frend, how shal myn wo ben lesse
Til this be doon? and goode, eek tel me this,
How wiltow seyn of me and my destresse?
Lest she be wrooth, this drede I most, y-wis,
Or nil not here or trowen how it is.
Al this drede I, and eek for the manere
Of thee, hir eem, she nil no swich thing here.'

147. Quod Pandarus, 'thou hast a ful gret care
Lest that the cherl may falle out of the mone!
Why, lord! I hate of thee thy nyce fare!

Why, entremete of that thou hast to done!
For goddes love, I bidde thee a bone,
So lat me alone, and it shal be thy beste.'—
'Why, freend,' quod he, 'now do right as thee leste.

148. 'But herke, Pandare, o word, for I nolde
That thou in me wendest so greet folye,
That to my lady I desiren sholde
That toucheth harm or any vilenye;
For dredelees, me were lever dye
Than she of me ought elles understode
But that, that mighte sounen in-to gode.'

149. Tho lough this Pandare, and anoon answerede,
'And I thy borw? fy! no wight dooth but so;
I roughte nought though that she stode and herde
How that thou seyst; but fare-wel, I wol go.
A-dieu! be glad! god spede us bothe two!
Yif me this labour and this besinesse,
And of my speed be thyn al that swetnesse.'

150. Tho Troilus gan doun on knees to falle,
And Pandare in his armes hente faste,
And seyde, 'now, fy on the Grekes alle!
Yet, pardee, god shal helpe us at the laste;
And dredelees, if that my lyf may laste,
And god to-forn, lo, som of hem shall smerte;
And yet me athinketh that this avaunt me asterte!

151. 'Now, Pandare, I can no more seye,
But thou wys, thou wost, thou mayst, thou art al!
My lyf, my deeth, hool in thyn honde I leye;
Help now,' quod he.   'Yis, by my trouthe, I shal.'
'God yelde thee, freend, and this in special,'
Quod Troilus, 'that thou me recomaunde
To hir that to the deeth me may comaunde.'

152. This Pandarus tho, desirous to serve
His fulle freend, than seyde in this manere,
'Far-wel, and thenk I wol thy thank deserve;
Have here my trouthe, and that thou shalt wel here.'—
And wente his wey, thenking on this matere,
And how he best mighte hir beseche of grace,
And finde a tyme ther-to, and a place.

153. For every wight that hath an hous to founde
Ne renneth nought the werk for to biginne
With rakel hond, but he wol byde a stounde,
And sende his hertes lyne out fro with-inne
Alderfirst his purpos for to winne.
Al this Pandare in his herte thoughte,
And caste his werk ful wysly, or he wroughte.

154. But Troilus lay tho no lenger doun,
But up anoon up-on his stede bay,
And in the feld he pleyde the leoun;
Wo was that Greek that with him mette that day.
And in the toun his maner tho forth ay
So goodly was, and gat him so in grace,
That ech him lovede that loked on his face.

155. For he bicom the frendlyeste wight,
The gentileste, and eek the moste free,
The thriftieste and oon the beste knight,
That in his tyme was, or mighte be.
Dede were his japes and his crueltee,
His heighe port and his manere estraunge,
And ech of tho gan for a vertu chaunge.

156. Now lat us stinte of Troilus a stounde,
That fareth lyk a man that hurt is sore,
And is somdel of akinge of his wounde
Y-lissed wel, but heled no del more:
And, as an esy pacient, the lore
Abit of him that gooth aboute his cure;
And thus he dryveth forth his aventure.

Explicit Liber Primus

BOOK II

Incipit prohemium Secundi Libri

1. OUT of these blake wawes for to sayle,
O wind, O wind, the weder ginneth clere;
For in this see the boot hath swich travayle,
Of my conning that unnethe I it stere:
This see clepe I the tempestous matere
Of desespeyr that Troilus was inne:
But now of hope the calendes biginne.

2. O lady myn, that called art Cleo,
Thou be my speed fro this forth, and my muse,
To ryme wel this book, til I have do;
Me nedeth here noon other art to use.
For-why to every lovere I me excuse,
That of no sentement I this endyte,
But out of Latin in my tonge it wryte.

3. Wherfore I nil have neither thank ne blame
Of all this werk, but pray yow mekely,
Disblameth me, if any word be lame,
For as myn auctor seyde, so seye I.
Eek though I speke of love unfelingly,
No wonder is, for it no-thing of newe is;
A blind man can nat juggen wel in hewis.

4. Ye knowe eek, that in forme of speche is chaunge
With-inne a thousand yeer, and wordes tho
That hadden prys, now wonder nyce and straunge
Us thinketh hem; and yet they spake hem so,
And spedde as wel in love as men now do;
Eek for to winne love in sondry ages,
In sondry londes, sondry been usages.

5. And for-thy if it happe in any wyse,
That here be any lovere in this place
That herkeneth, as the story wol devyse,
How Troilus com to his lady grace,
And thenketh, so nolde I nat love purchace,
Or wondreth on his speche and his doinge,
I noot; but it is me no wonderinge;

6. For every wight which that to Rome went,
Halt nat o path, or alwey o manere;
Eek in som lond were al the gamen shent,
If that they ferde in love as men don here,
As thus, in open doing or in chere,
In visitinge, in forme, or seyde hir sawes;
For-thy men seyn, ech contree hath his lawes.

7. Eek scarsly been ther in this place three
That han in love seyd lyk and doon in al;
For to thy purpos this may lyken thee,
And thee right nought, yet al is seyd or shal;
Eek som men grave in tree, som in stoon wal,
As it bitit; but sin I have begonne,
Myn auctor shal I folwen, if I conne.

Explicit prohemium Secundi Libri

Incipit Liber Secundus

8. In May, that moder is of monthes glade,
That fresshe floures, blewe, and whyte, and rede,
Ben quike agayn, that winter dede made,
And ful of bawme is fletinge every mede;
Whan Phebus doth his brighte bemes sprede
Right in the whyte Bole, it so bitidde
As I shal singe, on Mayes day the thridde,

9. That Pandarus, for al his wyse speche,
Felte eek his part of loves shottes kene,
That, coude he never so wel of loving preche,
It made his hewe a-day ful ofte grene;
So shoop it, that him fil that day a tene
In love, for which in wo to bedde he wente,
And made, er it was day, ful many a wente.

10. The swalwe Proignè, with a sorwful lay,
Whan morwe com, gan make hir weymentinge,
Why she forshapen was; and ever lay
Pandare a-bedde, half in a slomeringe,
Til she so neigh him made hir chiteringe
How Tereus gan forth hir suster take,
That with the noyse of hir he gan a-wake;

11. And gan to calle, and dresse him up to ryse,
Remembringe him his erand was to done
From Troilus, and eek his greet empryse;
And caste and knew in good plyt was the mone
To doon viage, and took his wey ful sone
Un-to his neces paleys ther bi-syde;
Now Janus, god of entree, thou him gyde!

12. Whan he was come un-to his neces place,
'Wher is my lady?' to hir folk seyde he;
And they him tolde; and he forth in gan pace,
And fond, two othere ladyes sete and she
With-inne a paved parlour; and they three
Herden a mayden reden hem the geste
Of the Sege of Thebes, whyl hem leste.

13. Quod Pandarus, 'ma dame, god yow see,
With al your book and al the companye!'
'Ey, uncle myn, welcome y-wis,' quod she,
And up she roos, and by the hond in hye
She took him faste, and seyde, 'this night thrye,
To goode mote it turne, of yow I mette!'
And with that word she doun on bench him sette.

14. 'Ye, nece, ye shal fare wel the bet,
If god wole, al this yeer,' quod Pandarus;
'But I am sory that I have yow let
To herknen of your book ye preysen thus;
For goddes love, what seith it? tel it us.
Is it of love? O, som good ye me lere!'
'Uncle,' quod she, 'your maistresse is not here!'

15. With that they gonnen laughe, and tho she seyde,
'This romaunce is of Thebes, that we rede;
And we han herd how that king Laius deyde
Thurgh Edippus his sone, and al that dede;
And here we stenten at these lettres rede,
How the bisshop, as the book can telle,
Amphiorax, fil thurgh the ground to helle.'

16. Quod Pandarus, 'al this knowe I my-selve,
And al th' assege of Thebes and the care;
For her-of been ther maked bokes twelve:—

But lat be this, and tel me how ye fare;
Do wey your barbe, and shew your face bare;
Do wey your book, rys up, and lat us daunce,
And lat us don to May som observaunce.'

17. 'A! god forbede!' quod she, 'be ye mad?
Is that a widwes lyf, so god you save?
By god, ye maken me right sore a-drad,
Ye ben so wilde, it semeth as ye rave!
It sete me wel bet ay in a cave
To bidde, and rede on holy seyntes lyves:
Lat maydens gon to daunce, and yonge wyves.'

18. 'As ever thryve I,' quod this Pandarus,
'Yet coude I telle a thing to doon you pleye.'
'Now uncle dere,' quod she, 'tel it us
For goddes love; is than th' assege aweye?
I am of Grekes so ferd that I deye.'
'Nay, nay,' quod he, 'as ever mote I thryve!
It is a thing wel bet than swiche fyve.'

19. 'Ye, holy god!' quod she, 'what thing is that?
What? bet than swiche fyve? ey, nay, y-wis!
For al this world ne can I reden what
It sholde been; som jape, I trowe, is this;
And but your-selven telle us what it is,
My wit is for to arede it al to lene;
As help me god, I noot nat what ye mene.'

20. 'And I your borow, ne never shal, for me,
This thing be told to yow, as mote I thryve!'
'And why so, uncle myn? why so?' quod she.
'By god,' quod he, 'that wole I telle as blyve;
For prouder womman were ther noon on-lyve,
And ye it wiste, in al the toun of Troye;
I jape nought, as ever have I joye!'

21. Tho gan she wondren more than biforn
A thousand fold, and doun hir eyen caste;
For never, sith the tyme that she was born,
To knowe thing desired she so faste;
And with a syk she seyde him at the laste,
'Now, uncle myn, I nil yow nought displese,
Nor axen more, that may do yow disese.'

22. So after this, with many wordes glade,
And freendly tales, and with mery chere,
Of this and that they pleyde, and gunnen wade
In many an unkouth glad and deep matere,
As freendes doon, whan they ben met y-fere;
Til she gan axen him how Ector ferde,
That was the tounes wal and Grekes yerde.

23. 'Ful wel, I thanke it god,' quod Pandarus,
'Save in his arm he hath a litel wounde;
And eek his fresshe brother Troilus,
The wyse worthy Ector the secounde,
In whom that every vertu list abounde,
As alle trouthe and alle gentillesse,
Wysdom, honour, fredom, and worthinesse.'

24. 'In good feith, eem,' quod she, 'that lyketh me;
They faren wel, god save hem bothe two!
For trewely I holde it greet deyntee
A kinges sone in armes wel to do,
And been of good condiciouns ther-to;
For greet power and moral vertu here
Is selde y-seye in o persone y-fere.'

25. 'In good feith, that is sooth,' quod Pandarus;
'But, by my trouthe, the king hath sones tweye,
That is to mene, Ector and Troilus,
That certainly, though that I sholde deye,
They been as voyde of vyces, dar I seye,
As any men that liveth under the sonne,
Hir might is wyde y-knowe, and what they conne.

26. 'Of Ector nedeth it nought for to telle;
In al this world ther nis a bettre knight
Than he, that is of worthinesse welle;
And he wel more vertu hath than might.
This knoweth many a wys and worthy wight.
The same prys of Troilus I seye,
God help me so, I knowe not swiche tweye.'

27. 'By god,' quod she, 'of Ector that is sooth;
Of Troilus the same thing trowe I;
For dredelees, men tellen that he dooth

In armes day by day so worthily,
And bereth him here at hoom so gentilly
To every wight, that al the prys hath he
Of hem that me were levest preysed be.'

28. 'Ye sey right sooth, y-wis,' quod Pandarus;
'For yesterday, who-so hadde with him been,
He might have wondred up-on Troilus;
For never yet so thikke a swarm of been
Ne fleigh, as Grekes fro him gonne fleen;
And thorugh the feld, in every wightes ere,
Ther nas no cry but "Troilus is there!"

29. 'Now here, now there, he hunted hem so faste,
Ther nas but Grekes blood; and Troilus,
Now hem he hurte, and hem alle doun he caste;
Ay where he wente it was arayed thus:
He was hir deeth, and sheld and lyf for us;
That as that day ther dorste noon withstonde,
Whyl that he held his blody swerd in honde.

30. 'Therto he is the freendlieste man
Of grete estat, that ever I saw my lyve;
And wher him list, best felawshipe can
To suche as him thinketh able for to thryve.'
And with that word tho Pandarus, as blyve,
He took his leve, and seyde, 'I wol go henne':
'Nay, blame have I, myn uncle,' quod she thenne.

31. 'What eyleth yow to be thus wery sone,
And namelich of wommen? wol ye so?
Nay, sitteth down; by god, I have to done
With yow, to speke of wisdom er ye go.'
And every wight that was a-boute hem tho,
That herde that, gan fer a-wey to stonde,
Whyl they two hadde al that hem liste in honde.

32. Whan that hir tale al brought was to an ende
Of hire estat and of hir governaunce,
Quod Pandarus, 'now is it tyme I wende;
But yet, I seye, aryseth, lat us daunce,
And cast your widwes habit to mischaunce:
What list yow thus your-self to disfigure,
Sith yow is tid thus fair an aventure?'

33. 'A! wel bithought! for love of god,' quod she,
'Shal I not witen ·vhat ye mene of this?'
'No, this thing axeth layser,' tho quod he,
'And eek me wolde muche greve, y-wis,
If I it tolde, and yet it toke amis.
Yet were it bet my tonge for to stille
Than seye a sooth that were ayeins your wille.

34. 'For, nece, by the goddesse Minerve,
And Juppiter, that maketh the thonder ringe,
And by the blisful Venus that I serve,
Ye been the womman in this world livinge,
With-oute paramours, to my witinge,
That I best love, and lothest am to greve,
And that ye witen wel your-self, I leve.'

35. 'Y-wis, myn uncle,' quod she, 'grant mercy;
Your freendship have I founden ever yit;
I am to no man holden trewely
So muche as yow, and have so litel quit;
And, with the grace of god, emforth my wit,
As in my gilt I shal you never offende;
And if I have er this, I wol amende.

36. 'But, for the love of god, I yow beseche,
As ye ben he that I most love and triste,
Lat be to me your fremde maner speche,
And sey to me, your nece, what yow liste':
And with that word hir uncle anoon hir kiste,
And seyde, 'gladly, leve nece dere,
Tak it for good that I shal seye yow here.'

37. With that she gan hir eyen doun to caste,
And Pandarus to coghe gan a lyte,
And seyde, 'nece, alwey, lo! to the laste,
How-so it be that som men hem delyte
With subtil art hir tales for to endyte,
Yet for al that, in hir entencioun,
Hir tale is al for som conclusioun.

38. 'And sithen th' ende is every tales strengthe,
And this matere is so bihovely,
What sholde I peynte or drawen it on lengthe

To yow, that been my freend so feithfully?'
And with that word he gan right inwardly
Biholden hir, and loken on hir face,
And seyde, 'on suche a mirour goode grace!'

39. Than thoughte he thus, 'if I my tale endyte
Ought hard, or make a proces any whyle,
She shal no savour han ther-in but lyte,
And trowe I wolde hir in my will bigyle.
For tendre wittes wenen al be wyle
Ther-as they can nat pleynly understonde;
For-thy hir wit to serven wol I fonde'—

40. And loked on hir in a besy wyse,
And she was war that he byheld hir so,
And seyde, 'lord! so faste ye me avyse!
Sey ye me never er now? what sey ye, no?'
'Yes, yes,' quod he, 'and bet wole er I go;
But, by my trouthe, I thoughte now if ye
Be fortunat, for now men shal it see.

41. 'For to every wight som goodly aventure
Som tyme is shape, if he it can receyven;
And if that he wol take of it no cure,
Whan that it cometh, but wilfully it weyven,
Lo, neither cas nor fortune him deceyven,
But right his verray slouthe and wrecchednesse;
And swich a wight is for to blame, I gesse.

42. 'Good aventure, O bele nece, have ye
Ful lightly founden, and ye conne it take;
And, for the love of god, and eek of me,
Cacche it anoon, lest aventure slake.
What sholde I lenger proces of it make?
Yif me your hond, for in this world is noon,
If that you list, a wight so wel begoon.

43. 'And sith I speke of good entencioun,
As I to yow have told wel here-biforn,
And love as wel your honour and renoun
As creature in al this world y-born;
By alle the othes that I have yow sworn,
And ye be wrooth therfore, or wene I lye,
Ne shal I never seen yow eft with yë.

44. 'Beth nought agast, ne quaketh nat; wher-to?
Ne chaungeth nat for fere so your hewe;
For hardely, the werste of this is do;
And though my tale as now be to yow newe,
Yet trist alwey, ye shal me finde trewe;
And were it thing that me thoughte unsittinge,
To yow nolde I no swiche tales bringe.'

45. 'Now, my good eem, for goddes love, I preye,'
Quod she, 'com of, and tell me what it is;
For bothe I am agast what ye wol seye,
And eek me longeth it to wite, y-wis,
For whether it be wel or be amis,
Sey on, lat me not in this fere dwelle.'
'So wol I doon, now herkneth, I shal telle:

46. 'Now, nece myn, the kinges dere sone,
The goode, wyse, worthy, fresshe, and free,
Which alwey for to do wel is his wone,
The noble Troilus, so loveth thee,
That, bot ye helpe, it wol his bane be.
Lo, here is al, what sholde I more seye?
Doth what yow list, to make him live or deye.

47. 'But if ye lete him deye, I wol sterve;
Have her my trouthe, nece, I nil not lyen;
Al sholde I with this knyf my throte kerve'—
With that the teres braste out of his yën,
And seyde, 'if that ye doon us bothe dyen,
Thus giltelees, than have ye fisshed faire;
What mende ye, though that we bothe apeyre?

48. 'Allas! he which that is my lord so dere,
That trewe man, that noble gentil knight,
That nought desireth but your freendly chere,
I see him deye, ther he goth up-right,
And hasteth him, with al his fulle might,
For to be slayn, if fortune wol assente;
Allas! that god yow swich a beautee sente!

49. 'If it be so that ye so cruel be,
That of his deeth yow liste nought to recche,
That is so trewe and worthy, as ye see,

No more than of a japere or a wrecche,
If ye be swich, your beautee may not strecche
To make amendes of so cruel a dede;
Avysement is good bifore the nede.

50. 'Wo worth the faire gemme vertulees!
Wo worth that herbe also that dooth no bote!
Wo worth that beautee that is routhelees!
Wo worth that wight that tret ech under fote!
And ye, that been of beautee crop and rote,
If therewith-al in you ther be no routhe,
Than is it harm ye liven, by my trouthe!

51. 'And also thenk wel, that this is no gaude;
For me were lever, thou and I and he
Were hanged, than I sholde been his baude,
As heye, as men mighte on us alle y-see:
I am thyn eem, the shame were to me,
As well as thee, if that I sholde assente,
Thorugh myn abet, that he thyn honour shente.

52. 'Now understand, for I yow nought requere
To binde yow to him thorugh no beheste,
But only that ye make him bettre chere
Than ye han doon er this, and more feste,
So that his lyf be saved, at the leste:
This al and som, and playnly our entente;
God helpe me so, I never other mente.

53. 'Lo, this request is not but skile, y-wis,
Ne doute of reson, pardee, is ther noon.
I sette the worste that ye dredden this,
Men wolden wondren seen him come or goon:
Ther-ayeins answere I thus a-noon,
That every wight, but he be fool of kinde,
Wol deme it love of freendship in his minde.

54. 'What? who wol deme, though he see a man
To temple go, that he the images eteth?
Thenk eek how wel and wysly that he can
Governe him-self, that he no-thing foryeteth,
That, wher he cometh, he prys and thank him geteth;
And eek ther-to, he shal come here so selde,
What fors were it though al the toun behelde?

55. 'Swich love of freendes regneth al this **toun**;
And wrye yow in that mantel ever-mo;
And, god so wis be my savacioun,
As I have seyd, your beste is to do so.
But alwey, goode nece, to stinte his wo,
So lat your daunger sucred ben a lyte,
That of his deeth ye be nought for to wyte.'

56. Criseyde, which that herde him in this wyse,
Thoughte, 'I shal fele what he meneth, y-wis.'
'Now, eem,' quod she, 'what wolde ye devyse,
What is your reed I sholde doon of this?'
'That is wel seyd,' quod he, 'certayn, best is
That ye him love ayein for his lovinge,
As love for love is skilful guerdoninge.

57. 'Thenk eek, how elde wasteth every houre
In eche of yow a party of beautee;
And therefore, er that age thee devoure,
Go love, for, olde, ther wol no wight of thee.
Lat this proverbe a lore un-to yow be;
"To late y-war, quod Beautee, whan it paste";
And elde daunteth daunger at the laste.

58. 'The kinges fool is woned to cryen loude,
Whan that him thinketh a womman bereth hir hyë,
"So longe mote ye live, and alle proude,
Til crowes feet be growe under your yë,
And sende yow thanne a mirour in to pryë
In whiche ye may see your face a-morwe!"
Nece, I bid wisshe yow no more sorwe.'

59. With this he stente, and caste adoun the heed,
And she bigan to breste a-wepe anoon,
And seyde, 'allas, for wo! why nere I deed?
For of this world the feith is al agoon!
Allas! what sholden straunge to me doon,
When he, that for my beste freend I wende
Ret me to love, and sholde it me defende?

60. 'Allas! I wolde han trusted, doutelees,
That if that I, thurgh my disaventure,
Had loved other him or Achilles,

Ector, or any mannes creature,
Ye nolde han had no mercy ne mesure
On me, but alwey had me in repreve;
This false world, allas! who may it leve?

61. 'What? is this al the joye and al the feste?
Is this your reed, is this my blisful cas?
Is this the verray mede of your beheste?
Is al this peynted proces seyd, allas!
Right for this fyn? O lady myn, Pallas!
Thou in this dredful cas for me purveye;
For so astonied am I that I deye!'

62. With that she gan ful sorwfully to syke;
'A! may it be no bet?' quod Pandarus;
'By god, I shal no-more come here this wyke,
And god to-forn, that am mistrusted thus;
I see ful wel that ye sette lyte of us,
Or of our deeth! Alias! I woful wrecche!
Mighte he yet live, of me is nought to recche.

63. 'O cruel god, O dispitouse Marte,
O Furies three of helle, on yow I crye!
So lat me never out of this hous departe,
If that I mente harm or vilanye!
But sith I see my lord mot nedes dye,
And I with him, here I me shryve, and seye
That wikkedly ye doon us bothe deye.

64. 'But sith it lyketh yow that I be deed,
By Neptunus, that god is of the see,
Fro this forth shal I never eten breed
Til I myn owene herte blood may see;
For certayn, I wole deye as soon as he'—
And up he sterte, and on his wey he raughte,
Til she agayn him by the lappe caughte.

65. Criseyde, which that wel neigh starf for fere,
So as she was the ferfulleste wight
That mighte be, and herde eek with hir ere,
And saw the sorwful ernest of the knight,
And in his preyere eek saw noon unright,
And for the harm that mighte eek fallen more,
She gan to rewe, and dradde hir wonder sore;

66. And thoughte thus, 'unhappes fallen thikke
Alday for love, and in swich manner cas,
As men ben cruel in hem-self and wikke;
And if this man slee here him-self, allas!
In my presence, it wol be no solas.
What men wolde of hit deme I can nat seye;
It nedeth me ful sleyly for to pleye.'

67. And with a sorwful syk she seyde thrye,
'A! lord! what me is tid a sory chaunce!
For myn estat now lyth in jupartye,
And eek myn emes lyf lyth in balaunce;
But nathelees, with goddes governaunce,
I shal so doon, myn honour shal I kepe,
And eek his lyf'; and stinte for to wepe.

68. 'Of harmes two, the lesse is for to chese;
Yet have I lever maken him good chere
In honour, than myn emes lyf to lese;
Ye seyn, ye no-thing elles me requere?'
'No, wis,' quod he, 'myn owene nece dere.'
'Now wel,' quod she, 'and I wol doon my peyne;
I shal myn herte ayeins my lust constreyne,

69. 'But that I nil not holden him in honde,
Ne love a man, ne can I not, ne may
Ayeins my wil; but elles wol I fonde,
Myn honour sauf, plese him fro day to day;
Ther-to nolde I nought ones have seyd nay,
But that I dredde, as in my fantasye;
But cesse cause, ay cesseth maladye.

70. 'And here I make a protestacioun,
That in this proces if ye depper go,
That certaynly, for no savacioun
Of yow, though that ye sterve bothe two,
Though al the world on o day be my fo,
Ne shal I never on him han other routhe.'—
'I graunte wel,' quod Pandare, 'by my trouthe.

71. 'But may I truste wel ther-to,' quod he,
'That, of this thing that ye han hight me here,
Ye wol it holden trewly un-to me?'

'Ye doutelees,' quod she, 'myn uncle dere.'
'Ne that I shal han cause in this matere,'
Quod he, 'to pleyne, or after yow to preche?'
'Why, no, pardee; what nedeth more speche?'

72. Tho fillen they in othere tales glade,
Til at the laste, 'O good eem,' quod she tho,
'For love of god, which that us bothe made,
Tel me how first ye wisten of his wo:
Wot noon of hit but ye?' He seyde, 'no.'
'Can he wel speke of love?' quod she, 'I preye,
Tel me, for I the bet me shal purveye.'

73. Tho Pandarus a litel gan to smyle,
And seyde, 'by my trouthe, I shal yow telle.
This other day, nought gon ful longe whyle,
In-with the paleys-gardyn, by a welle,
Gan he and I wel half a day to dwelle,
Right for to speken of an ordenaunce,
How we the Grekes mighte disavaunce.

74. 'Sone after that bigonne we to lepe,
And casten with our dartes to and fro,
Til at the laste he seyde, he wolde slepe,
And on the gres a-doun he leyde him tho;
And I after gan rome to and fro
Til that I herde, as that I welk allone,
How he bigan ful wofully to grone.

75. 'Tho gan I stalke him softely bihinde,
And sikerly, the sothe for to seyne,
As I can clepe ayein now to my minde,
Right thus to Love he gan him for to pleyne;
He seyde, "lord! have routhe up-on my peyne,
Al have I been rebel in myn entente;
Now, *mea culpa*, lord! I me repente.

76. '"O god, that at thy disposicioun
Ledest the fyn, by juste purveyaunce,
Of every wight, my lowe confessioun
Accepte in gree, and send me swich penaunce
As lyketh thee, but from desesperaunce,
That may my goost departe awey fro thee,
Thou be my sheld, for thy benignitee.

77. '"For certes, lord, so sore hath she me wounded
That stod in blak, with loking of hir yën,
That to myn hertes botme it is y-sounded,
Thorugh which I woot that I mot nedes dyen;
This is the worste, I dar me not bi-wryen;
And wel the hotter been the gledes rede,
That men hem wryen with asshen pale and dede."

78. 'With that he smoot his heed adoun anoon,
And gan to motre, I noot what, trewely.
And I with that gan stille awey to goon,
And leet ther-of as no-thing wist hadde I,
And come ayein anoon and stood him by,
And seyde, "a-wake, ye slepen al to longe;
It semeth nat that love dooth yow longe,

79. '"That slepen so that no man may yow wake.
Who sey ever or this so dull a man?"
"Ye, freend," quod he, "do ye your hedes ake
For love, and lat me liven as I can."
But though that he for wo was pale and wan,
Yet made he tho as fresh a contenaunce
As though he shulde have led the newe daunce.

80. 'This passed forth, till now, this other day,
It fel that I com roming al allone
Into his chaumbre, and fond how that he lay
Up-on his bed; but man so sore grone
Ne herde I never, and what that was his mone,
Ne wiste I nought; for, as I was cominge,
Al sodeynly he lefte his compleyninge.

81. 'Of which I took somwhat suspecioun,
And neer I com, and fond he wepte sore;
And god so wis be my savacioun,
As never of thing hadde I no routhe more.
For neither with engyn, ne with no lore,
Unethes mighte I fro the deeth him kepe;
That yet fele I myn herte for him wepe.

82. 'And god wot, never, sith that I was born,
Was I so bisy no man for to preche,
Ne never was to wight so depe y-sworn,

Or he me tolde who mighte been his leche,
But now to yow rehersen al his speche,
Or alle his woful wordes for to soune,
Ne bid me not, but ye wol see me swowne.

83. 'But for to save his lyf, and elles nought,
And to non harm of yow, thus am I driven;
And for the love of god that us hath wrought,
Swich chere him dooth, that he and I may liven.
Now have I plat to yow myn herte schriven;
And sin ye woot that myn entente is clene,
Tak hede ther-of, for I non yvel mene.

84. 'And right good thrift, I pray to god, have ye,
That han swich oon y-caught with-oute net;
And be ye wys, as ye ben fair to see,
Wel in the ring than is the ruby set.
Ther were never two so well y-met,
Whan ye ben his al hool, as he is youre:
Ther mighty god yet graunte us see that houre!'

85. 'Nay, therof spak I not, a, ha!' quod she,
'As helpe me god, ye shenden every deel!'
'O mercy, dere nece,' anoon quod he,
'What-so I spak, I mente nought but weel,
By Mars the god, that helmed is of steel;
Now beth nought wrooth, my blood, my nece dere.'
'Now wel,' quod she, 'foryeven be it here!'

86. With this he took his leve, and hoom he wente;
And lord, how he was glad and wel bigoon!
Criseyde aroos, no lenger she ne stente,
But straight in-to hir closet wente anoon,
And sette here doun as stille as any stoon,
And every word gan up and doun to winde,
That he hadde seyd, as it com hir to minde;

87. And wex somdel astonied in hir thought,
Right for the newe cas; but whan that she
Was ful avysed, tho fond she right nought
Of peril, why she oughte afered be.
For man may love, of possibilitee,
A womman so, his herte may to-breste,
And she nought love ayein, but-if hir leste.

88. But as she sat allone and thoughte thus,
Th' ascry aroos at skarmish al with-oute,
And men cryde in the strete, 'see, Troilus
Hath right now put to flight the Grekes route!'
With that gan al hir meynee for to shoute,
'A! go we see, caste up the latis wyde;
For thurgh this strete he moot to palays ryde;

89. 'For other wey is fro the yate noon
Of Dardanus, ther open is the cheyne.'
With that com he and all his folk anoon
An esy pas rydinge, in routes tweyne,
Right as his happy day was, sooth to seyne,
For which, men say, may nought disturbed be
That shal bityden of necessitee.

90. This Troilus sat on his baye stede,
Al armed, save his heed, ful richely,
And wounded was his hors, and gan to blede,
On which he rood a pas, ful softely;
But swich a knightly sighte, trewely,
As was on him, was nought, with-outen faile,
To loke on Mars, that god is of batayle.

91. So lyk a man of armes and a knight
He was to seen, fulfild of heigh prowesse;
For bothe he hadde a body and a might
To doon that thing, as wel as hardinesse;
And eek to seen him in his gere him dresse,
So fresh, so yong, so weldy semed he,
It was an heven up-on him for to see.

92. His helm to-hewen was in twenty places,
That by a tissew heng, his bak bihinde,
His sheld to-dasshed was with swerdes and maces,
In which men mighte many an arwe finde
That thirled hadde horn and nerf and rinde;
And ay the peple cryde, 'here cometh our joye,
And, next his brother, holdere up of Troye!'

93. For which he wex a litel reed for shame,
Whan he the peple up-on him herde cryen,
That to biholde it was a noble game,

How sobreliche he caste doun his yën.
Cryseyda gan al his chere aspyen,
And leet so softe it in hir herte sinke,
That to hir-self she seyde, 'who yaf me drinke?'

94. For of hir owene thought she wex al reed,
Remembringe hir right thus, 'lo, this is he
Which that myn uncle swereth he moot be deed,
But I on him have mercy and pitee';
And with that thought, for pure a-shamed, she
Gan in hir heed to pulle, and that as faste,
Whyl he and al the peple for-by paste,

95. And gan to caste and rollen up and doun
With-inne hir thought his excellent prowesse,
And his estat, and also his renoun,
His wit, his shap, and eek his gentilesse;
But most hir favour was, for his distresse
Was al for hir, and thoughte it was a routhe
To sleen swich oon, if that he mente trouthe.

96. Now mighte som envyous jangle thus,
'This was a sodeyn love, how mighte it be
That she so lightly lovede Troilus
Right for the firste sighte; ye, pardee?'
Now who-so seyth so, mote he never thee!
For every thing, a ginning hath it nede
Er al be wrought, with-outen any drede.

97. For I sey nought that she so sodeynly
Yaf him hir love, but that she gan enclyne
To lyke him first, and I have told yow why;
And after that, his manhod and his pyne
Made love with-inne hir for to myne,
For which, by proces and by good servyse,
He gat hir love, and in no sodeyn wyse.

98. And also blisful Venus, wel arayed,
Sat in hir seventhe hous of hevene tho,
Disposed wel, and with aspectes payed,
To helpen sely Troilus of his wo.
And, sooth to seyn, she nas nat al a fo
To Troilus in his nativitee;
God woot that wel the soner spedde he.

99. Now lat us stinte of Troilus a throwe,
That rydeth forth, and lat us tourne faste
Un-to Criseyde, that heng hir heed ful lowe,
Ther-as she sat allone, and gan to caste
Wher-on she wolde apoynte hir at the laste,
If it so were hir eem ne wolde cesse,
For Troilus, up-on hir for to presse.

100. And, lord! so she gan in hir thought argue
In this matere of which I have yow told,
And what to doon best were, and what eschue,
That plyted she ful ofte in many fold.
Now was hir herte warm, now was it cold,
And what she thoughte somewhat shal I wryte,
As to myn auctor listeth for to endyte.

101. She thoughte wel, that Troilus persone
She knew by sighte and eek his gentillesse,
And thus she seyde, 'al were it nought to done,
To graunte him love, yet, for his worthinesse,
It were honour, with pley and with gladnesse,
In honestee, with swich a lord to dele,
For myn estat, and also for his hele.

102. 'Eek, wel wot I my kinges sone is he;
And sith he hath to see me swich delyt,
If I wolde utterly his sighte flee,
Paraunter he mighte have me in dispyt,
Thurgh which I mighte stonde in worse plyt;
Now were I wys, me hate to purchace,
With-outen nede, ther I may stonde in grace?

103. 'In every thing, I woot, ther lyth mesure.
For though a man forbede dronkenesse,
He nought for-bet that every creature
Be drinkelees for alwey, as I gesse;
Eek sith I woot for me is his distresse,
I ne oughte not for that thing him despyse,
Sith it is so, he meneth in good wyse.

104. 'And eek I knowe, of longe tyme agoon,
His thewes goode, and that he is not nyce.
Ne avauntour, seyth men, certein, is he noon;

To wys is he to do so gret a vyce;
Ne als I nil him never so cheryce,
That he may make avaunt, by juste cause;
He shal me never binde in swiche a clause.

105. 'Now set a cas, the hardest is, y-wis,
Men mighten deme that he loveth me:
What dishonour were it un-to me, this?
May I him lette of that? why nay, pardee!
I knowe also, and alday here and see,
Men loven wommen al this toun aboute;
Be they the wers? why, nay, with-outen doute.

106. 'I thenk eek how he able is for to have
Of al this noble toun the thriftieste,
To been his love, so she hir honour save;
For out and out he is the worthieste,
Save only Ector, which that is the beste.
And yet his lyf al lyth now in my cure,
But swich is love, and eek myn aventure.

107. 'Ne me to love, a wonder is it nought;
For wel wot I my-self, so god me spede,
Al wolde I that noon wiste of this thought,
I am oon the fayreste, out of drede,
And goodlieste, who-so taketh hede;
And so men seyn in al the toun of Troye.
What wonder is it though he of me have joye?

108. 'I am myn owene woman, wel at ese,
I thanke it god, as after myn estat;
Right yong, and stonde unteyd in lusty lese,
With-outen jalousye or swich debat;
Shal noon housbonde seyn to me "chekmat!——"
Fo either they ben ful of jalousye,
Or maisterful, or loven novelrye.

109. 'What shall I doon? to what fyn live I thus?
Shal I nat loven, in cas if that me leste?
What, *par dieux*! I am nought religious!
And though that I myn herte sette at reste
Upon this knight, that is the worthieste,
And kepe alwey myn honour and my name,
By alle right, it may do me no shame.'

110. But right as whan the sonne shyneth brighte,
In March, that chaungeth ofte tyme his face,
And that a cloud is put with wind to flighte
Which over-sprat the sonne as for a space,
A cloudy thought gan thorugh hir soule pace,
That over-spradde hir brighte thoughtes alle,
So that for fere almost she gan to falle.

111. That thought was this, 'allas! sin I am free,
Sholde I now love, and putte in jupartye
My sikernesse, and thrallen libertee?
Allas! how dorste I thenken that folye?
May I nought well in other folk aspye
Hir dredful joye, hir constreynt, and hir peyne?
Ther loveth noon, that she nath why to pleyne.

112. 'For love is yet the moste stormy lyf,
Right of him-self, that ever was bigonne;
For ever som mistrust, or nyce stryf,
Ther is in love, som cloud is over the sonne:
Ther-to we wrecched wommen no-thing conne,
Whan us is wo, but wepe and sitte and thinke;
Our wreche is this, our owene wo to drinke.

113. 'Also these wikked tonges been so prest
To speke us harm, eek men be so untrewe,
That, right anoon as cessed is hir lest,
So cesseth love, and forth to love a newe:
But harm y-doon, is doon, who-so it rewe.
For though these men for love hem first to-rende,
Ful sharp biginning breketh ofte at ende.

114. 'How ofte tyme hath it y-knowen be,
The treson, that to womman hath be do?
To what fyn is swich love, I can nat see,
Or wher bicomth it, whan it is ago;
Ther is no wight that woot, I trowe so,
Wher it bycomth; lo, no wight on it sporneth;
That erst was no-thing, in-to nought it torneth.

115. 'How bisy, if I love, eek moste I be
To plesen hem that jangle of love, and demen,
And coye hem, that they sey non harm of me?

For though ther be no cause, yet hem semen
Al be for harm that folk hir freendes quemen;
And who may stoppen every wikked tonge,
Or soun of belles whyl that they be ronge?'

116. And after that, hir thought bigan to clere,
And seyde, 'he which that no-thing under-taketh,
No-thing ne acheveth, be him looth or dere.'
And with an other thought hir herte quaketh;
Than slepeth hope, and after dreed awaketh;
Now hoot, now cold; but thus, bi-twixen tweye,
She rist hir up, and went hir for to pleye.

117. Adoun the steyre anoon-right tho she wente
In-to the gardin, with hir neces three,
And up and doun ther made many a wente,
Flexippe, she, Tharbe, and Antigone,
To pleyen, that it joye was to see;
And othere of hir wommen, a gret route
Hir folwede in the gardin al aboute.

118. This yerd was large, and rayled alle the aleyes,
And shadwed wel with blosmy bowes grene,
And benched newe, and sonded alle the weyes,
In which she walketh arm in arm bitwene;
Til at the laste Antigone the shene
Gan on a Trojan song to singe clere,
That it an heven was hir voys to here.—

119. She seyde, 'O Love, to whom I have and shal
Ben humble subgit, trewe in myn entente,
As I best can, to yow, lord, yeve ich al
For ever-more, myn hertes lust to rente.
For never yet thy grace no wight sente
So blisful cause as me, my lyf to lede
In alle joye and seurtee, out of drede.

120. 'Ye, blisful god, han me so wel beset
In love, y-wis, that al that bereth lyf
Imaginen ne cowde how to ben bet;
For, lord, with-outen jalousye or stryf,
I love oon which that is most ententyf
To serven wel, unwery or unfeyned,
That ever was, and leest with harm distreyned.

121. 'As he that is the welle of worthinesse,
Of trouthe ground, mirour of goodliheed,
Of wit Appollo, stoon of sikernesse,
Of vertu rote, of luste findere and heed,
Thurgh which is alle sorwe fro me deed,
Y-wis, I love him best, so doth he me;
Now good thrift have he, wher-so that he be!

122. 'Whom sholde I thanke but yow, god of love,
Of al this blisse, in which to bathe I ginne?
And thanked be ye, lord, for that I love!
This is the righte lyf that I am inne,
To flemen alle manere vyce and sinne:
This doth me so to vertu for to entende,
That day by day I in my wil amende.

123. 'And who-so seyth that for to love is vyce,
Or thraldom, though he fele in it distresse,
He outher is envyous, or right nyce,
Or is unmighty, for his shrewednesse,
To loven; for swich maner folk, I gesse,
Defamen Love, as no-thing of him knowe;
They speken, but they bente never his bowe.

124. 'What is the sonne wers, of kinde righte,
Though that a man, for feblesse of his yën,
May nought endure on it to see for brighte?
Or love the wers, though wrecches on it cryen?
No wele is worth, that may no sorwe dryen.
And for-thy, who that hath an heed of verre,
Fro cast of stones war him in the werre!

125. 'But I with al myn herte and al my might,
As I have seyd, wol love, un-to my laste,
My dere herte, and al myn owene knight,
In which myn herte growen is so faste,
And his in me, that it shal ever laste.
Al dredde I first to love him to biginne,
Now woot I wel, ther is no peril inne.'

126. And of hir song right with that word she stente,
And therwith-al, 'now, nece,' quod Criseyde,
'Who made this song with so good entente?'

Antigone answerde anoon, and seyde,
'Ma dame, y-wis, the goodliest mayde
Of greet estat in al the toun of Troye;
And let hir lyf in most honour and joye.'

127. 'Forsothe, so it semeth by hir song,'
Quod tho Criseyde, and gan ther-with to syke,
And seyde, 'lord, is there swich blisse among
These lovers, as they conne fair endyte?'
'Ye, wis,' quod fresh Antigone the whyte,
'For alle the folk that han or been on lyve
Ne conne wel the blisse of love discryve.

128. 'But wene ye that every wrecche woot
The parfit blisse of love? why, nay, y-wis;
They wenen al be love, if oon be hoot;
Do wey, do wey, they woot no-thing of this!
Men mosten axe at seyntes if it is
Aught fair in hevene; why? for they conne telle;
And axen fendes, is it foul in helle.'

129. Criseyde un-to that purpos nought answerde,
But seyde, 'y-wis, it wol be night as faste.'
But every word which that she of hir herde,
She gan to prenten in hir herte faste;
And ay gan love hir lasse for to agaste
Than it dide erst, and sinken in hir herte,
That she wex somwhat able to converte.

130. The dayes honour, and the hevenes yë,
The nightes fo, al this clepe I the sonne,
Gan westren faste, and dounward for to wrye,
As he that hadde his dayes cours y-ronne;
And whyte thinges wexen dimme and donne
For lak of light, and sterres for to appere,
That she and al hir folk in wente y-fere.

131. So whan it lyked hir to goon to reste,
And voyded weren they that voyden oughte,
She seyde, that to slepe wel hir leste.
Hir wommen sone til hir bed hir broughte.
Whan al was hust, than lay she stille, and thoughte
Of al this thing the manere and the wyse.
Reherce it nedeth nought, for ye ben wyse.

132. A nightingale, upon a cedre grene,
Under the chambre-wal ther as she lay,
Ful loude sang ayein the mone shene,
Paraunter, in his briddes wyse, a lay
Of love, that made hir herte fresh and gay,
That herkned she so longe in good entente,
Til at the laste the dede sleep hir hente.

133. And, as she sleep, anoon-right tho hir mette,
How that an egle, fethered whyt as boon,
Under hir brest his longe clawes sette,
And out hir herte he rente, and that a-noon,
And dide his herte in-to hir brest to goon,
Of which she nought agroos ne no-thing smerte,
And forth he fleigh, with herte left for herte.

134. Now lat hir slepe, and we our tales holde
Of Troilus, that is to paleys riden,
Fro the scarmuch, of the whiche I tolde,
And in his chambre sit, and hath abiden
Till two or three of his messages yeden
For Pandarus, and soughten him ful faste,
Til they him founde, and broughte him at the laste.

135. This Pandarus com leping in at ones
And seide thus, 'who hath ben wel y-bete
To-day with swerdes, and with slinge-stones,
But Troilus, that hath caught him an hete?'
And gan to jape, and seyde, 'lord, so ye swete!
But rys, and lat us soupe and go to reste';
And he answerde him, 'do we as thee leste.'

136. With al the haste goodly that they mighte,
They spedde hem fro the souper un-to bedde;
And every wight out at the dore him dighte,
And wher him list upon his wey he spedde;
But Troilus, that thoughte his herte bledde
For wo, till that he herde som tydinge,
He seyde, 'freend, shal I now wepe or singe?'

137. Quod Pandarus, 'ly stille, and lat me slepe,
And don thyn hood, thy nedes spedde be;
And chese, if thou wolt singe or daunce or lepe;

At shorte wordes, thow shalt trowe me.—
Sire, my nece wol do wel by thee,
And love thee best, by god and by my trouthe,
But lak of pursuit make it in thy slouthe.

138. 'For thus ferforth I have thy work bigonne,
Fro day to day, til this day, by the morwe,
Hir love of freendship have I to thee wonne,
And also hath she leyd hir feyth to borwe.
Algate a foot is hameled of thy sorwe.'
What sholde I lenger sermon of it holde?
As ye han herd bifore, al he him tolde.

139. But right as floures, thorugh the colde of nighte
Y-closed, stoupen on hir stalkes lowe,
Redressen hem a-yein the sonne bright,
And spreden on hir kinde cours by rowe;
Right so gan tho his eyen up to throwe
This Troilus, and seyde, 'O Venus dere,
Thy might, thy grace, y-heried be it here!'

140. And to Pandare he held up bothe his hondes,
And seyde, 'lord, al thyn be that I have;
For I am hool, al brosten been my bondes;
A thousand Troians who so that me yave,
Eche after other, god so wis me save,
Ne mighte me so gladen; lo, myn herte,
It spredeth so for joye, it wol to-sterte!

141. 'But lord, how shal I doon, how shal I liven?
Whan shal I next my dere herte see?
How shal this longe tyme a-wey be driven,
Til that thou be ayein at hir fro me?
Thou mayst answere, "a-byd, a-byd," but he
That hangeth by the nekke, soothe to seyne,
In grete disese abydeth for the peyne.'

142. 'Al esily, now, for the love of Marte,'
Quod Pandarus, 'for every thing hath tyme;
So longe abyd til that the night departe;
For al so siker as thow lyst here by me,
And god toforn, I wol be there at pryme,
And for thy werk somwhat as I shal seye,
Or on som other wight this charge leye.

143. 'For pardee, god wot, I have ever yit
Ben redy thee to serve, and to this night
Have I nought fayned, but emforth my wit
Don al thy lust, and shal with al my might.
Do now as I shal seye, and fare a-right;
And if thou nilt, wyte al thy-self thy care,
On me is nought along thyn yvel fare.

144. 'I woot wel that thow wyser art than I
A thousand fold, but if I were as thou,
God helpe me so, as I wolde outrely,
Right of myn owene hond, wryte hir right now
A lettre, in which I wolde hir tellen how
I ferde amis, and hir beseche of routhe;
Now help thy-self, and leve it not for slouthe.

145. 'And I my-self shal ther-with to hir goon;
And whan thou wost that I am with hir there,
Worth thou up-on a courser right anoon,
Ye, hardily, right in thy beste gere,
And ryd forth by the place, as nought ne were,
And thou shalt finde us, if I may, sittinge
At som windowe, in-to the strete lokinge.

146. 'And if thee list, than maystow us saluwe,
And up-on me makë thy contenaunce;
But, by thy lyf, be war and faste eschuwe
To tarien ought, god shilde us fro mischaunce!
Ryd forth thy wey, and hold thy governaunce;
And we shal speke of thee som-what, I trowe,
Whan thou art goon, to do thyne eres glowe!

147. 'Touching thy lettre, thou art wys y-nough,
I woot thow nilt it digneliche endyte;
As make it with thise argumentes tough;
Ne scrivenish or craftily thou it wryte;
Beblotte it with thy teres eek a lyte;
And if thou wryte a goodly word al softe,
Though it be good, reherce it not to ofte.

148. 'For though the beste harpour upon lyve
Wolde on the beste souned joly harpe
That ever was, with alle his fingres fyve,

Touche ay o streng, or ay o werbul harpe,
Were his nayles poynted never so sharpe,
It shulde maken every wight to dulle,
To here his glee, and of his strokes fulle.

149. 'Ne jompre eek no discordaunt thing y-fere,
As thus, to usen termes of phisyk;
In loves termes, hold of thy matere
The forme alwey, and do that it be lyk;
For if a peyntour wolde peynte a pyk
With asses feet, and hede it as an ape,
It cordeth nought; so nere it but a jape.'

150. This counseyl lyked wel to Troilus;
But as a dreedful lover, he seyde this:—
'Allas, my dere brother Pandarus,
I am ashamed for to wryte, y-wis,
Lest of myn innocence I seyde a-mis,
Or that she nolde it for despyt receyve;
Thanne were I deed, ther mighte it nothing weyve.'

151. To that Pandare answerde, 'if thee lest,
Do that I seye, and lat me therwith goon;
For by that lord that formed est and west,
I hope of it to bringe answere anoon
Right of hir hond, and if that thou nilt noon,
Lat be; and sory mote he been his lyve,
Ayeins thy lust that helpeth thee to thryve.'

152. Quod Troilus, '*Depardieux*, I assente;
Sin that thee list, I will aryse and wryte;
And blisful god preye ich, with good entente,
The vyage, and the lettre I shal endyte,
So spede it; and thou, Minerva, the whyte,
Yif thou me wit my lettre to devyse':
And sette him doun, and wroot right in this wyse.—

153. First he gan hir his righte lady calle,
His hertes lyf, his lust, his sorwes leche,
His blisse, and eek this othere termes alle,
That in swich cas these loveres alle seche;
And in ful humble wyse, as in his speche,
He gan him recomaunde un-to hir grace;
To telle al how, it axeth muchel space.

154. And after this, ful lowly he hir prayde
To be nought wrooth, though he, of his folye,
So hardy was to hir to wryte, and seyde,
That love it made, or elles moste he dye,
And pitously gan mercy for to crye;
And after that he seyde, and ley ful loude,
Him-self was litel worth, and lesse he coude;

155. And that she sholde han his conning excused,
That litel was, and eek he dredde hir so,
And his unworthinesse he ay acused;
And after that, than gan he telle his wo;
But that was endeles, with-outen ho;
And seyde, he wolde in trouthe alwey him holde;—
And radde it over, and gan the lettre folde.

156. And with his salte teres gan he bathe
The ruby in his signet, and it sette
Upon the wex deliverliche and rathe;
Ther-with a thousand tymes, er he lette,
He kiste tho the lettre that he shette,
And seyde, 'lettre, a blisful destenee
Thee shapen is, my lady shal thee see.'

157. This Pandare took the lettre, and that by tyme
A-morwe, and to his neces paleys sterte,
And faste he swoor, that it was passed pryme,
And gan to jape, and seyde, 'y-wis, myn herte,
So fresh it is, al-though it sore smerte,
I may not slepe never a Mayes morwe;
I have a joly wo, a lusty sorwe.'

158. Criseyde, whan that she hir uncle herde,
With dreedful herte, and desirous to here
The cause of his cominge, thus answerde,
'Now by your feyth, myn uncle,' quod she, 'dere,
What maner windes gydeth yow now here?
Tel us your joly wo and your penaunce,
How ferforth be ye put in loves daunce.'

159. 'By god,' quod he, 'I hoppe alwey bihinde!'
And she to-laugh, it thoughte hir herte breste.
Quod Pandarus, 'loke alwey that ye finde

Game in myn hood, but herkneth, if yow leste;
Ther is right now come in-to toune a geste,
A Greek espye, and telleth newe thinges,
For which come I to telle yow tydinges.

160. 'Into the gardin go we, and we shal here,
Al prevely, of this a long sermoun.'
With that they wenten arm in arm y-fere
In-to the gardin from the chaumbre doun.
And whan that he so fer was that the soun
Of that he speke, no man here mighte,
He seyde hir thus, and out the lettre plighte,

161. 'Lo, he that is al hoolly youres free
Him recomaundeth lowly to your grace,
And sent to you this lettre here by me;
Avyseth you on it, whan ye han space,
And of som goodly answere yow purchace;
Or, helpe me god, so pleynly for to seyne,
He may not longe liven for his peyne.'

162. Ful dredfully tho gan she stonde stille,
And took it nought, but al hir humble chere
Gan for to chaunge, and seyde, 'scrit ne bille,
For love of god, that toucheth swich matere,
Ne bring me noon; and also, uncle dere,
To myn estat have more reward, I preye,
Than to his lust; what sholde I more seye?

163. 'And loketh now if this be resonable,
And letteth nought, for favour ne for slouthe,
To seyn a sooth; now were it convenable
To myn estat, by god, and by your trouthe,
To taken it, or to han of him routhe,
In harming of my-self or in repreve?
Ber it a-yein, for him that ye on leve!'

164. This Pandarus gan on hir for to stare,
And seyde, 'now is this the grettest wonder
That ever I sey! lat be this nyce fare!
To deethe mote I smiten be with thonder,
If, for the citee which that stondeth yonder,
Wolde I a lettre un-to yow bringe or take
To harm of yow; what list yow thus it make?

165. 'But thus ye faren, wel neigh alle and some,
That he that most desireth yow to serve,
Of him ye recche leest wher he bicome,
And whether that he live or elles sterve.
But for al that that ever I may deserve,
Refuse it nought,' quod he, and hente hir faste,
And in hir bosom the lettre doun he thraste,

166. And seyde hir, 'now cast it away anoon,
That folk may seen and gauren on us tweye.'
Quod she, 'I can abyde till they be goon,'
And gan to smyle, and seyde him, 'eem, I preye,
Swich answere as yow list your-self purveye,
For trewely I nil no lettre wryte.'
'No? than wol I,' quod he, 'so ye endyte.'

167. Therwith she lough, and seyde, 'go we dyne.'
And he gan at him-self to jape faste,
And seyde, 'nece, I have so greet a pyne
For love, that every other day I faste'—
And gan his beste japes forth to caste;
And made hir so to laughe at his folye,
That she for laughter wende for to dye.

168. And whan that she was comen in-to halle,
'Now, eem,' quod she, 'we wol go dyne anoon';
And gan some of hir women to hir calle,
And streyght in-to hir chaumbre gan she goon;
But of hir besinesses, this was oon
A-monges othere thinges, out of drede,
Ful prively this lettre for to rede;

169. Avysed word by word in every lyne,
And fond no lak, she thoughte he coude good;
And up it putte, and went hir in to dyne.
And Pandarus, that in a study stood,
Er he was war, she took him by the hood,
And seyde, 'ye were caught er that ye wiste';
'I vouche sauf,' quod he, 'do what yow liste.'

170. Tho wesshen they, and sette hem doun and etc;
And after noon ful sleyly Pandarus
Gan drawe him to the window next the strete,

And seyde, 'nece, who hath arayed thus
The yonder hous, that stant afor-yeyn us?'
'Which hous?' quod she, and gan for to biholde,
And knew it wel, and whos it was him tolde,

171. And fillen forth in speche of thinges smale,
And seten in the window bothe tweye,
Whan Pandarus saw tyme un-to his tale,
And saw wel that hir folk were alle aweye,
'Now, nece myn, tel on,' quod he, 'I seye,
How lyketh yow the lettre that ye woot?
Can he ther-on? for, by my trouthe, I noot.'

172. Therwith al rosy hewed tho wex she,
And gan to humme, and seyde, 'so I trowe.'
'Aquyte him wel, for goddes love,' quod he;
'My-self to medes wol the lettre sowe,'
And held his hondes up, and sat on knowe,
'Now, goode nece, be it never so lyte,
Yif me the labour, it to sowe and plyte.'

173. 'Ye, for I can so wryte,' quod she tho;
'And eek I noot what I sholde to him seye.'
'Nay, nece,' quod Pandare, 'sey not so;
Yet at the leste thanketh him, I preye,
Of his good wil, and doth him not to deye.
Now for the love of me, my nece dere,
Refuseth not at this tyme my preyere.'

174. 'Depardieux,' quod she, 'god leve al be wel!
God helpe me so, this is the firste lettre
That ever I wroot, ye, al or any del.'
And in-to a closet, for to avyse hir bettre,
She wente allone, and gan hir herte unfettre
Out of disdaynes prison but a lyte;
And sette hir doun, and gan a lettre wryte,

175. Of which to tell in short is myn entente
Th' effect, as fer as I can understonde:—
She thonked him of al that he wel mente
Towardes hir, but holden him in honde
She nolde nought, ne make hir-selven bonde
In love, but as his suster, him to plese,
She wolde fayn, to doon his herte an ese.

176. She shette it, and to Pandarus gan goon,
There as he sat and loked in-to strete,
And doun she sette hir by him on a stoon
Of jaspre, up-on a quisshin gold y-bete,
And seyde, 'as wisly helpe me god the grete,
I never dide a thing with more peyne
Than wryte this, to which ye me constreyne';

177. And took it him: he thonked hir and seyde,
'God woot, of thing ful ofte looth bigonne
Cometh ende good; and nece myn, Criseyde,
That ye to him of hard now ben y-wonne
Oughte he be glad, by god and yonder sonne!
For-why men seyth, "impressioun[e]s lighte
Ful lightly been ay redy to the flighte."

178. 'But ye han pleyed tyraunt neigh to longe,
And hard was it your herte for to grave;
Now stint, that ye no longer on it honge,
Al wolde ye the forme of daunger save.
But hasteth yow to doon him joye have;
For trusteth wel, to longe y-doon hardnesse
Causeth despyt ful often, for distresse.'

179. And right as they declamed this matere,
Lo, Troilus, right at the stretes ende,
Com ryding with his tenthe some y-fere,
Al softely, and thiderward gan bende
Ther-as they sete, as was his wey to wende
To paleys-ward; and Pandare him aspyde,
And seyde, 'nece, y-see who cometh here ryde!

180. 'O flee not in, he seeth us, I suppose;
Lest he may thinke that ye him eschuwe.'
'Nay, nay,' quod she, and wex as reed as rose.
With that he gan hir humbly to saluwe,
With dreedful chere, and ofte his hewes muwe;
And up his look debonairly he caste,
And bekked on Pandare, and forth he paste.

181. God woot if he sat on his hors a-right,
Or goodly was beseyn, that ilke day!
God woot wher he was lyk a manly knight!

What sholde I drecche, or telle of his aray?
Criseyde, which that alle these thinges say,
To telle in short, hir lyked al y-fere,
His persone, his aray, his look, his chere,

182. His goodly manere and his gentillesse,
So wel, that never, sith that she was born,
Ne hadde she swich routhe of his distresse;
And how-so she hath hard ben her-biforn,
To god hope I, she hath now caught a thorn.
She shal not pulle it out this nexte wyke;
God sende mo swich thornes on to pyke!

183. Pandare, which that stood hir faste by,
Felte iren hoot, and he bigan to smyte,
And seyde, 'nece, I pray yow hertely,
Tel me that I shal axen yow a lyte.
A womman, that were of his deeth to wyte,
With-outen his gilt, but for hir lakked routhe,
Were it wel doon?' Quod she, 'nay, by my trouthe!'

184. 'God helpe me so,' quod he, 'ye sey me sooth.
Ye felen wel your-self that I not lye;
Lo, yond he rit!' Quod she, 'ye, so he dooth.'
'Wel,' quod Pandare, 'as I have told yow thrye,
Lat be your nyce shame and your folye,
And spek with him in esing of his herte;
Lat nycetee not do yow bothe smerte.'

185. But ther-on was to heven and to done;
Considered al thing, it may not be;
And why, for shame; and it were eek to sone
To graunten him so greet a libertee;
'For playnly hir entente,' as seyde she,
'Was for to love him unwist, if she mighte,
And guerdon him with no-thing but with sighte.'

186. But Pandarus thoughte, 'it shal not be so,
If that I may; this nyce opinioun
Shal not be holden fully yeres two.'
What sholde I make of this a long sermoun?
He moste assente on that conclusioun
As for the tyme; and whan that it was eve,
And al was wel, he roos and took his leve.

187. And on his wey ful faste homward he spedde,
And right for joye he felte his herte daunce;
And Troilus he fond alone a-bedde,
That lay as dooth these loveres, in a traunce,
Bitwixen hope and dark desesperaunce.
But Pandarus, right at his in-cominge,
He song, as who seyth, 'lo! sumwhat I bringe.'

188. And seyde, 'who is in his bed so sone
Y-buried thus?' 'It am I, freend,' quod he.
'Who, Troilus? nay helpe me so the mone,'
Quod Pandarus, 'thou shalt aryse and see
A charme that was sent right now to thee,
The which can helen thee of thyn accesse,
If thou do forth-with al thy besinesse.'

189. 'Ye, through the might of god!' quod Troilus.
And Pandarus gan him the lettre take,
And seyde, 'pardee, god hath holpen us;
Have here a light, and loke on al this blake.'
But ofte gan the herte glade and quake
Of Troilus, whyl that he gan it rede,
So as the wordes yave him hope or drede.

190. But fynally, he tok al for the beste
That she him wroot, for sumwhat he biheld
On which, him thoughte, he mighte his herte reste,
Al covered she the wordes under sheld.
Thus to the more worthy part he held,
That, what for hope and Pandarus biheste,
His grete wo for-yede he at the leste.

191. But as we may alday our-selven see,
Through more wode or col, the more fyr;
Right so encrees of hope, of what it be,
Therwith ful ofte encreseth eek desyr;
Or, as an ook cometh of a litel spyr,
So through this lettre, which that she him sente,
Encresen gan desyr, of which he brente.

192. Wherfore I seye alwey, that day and night
This Troilus gan to desiren more
Than he dide erst, thurgh hope, and dide his might

To pressen on, as by Pandarus lore,
And wryten to hir of his sorwes sore
Fro day to day; he leet it not refreyde,
That by Pandare he wroot somwhat or seyde;

193. And dide also his othere observaunces
That to a lovere longeth in this cas;
And, after that these dees turnede on chaunces,
So was he outher glad or seyde 'allas!'
And held after his gestes ay his pas;
And aftir swiche answeres as he hadde,
So were his dayes sory outher gladde.

194. But to Pandare alwey was his recours,
And pitously gan ay til him to pleyne,
And him bisoughte of rede and som socours;
And Pandarus, that sey his wode peyne,
Wex wel neigh deed for routhe, sooth to seyne,
And bisily with al his herte caste
Som of his wo to sleen, and that as faste;

195. And seyde, 'lord, and freend, and brother dere,
God woot that thy disese doth me wo.
But woltow stinten al this woful chere,
And, by my trouthe, or it be dayes two,
And god to-forn, yet shal I shape it so,
That thou shalt come in-to a certayn place,
Ther-as thou mayst thy-self hir preye of grace.

196. 'And certainly, I noot if thou it wost,
But tho that been expert in love it seye,
It is oon of the thinges that furthereth most,
A man to have a leyser for to preye,
And siker place his wo for to biwreye;
For in good herte it moot som routhe impresse,
To here and see the giltles in distresse.

197. 'Paraunter thenkestow: though it be so
That kinde wolde doon hir to biginne
To han a maner routhe up-on my wo.
Seyth Daunger, "Nay, thou shalt me never winne;
So reuleth hir hir hertes goost with-inne,
That, though she bende, yet she stant on rote;
What in effect is this un-to my bote?"

198. 'Thenk here-ayeins, whan that the sturdy ook,
On which men hakketh ofte, for the nones,
Receyved hath the happy falling strook,
The grete sweigh doth it come al at ones,
As doon these rokkes or these milne-stones.
For swifter cours cometh thing that is of wighte,
Whan it descendeth, than don thinges lighte.

199. 'And reed that boweth doun for every blast,
Ful lightly, cesse wind, it wol aryse;
But so nil not an ook whan it is cast;
It nedeth me nought thee longe to forbyse.
Men shal rejoysen of a greet empryse
Acheved wel, and stant with-outen doute,
Al han men been the lenger ther-aboute.

200. 'But, Troilus, yet tel me, if thee lest,
A thing now which that I shal axen thee;
Which is thy brother that thou lovest best
As in thy verray hertes privitee?'
'Y-wis, my brother Deiphebus,' quod he.
'Now,' quod Pandare, 'er houres twyes twelve,
He shal thee ese, unwist of it him-selve.

201. 'Now lat me allone, and werken as I may,'
Quod he; and to Deiphebus wente he tho
Which hadde his lord and grete freend ben ay;
Save Troilus, no man he lovede so.
To telle in short, with-outen wordes mo,
Quod Pandarus, 'I pray yow that ye be
Freend to a cause which that toucheth me.'

202. 'Yis, pardee,' quod Deiphebus, 'wel thow wost,
In al that ever I may, and god to-fore,
Al nere it but for man I love most,
My brother Troilus; but sey wherfore
It is; for sith that day that I was bore,
I nas, ne never-mo to been I thinke,
Ayeins a thing that mighte thee for-thinke.'

203. Pandare gan him thonke, and to him seyde,
'Lo, sire, I have a lady in this toun,
That is my nece, and called is Criseyde,

Which som men wolden doon oppressioun,
And wrongfully have hir possessioun:
Wherfor I of your lordship yow biseche
To been our freend, with-oute more speche.'

204. Deiphebus him answerde, 'O, is not this,
That thow spekest of to me thus straungely,
Crisëyda, my freend?' He seyde, 'Yis.'
'Than nedeth,' quod Deiphebus hardely,
'Na-more to speke, for trusteth wel, that I
Wol be hir champioun with spore and yerde;
I roughte nought though alle hir foos it herde.

205. 'But tel me, thou that woost al this matere,
How I might best avaylen? now lat see.'
Quod Pandarus, 'if ye, my lord so dere,
Wolden as now don this honour to me,
To prayen hir to-morwe, lo, that she
Com un-to yow hir pleyntes to devyse,
Hir adversaries wolde of hit agryse.

206. 'And if I more dorste preye as now,
And chargen yow to have so greet travayle,
To han som of your bretheren here with yow,
That mighten to hir cause bet avayle,
Than, woot I wel, she mighte never fayle
For to holpen, what at your instaunce,
What with hir othere freendes governaunce.'

207. Deiphebus, which that comen was, of kinde,
To al honour and bountee to consente,
Answerde, 'it shal be doon; and I can finde
Yet gretter help to this in myn entente.
What wolt thow seyn, if I for Eleyne sente
To speke of this? I trow it be the beste;
For she may leden Paris as hir leste.

208. 'Of Ector, which that is my lord, my brother,
It nedeth nought to preye him freend to be;
For I have herd him, o tyme and eek other,
Speke of Criseyde swich honour, that he
May seyn no bet, swich hap to him hath she.
It nedeth nought his helpes for to crave;
He shal be swich, right as we wole him have.

209. 'Speke thou thy-self also to Troilus
On my bihalve, and pray him with us dyne.'
'Sire, al this shal be doon,' quod Pandarus;
And took his leve, and never gan to fyne,
But to his neces hous, as streght as lyne,
He com; and fond hir fro the mete aryse;
And sette him doun, and spak right in this wyse.

210. He seyde, 'O veray god, so have I ronne!
Lo, nece myn, see ye nought how I swete?
I noot whether ye the more thank me conne.
Be ye nought war how that fals Poliphete
Is now aboute eft-sones for to plete,
And bringe on yow advocacyës newe?'
'I? no,' quod she, and chaunged al hir hewe.

211. 'What is he more aboute, me to drecche
And doon me wrong? what shal I do, allas?
Yet of him-self no-thing ne wolde I recche,
Nere it for Antenor and Eneas,
That been his freendes in swich maner cas;
But, for the love of god, myn uncle dere,
No fors of that, lat him have al y-fere;

212. 'With-outen that, I have ynough for us.'
'Nay,' quod Pandare, 'it shal no-thing be so.
For I have been right now at Deiphebus,
And Ector, and myne othere lordes mo,
And shortly maked eche of hem his fo;
That, by my thrift, he shal it never winne
For ought he can, whan that so he biginne.'

213. And as they casten what was best to done,
Deiphebus, of his owene curtasye,
Com hir to preye, in his propre persone,
To holde him on the morwe companye
At diner, which she nolde not denye,
But goodly gan to his preyere obeye,
He thonked hir, and wente up-on his weye.

214. Whanne this was doon, this Pandare up a-noon,
To telle in short, and forth gan for to wende
To Troilus, as stille as any stoon,

And al this thing he tolde him, word and ende;
And how that he Deiphebus gan to blende;
And seyde him, 'now is tyme, if that thou conne,
To bere thee wel to-morwe, and al is wonne.

215. 'Now spek, now prey, now pitously compleyne;
Lat not for nyce shame, or drede, or slouthe;
Som-tyme a man mot telle his owene peyne;
Bileve it, and she shal han on thee routhe;
Thou shalt be saved by thy feyth, in trouthe.
But wel wot I, thou art now in a drede;
And what it is, I leye, I can arede.

216. 'Thow thinkest now, "how sholde I doon al this?
For by my cheres mosten folk aspye,
That for hir love is that I fare a-mis;
Yet hadde I lever unwist for sorwe dye."
Now thenk not so, for thou dost greet folye.
For right now have I founden o manere
Of sleighte, for to coveren al thy chere.

217. 'Thow shalt gon over night, and that as blyve,
Un-to Deiphebus hous, as thee to pleye,
Thy maladye a-wey the bet to dryve,
For-why thou semest syk, soth for to seye,
Sone after that, doun in thy bed thee leye,
And sey, thow mayst no lenger up endure,
And lye right there, and byde thyn aventure.

218. 'Sey that thy fever is wont thee for to take
The same tyme, and lasten til a-morwe;
And lat see now how wel thou canst it make,
For, par-dee, syk is he that is in sorwe.
Go now, farewel! and, Venus here to borwe,
I hope, and thou this purpos holde ferme,
Thy grace she shal fully ther conferme.'

219. Quod Troilus, 'y-wis, thou nedelees
Counseylest me, that sykliche I me feyne!
For I am syk in ernest, douteless,
So that wel neigh I sterve for the peyne.'
Quod Pandarus, 'thou shalt the bettre pleyne,
And hast the lasse nede to countrefete;
For him men demen hoot that men seen swete.

220. 'Lo, holde thee at thy triste cloos, and I
Shal wel the deer un-to thy bowe dryve.'
Therwith he took his leve al softely,
And Troilus to paleys wente blyve.
So glad ne was he never in al his lyve;
And to Pandarus reed gan al assente,
And to Deiphebus hous at night he wente.

221. What nedeth yow to tellen al the chere
That Deiphebus un-to his brother made,
Or his accesse, or his syklich manere,
How men gan him with clothes for to lade,
Whan he was leyd, and how men wolde him glade?
But al for nought, he held forth ay the wyse
That ye han herd Pandare er this devyse.

222. But certeyn is, er Troilus him leyde,
Deiphebus had him prayed, over night,
To been a freend and helping to Criseyde.
God woot, that he it grauntede anon-right,
To been hir fulle freend with al his might.
But swich a nede was to preye him thenne,
As for to bidde a wood man for to renne.

223. The morwen com, and neighen gan the tyme
Of meel-tyd, that the faire quene Eleyne
Shoop hir to been, an houre after the pryme,
With Deiphebus, to whom she nolde feyne;
But as his suster, hoomly, sooth to seyne,
She com to diner in hir playn entente.
But god and Pandare wiste al what this mente.

224. Come eek Criseyde, all innocent of this,
Antigone, hir sister Tarbe also;
But flee we now prolixitee best is,
For love of god, and lat us faste go
Right to the effect, with-oute tales mo,
Why al this folk assembled in this place;
And lat us of hir saluinges pace.

225. Gret honour dide hem Deiphebus, certeyn,
And fedde hem wel with al that mighte lyke.
But ever-more, 'allas!' was his refreyn,

'My goode brother Troilus, the syke,
Lyth yet'—and therwith-al he gan to syke;
And after that, he peyned him to glade
Hem as he mighte, and chere good he made.

226. Compleyned eek Eleyne of his syknesse
So feithfully, that pitee was to here,
And every wight gan waxen for accesse
A leche anoon, and seyde, 'in this manere
Men curen folk: this charme I wol yow lere.'
But there sat oon, al list hir nought to teche,
That thoughte, best coude I yet been his leche.

227. After compleynt, him gonnen they to preyse,
As folk don yet, whan som wight hath bigonne
To preyse a man, and up with prys him reyse
A thousand fold yet hyer than the sonne:—
'He is, he can, that fewe lordes conne.'
And Pandarus, of that they wolde afferme,
He not for-gat hir preysing to conferme.

228. Herde al this thing Criseyde wel y-nough,
And every word gan for to notifye;
For which with sobre chere hir herte lough;
For who is that ne wolde hir glorifye,
To mowen swich a knight don live or dye?
But al passe I, lest ye to longe dwelle;
For for o fyn is al that ever I telle.

229. The tyme com, fro diner for to ryse,
And, as hem oughte, arisen everychoon,
And gonne a whyl of this and that devyse.
But Pandarus brak al this speche anoon,
And seyde to Deiphebus, 'wole ye goon,
If yourë wille be, as I yow preyde,
To speke here of the nedes of Criseyde?'

230. Eleyne, which that by the hond hir held,
Took first the tale, and seyde, 'go we blyve';
And goodly on Criseyde she biheld,
And seyde, 'Joves lat him never thryve,
That dooth yow harm, and bringe him sone of lyve!
And yeve me sorwe, but he shal it rewe,
If that I may, and alle folk be trewe.'

231. 'Tel thou thy neces cas,' quod Deiphebus
To Pandarus, 'for thou canst best it telle.'—
'My lordes and my ladyes, it stant thus;
What sholde I lenger,' quod he, 'do you dwelle?'
He rong hem out a proces lyk a belle,
Up-on hir fo, that highte Poliphete,
So hëynous, that men mighte on it spete.

232. Answerde of this ech worse of hem than other,
And Poliphete they gonnen thus to warien,
'An-honged be swich oon, were he my brother;
And so he shal, for it ne may not varien.'
What sholde I lenger in this tale tarien?
Pleynly, alle at ones, they hir highten,
To been hir helpe in al that ever they mighten.

233. Spak than Eleyne, and seyde, 'Pandarus,
Woot ought my lord, my brother, this matere,
I mene, Ector? or woot it Troilus?'
He seyde, 'ye, but wole ye now me here?
Me thinketh this, sith Troilus is here,
It were good, if that ye wolde assente,
She tolde hir-self him al this, er she wente.

234. 'For he wole have the more hir grief at herte,
By cause, lo, that she a lady is;
And, by your leve, I wol but right in sterte,
And do yow wite, and that anoon, y-wis,
If that he slepe, or wole ought here of this.'
And in he lepte, and seyde him in his ere,
'God have thy soule, y-brought have I thy bere!'

235. To smylen of this gan tho Troilus,
And Pandarus, with-oute rekeninge,
Out went anoon t' Eleyne and Deiphebus,
And seyde hem, 'so there be no taryinge,
Ne more pres, he wol wel that ye bringe
Crisëyda, my lady, that is here;
And as he may enduren, he wole here.

236. 'But wel ye woot, the chaumbre is but lyte,
And fewe folk may lightly make it warm;
Now loketh ye (for I wol have no wyte,

To bringe in prees that mighte doon him harm
Or him disesen, for my bettre arm),
Wher it be bet she byde til eft-sones;
Now loketh ye, that knowen what to doon is.

237. 'I sey for me, best is, as I can knowe,
That no wight in ne wente but ye tweye,
But it were I, for I can, in a throwe,
Reherce hir cas, unlyk that she can seye;
And after this, she may him ones preye
To ben good lord, in short, and take hir leve;
This may not muchel of his ese him reve.

238. 'And eek, for she is straunge, he wol forbere
His ese, which that him thar nought for yow;
Eek other thing, that toucheth not to here,
He wol me telle, I woot it wel right now,
That secret is, and for the tounes prow.'
And they, that no-thing knewe of this entente,
With-oute more, to Troilus in they wente.

239. Eleyne in al hir goodly softe wyse,
Gan him saluwe, and womanly to pleye,
And seyde, 'ywis, ye moste alweyes aryse!
Now fayre brother, beth al hool, I preye!'
And gan hir arm right over his sholder leye,
And him with al hir wit to recomforte;
As she best coude, she gan him to disporte.

240. So after this quod she, 'we yow biseke,
My dere brother, Deiphebus, and I,
For love of god, and so doth Pandare eke,
To been good lord and freend, right hertely,
Un-to Criseyde, which that certeinly
Receyveth wrong, as woot wel here Pandare
That can hir cas wel bet than I declare.'

241. This Pandarus gan newe his tunge affyle,
And al hir cas reherce, and that anoon;
Whan it was seyd, sone after, in a whyle,
Quod Troilus, 'as sone as I may goon,
I wol right fayn with al my might ben oon,
Have god my trouthe, hir cause to sustene.'
'Good thrift have ye,' quod Eleyne the quene.

242. Quod Pandarus, 'and it your wille be,
That she may take hir leve, er that she go?'
'Or elles god for-bede,' tho quod he,
'If that she vouche sauf for to do so.'
And with that word quod Troilus, 'ye two,
Deiphebus, and my suster leef and dere,
To yow have I to speke of o matere,

243. 'To been avysed by your reed the bettre':—
And fond, as hap was, at his beddes heed,
The copie of a tretis and a lettre,
That Ector hadde him sent to axen reed,
If swich a man was worthy to ben deed,
Woot I nought who; but in a grisly wyse
He preyede hem anoon on it avyse.

244. Deiphebus gan this lettre to unfolde
In ernest greet; so dide Eleyne the quene;
And rominge outward, fast it gan biholde,
Downward a steyre, in-to an herber grene,
This ilke thing they redden hem bi-twene;
And largely, the mountaunce of an houre,
They gonne on it to reden and to poure.

245. Now lat hem rede, and turne we anoon
To Pandarus, that gan ful faste prye
That al was wel, and out he gan to goon
In-to the grete chambre, and that in hye,
And seyde, 'god save al this companye!
Com, nece myn; my lady quene Eleyne
Abydeth yow, and eek my lordes tweyne.

246. 'Rys, take with yow your nece Antigone,
Or whom yow list, or no fors, hardily;
The lasse prees, the bet; com forth with me,
And loke that ye thonke humblely
Hem alle three, and, whan ye may goodly
Your tyme y-see, taketh of hem your leve,
Lest we to longe his restes him bireve.'

247. Al innocent of Pandarus entente,
Quod tho Criseyde, 'go we, uncle dere';
And arm in arm inward with him she wente,

Avysed wel hir wordes and hir chere;
And Pandarus, in ernestful manere,
Seyde, 'alle folk, for goddes love, I preye,
Stinteth right here, and softely yow pleye.

248. 'Aviseth yow what folk ben here with-inne,
And in what plyt oon is, god him amende!
And inward thus ful softely biginne;
Nece, I conjure and heighly yow defende,
On his half, which that sowle us alle sende,
And in the vertue of corounes tweyne,
Slee nought this man, that hath for yow this peyne!

249. 'Fy on the devel! thenk which oon he is,
And in what plyt he lyth; com of anoon;
Thenk al swich taried tyd, but lost it nis!
That wol ye bothe seyn, whan ye ben oon.
Secoundelich, ther yet devyneth noon
Up-on yow two; com of now, if ye conne;
Whyl folk is blent, lo, al the tyme is wonne!

250. 'In titering, and pursuite, and delayes,
The folk devyne at wagginge of a stree;
And though ye wolde han after merye dayes,
Than dar ye nought, and why? for she, and she
Spak swich a word; thus loked he, and he;
Lest tyme I loste, I dar not with yow dele;
Com of therfore, and bringeth him to hele.'

251. But now to yow, ye lovers that ben here,
Was Troilus nought in a cankedort,
That lay, and mighte whispringe of hem here,
And thoughte, 'O lord, right now renneth my sort
Fully to dye, or han anoon comfort';
And was the firste tyme he shulde hir preye
Of love; O mighty god, what shal he seye?

Explicit Secundus Liber

BOOK III

Incipit prohemium Tercii Libri

1. O BLISFUL light, of whiche the bemes clere
Adorneth al the thridde hevene faire!
O sonnes leef, O Joves doughter dere,
Plesaunce of love, O goodly debonaire,
In gentil hertes ay redy to repaire!
O verray cause of hele and of gladnesse,
Y-heried be thy might and thy goodnesse!

2. In hevene and helle, in erthe and salte see
Is felt thy might, if that I wel descerne;
As man, brid, best, fish, herbe and grene tree
Thee fele in tymes with vapour eterne.
God loveth, and to love wol nought werne;
And in this world no lyves creature,
With-outen love, is worth, or may endure.

3. Ye Joves first to thilke effectes glade,
Thorugh which that thinges liven alle and be,
Comeveden, and amorous him made
On mortal thing, and as yow list, ay ye
Yeve him in love ese or adversitee;
And in a thousand formes doun him sente
For love in erthe, and whom yow liste, he hente.

4. Ye fierse Mars apeysen of his ire,
And, as yow list, ye maken hertes digne;
Algates, hem that ye wol sette a-fyre,
They dreden shame, and vices they resigne;
Ye do hem corteys be, fresshe and benigne,
And hye or lowe, after a wight entendeth;
The joyes that he hath, your might him sendeth.

5. Ye holden regne and hous in unitee;
Ye soothfast cause of frendship been also;
Ye knowe al thilke covered qualitee
Of thinges which that folk on wondren so,
Whan they can not construe how it may jo,
She loveth him, or why he loveth here;
As why this fish, and nought that, cometh to were.

6. Ye folk a lawe han set in universe,
And this knowe I by hem that loveres be,
That who-so stryveth with yow hath the werse:
Now, lady bright, for thy benignitee,
At reverence of hem that serven thee,
Whos clerk I am, so techeth me devyse
Som joye of that is felt in thy servyse.

7. Ye in my naked herte sentement
Inhelde, and do me shewe of thy swetnesse.—
Caliope, thy vois be now present,
For now is nede; sestow not my destresse,
How I mot telle anon-right the gladnesse
Of Troilus, to Venus heryinge?
To which gladnes, who nede hath, god him bringe!

Explicit prohemium Tercii Libri

Incipit Liber Tercius

8. Lay al this mene whyle Troilus,
Recordinge his lessoun in this manere,
'Ma fey!' thought he, 'thus wole I seye and thus;
Thus wole I pleyne un-to my lady dere;
That word is good, and this shal be my chere;
This nil I not foryeten in no wyse.'
God leve him werken as he gan devyse.

9. And lord, so that his herte gan to quappe,
Heringe hir come, and shorte for to syke!
And Pandarus, that ladde hir by the lappe,
Com neer, and gan in at the curtin pyke,
And seyd, 'god do bote on alle syke!
See, who is here yow comen to visyte;
Lo, here is she that is your deeth to wyte.'

10. Ther-with it seemed as he wepte almost;
'A ha,' quod Troilus so rewfully,
'Wher me be wo, O mighty god, thou wost!
Who is al there? I see nought trewely.'
'Sire,' quod Criseyde, 'it is Pandare and I.'
'Ye, swete herte? allas, I may nought ryse
To knele, and do yow honour in som wyse.'

11. And dressede him upward, and she right tho
Gan bothe here hondes softe upon him leye,
⸵'O, for the love of god, do ye not so
To me,' quod she, 'ey! what is this to seye?
Sire, come am I to yow for causes tweye;
First, yow to thonke, and of your lordshipe eke
Continuaunce I wolde yow biseke.'

12. This Troilus, that herde his lady preye
Of lordship him, wex neither quik ne deed,
Ne mighte a word for shame to it seye,
Al-though men sholde smyten of his heed.
But lord, so he wex sodeinliche reed,
And sire, his lesson, that he wende conne,
To preyen hir, is thurgh his wit y-ronne.

13. Criseyde al this aspyede wel y-nough,
For she was wys, and lovede him never-the-lasse,
Al nere he malapert, or made it tough,
Or was to bold, to singe a fool a masse.
But whan his shame gan somwhat to passe,
His resons, as I may my rymes holde,
I yow wol telle, as techen bokes olde.

14. In chaunged vois, right for his verrey drede,
Which vois eek quook, and ther-to his manere
Goodly abayst, and now his hewes rede,
Now pale, un-to Criseyde, his lady dere,
With look doun cast and humble yolden chere,
Lo, th' alderfirste word that him asterte
Was, twyes, 'mercy, mercy, swete herte!'

15. And stinte a whyl, and whan he mighte out-bringe,
The nexte word was, 'god wot, for I have,
As feythfully, as I have had konninge,
Ben youres, also god my sowle save;
And shal, til that I, woful wight, be grave.
And though I dar ne can un-to yow pleyne,
Y-wis, I suffre nought the lasse peyne.

16. 'Thus muche as now, O wommanliche wyf,
I may out-bringe, and if this yow displese,
That shal I wreke upon myn owne lyf

Right sone, I trowe, and doon your herte an ese,
If with my deeth your herte I may apese.
But sin that ye han herd me som-what seye,
Now recche I never how sone that I deye.'

17. Ther-with his manly sorwe to biholde,
It mighte han maad an herte of stoon to rewe;
And Pandare weep as he to watre wolde,
And poked ever his nece newe and newe,
And seyde, 'wo bigon ben hertes trewe!
For love of god, make of this thing an ende,
Or slee us bothe at ones, er that ye wende.'

18. 'I? what?' quod she, 'by god and by my trouthe,
I noot nought what ye wilne that I seye.'
'I? what?' quod he, 'that ye han on him routhe,
For goddes love, and doth him nought to deye.'
'Now thanne thus,' quod she, 'I wolde him preye
To telle me the fyn of his entente;
Yet wiste I never wel what that he mente.'

19. 'What that I mene, O swete herte dere?'
Quod Troilus, 'O goodly fresshe free!
That, with the stremes of your eyen clere,
Ye wolde som-tyme freendly on me see,
And thanne agreën that I may ben he,
With-oute braunche of vyce in any wyse,
In trouthe alwey to doon yow my servyse

20. 'As to my lady right and chief resort,
With al my wit and al my diligence,
And I to han, right as yow list, comfort,
Under your yerde, egal to myn offence,
As deeth, if that I breke your defence;
And that ye deigne me so muche honoure,
Me to comaunden ought in any houre.

21. 'And I to been your verray humble trewe,
Secret, and in my paynes pacient,
And ever-mo desire freshly newe,
To serven, and been y-lyke ay diligent,
And, with good herte, al holly your talent
Receyven wel, how sore that me smerte,
Lo, this mene I, myn owene swete herte.'

22. Quod Pandarus, 'lo, here an hard request,
And resonable, a lady for to werne!
Now, nece myn, by natal Joves fest,
Were I a god, ye sholde sterve as yerne,
That heren wel, this man wol no-thing yerne
But your honour, and seen him almost sterve,
And been so looth to suffren him yow serve.'

23. With that she gan hir eyen on him caste
Ful esily, and ful debonairly,
Avysing hir, and hyed not to faste
With never a word, but seyde him softely,
'Myn honour sauf, I wol wel trewely,
And in swiche forme as he can now devyse,
Receyven him fully to my servyse,

24. 'Biseching him, for goddes love, that he
Wolde, in honour of trouthe and gentilesse,
As I wel mene, eek mene wel to me,
And myn honour, with wit and besinesse,
Ay kepe; and if I may don him gladnesse,
From hennes-forth, y-wis, I nil not feyne:
Now beeth al hool, no lenger ye ne pleyne.

25. 'But nathelees, this warne I yow,' quod she,
'A kinges sone al-though ye be, y-wis,
Ye shul na-more have soverainetee
Of me in love, than right in that cas is;
Ne I nil forbere, if that ye doon a-mis,
To wrathen yow; and whyl that ye me serve,
Cherycen yow right after ye deserve.

26. 'And shortly, derë herte and al my knight,
Beth glad, and draweth yow to lustinesse,
And I shal trewely, with al my might,
Your bittre tornen al in-to swetnesse;
If I be she that may yow do gladnesse,
For every wo ye shal recovere a blisse';
And him in armes took, and gan him kisse.

27. Fil Pandarus on knees, and up his yën
To hevene threw, and held his hondes hye,
'Immortal god!' quod he, 'that mayst nought dyen,

Cupide I mene, of this mayst glorifye;
And Venus, thou mayst make melodye;
With-outen hond, me semeth that in towne,
For this merveyle, I here ech belle sowne.

28. 'But ho! no more as now of this matere,
For-why this folk wol comen up anoon,
That han the lettre red: lo, I hem here.
But I conjure thee, Criseyde, and oon,
And two, thou Troilus, whan thow mayst goon,
That at myn hous ye been at my warninge,
For I ful wel shal shape your cominge;

29. And eseth ther your hertes right y-nough;
And lat see which of yow shal bere the belle
To speke of love a-right!' ther-with he lough,
'For ther have ye a layser for to telle.'
Quod Troilus, 'how longe shal I dwelle
Er this be doon?'   Quod he, 'whan thou mayst ryse,
This thing shal be right as I yow devyse.'

30. With that Eleyne and also Deiphebus
Tho comen upward, right at the steyres ende;
And lord, so than gan grone Troilus,
His brother and his suster for to blende.
Quod Pandarus, 'it tyme is that we wende;
Tak, nece myn, your leve at alle three,
And lat hem speke, and cometh forth with me.'

31. She took hir leve at hem ful thriftily,
As she wel coude, and they hir reverence
Un-to the fulle diden hardely,
And speken wonder wel, in hir absence,
Of hir, in preysing of hir excellence,
Hir governaunce, hir wit; and hir manere
Commendeden, it joye was to here.

32. Now lat hir wende un-to hir owne place,
And torne we to Troilus a-yein,
That gan ful lightly of the lettre passe
That Deiphebus hadde in the gardin seyn.
And of Eleyne and him he wolde fayn
Delivered been, and seyde, that him leste
To slepe, and after tales have reste.

33. Eleyne him kiste, and took hir leve blyve,
Deiphebus eek, and hoom wente every wight;
And Pandarus, as faste as he may dryve,
To Troilus tho com, as lyne right;
And on a paillet, al that glade night,
By Troilus he lay, with mery chere,
To tale; and wel was hem they were y-fere.

34. Whan every wight was voided but they two,
And alle the dores were faste y-shette,
To telle in short, with-oute wordes mo,
This Pandarus, with-outen any lette,
Up roos, and on his beddes syde him sette,
And gan to speken in a sobre wyse
To Troilus, as I shal yow devyse.

35. 'Myn alderlevest lord, and brother dere,
God woot, and thou, that it sat me so sore,
When I thee saw so languisshing to-yere,
For love, of which thy wo wex alwey more;
That I, with al my might and al my lore,
Hath ever sithen doon my bisinesse
To bringe thee to joye out of distresse;

36. 'And have it brought to swich plyt as thou wost,
So that, thorugh me, thow stondest now in weye
To fare wel, I seye it for no bost,
And wostow why? for shame it is to seye,
For thee have I bigonne a gamen pleye
Which that I never doon shal eft for other,
Al-though he were a thousand fold my brother.

37. 'That is to seye, for thee am I bicomen,
Bitwixen game and ernest, swich a mene
As maken wommen un-to men to comen;
Al sey I nought, thou wost wel what I mene.
For thee have I my nece, of vyces clene,
So fully maad thy gentilesse triste,
That al shal been right as thy-selve liste.

38. 'But god, that al wot, take I to witnesse,
That never I this for coveityse wroughte,
But only for to abregge that distresse,

For which wel nygh thou deydest, as me thoughte.
But gode brother, do now as thee oughte,
For goddes love, and keep hir out of blame,
Sin thou art wys, and save alwey hir name.

39. 'For wel thou wost, the name as yet of here
Among the peple, as who seyth, halwed is;
For that man is unbore, I dar wel swere,
That ever wiste that she dide amis.
But wo is me, that I, that cause al this,
May thenken that she is my nece dere,
And I hir eem, and traytor eek y-fere!

40. 'And were it wist that I, through myn engyn,
Hadde in my nece y-put this fantasye,
To do thy lust, and hoolly to be thyn,
Why, al the world up-on it wolde crye,
And seye, that I the worste trecherye
Dide in this cas, that ever was bigonne,
And she for-lost, and thou right nought y-wonne.

41. 'Wher-fore, er I wol ferther goon a pas,
Yet eft I thee biseche and fully seye,
That privetee go with us in this cas,
That is to seye, that thou us never wreye;
And be nought wrooth, though I thee ofte preye
To holden secree swich an heigh matere;
For skilful is, thow wost wel, my preyere.

42. 'And thenk what wo ther hath bitid er this,
For makinge of avauntes, as men rede;
And what mischaunce in this world yet ther is,
Fro day to day, right for that wikked dede;
For which these wyse clerkes that ben dede
Han ever yet proverbed to us yonge,
That "firste vertu is to kepe tonge."

43. 'And, nere it that I wilne as now t' abregge
Diffusion of speche, I coude almost
A thousand olde stories thee alegge
Of wommen lost, thorugh fals and foles bost;
Proverbes canst thy-self y-nowe, and wost,
Ayeins that vyce, for to been a labbe,
Al seyde men sooth as often as they gabbe.

44. 'O tonge, allas! so often here-biforn
Hastow made many a lady bright of hewe
Seyd, "welawey! the day that I was born!"
And many a maydes sorwes for to newe;
And, for the more part, al is untrewe
That men of yelpe, and it were brought to preve;
Of kinde non avauntour is to leve.

45. 'Avauntour and a lyere, al is on;
As thus: I pose, a womman graunte me
Hir love, and seyth that other wol she non,
And I am sworn to holden it secree,
And after I go telle it two or three;
Y-wis, I am avauntour at the leste,
And lyere, for I breke my biheste.

46. 'Now loke thanne, if they be nought to blame,
Swich maner folk; what shal I clepe hem, what,
That hem avaunte of wommen, and by name,
That never yet bihighte hem this ne that,
Ne knewe hem more than myn olde hat?
No wonder is, so god me sende hele,
Though wommen drede with us men to dele.

47. 'I sey not this for no mistrust of yow,
Ne for no wys man, but for foles nyce,
And for the harm that in the world is now,
As wel for foly ofte as for malyce;
For wel wot I, in wyse folk, that vyce
No womman drat, if she be wel avysed;
For wyse ben by foles harm chastysed.

48. 'But now to purpos; leve brother dere,
Have al this thing that I have seyd in minde,
And keep thee clos, and be now of good chere,
For at thy day thou shalt me trewe finde.
I shal thy proces sette in swich a kinde,
And god to-forn, that it shall thee suffyse,
For it shal been right as thou wolt devyse.

49. 'For wel I woot, thou menest wel, parde;
Therfore I dar this fully undertake.
Thou wost eek what thy lady graunted thee,

And day is set, the chartres up to make.
Have now good night, I may no lenger wake;
And bid for me, sin thou art now in blisse,
That god me sende deeth or sone lisse.'

50. Who mighte telle half the joye or feste
Which that the sowle of Troilus tho felte,
Heringe th' effect of Pandarus biheste?
His olde wo, that made his herte swelte,
Gan tho for joye wasten and to-melte,
And al the richesse of his sykes sore
At ones fledde, he felte of hem no more.

51. But right so as these holtes and these hayes,
That han in winter dede been and dreye,
Revesten hem in grene, whan that May is,
Whan every lusty lyketh best to pleye:
Right in that selve wyse, sooth to seye,
Wex sodeynliche his herte ful of joye,
That gladder was ther never man in Troye.

52. And gan his look on Pandarus up caste
Ful sobrely, and frendly for to see,
And seyde, 'freend, in Aprille the laste,
As wel thou wost, if it remembre thee,
How neigh the deeth for wo thou founde me;
And how thou didest al thy bisinesse
To knowe of me the cause of my distresse.

53. 'Thou wost how longe I it for-bar to seye
To thee, that art the man that I best triste;
And peril was it noon to thee by-wreye,
That wiste I wel; but tel me, if thee liste,
Sith I so looth was that thy-self it wiste,
How dorste I mo tellen of this matere,
That quake now, and no wight may us here?

54. 'But natheles, by that god I thee swere,
That, as him list, may al this world governe,
And, if I lye, Achilles with his spere
Myn herte cleve, al were my lyf eterne,
As I am mortal, if I late or yerne
Wolde it biwreye, or dorste, or sholde conne,
For al the good that god made under sonne;

55. 'That rather deye I wolde, and determyne,
As thinketh me, now stokked in presoun,
In wrecchednesse, in filthe, and in vermyne,
Catif to cruel king Agamenoun;
And this, in alle the temples of this toun,
Upon the goddes alle, I wol thee swere,
To-morwe day, if that thee lyketh here.

56. 'And that thou hast so muche y-doon for me,
That I ne may it never-more deserve,
This knowe I wel, al mighte I now for thee
A thousand tymes on a morwen sterve,
I can no more, but that I wol thee serve
Right as thy sclave, whider-so thou wende,
For ever-more, un-to my lyves ende!

57. 'But here, with al myn herte, I thee biseche,
That never in me thou deme swich folye
As I shal seyn; me thoughte, by thy speche,
That this, which thou me dost for companye,
I sholde wene it were a bauderye;
I am nought wood, al-if I lewed be;
It is not so, that woot I wel, pardee.

58. 'But he that goth, for gold or for richesse,
On swich message, calle him what thee list;
And this that thou dost, calle it gentilesse,
Compassioun, and felawship, and trist;
Departe it so, for wyde-where is wist
How that there is dyversitee requered
Bitwixen thinges lyke, as I have lered.

59. 'And, that thou knowe I thenke nought ne wene
That this servyse a shame be or jape,
I have my faire suster Polixene,
Cassandre, Eleyne, or any of the frape;
Be she never so faire or wel y-shape,
Tel me, which thou wilt of everichone,
To han for thyn, and lat me thanne allone.

60. 'But sin that thou hast don me this servyse,
My lyf to save, and for noon hope of mede,
So, for the love of god, this grete empryse

Parforme it out; for now is moste nede.
For high and low, with-outen any drede,
I wol alwey thyne hestes alle kepe;
Have now good night, and lat us bothe slepe.'

61. Thus held him ech with other wel apayed,
That al the world ne mighte it bet amende;
And, on the morwe, whan they were arayed,
Ech to his owene nedes gan entende.
But Troilus, though as the fyr he brende
For sharp desyr of hope and of plesaunce,
He not for-gat his gode governaunce.

62. But in him-self with manhod gan restreyne
Ech rakel dede and ech unbrydled chere,
That alle tho that liven, sooth to seyne,
Ne sholde han wist, by word or by manere,
What that he mente, as touching this matere.
From every wight as fer as is the cloude
He was, so wel dissimulen he coude.

63. And al the whyl which that I yow devyse,
This was his lyf; with al his fulle might,
By day he was in Martes high servyse,
This is to seyn, in armes as a knight;
And for the more part, the longe night
He lay, and thoughte how that he mighte serve
His lady best, hir thank for to deserve.

64. Nil I nought swerë, al-though he lay softe,
That in his thought he nas sumwhat disesed,
Ne that he tornede on his pilwes ofte,
And wolde of that him missed han ben sesed;
But in swich cas man is nought alwey plesed,
For ought I wot, no more than was he;
That can I deme of possibilitee.

65. But certeyn is, to purpos for to go,
That in this whyle, as writen is in geste,
He say his lady som-tyme; and also
She with him spak, whan that she dorste or leste,
And by hir bothe avys, as was the beste,
Apoynteden ful warly in this nede,
So as they dorste, how they wolde procede.

66. But it was spoken in so short a wyse,
In swich awayt alwey, and in swich fere,
Lest any wyght divynen or devyse
Wolde of hem two, or to it leye an ere,
That al this world so leef to hem ne were
As that Cupido wolde hem grace sende
To maken of hir speche aright an ende.

67. But thilke litel that they speke or wroughte,
His wyse goost took ay of al swich hede,
It semed hir, he wiste that she thoughte
With-outen word, so that it was no nede
To bidde him ought to done, or ought forbede;
For which she thoughte that love, al come it late,
Of alle joye hadde opned hir the yate.

68. And shortly of this proces for to pace,
So wel his werk and wordes he bisette,
That he so ful stood in his lady grace,
That twenty thousand tymes, or she lette,
She thonked god she ever with him mette;
So coude he him governe in swich servyse,
That al the world ne mighte it bet devyse.

69. For-why she fond him so discreet in al,
So secret, and of swich obëisaunce,
That wel she felte he was to hir a wal
Of steel, and sheld from every displesaunce;
That, to ben in his gode governaunce,
So wys he was, she was no more afered,
I mene, as fer as oughte ben requered.

70. And Pandarus, to quike alwey the fyr,
Was ever y-lyke prest and diligent;
To ese his frend was set al his desyr.
He shoof ay on, he to and fro was sent;
He lettres bar whan Troilus was absent.
That never man, as in his freendes nede,
Ne bar him bet than he, with-outen drede.

71. But now, paraunter, som man wayten wolde
That every word, or sonde, or look, or chere
Of Troilus that I rehersen sholde,

In al this whyle, un-to his lady dere;
I trowe it were a long thing for to here;
Or of what wight that stant in swich disjoynte,
His wordes alle, or every look, to poynte.

72. For sothe, I have not herd it doon er this,
In storye noon, ne no man, here, I wene;
And though I wolde I coude not, y-wis;
For ther was som epistel hem bitwene,
That wolde, as seyth myn auctor, wel contene
Neigh half this book, of which him list not wryte;
How sholde I thanne a lyne of it endyte?

73. But to the grete effect: than sey I thus,
That stonding in concord and in quiete
Thise ilke two, Criseyde and Troilus,
As I have told, and in this tyme swete,
Save only often mighte they not mete,
Ne layser have hir speches to fulfelle,
That it befel right as I shal yow telle,

74. That Pandarus, that ever dide his might
Right for the fyn that I shal speke of here,
As for to bringe to his hous som night
His faire nece, and Troilus y-fere,
Wher-as at leyser al this heigh matere,
Touching hir love, were at the fulle up-bounde,
Hadde out of doute a tyme to it founde.

75. For he with greet deliberacioun
Hadde every thing that her-to mighte avayle
Forn-cast, and put in execucioun,
And neither laft for cost ne for travayle;
Come if hem lest, hem sholde no-thing fayle;
And for to been in ought espyed there,
That, wiste he wel, an inpossible were.

76. Dredelees, it cleer was in the wind
Of every pye and every lette-game;
Now al is wel, for al the world is blind
In this matere, bothe fremed and tame.
This timber is al redy up to frame;
Us lakketh nought but that we witen wolde
A certein houre, in whiche she comen sholde.

77. And Troilus, that al this purveyaunce
Knew at the fulle, and waytede on it ay,
Hadde here-up-on eek made gret ordenaunce,
And founde his cause, and ther-to his aray,
If that he were missed, night or day,
Ther-whyle he was aboute this servyse,
That he was goon to doon his sacrifyse,

78. And moste at swich a temple alone wake,
Answered of Appollo for to be;
And first, to seen the holy laurer quake,
Er that Apollo spak out of the tree,
To telle him next whan Grekes sholden flee;
And forthy lette him no man, god forbede,
But preye Apollo helpen in this nede.

79. Now is ther litel more to for done,
But Pandare up, and shortly for to seyne,
Right sone upon the chaunging of the mone,
Whan lightles is the world a night or tweyne,
And that the welken shoop him for to reyne,
He streight a-morwe un-to his nece wente;
Ye han wel herd the fyn of his entente.

80. Whan he was come, he gan anoon to pleye
As he was wont, and of him-self to jape;
And fynally, he swor and gan hir seye,
By this and that, she sholde him not escape,
Ne lenger doon him after hir to gape;
But certeynly she moste, by hir leve,
Come soupen in his hous with him at eve.

81. At whiche she lough, and gan hir faste excuse,
And seyde, 'it rayneth; lo, how sholde I goon?'
'Lat be,' quod he, 'ne stond not thus to muse;
This moot be doon, ye shal be ther anoon.'
So at the laste her-of they felle at oon,
Or elles, softe he swor hir in hir ere,
He nolde never come ther she were.

82. Sone after this, to him she gan to rowne,
And asked him if Troilus were there?
He swor hir, 'nay, for he was out of towne,'

And seyde, 'nece, I pose that he were,
Yow thurfte never have the more fere.
For rather than men mighte him ther aspye,
Me were lever a thousand-fold to dye.'

83. Nought list myn auctor fully to declare
What that she thoughte whan he seyde so,
That Troilus was out of town y-fare,
As if he seyde ther-of sooth or no;
But that, with-oute awayt, with him to go,
She graunted him, sith he hir that bisoughte,
And, as his nece, obeyed as hir oughte.

84. But nathelees, yet gan she him biseche,
Al-though with him to goon it was no fere,
For to be war of goosish peples speche,
That dremen thinges whiche that never were,
And wel avyse him whom he broughte there;
And seyde him, 'eem, sin I mot on yow triste,
Loke al be wel, and do now as yow liste.'

85. He swor hir, 'yis, by stokkes and by stones,
And by the goddes that in hevene dwelle,
Or elles were him lever, soule and bones,
With Pluto king as depe been in helle
As Tantalus!' What sholde I more telle?
Whan al was wel, he roos and took his leve,
And she to souper com, whan it was eve,

86. With a certayn of hir owene men,
And with hir faire nece Antigone,
And othere of hir wommen nyne or ten;
But who was glad now, who, as trowe ye,
But Troilus, that stood and mighte it see
Thurgh-out a litel windowe in a stewe,
Ther he bishet, sin midnight, was in mewe,

87. Unwist of every wight but of Pandare?
But to the poynt; now whan she was y-come
With alle joye, and alle frendes fare,
Hir eem anoon in armes hath hir nome,
And after to the souper, alle and some,
Whan tyme was, ful softe they hem sette;
God wot, ther was no deyntee for to fette

88. And after souper gonnen they to ryse,
At ese wel, with hertes fresshe and glade,
And wel was him that coude best devyse
To lyken hir, or that hir laughen made.
He song; she pleyde; he tolde tale of Wade.
But at the laste, as every thing hath ende,
She took hir leve, and nedes wolde wende.

89. But O, Fortune, executrice of wierdes,
O influences of thise hevenes hye!
Soth is, that, under god, ye ben our hierdes,
Though to us bestes been the causes wrye.
This mene I now, for she gan hoomward hye,
But execut was al bisyde hir leve,
At the goddes wil; for which she moste bleve.

90. The bente mone with hir hornes pale,
Saturne, and Jove, in Cancro joyned were,
That swich a rayn from hevene gan avale,
That every maner womman that was there
Hadde of that smoky reyn a verray fere;
At which Pandare tho lough, and seyde thenne,
'Now were it tyme a lady to go henne!

91. 'But goode nece, if I mighte ever plese
Yow any-thing, than prey I yow,' quod he,
'To doon myn herte as now so greet an ese
As for to dwelle here al this night with me,
For-why this is your owene hous, pardee.
For, by my trouthe, I sey it nought a-game,
To wende as now, it were to me a shame.'

92. Criseyde, whiche that coude as muche good
As half a world, tok hede of his preyere;
And sin it ron, and al was on a flood,
She thoughte, as good chep may I dwellen here,
And graunte it gladly with a freendes chere,
And have a thank, as grucche and thanne abyde;
For hoom to goon it may nought wel bityde.

93. 'I wol,' quod she, 'myn uncle leef and dere,
Sin that yow list, it skile is to be so;
I am right glad with yow to dwellen here;

I seyde but a-game, I wolde go.'
'Y-wis, graunt mercy, nece!' quod he tho;
'Were it a game or no, soth for to telle,
Now am I glad, sin that yow list to dwelle.'

94. Thus al is wel; but tho bigan aright
The newe joye, and al the feste agayn;
But Pandarus, if goodly hadde he might,
He wolde han hyed hir to bedde fayn,
And seyde, 'lord, this is an huge rayn!
This were a weder for to slepen inne;
And that I rede us sone to biginne.

95. 'And nece, woot ye wher I wol yow leye,
For that we shul not liggen fer asonder,
And for ye neither shullen, dar I seye,
Heren noise of reynes nor of thonder?
By god, right in my lyte closet yonder.
And I wol in that outer hous allone
Be wardeyn of your wommen everichone.

96. 'And in this middel chaumbre that ye see
Shul youre wommen slepen wel and softe;
And ther I seyde shal your-selve be;
And if ye liggen wel to-night, com lofte,
And careth not what weder is on-lofte.
The wyn anon, and whan so that yow leste,
So go we slepe, I trowe it be the beste.'

97. Ther nis no more, but here-after sone,
The voydè dronke, and travers drawe anon,
Gan every wight, that hadde nought to done
More in that place, out of the chaumber gon.
And ever-mo so sternelich it ron,
And blew ther-with so wonderliche loude,
That wel neigh no man heren other coude.

98. Tho Pandarus, hir eem, right as him oughte,
With women swiche as were hir most aboute,
Ful glad un-to hir beddes syde hir broughte,
And took his leve, and gan ful lowe loute,
And seyde, 'here at this closet-dore with-oute,
Right over-thwart, your wommen liggen alle,
That, whom yow liste of hem, ye may here calle.'

99. So whan that she was in the closet leyd,
And alle hir wommen forth by ordenaunce
A-bedde weren, ther as I have seyd,
There was no more to skippen nor to traunce,
But boden go to bedde, with mischaunce,
If any wight was steringe any-where,
And late hem slepe that a-bedde were.

100. But Pandarus, that wel coude eche a del
The olde daunce, and every poynt ther-inne,
Whan that he sey that alle thing was wel,
He thoughte he wolde up-on his werk biginne,
And gan the stewe-dore al softe un-pinne,
And stille as stoon, with-outen lenger lette,
By Troilus a-doun right he him sette.

101. And, shortly to the poynt right for to gon,
Of al this werk he tolde him word and ende,
And seyde, 'make thee redy right anon,
For thou shalt in-to hevene blisse wende.'
'Now blisful Venus, thou me grace sende,'
Quod Troilus, 'for never yet no nede
Hadde I er now, ne halvendel the drede.'

102. Quod Pandarus, 'ne drede thee never a del,
For it shal been right as thou wilt desyre;
So thryve I, this night shal I make it wel,
Or casten al the gruwel in the fyre.'
'Yit blisful Venus, this night thou me enspyre,'
Quod Troilus, 'as wis as I thee serve,
And ever bet and bet shal, til I sterve.

103. 'And if I hadde, O Venus ful of mirthe,
Aspectes badde of Mars or of Saturne,
Or thou combust or let were in my birthe,
Thy fader pray al thilke harm disturne
Of grace, and that I glad ayein may turne,
For love of him thou lovedest in the shawe,
I mene Adoon, that with the boor was slawe.

104. 'O Jove, eek for the love of faire Europe,
The whiche in forme of bole away thou fette;
Now help, O Mars, thou with thy blody cope,

For love of Cipris, thou me nought ne lette;
O Phebus, thenk whan Dane hir-selven shette
Under the bark, and laurer wex for drede,
Yet for hir love, O help now at this nede!

105. 'Mercurie, for the love of Hiersè eke,
For which Pallas was with Aglauros wrooth,
Now help, and eek Diane, I thee biseke,
That this viage be not to thee looth.
O fatal sustren, which, er any clooth
Me shapen was, my destenè me sponne,
So helpeth to this werk that is bi-gonne!'

106. Quod Pandarus, 'thou wrecched mouses herte,
Art thou agast so that she wol thee byte?
Why, don this furred cloke up-on thy sherte,
And folowe me, for I wol han the wyte;
But byd, and lat me go bifore a lyte.'
And with that word he gan un-do a trappe,
And Troilus he broughte in by the lappe.

107. The sterne wind so loude gan to route
That no wight other noyse mighte here;
And they they layen at the dore with-oute,
Ful sikerly they slepten alle y-fere;
And Pandarus, with a ful sobre chere,
Goth to the dore anon with-outen lette,
Ther-as they laye, and softely it shette.

108. And as he com ayeinward prively,
His nece awook, and asked 'who goth there?'
'My dere nece,' quod he, 'it am I;
Ne wondreth not, ne have of it no fere';
And ner he com, and seyde hir in hir ere,
'No word, for love of god I yow biseche;
Lat no wight ryse and heren of our speche.'

109. 'What! which wey be ye comen, *benedicite*?'
Quod she, 'and how thus unwist of hem alle?'
'Here at this secree trappe-door,' quod he.
Quod tho Criseyde, 'lat me som wight calle.'
'Ey! god forbede that it sholde falle,'
Quod Pandarus, 'that ye swich foly wroughte!
They mighte deme thing they never er thoughte!

110. 'It is nought good a sleping hound to wake,
Ne yeve a wight a cause to devyne;
Your wommen slepen alle, I under-take,
So that, for hem, the hous men mighte myne;
And slepen wolen til the sonne shyne.
And whan my tale al brought is to an ende,
Unwist, right as I com, so wol I wende.

111. 'Now nece myn, ye shul wel understonde,'
Quod he, 'so as ye wommen demen alle,
That for to holde in love a man in honde,
And him hir "leef" and "dere herte" calle,
And maken him an howve above a calle,
I mene, as love an other in this whyle,
She doth hir-self a shame, and him a gyle.

112. 'Now wherby that I telle yow al this?
Ye woot your-self, as wel as any wight,
How that your love al fully graunted is
To Troilus, the worthieste knight,
Oon of this world, and ther-to trouthe plyght,
That, but it were on him along, ye nolde
Him never falsen, whyl ye liven sholde.

113. 'Now stant it thus, that sith I fro yow wente,
This Troilus, right platly for to seyn,
Is thurgh a goter, by a privè wente,
In-to my chaumbre come in al this reyn,
Unwist of every maner wight, certeyn,
Save of my-self, as wisly have I joye,
And by that feith I shal Pryam of Troye!

114. 'And he is come in swich peyne and distresse
That, but he be al fully wood by this,
He sodeynly mot falle in-to wodnesse,
But-if god helpe; and cause why this is,
He seyth him told is, of a freend of his,
How that ye sholde love oon that hatte Horaste,
For sorwe of which this night shalt been his laste.'

115. Criseyde, which that al this wonder herde,
Gan sodeynly aboute hir herte colde,
And with a syk she sorwfully answerde,

'Allas! I wende, who-so tales tolde,
My dere herte wolde me not holde
So lightly fals! allas! conceytes wronge,
What harm they doon, for now live I to longe!

116. 'Horaste! allas! and falsen Troilus?
I knowe him not, god helpe me so,' quod she;
'Alas! what wikked spirit tolde him thus?
Now certes, eem, to-morwe, and I him see,
I shall ther-of as ful excusen me
As ever dide womman, if him lyke';
And with that word she gan ful sore syke.

117. 'O god!' quod she, 'so worldly selinesse,
Which clerkes callen fals felicitee,
Y-medled is with many a bitternesse!
Ful anguisshous than is, god woot,' quod she,
'Condicioun of veyn prosperitee;
For either joyes comen nought y-fere,
Or elles no wight hath hem alwey here.

118. 'O brotel wele of mannes joye unstable!
With what wight so thou be, or how thou pleye,
Either he woot that thou, joye, art muable,
Or woot it not, it moot ben oon of tweye;
Now if he woot it not, how may he seye
That he hath verray joye and selinesse,
That is of ignoraunce ay in derknesse?

119. 'Now if he woot that joye is transitorie,
As every joye of worldly thing mot flee,
Than every tyme he that hath in memorie,
The drede of lesing maketh him that he
May in no parfit selinesse be.
And if to lese his joye he set a myte,
Than semeth it that joye is worth ful lyte.

120. 'Wherfore I wol deffyne in this matere,
That trewely, for ought I can espye,
Ther is no verray wele in this world here.
But O, thou wikked serpent Jalousye,
Thou misbeleved and envious folye,
Why hastow Troilus me mad untriste,
That never yet agilte him, that I wiste?'

121. Quod Pandarus, 'thus fallen is this cas.'
'Why, uncle myn,' quod she, 'who tolde him this?
Why doth my dere herte thus, allas?'
'Ye woot, ye nece myn,' quod he, 'what is;
I hope al shal be wel that is amis.
For ye may quenche al this, if that yow leste,
And doth right so, for I holde it the beste.'

122. 'So shal I do to-morwe, y-wis,' quod she,
'And god to-forn, so that it shal suffyse.'
'To-morwe? allas, that were a fayr,' quod he,
'Nay, nay, it may not stonden in this wyse;
For, nece myn, thus wryten clerkes wyse,
That peril is with drecching in y-drawe;
Nay, swich abodes been nought worth an hawe.

123. 'Nece, al thing hath tyme, I dar avowe;
For whan a chaumber a-fyr is, or an halle,
Wel more nede is, it sodeynly rescowe
Than to dispute, and axe amonges alle
How is this candel in the straw y-falle?
A! *benedicite !* for al among that fare
The harm is doon, and fare-wel feldefare!

124. 'And, nece myn, ne take it not a-greef,
If that ye suffre him al night in this wo,
God help me so, ye hadde him never leef,
That dar I seyn, now there is but we two;
But wel I woot, that ye wol not do so;
Ye been to wys to do so gret folye,
To putte his lyf al night in jupartye.'

125. 'Hadde I him never leef? By god, I wene
Ye hadde never thing so leef,' quod she.
'Now by my thrift,' quod he, 'that shal be sene;
For, sin ye make this ensample of me,
If I al night wolde him in sorwe see
For al the tresour in the toun of Troye,
I bidde god, I never mote have joye!

126. 'Now loke thanne, if ye, that been his love,
Shul putte al night his lyf in jupartye
For thing of nought! Now, by that god above,

Nought only this delay comth of folye,
But of malyce, if that I shall nought lye.
What, platly, and ye suffre him in distresse,
Ye neither bountee doon ne gentilesse!'

127. Quod tho Criseyde, 'wol ye doon o thing,
And ye therwith shal stinte al his disese;
Have here, and bereth him this blewe ring,
For ther is no-thing mighte him bettre plese,
Save I my-self, ne more his herte apese;
And sey my dere herte, that his sorwe
Is causeles, that shal be seen to-morwe.'

128. 'A ring?' quod he, 'ye, hasel-wodes shaken!
Ye, nece myn, that ring moste han a stoon
That mighte dede men alyve maken;
And swich a ring, trowe I that ye have noon.
Discrecioun out of your heed is goon;
That fele I now,' quod he, 'and that is routhe;
O tyme y-lost, wel maystow cursen slouthe!

129. 'Wot ye not wel that noble and heigh corage
Ne sorweth not, ne stinteth eek for lyte?
But if a fool were in a jalous rage,
I nolde setten at his sorwe a myte,
But feffe him with a fewe wordes whyte
Another day, whan that I mighte him finde:
But this thing stont al in another kinde.

130. 'This is so gentil and so tendre of herte,
That with his deeth he wol his sorwes wreke;
For trusteth wel, how sore that him smerte,
He wol to yow no jalouse wordes speke.
And for-thy, nece, er that his herte breke,
So spek your-self to him of this matere;
For with o word ye may his herte stere.

131. 'Now have I told what peril he is inne,
And his coming unwist is t' every wight;
Ne, pardee, harm may ther be noon ne sinne;
I wol my-self be with yow al this night.
Ye knowe eek how it is your owne knight,
And that, by right, ye moste upon him triste,
And I al prest to fecche him whan yow liste.'

132. This accident so pitous was to here,
And eek so lyk a sooth, at pryme face,
And Troilus hir knight to hir so dere,
His privè coming, and the siker place,
That, though that she dide him as thanne a grace,
Considered alle thinges as they stode,
No wonder is, sin she dide al for gode.

133. Cryseyde answerde, 'as wisly god at reste
My sowle bringe, as me is for him wo!
And eem, y-wis, fayn wolde I doon the beste,
If that I hadde grace to do so.
But whether that ye dwelle or for him go,
I am, til god me bettre minde sende,
At dulcarnon, right at my wittes ende.'

134. Quod Pandarus, 'ye, nece, wol ye here?
Dulcarnon called is "fleminge of wrecches";
It semeth hard, for wrecches wol not lere
For verray slouthe or othere wilful tecches;
This seyd by hem that be not worth two fecches.
But ye ben wys, and that we han on honde
Nis neither hard, ne skilful to withstonde.'

135. 'Thanne, eem,' quod she, 'doth her-of as yow list;
But er he come I wil up first aryse;
And, for the love of god, sin al my trist
Is on yow two, and ye ben bothe wyse,
So wircheth now in so discreet a wyse,
That I honour may have, and he plesaunce
For I am here al in your governaunce.'

136. 'That is wel seyd,' quod he, 'my nece dere,
Ther good thrift on that wyse gentil herte!
But liggeth stille, and taketh him right here,
It nedeth not no ferther for him sterte;
And ech of yow ese otheres sorwes smerte,
For love of god; and, Venus, I thee herie;
For sone hope I we shulle ben alle merie.'

137. This Troilus ful sone on knees him sette
Ful sobrely, right by hir beddes heed,
And in his beste wyse his lady grette;

But lord, so she wex sodeynliche reed!
Ne, though men sholden smyten of hir heed,
She coude nought a word a-right out-bringe
So sodeynly, for his sodeyn cominge.

138. But Pandarus, that so wel coude fele
In every thing, to pleye anoon bigan,
And seyde, 'nece, see how this lord can knele!
Now, for your trouthe, seeth this gentil man!'
And with that word he for a quisshen ran,
And seyde, 'kneleth now, whyl that yow leste,
Ther god your hertes bringe sone at reste!'

139. Can I not seyn, for she bad him not ryse,
If sorwe it putte out of hir remembraunce,
Or elles if she toke it in the wyse
Of duëtee, as for his observaunce;
But wel finde I she dide him this plesaunce,
That she him kiste, al-though she syked sore;
And bad him sitte a-doun with-outen more.

140. Quod Pandarus, 'now wol ye wel biginne;
Now doth him sitte, gode nece dere,
Upon your beddes syde al there with-inne,
That ech of yow the bet may other here.'
And with that word he drow him to the fere,
And took a light, and fond his contenaunce
As for to loke up-on an old romaunce.

141. Criseyde, that was Troilus lady right,
And cleer stood on a ground of sikernesse,
Al thoughte she, hir servaunt and hir knight
Ne sholde of right non untrouthe in hir gesse,
Yet nathelees, considered his distresse,
And that love is in cause of swich folye,
Thus to him spak she of his jelousye:

142. 'Lo, herte myn, as wolde the excellence
Of love, ayeins the which that no man may,
Ne oughte eek goodly maken resistence;
And eek bycause I felte wel and say
Your grete trouthe, and servyse every day;
And that your herte al myn was, sooth to seyne,
This droof me for to rewe up-on your peyne.

143. 'And your goodnesse have I founde alwey yit,
Of whiche, my dere herte and al my knight,
I thonke it yow, as fer as I have wit,
Al can I nought as muche as it were right;
And I, emforth my conninge and my might,
Have and ay shal, how sore that me smerte,
Ben to yow trewe and hool, with al myn herte;

144. 'And dredelees, that shal be founde at preve.—
But, herte myn, what al this is to seyne
Shal wel be told, so that ye noght yow greve,
Though I to yow right on your-self compleyne.
For ther-with mene I fynally the peyne,
That halt your herte and myn in hevinesse,
Fully to sleen, and every wrong redresse.

145. 'My goode, myn, not I for-why ne how
That Jalousye, allas! that wikked wivere,
Thus causelees is cropen in-to yow;
The harm of which I wolde fayn delivere!
Allas! that he, al hool, or of him slivere,
Shuld have his refut in so digne a place,
Ther Jove him sone out of your herte arace!

146. 'But O, thou Jove, O auctor of nature,
Is this an honour to thy deitee,
That folk ungiltif suffren here injure,
And who that giltif is, al quit goth he?
O were it leful for to pleyne on thee,
That undeserved suffrest jalousye,
And that I wolde up-on thee pleyne and crye!

147. 'Eek al my wo is this, that folk now usen
To seyn right thus, "ye, Jalousye is Love!"
And wolde a busshel venim al excusen,
For that o greyn of love is on it shove!
But that wot heighe god that sit above,
If it be lyker love, or hate, or grame;
And after that, it oughte bere his name.

148. 'But certyn is, som maner jalousye
Is excusable more than som, y-wis.
As whan cause is, and som swich fantasye

With pietee so wel repressed is,
That it unnethe dooth or seyth amis,
But goodly drinketh up al his distresse;
And that excuse I, for the gentilesse.

149. 'And som so ful of furie is and despyt,
That it sourmounteth his repressioun;
But herte myn, ye be not in that plyt,
That thanke I god, for whiche your passioun
I wol not calle it but illusioun,
Of habundaunce of love and bisy cure,
That dooth your herte this disese endure.

150. 'Of which I am right sory, but not wrooth;
But, for my devoir and your hertes reste,
Wher-so yow list, by ordal or by ooth,
By sort, or in what wyse so yow leste,
For love of god, lat preve it for the beste!
And if that I be giltif, do me deye,
Allas! what mighte I more doon or seye?'

151. With that a fewe brighte teres newe
Out of hir eyen fille, and thus she seyde,
'Now god, thou wost, in thought ne dede untrewe
To Troilus was never yet Criseyde.'
With that hir heed doun in the bed she leyde,
And with the shete it wreigh, and syghed sore,
And held hir pees; not o word spak she more.

152. But now help god to quenchen al this sorwe,
So hope I that he shal, for he best may;
For I have seyn, of a ful misty morwe
Folwen ful ofte a mery someres day;
And after winter folweth grene May.
Men seen alday, and reden eek in stories,
That after sharpe shoures been victories.

153. This Troilus, whan he hir wordes herde,
Have ye no care, him liste not to slepe;
For it thoughte him no strokes of a yerde
To here or seen Criseyde his lady wepe;
But wel he felte aboute his herte crepe,
For every tere which that Criseyde a-sterte,
The crampe of deeth, to streyne him by the herte.

154. And in his minde he gan the tyme acurse
That he cam therë, and that he was born;
For now is wikke y-turned in-to worse,
And al that labour he hath doon biforn,
He wende it lost, he thoughte he nas but lorn.
'O Pandarus,' thoughte he, 'allas! thy wyle
Serveth of nought, so weylawey the whyle!'

155. And therwithal he heng a-doun the heed,
And fil on knees, and sorwfully he sighte;
What mighte he seyn? he felte he nas but deed,
For wrooth was she that shulde his sorwes lighte.
But nathelees, whan that he speken mighte,
Than seyde he thus, 'god woot, that of this game,
Whan al is wist, than am I not to blame!'

156. Ther-with the sorwe so his herte shette,
That from his eyen fil ther not a tere,
And every spirit his vigour in-knette,
So they astoned and oppressed were.
The feling of his sorwe, or of his fere,
Or of ought elles, fled was out of towne;
And doun he fel al sodeynly a-swowne.

157. This was no litel sorwe for to see;
But al was hust, and Pandare up as faste,
'O nece, pees, or we be lost,' quod he,
'Beth nought agast'; but certeyn, at the laste,
For this or that, he in-to bedde him caste,
And seyde, 'O theef, is this a mannes herte?'
And of he rente al to his bare sherte;

158. And seyde, 'nece, but ye helpe us now,
Allas, your owne Troilus is lorn!'
'Y-wis, so wolde I, and I wiste how,
Ful fayn,' quod she; 'allas! that I was born!'
'Ye, nece, wol ye pullen out the thorn
That stiketh in his herte?' quod Pandare;
'Sey "al foryeve," and stint is al this fare!'

159. 'Ye, that to me,' quod she, 'ful lever were
Than all the good the sonne aboute gooth';
And therwith-al she swoor him in his ere,

'Y-wis, my dere herte, I am nought wrooth,
Have here my trouthe and many another ooth;
Now speek to me, for it am I, Criseyde!'
But al for nought; yet mighte he not a-breyde.

160. Therwith his pous and pawmes of his hondes
They gan to frote, and wete his temples tweyne,
And, to deliveren him from bittre bondes,
She ofte him kiste; and, shortly for to seyne,
Him to revoken she dide al hir peyne.
And at the laste, he gan his breeth to drawe,
And of his swough sone after that adawe,

161. And gan bet minde and reson to him take,
But wonder sore he was abayst, y-wis.
And with a syk, whan he gan bet a-wake,
He seyde, 'O mercy, god, what thing is this?'
'Why do ye with your-selven thus amis?'
Quod tho Criseyde, 'is this a mannes game?
What, Troilus! wol ye do thus, for shame?'

162. And therwith-al hir arm over him she leyde,
And al foryaf, and ofte tyme him keste.
He thonked hir, and to hir spak, and seyde
As fil to purpos for his herte reste.
And she to that answerde him as hir leste;
And with hir goodly wordes him disporte
She gan, and ofte his sorwes to comforte.

163. Quod Pandarus, 'for ought I can espyen,
This light nor I ne serven here of nought;
Light is not good for syke folkes yën.
But for the love of god, sin ye be brought
In thus good plyt, lat now non hevy thought
Ben hanginge in the hertes of yow tweye':
And bar the candel to the chimeneye.

164. Sone after this, though it no nede were,
Whan she swich othes as hir list devyse
Hadde of him take, hir thoughte tho no fere,
Ne cause eek non, to bidde him thennes ryse.
Yet lesse thing than othes may suffyse
In many a cas; for every wight, I gesse,
That loveth wel meneth but gentilesse.

165. But in effect she wolde wite anoon
Of what man, and eek where, and also why
He jelous was, sin ther was cause noon;
And eek the signe, that he took it by,
She bad him that to telle hir bisily,
Or elles, certeyn, she bar him on honde,
That this was doon of malis, hir to fonde.

166. With-outen more, shortly for to seyne,
He moste obeye un-to his lady heste;
And for the lasse harm, he moste feyne.
He seyde hir, whan she was at swiche a feste
She mighte on him han loked at the leste;
Not I not what, al dere y-nough a risshe,
As he that nedes moste a cause fisshe.

167. And she answerde, 'swete, al were it so,
What harm was that, sin I non yvel mene?
For, by that god that boughte us bothe two,
In alle thinge is myn entente clene.
Swich arguments ne been not worth a bene;
Wol ye the childish jalous contrefete?
Now were it worthy that ye were y-bete.'

168. Tho Troilus gan sorwfully to syke,
Lest she be wrooth, him thoughte his herte deyde;
And seyde, 'allas! upon my sorwes syke
Have mercy, swete herte myn, Criseyde!
And if that, in tho wordes that I seyde,
Be any wrong, I wol no more trespace;
Do what yow list, I am al in your grace.'

169. And she answerde, 'of gilt misericorde!
That is to seyn, that I foryeve al this;
And ever-more on this night yow recorde,
And beth wel war ye do no more amis.'
'Nay, dere herte myn,' quod he, 'y-wis.'
'And now,' quod she, 'that I have do yow smerte,
Foryeve it me, myn owene swete herte.'

170. This Troilus, with blisse of that supprysed,
Put al in goddes hond, as he that mente
No-thing but wel; and, sodeynly avysed,

He hir in armes faste to him hente.
And Pandarus, with a ful good entente,
Leyde him to slepe, and seyde, 'if ye ben wyse,
Swowneth not now, lest more folk aryse.'

171. What mighte or may the sely larke seye,
Whan that the sparhauk hath it in his foot?
I can no more, but of thise ilke tweye,
To whom this tale sucre be or soot,
Though that I tarie a yeer, som-tyme I moot,
After myn auctor, tellen hir gladnesse,
As wel as I have told hir hevinesse.

172. Criseyde, which that felte hir thus y-take,
As writen clerkes in hir bokes olde,
Right as an aspen leef she gan to quake,
Whan she him felte hir in his armes folde.
But Troilus, al hool of cares colde,
Gan thanken tho the blisful goddes sevene;
Thus sondry peynes bringen folk to hevene.

173. This Troilus in armes gan hir streyne,
And seyde, 'O swete, as ever mote I goon,
Now be ye caught, now is ther but we tweyne;
Now yeldeth yow, for other boot is noon.'
To that Criseyde answerde thus anoon,
'Ne hadde I er now, my swete herte dere,
Ben yolde, y-wis, I were now not here!'

174. O! sooth is seyd, that heled for to be
As of a fevre or othere greet syknesse,
Men moste drinke, as men may often see,
Ful bittre drink; and for to han gladnesse,
Men drinken often peyne and greet distresse;
I mene it here, as for this aventure,
That thourgh a peyne hath founden al his cure.

175. And now swetnesse semeth more swete,
That bitternesse assayed was biforn;
For out of wo in blisse now they flete.
Non swich they felten, sith they were born;
Now is this bet, than bothe two be lorn!
For love of god, take every womman hede
To werken thus, if it comth to the nede.

176. Criseyde, al quit from every drede and tene,
As she that juste cause hadde him to triste,
Made him swich feste, it joye was to sene,
Whan she his trouthe and clene entente wiste.
And as aboute a tree, with many a twiste,
Bitrent and wryth the sote wode-binde,
Gan eche of hem in armes other winde.

177. And as the newe abaysshed nightingale,
That stinteth first whan she biginneth singe,
Whan that she hereth any herde tale,
Or in the hegges any wight steringe,
And after siker dooth hir voys out-ringe;
Right so Criseyde, whan hir drede stente,
Opned hir herte, and tolde him hir entente.

178. And right as he that seeth his deeth y-shapen,
And deye moot, in ought that he may gesse,
And sodeynly rescous doth him escapen,
And from his deeth is brought in sikernesse,
For al this world, in swich present gladnesse
Was Troilus, and hath his lady swete;
With worse hap god lat us never mete!

179. Hir armes smale, hir streyghte bak and softe,
Hir sydes longe, fleshly, smothe, and whyte
He gan to stroke, and good thrift bad ful ofte
Hir snowish throte, hir brestes rounde and lyte;
Thus in this hevene he gan him to delyte,
And there-with-al a thousand tyme hir kiste;
That, what to done, for joye unnethe he wiste.

180. Then seyde he thus, 'O, Love, O, Charitee,
Thy moder eek, Citherea the swete,
After thy-self next heried be she,
Venus mene I, the wel-willy planete;
And next that, Imenëus, I thee grete;
For never man was to yow goddes holde
As I, which ye han brought fro cares colde.

181. 'Benigne Love, thou holy bond of thinges,
Who-so wol grace, and list thee nought honouren,
Lo, his desyr wol flee with-outen winges.

For, noldestow of bountee hem socouren
That serven best and most alwey labouren,
Yet were al lost, that dar I wel seyn, certes,
But-if thy grace passed our desertes.

182. 'And for thou me, that coude leest deserve
Of hem that nombred been un-to thy grace,
Hast holpen, ther I lykly was to sterve,
And me bistowed in so heygh a place
That thilke boundes may no blisse pace,
I can no more, but laude and reverence
Be to thy bounte and thyn excellence!'

183. And therwith-al Criseyde anoon he kiste,
Of which, certeyn, she felte no disese.
And thus seyde he, 'now wolde god I wiste,
Myn herte swete, how I yow mighte plese!
What man,' quod he, 'was ever thus at ese
As I, on whiche the faireste and the beste
That ever I say, deyneth hir herte reste.

184. 'Here may men seen that mercy passeth right;
The experience of that is felt in me,
That am unworthy to so swete a wight.
But herte myn, of your benignitee,
So thenketh, though that I unworthy be,
Yet mot I nede amenden in som wyse,
Right thourgh the vertu of your heyghe servyse.

185. And for the love of god, my lady dere,
Sin god hath wrought me for I shal yow serve,
As thus I mene, that ye wol be my stere,
To do me live, if that yow liste, or sterve,
So techeth me how that I may deserve
Your thank, so that I, thurgh myn ignoraunce,
Ne do no-thing that yow be displesaunce.

186. 'For certes, fresshe wommanliche wyf,
This dar I seye, that trouthe and diligence,
That shal ye finden in me al my lyf,
Ne I wol not, certeyn, breken your defence;
And if I do, present or in absence,
For love of god, lat slee me with the dede,
If that it lyke un-to your womanhede.'

187. 'Y-wis,' quod she, 'myn owne hertes list,
My ground of ese, and al myn herte dere,
Graunt mercy, for on that is al my trist;
But late us falle awey fro this matere;
For it suffyseth, this that seyd is here.
And at o word, with-outen repentaunce,
Wel-come, my knight, my pees, my suffisaunce!'

188. Of hir delyt, or joyes oon the leste
Were impossible to my wit to seye;
But juggeth, ye that han ben at the feste
Of swich gladnesse, if that hem liste pleye!
I can no more, but thus thise ilke tweye
That night, be-twixen dreed and sikernesse,
Felten in love the grete worthinesse.

189. O blisful night, of hem so longe y-sought,
How blithe un-to hem bothe two thou were!
Why ne hadde I swich on with my soule y-bought,
Ye, or the leeste joye that was there?
A-wey, thou foule daunger and thou fere,
And lat hem in this hevene blisse dwelle,
That is so heygh, that al ne can I telle!

190. But sooth is, though I can not tellen al,
As can myn auctor, of his excellence,
Yet have I seyd, and, god to-forn, I shal
In every thing al hoolly his sentence.
And if that I, at loves reverence,
Have any word in eched for the beste,
Doth therwith-al right as your-selven leste.

191. For myne wordes, here and every part,
I speke hem alle under correccioun
Of yow, that feling han in loves art,
And putte it al in your discrecioun
T' encrese or maken diminucioun
Of my langage, and that I yow bi-seche;
But now to purpos of my rather speche.

192. Thise ilke two, that ben in armes laft,
So looth to hem a-sonder goon it were,
That ech from other wende been biraft,

Or elles, lo, this was hir moste fere,
That al this thing but nyce dremes were;
For which ful ofte ech of hem seyde, 'O swete,
Clippe ich yow thus, or elles I it mete?'

193. And, lord! so he gan goodly on hir see,
That never his look ne bleynte from hir face,
And seyde, 'O dere herte, may it be
That it be sooth, that ye ben in this place?'
'Ye, herte myn, god thank I of his grace!'
Quod tho Criseyde, and therwith-al him kiste,
That where his spirit was, for joye he niste.

194. This Troilus ful ofte hir eyen two
Gan for to kisse, and seyde, 'O eyen clere,
It were ye that wroughte me swich wo,
Ye humble nettes of my lady dere!
Though ther be mercy writen in your chere,
God wot, the text ful hard is, sooth, to finde,
How coude ye with-outen bond me binde?'

195. Therwith he gan hir faste in armes take,
And wel an hundred tymes gan he syke,
Nought swiche sorwful sykes as men make
For wo, or elles whan that folk ben syke,
But esy sykes, swiche as been to lyke,
That shewed his affeccioun with-inne;
Of swiche sykes coude he nought bilinne.

196. Sone after this they speke of sondry thinges,
As fil to purpos of this aventure,
And pleyinge entrechaungeden hir ringes,
Of which I can nought tellen no scripture;
But wel I woot a broche, gold and asure,
In whiche a ruby set was lyk an herte,
Criseyde him yaf, and stak it on his sherte.

197. Lord! trowe ye, a coveitous, a wrecche,
That blameth love and holt of it despyt,
That, of tho pens that he can mokre and kecche,
Was ever yet y-yeve him swich delyt,
As is in love, in oo poynt, in som plyt?
Nay, doutelees, for also god me save,
So parfit joye may no nigard have!

198. They wol sey 'yis,' but lord! so that they lye,
Tho bisy wrecches, ful of wo and drede!
They callen love a woodnesse or folye,
But it shal falle hem as I shal yow rede;
They shul forgo the whyte and eke the rede,
And live in wo, ther god yeve hem mischaunce,
And every lover in his trouthe avaunce!

199. As wolde god, tho wrecches, that dispyse
Servyse of love, hadde eres al-so longe
As hadde Myda, ful of coveityse;
And ther-to dronken hadde as hoot and stronge
As Crassus dide for his affectis wronge,
To techen hem that they ben in the vyce,
And loveres nought, al-though they holde hem nyce!

200. Thise ilke two, of whom that I yow seye,
Whan that hir hertes wel assured were,
Tho gonne they to speken and to pleye,
And eek rehercen how, and whanne, and where,
They knewe hem first, and every wo and fere
That passed was; but al swich hevinesse.
I thanke it god, was tourned to gladnesse.

201. And ever-mo, whan that hem fel to speke
Of any thing of swich a tyme agoon,
With kissing al that tale sholde breke,
And fallen in a newe joye anoon,
And diden al hir might, sin they were oon,
For to recoveren blisse and been at ese,
And passed wo with joye countrepeyse.

202. Reson wil not that I speke of sleep,
For it accordeth nought to my matere;
God woot, they toke of that ful litel keep,
But lest this night, that was to hem so dere,
Ne sholde in veyn escape in no manere,
It was biset in joye and bisinesse
Of al that souneth in-to gentilnesse.

203. But whan the cok, comune astrologer,
Gan on his brest to bete, and after crowe,
And Lucifer, the dayes messager,

Gan for to ryse, and out hir bemes throwe;
And estward roos, to him that coude it knowe,
Fortuna maior, than anoon Criseyde,
With herte sore, to Troilus thus seyde:

204. 'Myn hertes lyf, my trist and my plesaunce,
That I was born, allas! what me is wo,
That day of us mot make desseveraunce!
For tyme it is to ryse, and hennes go,
Or elles I am lost for evermo!
O night, allas! why niltow over us hove,
As longe as whanne Almena lay by Jove?

205. 'O blake night, as folk in bokes rede,
That shapen art by god this world to hyde
At certeyn tymes with thy derk wede,
That under that men mighte in reste abyde,
Wel oughte bestes pleyne, and folk thee chyde,
That there-as day with labour wolde us breste,
That thou thus fleest, and deynest us nought reste!

206. 'Thou dost, allas! to shortly thyn offyce,
Thou rakel night, ther god, makere of kinde,
Thee, for thyn hast and thyn unkinde vyce,
So faste ay to our hemi-spere binde,
That never-more under the ground thou winde!
For now, for thou so hyest out of Troye,
Have I forgon thus hastily my joye!'

207. This Troilus, that with tho wordes felte,
As thoughte him tho, for piëtous distresse,
The blody teres from his herte melte,
As he that never yet swich hevinesse
Assayed hadde, out of so greet gladnesse,
Gan therwith-al Criseyde his lady dere
In armes streyne, and seyde in this manere:

208. 'O cruel day, accusour of the joye
That night and love han stole and faste y-wryen,
A-cursed be thy coming in-to Troye,
For every bore hath oon of thy bright yën!
Envyous day, what list thee so to spyen?
What hastow lost, why sekestow this place,
Ther god thy lyght so quenche, for his grace?

209. 'Allas! what han thise loveres thee agilt,
Dispitous day? thyn be the pyne of helle!
For many a lovere hastow shent, and wilt;
Thy pouring in wol no-where lete hem dwelle.
What proferestow thy light here for to selle?
Go selle it hem that smale seles graven,
We wol thee nought, us nedeth no day haven.'

210. And eek the sonne Tytan gan he chyde,
And seyde, 'O fool, wel may men thee dispyse,
That hast the Dawing al night by thy syde,
And suffrest hir so sone up fro thee ryse,
For to disesen loveres in this wyse.
What! hold your bed there, thou, and eek thy Morwe!
I bidde god, so yeve yow bothe sorwe!'

211. Therwith ful sore he sighte, and thus he seyde,
'My lady right, and of my wele or wo
The welle and rote, O goodly myn, Criseyde,
And shall I ryse, allas! and shal I go?
Now fele I that myn herte moot a-two!
For how sholde I my lyf an houre save,
Sin that with yow is al the lyf I have?

212. 'What shal I doon, for certes, I not how,
Ne whanne, allas! I shall the tyme see,
That in this plyt, I may be eft with yow;
And of my lyf, god woot how that shal be,
Sin that desyr right now so byteth me,
That I am deed anoon, but I retourne.
How sholde I longe, allas! fro yow sojourne?

213. 'But nathelees, myn owene lady bright,
Yit were it so that I wiste outrely,
That I, your humble servaunt and your knight,
Were in your herte set so fermely
As ye in myn, the which thing, trewely,
Me lever were than thise worldes tweyne,
Yet sholde I bet enduren al my peyne.'

214. To that Criseyde answerde right anoon,
And with a syk she seyde, 'O herte dere,
The game, y-wis, so ferforth now is goon,

That first shal Phebus falle fro his spere,
And every egle been the dowves fere,
And every roche out of his place sterte,
Er Troilus out of Criseydes herte!

215. 'Ye be so depe in with myn herte grave,
That, though I wolde it turne out of my thought,
As wisly verray god my soule save,
To dyen in the peyne, I coude nought!
And, for the love of god that us hath wrought,
Lat in your brayn non other fantasye
So crepe, that it cause me to dye!

216. 'And that ye me wolde han as faste in minde
As I have yow, that wolde I yow bi-seche;
And, if I wiste soothly that to finde,
God mighte not a poynt my joyes eche!
But, herte myn, with-oute more speche,
Beth to me trewe, or elles were it routhe;
For I am thyn, by god and by my trouthe!

217. 'Beth glad for-thy, and live in sikernesse;
Thus seyde I never er this, ne shal to mo;
And if to yow it were a gret gladnesse
To turne ayein, soone after that ye go,
As fayn wolde I as ye, it were so,
As wisly god myn herte bringe at reste!'
And him in armes took, and ofte keste.

218. Agayns his wil, sin it mot nedes be,
This Troilus up roos, and faste him cledde,
And in his armes took his lady free
An hundred tyme, and on his wey him spedde,
And with swich wordes as his herte bledde,
He seyde, 'farewel, my dere herte swete,
Ther god us graunte sounde and sone to mete!'

219. To which no word for sorwe she answerde,
So sore gan his parting hir destreyne;
And Troilus un-to his palays ferde,
As woo bigon as she was, sooth to seyne;
So hard him wrong of sharp desyr the peyne
For to ben eft there he was in plesaunce,
That it may never out of his remembraunce.

220. Retorned to his rëal palais, sone
He softe in-to his bed gan for to slinke,
To slepe longe, as he was wont to done,
But al for nought; he may wel ligge and winke,
But sleep ne may ther in his herte sinke;
Thenkinge how she, for whom desyr him brende,
A thousand-fold was worth more than he wende.

221. And in his thought gan up and doun to winde
Hir wordes alle, and every contenaunce,
And fermely impressen in his minde
The leste poynt that to him was plesaunce;
And verrayliche, of thilke remembraunce,
Desyr al newe him brende, and lust to brede
Gan more than erst, and yet took he non hede.

222. Criseyde also, right in the same wyse,
Of Troilus gan in hir herte shette
His worthinesse, his lust, his dedes wyse,
His gentilesse, and how she with him mette,
Thonkinge love he so wel hir bisette;
Desyring eft to have hir herte dere
In swich a plyt, she dorste make him chere.

223. Pandare, a-morwe which that comen was
Un-to his nece, and gan hir fayre grete,
Seyde, 'al this night so reyned it, allas!
That al my drede is that ye, nece swete,
Han litel layser had to slepe and mete;
Al night,' quod he, 'hath reyn so do me wake,
That som of us, I trowe, hir hedes ake.'

224. And ner he com, and seyde, 'how stont it now
This mery morwe, nece, how can ye fare?'
Criseyde answerde, 'never the bet for yow,
Fox that ye been, god yeve your herte care!
God helpe me so, ye caused al this fare,
Trow I,' quod she, 'for alle your wordes whyte;
O! who-so seeth yow knoweth yow ful lyte!'

225. With that she gan hir face for to wrye
With the shete, and wex for shame al reed;
And Pandarus gan under for to prye,

And seyde, 'nece, if that I shal ben deed,
Have here a swerd, and smyteth of myn heed.'
With that his arm al sodeynly he thriste
Under hir nekke, and at the laste hir kiste.

226. I passe al that which chargeth nought to seye,
What! God foryaf his deeth, and she al-so
Foryaf, and with hir uncle gan to pleye,
For other cause was ther noon than so.
But of this thing right to the effect to go,
Whan tyme was, hom til hir hous she wente,
And Pandarus hath fully his entente.

227. Now torne we ayein to Troilus,
That restelees ful loneg a-bedde lay,
And prevely sente after Pandarus,
To him to come in al the haste he may.
He com anoon, nought ones seyde he 'nay,'
And Troilus ful sobrely he grette,
And doun upon his beddes syde him sette.

228. This Troilus, with al the affeccioun
Of frendes love that herte may devyse,
To Pandarus on kneës fil adoun,
And er that he wolde of the place aryse,
He gan him thonken in his beste wyse;
A hondred sythe he gan the tyme blesse,
That he was born to bringe him fro distresse.

229. He seyde, 'O frend, of frendes th' alderbeste
That ever was, the sothe for to telle,
Thou hast in hevene y-brought my soule at reste
Fro Flegiton, the fery flood of helle;
That, though I mighte a thousand tymes selle,
Upon a day, my lyf in thy servyse,
It mighte nought a mote in that suffyse.

230. 'The sonne, which that al the world may see,
Saw never yet, my lyf, that dar I leye,
So inly fair and goodly as is she,
Whos I am al, and shal, til that I deye;
And, that I thus am hires, dar I seye,
That thanked be the heighe worthinesse
Of love, and eek thy kinde bisinesse.

231. 'Thus hastow me no litel thing y-yive,
For which to thee obliged be for ay
My lyf, and why? for thorugh thyn help I live;
For elles deed hadde I be many a day.'
And with that word doun in his bed he lay,
And Pandarus ful sobrely him herde
Til al was seyd, and thanne he him answerde:

232. 'My dere frend, if I have doon for thee
In any cas, god wot, it is me leef;
And am as glad as man may of it be,
God help me so; but tak now not a-greef
That I shal seyn, be war of this myscheef,
That, there-as thou now brought art in-to blisse,
That thou thy-self ne cause it nought to misse.

233. 'For of fortunes sharp adversitee
The worst kinde of infortune is this,
A man to have ben in prosperitee,
And it remembren, whan it passed is.
Thou art wys y-nough, for-thy do nought amis;
Be not to rakel, though thou sitte warme,
For if thou be, certeyn, it wol thee harme.

234. 'Thou art at ese, and hold thee wel ther-inne.
For also seur as reed is every fyr,
As greet a craft is kepe wel as winne;
Brydle alwey wel thy speche and thy desyr.
For worldly joye halt not but by a wyr;
That preveth wel, it brest alday so ofte;
For-thy nede is to werke with it softe.'

235. Quod Troilus, 'I hope, and god to-forn,
My dere frend, that I shal so me bere,
That in my gilt ther shal no thing be lorn,
N' I nil not rakle as for to greven here;
It nedeth not this matere ofte tere;
For wistestow myn herte wel, Pandare,
God woot, of this thou woldest litel care.'

236. Tho gan he telle him of his glade night,
And wher-of first his herte dredde, and how,
And seyde, 'freend, as I am trewe knight,

And by that feyth I shal to god and yow,
I hadde it never half so hote as now;
And ay the more that desyr me byteth
To love hir best, the more it me delyteth.

237. 'I noot my-self not wisly what it is;
But now I fele a newe qualitee,
Ye, al another than I dide er this.'
Pandare answerde, and seyde thus, that he
That ones may in heven blisse be,
He feleth other weyes, dar I leye,
Than thilke tyme he first herde of it seye.

238. This is o word for al; this Troilus
Was never ful, to speke of this matere,
And for to preysen un-to Pandarus
The bountee of his righte lady dere,
And Pandarus to thanke and maken chere.
This tale ay was span-newe to biginne
Til that the night departed hem a-twinne.

239. Sone after this, for that fortune it wolde,
I-comen was the blisful tyme swete,
That Troilus was warned that he sholde,
Ther he was erst, Criseyde his lady mete;
For which he felte his herte in joye flete;
And feythfully gan alle the goddes herie;
And lat see now if that he can be merie.

240. And holden was the forme and al the wyse,
Of hir cominge, and eek of his also,
As it was erst, which nedeth nought devyse.
But playnly to the effect right for to go,
In joye and seurte Pandarus hem two
A-bedde broughte, whan hem both leste,
And thus they ben in quiete and in reste.

241. Nought nedeth it to yow, sin they ben met,
To aske at me if that they blythe were;
For if it erst were wel, tho was it bet
A thousand fold, this nedeth not enquere.
A-gon was every sorwe and every fere;
And bothe, y-wis, they hadde, and so they wende,
As muche joye as herte may comprende.

242. This is no litel thing of for to seye,
This passeth every wit for to devyse;
For eche of hem gan otheres lust obeye;
Felicitee, which that thise clerkes wyse
Commenden so, ne may not here suffyse.
This joye may not writen been with inke,
This passeth al that herte may bithinke.

243. But cruel day, so wel-awey the stounde!
Gan for to aproche, as they by signes knewe,
For whiche hem thoughte felen dethes wounde:
So wo was hem, that changen gan hir hewe,
And day they gonnen to dispyse al newe,
Calling it traytour, envyous, and worse,
And bitterly the dayes lights they curse.

244. Quod Troilus, 'allas! now am I war
That Pirous and tho swifte stedes three,
Whiche that drawen forth the sonnes char,
Han goon som by-path in despyt of me;
That maketh it so sone day to be;
And, for the sonne him hasteth thus to ryse,
Ne shal I never doon him sacrifyse!'

245. But nedes day departe moste hem sone;
And whanne hir speche doon was and hir chere,
They twinne anoon as they were wont to done,
And setten tyme of meting eft y-fere;
And many a night they wroughte in this manere.
And thus Fortune a tyme ladde in joye
Criseyde, and eek this kinges sone of Troye.

246. In suffisaunce, in blisse, and in singinges,
This Troilus gan al his lyf to lede;
He spendeth, justeth, maketh festeyinges;
He yeveth frely ofte, and chaungeth wede,
And held aboute him alwey, out of drede,
A world of folk, as cam him wel of kinde,
The fressheste and the beste he coude finde;

247. That swich a voys was of him and a stevene
Through-out the world, of honour and largesse,
That it up rong un-to the yate of hevene.

And, as in love, he was in swich gladnesse,
That, in his herte he demede, as I gesse,
That there nis lovere in this world at ese
So wel as he, and thus gan love him plese.

248. The godlihede or beautee which that kinde
In any other lady hadde y-set
Can not the mountaunce of a knot unbinde,
A-boute his herte, of al Criseydes net.
He was so narwe y-masked and y-knet,
That it undoon on any manere syde,
That nil not been, for ought that may betyde.

249. And by the hond ful ofte he wolde take
This Pandarus, and in-to gardin lede,
And swich a feste and swich a proces make
Him of Criseyde, and of hir womanhede,
And of hir beautee, that, with-outen drede,
It was an hevene his wordes for to here;
And thanne he wolde singe in this manere:

250. 'Love, that of erthe and see hath governaunce,
Love, that his hestes hath in heven hye,
Love, that with an holsom alliaunce
Halt peples joyned, as him list hem gye,
Love, that knetteth lawe of companye,
And couples doth in vertu for to dwelle,
Bind this acord, that I have told and telle;

251. 'That that the world with feyth, which that is stable,
Dyverseth so his stoundes concordinge,
That elements that been so discordable
Holden a bond perpetuely duringe,
That Phebus mote his rosy day forth bringe,
And that the mone hath lordship over the nightes,
Al this doth Love; ay heried be his mightes!

252. 'That that the see, that gredy is to flowen,
Constreyneth to a certeyn ende so
His flodes, that so fersly they ne growen
To drenchen erthe and al for ever-mo;
And if that Love ought lete his brydel go,
Al that now loveth a-sonder sholde lepe,
And lost were al, that Love halt now to-hepe.

253. 'So wolde god, that auctor is of kinde,
That, with his bond, Love of his vertu liste
To cerclen hertes alle, and faste binde,
That from his bond no wight the wey out wiste.
And hertes colde, hem wolde I that he twiste
To make hem love, and that hem leste ay rewe
On hertes sore, and kep hem that ben trewe.'

254. In alle nedes, for the tounes werre,
He was, and ay the firste in armes dight;
And certeynly, but-if that bokes erre,
Save Ector, most y-drad of any wight;
And this encrees of hardinesse and might
Cam him of love, his ladies thank to winne,
That altered his spirit so with-inne.

255. In tyme of trewe, on haukinge wolde he ryde,
Or elles hunten boor, bere, or lyoun;
The smale bestes leet he gon bi-syde.
And whan that he com rydinge in-to toun,
Ful ofte his lady, from hir window doun,
As fresh as faucon comen out of muwe,
Ful redy was, him goodly to saluwe.

256. And most of love and vertu was his speeche,
And in despyt hadde alle wrecchednesse;
And doutelees, no nede was him biseche
To honouren hem that hadde worthinesse,
And esen hem that weren in distresse.
And glad was he if any wight wel ferde,
That lover was, whan he it wiste or herde.

257. For sooth to seyn, he lost held every wight
But-if he were in loves heigh servyse,
I mene folk that oughte it been of right.
And over al this, so wel coude he devyse
Of sentement, and in so unkouth wyse
Al his array, that every lover thoughte,
That al was wel, what-so he seyde or wroughte.

258. And though that he be come of blood royal,
Him liste of pryde at no wight for to chase;
Benigne he was to ech in general,

For which he gat him thank in every place.
Thus wolde Love, y-heried be his grace,
That Pryde, Envye, Ire, and Avaryce
He gan to flee, and every other vyce.

259. Thou lady bright, the daughter to Dione,
Thy blinde and winged sone eek, daun Cupyde;
Ye sustren nyne eek, that by Elicone
In hil Parnaso listen for to abyde,
That ye thus fer han deyned me to gyde,
I can no more, but sin that ye wol wende,
Ye heried been for ay, with-outen ende!

260. Thourgh yow have I seyd fully in my song
Th' effect and joye of Troilus servyse,
Al be that ther was som disese among,
As to myn auctor listeth to devyse.
My thridde book now ende ich in this wyse;
And Troilus in luste and in quiete
Is with Criseyde, his owne herte swete.

Explicit Liber Tercius

BOOK IV

[*Prohemium*]

1. But al to litel, weylawey the whyle,
Lasteth swich joye, y-thonked be Fortune!
That semeth trewest, whan she wol bygyle,
And can to foles so hir song entune,
That she hem hent and blent, traytour comune;
And whan a wight is from hir wheel y-throwe,
Than laugheth she, and maketh him the mowe.

2. From Troilus she gan hir brighte face
Awey to wrythe, and took of him non hede,
But caste him clene oute of his lady grace,
And on hir wheel she sette up Diomede;
For which right now myn herte ginneth blede,
And now my penne, allas! with which I wryte,
Quaketh for drede of that I moot endyte.

3. For how Criseyde Troilus forsook,
Or at the leste, how that she was unkinde,
Mot hennes-forth ben matere of my book,
As wryten folk thorugh which it is in minde.
Allas! that they shulde ever cause finde
To speke hir harm; and if they on hir lye,
Y-wis, hem-self sholde han the vilanye.

4. O ye Herines, Nightes doughtren three,
That endelees compleynen ever in pyne,
Megera, Alete, and eek Thesiphone;
Thou cruel Mars eek, fader to Quiryne,
This ilke ferthe book me helpeth fyne,
So that the los of lyf and love y-fere
Of Troilus be fully shewed here.

Explicit prohemium.　Incipit Quartus Liber

5. Ligginge in ost, as I have seyd er this,
The Grekes stronge, aboute Troye toun,
Bifel that, whan that Phebus shyning is

Up-on the brest of Hercules Lyoun,
That Ector, with ful many a bold baroun,
Caste on a day with Grekes for to fighte,
As he was wont to greve hem what he mighte.

6. Not I how longe or short it was bitwene
This purpos and that day they fighte mente;
But on a day wel armed, bright and shene,
Ector, and many a worthy wight out wente,
With spere in hond and bigge bowes bente;
And in the berd, with-oute lenger lette,
Hir fomen in the feld anoon hem mette.

7. The longe day, with speres sharpe y-grounde,
With arwes, dartes, swerdes, maces felle,
They fighte and bringen hors and man to grounde,
And with hir axes out the braynes quelle.
But in the laste shour, sooth for to telle,
The folk of Troye hem-selven so misledden,
That with the worse at night homward they fledden.

8. At whiche day was taken Antenor,
Maugre Polydamas or Monesteo,
Santippe, Sarpedon, Polynestor,
Polyte, or eek the Trojan daun Ripheo,
And othere lasse folk, as Phebuseo.
So that, for harm, that day the folk of Troye
Dredden to lese a greet part of hir joye.

9. Of Pryamus was yeve, at Greek requeste,
A tyme of trewe, and tho they gonnen trete,
Hir prisoneres to chaungen, moste and leste,
And for the surplus yeven sommes grete.
This thing anoon was couth in every strete,
Bothe in th' assege, in toune, and every-where,
And with the firste it cam to Calkas ere.

10. Whan Calkas knew this tretis sholde holde,
In consistorie, among the Grekes, sone
He gan in thringe forth, with lordes olde,
And sette him there-as he was wont to done;
And with a chaunged face hem bad a bone,
For love of god, to don that reverence,
To stinte noyse, and yeve him audience.

11. Thanne seyde he thus, 'lo! lordes myne, I was
Trojan, as it is knowen out of drede;
And if that yow remembre, I am Calkas,
That alderfirst yaf comfort to your nede,
And tolde wel how that ye sholden spede.
For dredelees, thorugh yow, shal, in a stounde,
Ben Troye y-brend, and beten doun to grounde.

12. 'And in what forme, or in what maner wyse
This town to shende, and al your lust to acheve,
Ye han er this wel herd it me devyse;
This knowe ye, my lordes, as I leve.
And for the Grekes weren me so leve,
I com my-self in my propre persone,
To teche in this how yow was best to done;

13. 'Havinge un-to my tresour ne my rente
Right no resport, to respect of your ese.
Thus al my good I loste and to yow wente,
Wening in this you, lordes, for to plese.
But al that los ne doth me no disese.
I vouche-sauf, as wisly have I joye.
For you to lese al that I have in Troye,

14. 'Save of a daughter, that I lafte, allas!
Slepinge at hoom, whanne out of Troye I sterte.
O sterne, O cruel fader that I was!
How might I have in that so hard an herte?
Allas! I ne hadde y-brought hir in hir sherte!
For sorwe of which I wol not live to morwe,
But-if ye lordes rewe up-on my sorwe.

15. 'For, by that cause I say no tyme er now
Hir to delivere, I holden have my pees;
But now or never, if that it lyke yow,
I may hir have right sone, doutelees.
O help and grace! amonges al this prees,
Rewe on this olde caitif in destresse,
Sin I through yow have al this hevinesse!

16. 'Ye have now caught and fetered in prisoun
Trojans y-nowe; and if your willes be
My child with oon may have redempcioun.

Now for the love of god and of bountee,
Oon of so fele, allas! so yeve him me.
What nede were it this preyere for to werne,
Sin ye shul bothe han folk and toun as yerne?

17. 'On peril of my lyf, I shal not lye,
Appollo hath me told it feithfully;
I have eek founde it by astronomye,
By sort, and by augurie eek trewely,
And dar wel seye, the tyme is faste by,
That fyr and flaumbe on al the toun shal sprede;
And thus shal Troye turne in asshen dede.

18. 'For certeyn, Phebus and Neptunus bothe,
That makeden the walles of the toun,
Ben with the folk of Troye alwey so wrothe,
That thei wol bringe it to confusioun,
Right in despyt of king Lameadoun.
By-cause he nolde payen hem hir hyre,
The toun of Troye shal ben set on-fyre.'

19. Telling his tale alwey, this olde greye,
Humble in speche, and in his lokinge eke,
The salte teres from his eyën tweye
Ful faste ronnen doun by eyther cheke.
So longe he gan of socour hem by-seke
That, for to hele him of his sorwes sore,
They yave him Antenor, with-oute more.

20. But who was glad y-nough but Calkas tho?
And of this thing ful sone his nedes leyde
On hem that sholden for the tretis go,
And hem for Antenor ful ofte preyde
To bringen hoom king Toas and Criseyde;
And whan Pryam his save-garde sente,
Th' embassadours to Troye streyght they wente.

21. The cause y-told of hir cominge, the olde
Pryam the king ful sone in general
Let here-upon his parlement to holde,
Of which the effect rehersen yow I shall.
Th' embassadours ben answered for fynal,
Th' eschaunge of prisoners and al this nede
Hem lyketh wel, and forth in they procede.

22. This Troilus was present in the place,
Whan axed was for Antenor Criseyde,
For which ful sone chaungen gan his face,
As he that with tho wordes wel neigh deyde.
But nathelees, he no word to it seyde,
Lest men sholde his affeccioun espye;
With mannes herte he gan his sorwes drye.

23. And ful of anguish and of grisly drede
Abood what lordes wolde un-to it seye;
And if they wolde graunte, as god forbede,
Th' eschaunge of hir, than thoughte he thinges tweye,
First, how to save hir honour, and what weye
He mighte best th' eschaunge of hir withstonde;
Ful faste he caste how al this mighte stonde.

24. Love him made al prest to doon hir byde,
And rather dye than she sholde go;
But resoun seyde him, on that other syde,
'With-oute assente of hir ne do not so,
Lest for thy werk she wolde be thy fo,
And seyn, that thorugh thy medling is y-blowe
Your bother love, there it was erst unknowe.'

25. For which he gan deliberen, for the beste,
That though the lordes wolde that she wente,
He wolde late hem graunte what hem leste,
And telle his lady first what that they mente.
And whan that she had seyd him hir entente,
Ther-after wolde he werken also blyve,
Though al the world ayein it wolde stryve.

26. Ector, which that wel the Grekes herde,
For Antenor how they wolde han Criseyde,
Gan it withstonde, and sobrely answerde:—
'Sires, she nis no prisoner,' he seyde;
'I noot on yow who that this charge leyde,
But, on my part, ye may eft-sone him telle,
We usen here no wommen for to selle.'

27. The noyse of peple up-stirte thanne at ones,
As breme as blase of straw y-set on fyre;
For infortune it wolde, for the nones,

They sholden hir confusioun desyre.
'Ector,' quod they, 'what goost may yow enspyre,
This womman thus to shilde and doon us lese
Daun Antenor?—a wrong wey now ye chese—

28. 'That is so wys, and eek so bold baroun,
And we han nede of folk, as men may see;
He is eek oon, the grettest of this toun;
O Ector, lat tho fantasyës be!
O king Pryam,' quod they, 'thus seggen we,
That al our voys is to for-gon Criseyde';
And to deliveren Antenor they preyde.

29. O Juvenal, lord! trewe is thy sentence,
That litel witen folk what is to yerne
That they ne finde in hir desyr offence;
For cloud of errour lat hem not descerne
What best is; and lo, here ensample as yerne.
This folk desiren now deliveraunce
Of Antenor, that broughte hem to mischaunce!

30. For he was after traytour to the toun
Of Troye; allas! they quitte him out to rathe;
O nyce world, lo, thy discrecioun!
Criseyde, which that never dide hem skathe,
Shal now no lenger in hir blisse bathe;
But Antenor, he shal com hoom to toune,
And she shal out: thus seyden here and howne.

31. For which delibered was by parlement,
For Antenor to yelden up Criseyde,
And it pronounced by the president,
Al-theigh that Ector 'nay' ful ofte preyde.
And fynaly, what wight that it withseyde,
It was for nought; it moste been, and sholde;
For substaunce of the parlement it wolde.

32. Departed out of parlement echone,
This Troilus, with-oute wordes mo,
Un-to his chaumbre spedde him faste allone,
But-if it were a man of his or two,
The whiche he bad out faste for to go,
By-cause he wolde slepen, as he seyde,
And hastely up-on his bed him leyde.

33. And as in winter leves been biraft,
Eche after other, til the tree be bare,
So that ther nis but bark and braunche y-laft,
Lyth Troilus, biraft of each wel-fare,
Y-bounden in the blake bark of care,
Disposed wood out of his wit to breyde,
So sore him sat the chaunginge of Criseyde.

34. He rist him up, and every dore he shette
And windowe eek, and tho this sorweful man
Up-on his beddes syde a-doun him sette,
Ful lyk a deed image pale and wan;
And in his brest the heped wo bigan
Out-breste, and he to werken in this wyse
In his woodnesse, as I shal yow devyse.

35. Right as the wilde bole biginneth springe
Now here, now there, y-darted to the herte,
And of his deeth roreth in compleyninge,
Right so gan he aboute the chaumbre sterte,
Smyting his brest ay with his festes smerte;
His heed to the wal, his body to the grounde
Ful ofte he swapte, him-selven to confounde.

36. His eyen two, for pitee of his herte,
Out stremeden as swifte welles tweye;
The heighe sobbes of his sorwes smerte
His speche him rafte, unnethes mighte he seye,
'O deeth, allas! why niltow do me deye?
A-cursed be the day which that nature
Shoop me to ben a lyves creature!'

37. But after, whan the furie and the rage
Which that his herte twiste and faste threste,
By lengthe of tyme somwhat gan asswage,
Up-on his bed he leyde him doun to reste;
But tho bigonne his teres more out-breste,
That wonder is, the body may suffyse
To half this wo, which that I yow devyse.

38. Then seyde he thus, 'Fortune! allas the whyle!
What have I doon, what have I thus a-gilt?
How mightestow for reuthe me bigyle?

Is ther no grace, and shal I thus be spilt?
Shal thus Criseyde awey, for that thou wilt?
Allas! how maystow in thyn herte finde
To been to me thus cruel and unkinde?

39. 'Have I thee nought honoured al my lyve,
As thou wel wost, above the goddes alle?
Why wiltow me fro joye thus depryve?
O Troilus, what may men now thee calle
But wrecche of wrecches, out of honour falle
In-to miserie, in which I wol biwayle
Criseyde, allas! til that the breeth me fayle?

40. 'Allas, Fortune! if that my lyf in joye
Displesed hadde un-to thy foule envye,
Why ne haddestow my fader, king of Troye,
By-raft the lyf, or doon my bretheren dye,
Or slayn my-self, that thus compleyne and crye,
I, combre-world, that may of no-thing serve,
But ever dye, and never fully sterve?

41. 'If that Criseyde allone were me laft,
Nought roughte I whider thou woldest me stere;
And hir, allas! than hastow me biraft.
But ever-more, lo! this is thy manere,
To reve a wight that most is to him dere,
To preve in that thy gerful violence.
Thus am I lost, ther helpeth no defence.

42. 'O verray lord of love, O god, allas!
That knowest best myn herte and al my thought,
What shal my sorwful lyf don in this cas
If I for-go that I so dere have bought?
Sin ye Cryseyde and me han fully brought
In-to your grace, and bothe our hertes seled,
How may ye suffre, allas! it be repeled?

43. 'What I may doon, I shal, whyl I may dure
On lyve in torment and in cruel peyne,
This infortune or this disaventure,
Allone as I was born, y-wis, compleyne;
Ne never wil I seen it shyne or reyne;
But ende I wil, as Edippe, in derknesse
My sorwful lyf, and dyen in distresse.

44. 'O wery goost, that errest to and fro,
Why niltow fleen out of the wofulleste
Body, that ever mighte on grounde go?
O soule, lurkinge in this wo, unneste,
Flee forth out of myn herte, and lat it breste,
And folwe alwey Criseyde, thy lady dere;
Thy righte place is now no lenger here!

45. 'O wofulle eyen two, sin your disport
Was al to seen Criseydes eyen brighte,
What shal ye doon but, for my discomfort,
Stonden for nought, and wepen out your sighte?
Sin she is queynt, that wont was yow to lighte,
In veyn fro-this-forth have I eyen tweye
Y-formed, sin your vertue is a-weye.

46. 'O my Criseyde, O lady sovereyne
Of thilke woful soule that thus cryeth,
Who shal now yeven comfort to my peyne?
Allas, no wight; but when myn herte dyeth,
My spirit, which that so un-to yow hyeth,
Receyve in gree, for that shal ay yow serve;
For-thy no fors is, though the body sterve.

47. 'O ye loveres, that heighe upon the wheel
Ben set of Fortune, in good aventure,
God leve that ye finde ay love of steel,
And longe mot your lyf in joye endure!
But whan ye comen by my sepulture,
Remembreth that your felawe resteth there;
For I lovede eek, though I unworthy were.

48. 'O olde unholsom and mislyved man,
Calkas I mene, allas! what eyleth thee
To been a Greek, sin thou art born Trojan?
O Calkas, which that wilt my bane be,
In cursed tyme was thou born for me!
As wolde blisful Jove, for his joye,
That I thee hadde, where I wolde, in Troye!'

49. A thousand sykes, hottere than the glede,
Out of his brest ech after other wente,
Medled with pleyntes newe, his wo to fede,

For which his woful teres never stente;
And shortly, so his peynes him to-rente,
And wex so mat, that joye nor penaunce
He feleth noon, but lyth forth in a traunce.

50. Pandare, which that in the parlement
Hadde herd what every lord and burgeys seyde,
And how ful graunted was, by oon assent,
For Antenor to yelden so Criseyde,
Gan wel neigh wood out of his wit to breyde,
So that, for wo, he niste what he mente;
But in a rees to Troilus he wente.

51. A certeyn knight, that for the tyme kepte
The chaumbre-dore, un-dide it him anoon;
And Pandare, that ful tendreliche wepte,
In-to the derke chaumbre, as stille as stoon,
Toward the bed gan softely to goon,
So confus, that he niste what to seye;
For verray wo his wit was neigh aweye.

52. And with his chere and loking al to-torn,
For sorwe of this, and with his armes folden,
He stood this woful Troilus biforn,
And on his pitous face he gan biholden;
But lord, so often gan his herte colden,
Seing his freend in wo, whos hevinesse
His herte slow, as thoughte him, for distresse.

53. This woful wight, this Troilus, that felte
His freend Pandare y-comen him to see,
Gan as the snow ayein the sonne melte,
For which this sorwful Pandare, of pitee,
Gan for to wepe as tendreliche as he;
And specheles thus been thise ilke tweye,
That neyther mighte o word for sorwe seye.

54. But at the laste this woful Troilus,
Ney deed for smert, gan bresten out to rore,
And with a sorwful noyse he seyde thus,
Among his sobbes and his sykes sore,
'Lo! Pandare, I am deed, with-outen more.
Hastow nought herd at parlement,' he seyde,
'For Antenor how lost is my Criseyde?'

55. This Pandarus, ful deed and pale of hewe,
Ful pitously answerde and seyde, 'yis!
As wisly were it fals as it is trewe,
That I have herd, and wot al how it is.
O mercy, god, who wolde have trowed this?
Who wolde have wend that, in so litel a throwe,
Fortune our joye wolde han over-throwe?

56. 'For in this world ther is no creature,
As to my doom, that ever saw ruyne
Straungere than this, thorugh cas or aventure.
But who may al eschewe or al devyne?
Swich is this world; for-thy I thus defyne,
Ne truste no wight finden in Fortune
Ay propretee; hir yeftes been comune.

57. 'But tel me this, why thou art now so mad
To sorwen thus? Why lystow in this wyse,
Sin thy desyr al holly hastow had,
So that, by right, it oughte y-now suffyse?
But I, that never felte in my servyse
A frendly chere or loking of an yë,
Lat me thus wepe and wayle, til I dye.

58. 'And over al this, as thou wel wost thy-selve,
This town is ful of ladies al aboute;
And, to my doom, fairer than swiche twelve
As ever she was, shal I finde, in som route,
Ye, oon or two, with-outen any doute.
For-thy be glad, myn owene dere brother,
If she be lost, we shul recovere another.

59. 'What, god for-bede alwey that ech plesaunce
In o thing were, and in non other wight!
If oon can singe, another can wel daunce;
If this be goodly, she is glad and light;
And this is fayr, and that can good a-right.
Ech for his vertu holden is for dere,
Bothe heroner and faucon for rivere.

60. 'And eek, as writ Zanzis, that was ful wys,
"The newe love out chaceth ofte the olde";
And up-on newe cas lyth newe avys.

Thenk eek, thy-self to saven artow holde;
Swich fyr, by proces, shal of kinde colde.
For sin it is but casuel plesaunce,
Som cas shal putte it out of remembraunce.

61. 'For al-so seur as day cometh after night,
The newe love, labour or other wo,
Or elles selde seinge of a wight,
Don olde affecciouns alle over-go.
And, for thy part, thou shalt have oon of tho
To abrigge with thy bittre peynes smerte;
Absence of hir shal dryve hir out of herte.'

62. Thise wordes seyde he for the nones alle,
To helpe his freend, lest he for sorwe deyde.
For doutelees, to doon his wo to falle,
He roughte not what unthrift that he seyde.
But Troilus, that neigh for sorwe deyde,
Tok litel hede of al that ever he mente;
Oon ere it herde, at the other out it wente:—

63. But at the laste answerde and seyde, 'freend,
This lechecraft, or heled thus to be,
Were wel sitting, if that I were a feend,
To traysen hir that trewe is unto me!
I pray god, lat this consayl never y-thee;
But do me rather sterve anon-right here
Er I thus do as thou me woldest lere.

64. 'She that I serve, y-wis, what so thou seye,
To whom myn herte enhabit is by right,
Shall han me holly hires til that I deye.
For, Pandarus, sin I have trouthe hir hight,
I wol not been untrewe for no wight;
But as hir man I wol ay live and sterve,
And never other creature serve.

65. 'And ther thou seyst, thou shalt as faire finde
As she, lat be, make no comparisoun
To creature y-formed here by kinde.
O leve Pandare, in conclusioun,
I wol not be of thyn opinioun,
Touching al this; for whiche I thee biseche,
So hold thy pees; thou sleest me with thy speche.

66. 'Thow biddest me I sholde love another
Al freshly newe, and lat Criseyde go!
It lyth not in my power, leve brother.
And though I mighte, I wolde not do so.
But canstow pleyen raket, to and fro,
Netle in, dokke out, now this, now that, Pandare?
Now foule falle hir, for thy wo that care!

67. 'Thow farest eek by me, thou Pandarus,
As he, that whan a wight is wo bi-goon,
He cometh to him a pas, and seyth right thus,
"Thenk not on smert, and thou shalt fele noon."
Thou most me first transmuwen in a stoon,
And reve me my passiounes alle,
Er thou so lightly do my wo to falle.

68. 'The deeth may wel out of my brest departe
The lyf, so longe may this sorwe myne;
But fro my soule shal Criseydes darte
Out never-mo; but doun with Proserpyne,
Whan I am deed, I wol go wone in pyne;
And ther I wol eternally compleyne
My wo, and how that twinned be we tweyne.

69. 'Thow hast here maad an argument, for fyn,
How that it sholde lasse peyne be
Criseyde to for-goon, for she was myn,
And live in ese and in felicitee.
Why gabbestow, that seydest thus to me
That "him is wors that is fro wele y-throwe,
Than he hadde erst non of that wele y-knowe"?

70. 'But tel me now, sin that thee thinketh so light
To chaungen so in love, ay to and fro,
Why hastow not don bisily thy might
To chaungen hir that doth thee al thy wo?
Why niltow lete hir fro thyn herte go?
Why niltow love an-other lady swete,
That may thyn herte setten in quiete?

71. 'If thou hast had in love ay yet mischaunce,
And canst it not out of thyn herte dryve,
I, that livede in lust and in plesaunce

With hir as muche as creature on-lyve,
How sholde I that foryete, and that so blyve?
O where hastow ben hid so longe in muwe,
That canst so wel and formely arguwe?

72. 'Nay, nay, god wot, nought worth is al thy reed,
For which, for what that ever may bifalle,
With-outen wordes mo, I wol be deed.
O deeth, that endere art of sorwes alle,
Com now, sin I so ofte after thee calle;
For sely is that deeth, soth for to seyne,
That, ofte y-cleped, cometh, and endeth peyne.

73. 'Wel wot I, whyl my lyf was in quiete,
Er thou me slowe, I wolde have yeven hyre;
But now thy cominge is to me so swete,
That in this world I no-thing so desyre.
O deeth, sin with this sorwe I am a-fyre,
Thou outher do me anoon in teres drenche,
Or with thy colde strook myn hete quenche!

74. 'Sin that thou sleest so fele in sondry wyse
Ayens hir wil, unpreyed, day and night,
Do me, at my requeste, this servyse,
Delivere now the world, so dostow right,
Of me, that am the wofulleste wight
That ever was; for tyme is that I sterve,
Sin in this world of right nought may I serve.'

75. This Troilus in teres gan distille,
As licour out of alambyk ful faste;
And Pandarus gan holde his tunge stille,
And to the ground his eyen doun he caste.
But nathelees, thus thoughte he at the laste,
'What, parde, rather than my felawe deye,
Yet shal I som-what more un-to him seye':

76. And seyde, 'freend, sin thou hast swich distresse,
And sin thee list myn arguments to blame,
Why nilt thy-selven helpen doon redresse,
And with thy manhod letten al this grame?
Go ravisshe hir ne canstow not for shame!
And outher lat hir out of toune fare,
Or hold hir stille, and leve thy nyce fare.

77. 'Artow in Troye, and hast non hardiment
To take a womman which that loveth thee,
And wolde hir-selven been of thyn assent?
Now is not this a nyce vanitee?
Rys up anoon, and lat this weping be,
And kyth thou art a man, for in this houre
I wil be deed, or she shal bleven oure.'

78. To this answerde him Troilus ful softe,
And seyde, 'parde, leve brother dere,
Al this have I my-self yet thought ful ofte,
And more thing than thou devysest here.
But why this thing is laft, thou shalt wel here;
And whan thou me hast yeve an audience,
Ther-after mayst thou telle al thy sentence.

79. 'First, sin thou wost this town hath al this werre
For ravisshing of wommen so by might,
It sholde not be suffred me to erre,
As it stant now, ne doon so gret unright.
I sholde han also blame of every wight,
My fadres graunt if that I so withstode,
Sin she is chaunged for the tounes goode.

80. 'I have eek thought, so it were hir assent,
To aske hir at my fader, of his grace;
Than thenke I, this were hir accusement,
Sin wel I woot I may hir not purchace.
For sin my fader, in so heigh a place
As parlement, hath hir eschaunge enseled,
He nil for me his lettre be repeled.

81. 'Yet drede I most hir herte to pertourbe
With violence, if I do swich a game;
For if I wolde it openly distourbe,
It moste been disclaundre to hir name.
And me were lever deed than hir defame,
As nolde god but-if I sholde have
Hir honour lever than my lyf to save!

82. 'Thus am I lost, for ought that I can see;
For certeyn is, sin that I am hir knight,
I moste hir honour lever han than me

In every cas, as lovere oughte of right.
Thus am I with desyr and reson twight;
Desyr for to distourben hir me redeth,
And reson nil not, so myn herte dredeth.'

83. Thus wepinge that he coude never cesse,
He seyde, 'allas! how shal I, wrecche, fare?
For wel fele I alwey my love encresse,
And hope is lasse and lasse alwey, Pandare!
Encressen eek the causes of my care;
So wel-a-wey, why nil myn herte breste?
For, as in love, ther is but litel reste.'

84. Pandare answerde, 'freend, thou mayst, for me,
Don as thee list; but hadde ich it so hote,
And thyn estat, she sholde go with me;
Though al this toun cryede on this thing by note,
I nolde sette at al that noyse a grote.
For when men han wel cryed, than wol they roune;
A wonder last but nyne night never in toune.

85. 'Devyne not in reson ay so depe
Ne curteysly, but help thy-self anoon;
Bet is that othere than thy-selven wepe,
And namely, sin ye two been al oon.
Rys up, for by myn heed, she shal not goon;
And rather be in blame a lyte y-founde
Than sterve here as a gnat, with-oute wounde.

86. 'It is no shame un-to yow, ne no vyce
Hir to with-holden, that ye loveth most.
Paraunter, she mighte holden thee for nyce
To lete hir go thus to the Grekes ost.
Thenk eek Fortune, as wel thy-selven wost,
Helpeth hardy man to his empryse,
And weyveth wrecches, for hir cowardyse.

87. 'And though thy lady wolde a litel hir greve,
Thou shalt thy pees ful wel here-after make,
But as for me, certayn, I can not leve
That she wolde it as now for yvel take.
Why sholde than for ferd thyn herte quake?
Thenk eek how Paris hath, that is thy brother,
A love; and why shaltow not have another?

88. 'And Troilus, o thing I dar thee swere,
That if Criseyde, whiche that is thy leef,
Now loveth thee as wel as thou dost here,
God helpe me so, she nil not take a-greef,
Though thou do bote a-noon in this mischeef.
And if she wilneth fro thee for to passe,
Thanne is she fals; so love hir wel the lasse.

89. 'For-thy tak herte, and thenk, right as a knight,
Thourgh love is broken alday every lawe.
Kyth now sumwhat thy corage and thy might,
Have mercy on thy-self, for any awe.
Lat not this wrecched wo thin herte gnawe,
But manly set the world on sixe and sevene;
And, if thou deye a martir, go to hevene.

90. 'I wol my-self be with thee at this dede,
Though ich and al my kin, up-on a stounde,
Shulle in a strete as dogges liggen dede,
Thourgh-girt with many a wyd and blody wounde.
In every cas I wol a freend be founde.
And if thee list here sterven as a wrecche,
A-dieu, the devel spede him that it recche!'

91. This Troilus gan with tho wordes quiken,
And seyde, 'freend, graunt mercy, ich assente;
But certaynly thou mayst not me so priken,
Ne peyne noon ne may me so tormente,
That, for no cas, it is not myn entente,
At shorte wordes, though I dyen sholde,
To ravisshe hir, but-if hir-self it wolde.'

92. 'Why, so mene I,' quod Pandarus, 'al this day.
But tel me than, hastow hir wel assayed,
That sorwest thus?'   And he answerde, 'nay.'
'Wher-of artow,' quod Pandare, 'than a-mayed,
That nost not that she wol ben yvel apayed
To ravisshe hir, sin thou hast not ben there,
But-if that Jove tolde it in thyn ere?

93. 'For-thy rys up, as nought ne were, anoon,
And wash thy face, and to the king thou wende,
Or he may wondren whider thou art goon.

Thou most with wisdom him and othere blende;
Or, up-on cas, he may after thee sende
Er thou be war; and shortly, brother dere,
Be glad, and let me werke in this matere.

94. 'For I shal shape it so, that sikerly
Thou shalt this night som tyme, in som manere.
Com speke with thy lady prevely,
And by hir wordes eek, and by hir chere,
Thou shalt ful sone aparceyve and wel here
Al hir entente, and in this cas the beste;'
And fare now wel, for in this point I reste.'

95. The swifte Fame, whiche that false thinges
Egal reporteth lyk the thinges trewe,
Was thorugh-out Troye y-fled with preste winges
Fro man to man, and made this tale al newe,
How Calkas doughter, with hir brighte hewe,
At parlement, with-oute wordes more,
I-graunted was in chaunge of Antenore.

96. The whiche tale anoon-right as Criseyde
Had herd, she which that of hir fader roughte,
As in this cas, right nought, ne whanne he deyde,
Ful bisily to Juppiter bisoughte
Yeve him mischaunce that this tretis broughte.
But shortly, lest thise tales sothe were,
She dorste at no wight asken it, for fere;

97. As she that hadde hir herte and al hir minde
On Troilus y-set so wonder faste,
That al this world ne might hir love unbinde,
Ne Troilus out of hir herte caste;
She wol ben his, whyl that hir lyf may laste.
And thus she brenneth bothe in love and drede,
So that she niste what was best to rede.

98. But as men seen in toune, and al aboute,
That wommen usen frendes to visyte,
So to Criseyde of wommen com a route
For pitous joye, and wenden hir delyte;
And with hir tales, dere y-nough a myte,
These wommen, whiche that in the cite dwelle,
They sette hem doun, and seyde as I shal telle.

99. Quod first that oon, 'I am glad, trewely,
By-cause of yow, that shal your fader see.'
A-nother seyde, 'y-wis, so nam not I;
For al to litel hath she with us be.'
Quod tho the thridde, 'I hope, y-wis, that she
Shal bringen us the pees on every syde,
That, whan she gooth, almighty god hir gyde!'

100. Tho wordes and tho wommannisshe thinges,
She herde hem right as though she thennes were;
For, god it wot, hir herte on other thing is,
Although the body sat among hem there.
Hir advertence is alwey elles-where;
For Troilus ful faste hir soule soughte;
With-outen word, alwey on him she thoughte.

101. Thise wommen, that thus wenden hir to plese,
Aboute nought gonne alle hir tales spende;
Swich vanitee ne can don hir non ese,
As she that, al this mene whyle, brende
Of other passioun than that they wende,
So that she felte almost hir herte dye
For wo, and wery of that companye.

102. For which no lenger mighte she restreyne
Hir teres, so they gonnen up to welle,
That yeven signes of the bitter peyne
In whiche hir spirit was, and moste dwelle;
Remembring hir, fro heven unto which helle
She fallen was, sith she forgoth the sighte
Of Troilus, and sorowfully she sighte.

103. And thilke foles sitting hir aboute
Wenden, that she wepte and syked sore
By-cause that she sholde out of that route
Departe, and never pleye with hem more.
And they that hadde y-knowen hir of yore
Seye hir so wepe, and thoughte it kindenesse,
And eche of hem wepte eek for hir distresse;

104. And bisily they gonnen hir conforten
Of thing, god wot, on which she litel thoughte;
And with hir tales wenden hir disporten,

And to be glad they often hir bisoughte.
But swich an ese ther-with they hir wroughte
Right as a man is esed for to fele,
For ache of heed, to clawen him on his hele!

105. But after al this nyce vanitee
They took hir leve, and hoom they wenten alle.
Criseyede, ful of sorweful pitee,
In-to hir chaumbre up wente out of the halle,
And on hir bed she gan for deed to falle,
In purpos never thennes for to ryse;
And thus she wroughte, as I shal yow devyse.

106. Hir ounded heer, that sonnish was of hewe,
She rente, and eek hir fingres longe and smale
She wrong ful ofte, and bad god on hir rewe,
And with the deeth to doon bote on hir bale.
Hir hewe, whylom bright, that tho was pale,
Bar witnes of hir wo and hir constreynte;
And thus she spak, sobbinge, in hir compleynte:

107. 'Alas!' quod she, 'out of this regioun
I, woful wrecche and infortuned wight,
And born in corsed constellacioun,
Mot goon, and thus departen fro my knight;
Wo worth, allas! that ilke dayes light
On which I saw him first with eyen tweyne,
That causeth me, and I him, al this peyne!'

108. Therwith the teres from hir eyen two
Doun fille, as shour in Aperill, ful swythe;
Hir whyte brest she bet, and for the wo
After the deeth she cryed a thousand sythe,
Sin he that wont hir wo was for to lythe,
She mot for-goon; for which disaventure
She held hir-self a forlost creature.

109. She seyde, 'how shal he doon, and I also?
How sholde I live, if that I from him twinne?
O dere herte eek, that I love so,
Who shal that sorwe sleen that ye ben inne?
O Calkas, fader, thyn be al this sinne!
O moder myn, that cleped were Argyve,
Wo worth that day that thou me bere on lyve!

110. 'To what fyn sholde I live and sorwen thus?
How sholde a fish with-oute water dure?
What is Criseyde worth, from Troilus?
How sholde a plaunte or lyves creature
Live, with-oute his kinde noriture?
For which ful oft a by-word here I seye,
That, "rotelees, mot grene sone deye."

111. 'I shal don thus, sin neither swerd ne darte
Dar I non handle, for the crueltee,
That ilke day that I from yow departe,
If sorwe of that nil not my bane be,
Than shal no mete or drinke come in me
Til I my soule out of my breste unshethe;
And thus my-selven wol I do to dethe.

112. 'And, Troilus, my clothes everichoon
Shul blake been, in tokeninge, herte swete,
That I am as out of this world agoon,
That wont was yow to setten in quiete;
And of myn ordre, ay til deeth me mete,
The observaunce ever, in your absence,
Shal sorwe been, compleynte, and abstinence.

113. 'Myn herte and eek the woful goost ther-inne
Biquethe I, with your spirit to compleyne
Eternally, for they shul never twinne.
For though in erthe y-twinned be we tweyne,
Yet in the feld of pitee, out of peyne,
That hight Elysos, shul we been y-fere,
As Orpheus and Erudice his fere.

114. 'Thus herte myn, for Antenor, allas!
I sone shal be chaunged, as I wene.
But how shul ye don in this sorwful cas,
How shal your tendre herte this sustene?
But herte myn, for-yet this sorwe and tene,
And me also; for, soothly for to seye,
So ye wel fare, I recche not to deye.'

115. How mighte it ever y-red ben or y-songe,
The pleynte that she made in hir distresse?
I noot; but, as for me, my litel tonge,

If I discreven wolde hir hevinesse,
It sholde make hir sorwe seme lesse
Than that it was, and childishly deface
Hir heigh compleynte, and therfore I it pace.

116. Pandare, which that sent from Troilus
Was to Criseyde, as ye han herd devyse,
That for the beste it was accorded thus,
And he ful glad to doon him that servyse,
Un-to Criseyde, in a ful secree wyse,
There-as she lay in torment and in rage,
Com hir to telle al hoolly his message.

117. And fond that she hir-selven gan to trete
Ful pitously; for with hir salte teres
Hir brest, hir face y-bathed was ful wete;
The mighty tresses of hir sonnish heres,
Unbroyden, hangen al about hir eres;
Which yaf him verray signal of martyre
Of deeth, which that hir herte gan desyre.

118. Whan she him saw, she gan for sorwe anoon
Her tery face a-twixe hir armes hyde,
For which this Pandare is so wo bi-goon,
That in the hous he mighte unnethe abyde,
As he that pitee felte on every syde.
For if Criseyde hadde erst compleyned sore,
Tho gan she pleyne a thousand tymes more.

119. And in hir aspre pleynte than she seyde,
'Pandare first of joyes mo than two
Was cause causinge un-to me, Criseyde,
That now transmuwed been in cruel wo.
Wher shal I seye to yow "wel come" or no,
That alderfirst me broughte in-to servyse
Of love, allas! that endeth in swich wyse?

120. 'Endeth than love in wo? Ye, or men lyeth!
And alle worldly blisse, as thinketh me,
The ende of blisse ay sorwe it occupyeth;
And who-so troweth not that it so be,
Lat him upon me, woful wrecche, y-see,
That my-self hate, and ay my birthe acorse,
Felinge alwey, fro wikke I go to worse.

121. 'Who-so me seeth, he seeth sorwe al at ones,
Peyne, torment, pleynte, wo, distresse.
Out of my woful body harm ther noon is,
As anguish, langour, cruel bitternesse,
A-noy, smert, drede, fury, and eek siknesse,
I trowe, y-wis, from hevene teres reyne,
For pitee of myn aspre and cruel peyne!'

122. 'And thou, my suster, ful of discomfort,'
Quod Pandarus, 'what thenkestow to do?
Why ne hastow to thy-selven som resport,
Why woltow thus thy-selve, allas, for-do?
Leef al this werk and tak now hede to
That I shal seyn, and herkne, of good entente,
This, which by me thy Troilus thee sente.'

123. Torned hir tho Criseyde, a wo makinge
So greet that it a deeth was for to see:—
'Allas!' quod she, 'what wordes may ye bringe?
What wol my dere herte seyn to me,
Which that I drede never-mo to see?
Wol he have pleynte or teres, er I wende?
I have y-nowe, if he ther-after sende!'

124. She was right swich to seen in hir visage
As is that wight that men on bere binde;
Hir face, lyk of Paradys the image,
Was al y-chaunged in another kinde.
The pleye, the laughtre men was wont to finde
In hir, and eek hir joyes everychone,
Ben fled, and thus lyth now Criseyde allone.

125. Aboute hir eyen two a purpre ring
Bi-trent, in sothfast tokninge of hir peyne,
That to biholde it was a dedly thing,
For which Pandare might not restreyne
The teres from his eyen for to reyne.
But nathelees, as he best mighte, he seyde
From Troilus thise wordes to Criseyde.

126. 'Lo, nece, I trowe ye han herd al how
The king, with othere lordes, for the beste,
Hath mad eschaunge of Antenor and yow,

That cause is of this sorwe and this unreste.
But how this cas doth Troilus moleste,
That may non erthely mannes tonge seye;
For verray wo his wit is al aweye.

127. 'For which we han so sorwed, he and I,
That in-to litel bothe it hadde us slawe;
But thurgh my conseil this day, fynally,
He somwhat is fro weping now withdrawe.
And semeth me that he desyreth fawe
With yow to been al night, for to devyse
Remede in this, if there were any wyse.

128. 'This, short and pleyne, th' effect of my message,
As ferforth as my wit can comprehende.
For ye, that been of torment in swich rage,
May to no long prologe as now entende;
And her-upon ye may answere him sende.
And, for the love of god, my nece dere,
So leef this wo er Troilus be here.'

129. 'Gret is my wo,' quod she, and sighte sore,
As she that feleth dedly sharp distresse;
'But yet to me his sorwe is muchel more,
That love him bet than he him-self, I gesse.
Allas! for me hath he swich hevinesse?
Can he for me so pitously compleyne?
Y-wis, this sorwe doubleth al my peyne.

130. 'Grevous to me, god wot, is for to twinne,'
Quod she, 'but yet it hardere is to me
To seen that sorwe which that he is inne;
For wel wot I, it wol my bane be;
And deye I wol in certayn,' tho quod she;
'But bidde him come, er deeth, that thus me threteth,
Dryve out that goost, which in myn herte beteth.'

131. Thise wordes seyd, she on hir armes two
Fil gruf, and gan to wepe pitously.
Quod Pandarus, 'allas! why do ye so,
Syn wel ye wot the tyme is faste by,
That he shal come?   Arys up hastely,
That he yow nat biwopen thus ne finde,
But ye wol han him wood out of his minde!

132. 'For wiste he that ye ferde in this manere,
He wolde him-selve slee; and if I wende
To han this fare, he sholde not come here
For al the good that Pryam may despende.
For to what fyn he wolde anoon pretende,
That knowe I wel; and for-thy yet I seye,
So leef this sorwe, or platly he wol deye.

133. 'And shapeth yow his sorwe for to abregge,
And nought encresse, leve nece swete;
Beth rather to him cause of flat than egge,
And with som wysdom ye his sorwes bete.
What helpeth it to wepen ful a strete,
Or though ye bothe in salte teres dreynte?
Bet is a tyme of cure ay than of pleynte.

134. 'I mene thus; whan I him hider bringe,
Sin ye ben wyse, and bothe of oon assent,
So shapeth how distourbe your goinge,
Or come ayen, sone after ye be went.
Wommen ben wyse in short avysement;
And lat sen how your wit shal now avayle;
And what that I may helpe, it shal not fayle.'

135. 'Go,' quod Criseyde, 'and uncle, trewely,
I shal don al my might, me to restreyne
From weping in his sight, and bisily,
Him for to glade, I shal don al my peyne,
And in myn herte seken every veyne;
If to this soor ther may be founden salve,
It shal not lakken, certain, on myn halve.'

136. Goth Pandarus, and Troilus he soughte,
Til in a temple he fond him allone,
As he that of his lyf no lenger roughte;
But to the pitouse goddes everichone
Ful tendrely he preyde, and made his mone,
To doon him sone out of this world to pace;
For wel he thoughte ther was non other grace.

137. And shortly, al the sothe for to seye,
He was so fallen in despeyr that day,
That outrely he shoop him for to deye.

For right thus was his argument alwey:
He seyde, he nas but loren, waylawey!
'For al that comth, comth by necessitee;
Thus to be lorn, it is my destinee.

138. 'For certaynly, this wot I wel,' he seyde,
'That for-sight of divyne purveyaunce
Hath seyn alwey me to for-gon Criseyde,
Sin god seeth every thing, out of doutaunce,
And hem desponeth, thourgh his ordenaunce,
In hir merytes sothly for to be,
As they shul comen by predestinee.

139. 'But nathelees, allas! whom shal I leve?
For ther ben grete clerkes many oon,
That destinee thorugh argumentes preve;
And som men seyn that nedely there is noon;
But that free chois is yeven us everichoon.
O, welaway! so sleye arn clerkes olde,
That I not whos opinion I may holde.

140. 'For som men seyn, if god seth al biforn,
Ne god may not deceyved ben, pardee,
Than moot it fallen, though men hadde it sworn,
That purveyaunce hath seyn bifore to be.
Wherefor I seye, that from eterne if he
Hath wist biforn our thought eek as our dede,
We have no free chois, as these clerkes rede.

141. 'For other thought nor other dede also
Might never be, but swich as purveyaunce,
Which may not ben deceyved never-mo,
Hath feled biforn, with-outen ignoraunce.
For if ther mighte been a variaunce
To wrythen out fro goddes purveyinge,
There nere no prescience of thing cominge;

142. 'But it were rather an opinioun
Uncerteyn, and no stedfast forseinge;
And certes, that were an abusioun,
That god shuld han no parfit cleer witinge
More than we men that han doutous weninge.
But swich an errour up-on god to gesse
Were fals and foul, and wikked corsednesse.

143. 'Eek this is an opinioun of somme
That han hir top ful heighe and smothe y-shore;
They seyn right thus, that thing is not to come
For that the prescience hath seyn bifore
That it shal come; but they seyn, that therfore
That it shal come, therfore the purveyaunce
Wot it biforn with-outen ignoraunce;

144. 'And in this manere this necessitee
Retorneth in his part contrarie agayn.
For needfully bihoveth it not to be
That thilke thinges fallen in certayn
That ben purveyed; but nedely, as they seyn,
Bihoveth it that thinges, whiche that falle,
That they in certayn ben purveyed alle.

145. 'I mene as though I laboured me in this,
To enqueren which thing cause of which thing be;
As whether that the prescience of god is
The certayn cause of the necessitee
Of thinges that to comen been, pardee;
Or if necessitee of thing cominge
Be cause certeyn of the purveyinge.

146. 'But now ne enforce I me nat in shewinge
How the ordre of causes stant; but wel wot I,
That it bihoveth that the bifallinge
Of thinges wist biforen certeynly
Be necessarie, al seme it not ther-by
That prescience put falling necessaire
To thing to come, al falle it foule or faire.

147. 'For if ther sit a man yond on a see,
Than by necessitee bihoveth it
That, certes, thyn opinioun soth be,
That wenest or conjectest that he sit;
And ferther-over now ayenward yit,
Lo, right so it is of the part contrarie,
As thus; (now herkne, for I wol not tarie):

148. 'I seye, that if the opinioun of thee
Be sooth, for that he sit, than seye I this,
That he mot sitten by necessitee;

And thus necessitee in either is.
For in him nede of sitting is, y-wis,
And in thee nede of sooth; and thus, forsothe,
Ther moot necessitee ben in yow bothe.

149. 'But thou mayst seyn, the man sit not therfore,
That thyn opinion of sitting soth is;
But rather, for the man sit there bifore,
Therfore is thyn opinion sooth, y-wis.
And I seye, though the cause of sooth of this
Comth of his sitting, yet necessitee
Is entrechaunged, bothe in him and thee.

150. 'Thus on this same wyse, out of doutaunce,
I may wel maken, as it semeth me,
My resoninge of goddes purveyaunce,
And of the thinges that to comen be;
By whiche reson men may wel y-see,
That thilke thinges that in erthe falle,
That by necessitee they comen alle.

151. 'For al-though that, for thing shal come, y-wis,
Therefore is it purveyed, certaynly,
Nat that it comth for it purveyed is:
Yet natheless, bihoveth it nedfully,
That thing to come be purveyed, trewely;
Or elles, thinges that purveyed be,
That they bityden by necessitee.

152. 'And this suffyseth right y-now, certeyn,
For to destroye our free chois every del.—
But now is this abusion to seyn,
That fallinge of the thinges temporel
Is cause of goddes prescience eternel.
Now trewely, that is a fals sentence,
That thing to come sholde cause his prescience.

153. 'What mighte I wene, and I hadde swich a thought,
But that god purveyth thing that is to come
For that it is to come, and elles nought?
So mighte I wene that thinges alle and some,
That whylom been bifalle and over-come,
Ben cause of thilke sovereyn purveyaunce,
That for-wot al with-outen ignoraunce.

154. 'And over al this, yet seye I more herto,
That right as whan I woot ther is a thing,
Y-wis, that thing mot nedefully be so;
Eek right so, whan I woot a thing coming,
So mot it come; and thus the bifalling
Of thinges that ben wist bifore the tyde,
They mowe not been eschewed on no syde.'

155. Than seyde he thus, 'almighty Jove in trone,
That wost of al this thing the soothfastnesse,
Rewe on my sorwe, or do me deye sone,
Or bring Criseyde and me fro this distresse.'
And whyl he was in al this hevinesse,
Disputinge with him-self in this matere,
Com Pandare in, and seyde as ye may here.

156. 'O mighty god,' quod Pandarus, 'in trone,
Ey! who seigh ever a wys man faren so?
Why, Troilus, what thenkestow to done?
Hastow swich lust to been thyn owene fo?
What, parde, yet is not Criseyde a-go!
Why lust thee so thy-self for-doon for drede,
That in thyn heed thyn eyen semen dede?

157. 'Hastow not lived many a yeer biforn
With-outen hir, and ferd ful wel at ese?
Artow for hir and for non other born?
Hath kind thee wroughte al-only hir to plese?
Lat be, and thenk right thus in thy disese:
That, in the dees right as ther fallen chaunces,
Right so in love, ther com and goon plesaunces.

158. 'And yet this is a wonder most of alle,
Why thou thus sorwest, sin thou nost not yit,
Touching hir goinge, how that it shal falle,
Ne if she can hir-self distorben it.
Thou hast not yet assayed al hir wit.
A man may al by tyme his nekke bede
Whan it shal of, and sorwen at the nede.

159. 'For-thy take hede of that that I shal seye;
I have with hir y-spoke and longe y-be,
So as accorded was bitwixe us tweye.

And ever-mo me thinketh thus, that she
Hath som-what in hir hertes prevetee,
Wher-with she can, if I shal right arede,
Distorbe al this, of which thou art in drede.

160. 'For which my counseil is, whan it is night,
Thou to hir go, and make of this an ende;
And blisful Juno, thourgh hir grete mighte,
Shal, as I hope, hir grace un-to us sende.
Myn herte seyth, "certeyn, she shal not wende";
And for-thy put thyn herte a whyle in reste;
And hold this purpos, for it is the beste.'

161. This Troilus answerde, and sighte sore,
'Thou seyst right wel, and I wil do right so';
And what him liste, he seyde un-to it more.
And whan that it was tyme for to go,
Ful prevely him-self, with-outen mo,
Un-to hir com, as he was wont to done;
And how they wroughte, I shal yow telle sone.

162. Soth is, that whan they gonne first to mete,
So gan the peyne hir hertes for to twiste,
That neither of hem other mighte grete,
But hem in armes toke and after kiste.
The lasse wofulle of hem bothe niste
Wher that he was, ne mighte o word out-bringe,
As I seyde erst, for wo and for sobbinge.

163. The woful teres that they leten falle
As bittre weren, out of teres kinde,
For peyne, as is ligne-aloës or galle.
So bittre teres weep nought, as I finde,
The woful Myrra through the bark and rinde.
That in this world ther nis so hard an herte,
That nolde han rewed on hir peynes smerte.

164. But whan hir woful wery gostes tweyne
Retorned been ther-as hem oughte dwelle,
And that som-what to wayken gan the peyne
By lengthe of pleynte, and ebben gan the welle
Of hire teres, and the herte unswelle,
With broken voys, al hoors for-shright, Criseyde
To Troilus thise ilke wordes seyde:

165. 'O Jove, I deye, and mercy I beseche!
Help, Troilus!' and ther-with-al hir face
Upon his brest she leyde, and loste speche;
Hir woful spirit from his propre place,
Right with the word, alwey up poynt to pace.
And thus she lyth with hewes pale and grene,
That whylom fresh and fairest was to sene.

166. This Troilus, that on hir gan biholde,
Clepinge hir name, (and she lay as for deed,
With-oute answere, and felte hir limes colde,
Hir eyen throwen upward to hir heed),
This sorwful man can now noon other reed,
But ofte tyme hir colde mouth he kiste;
Wher him was wo, god and him-self it wiste!

167. He rist him up, and long streight he hir leyde;
For signe of lyf, for ought he can or may,
Can he noon finde in no-thing on Criseyde,
For which his song ful ofte is 'weylaway!'
But whan he saugh that specheles she lay,
With sorwful voys, and herte of blisse al bare,
He seyde how she was fro this world y-fare!

168. So after that he longe hadde hir compleyned,
His hondes wronge, and seyd that was to seye,
And with his teres salte hir brest bireyned,
He gan tho teres wypen of ful dreye,
And pitously gan for the soule preye,
And seyde, 'O lord, that set art in thy trone,
Rewe eek on me, for I shal folwe hir sone!'

169. She cold was and with-outen sentement,
For aught he woot, for breeth ne felte he noon;
And this was him a preignant argument
That she was forth out of this world agoon;
And whan he seigh ther was non other woon,
He gan hir limes dresse in swich manere
As men don hem that shul be leyd on bere.

170. And after this, with sterne and cruel herte,
His swerd a-noon out of his shethe he twighte,
Him-self to sleen. how sore that him smerte,

So that his sowle hir sowle folwen mighte,
Ther-as the doom of Mynos wolde it dighte;
Sin love and cruel Fortune it ne wolde,
That in this world he lenger liven sholde.

171. Thanne seyde he thus, fulfild of heigh desdayn,
'O cruel Jove, and thou, Fortune adverse,
This al and som, that falsly have ye slayn
Criseyde, and sin ye may do me no werse,
Fy on your might and werkes so diverse!
Thus cowardly ye shul me never winne;
Ther shal no deeth me fro my lady twinne.

172. 'For I this world, sin ye han slayn hir thus,
Wol lete, and folowe hir spirit lowe or hye;
Shal never lover seyn that Troilus
Dar not, for fere, with his lady dye;
For certeyn, I wol bere hir companye.
But sin ye wol not suffre us liven here,
Yet suffreth that our soules ben y-fere.

173. 'And thou, citee, whiche that I leve in wo,
And thou, Pryam, and bretheren al y-fere,
And thou, my moder, farewel! for I go;
And Attropos, make redy thou my bere!
And thou, Criseyde, o swete herte dere,
Receyve now my spirit!' wolde he seye,
With swerd at herte, al redy for to deye.

174. But as god wolde, of swough therwith she abreyde,
And gan to syke, and 'Troilus' she cryde;
And he answerde, 'lady myn Criseyde,
Live ye yet?' and leet his swerd doun glyde.
'Ye, herte myn, that thanked be Cupyde!'
Quod she, and ther-with-al she sore sighte;
And he bigan to glade hir as he mighte;

175. Took hir in armes two, and kiste hir ofte,
And hir to glade he dide al his entente;
For which hir goost, that flikered ay on-lofte,
In-to hir woful herte ayein it wente.
But at the laste, as that hir eyen glente
A-syde, anoon she gan his swerd aspye,
As it lay bare, and gan for fere crye,

176. And asked him, why he it hadde out-drawe?
And Troilus anoon the cause hir tolde,
And how himself ther-with he wolde have slawe.
For which Criseyde up-on him gan biholde,
And gan him in hir armes faste folde,
And seyde, 'O mercy, god, lo, which a dede!
Allas! how neigh we were bothe dede!

177. 'Thanne if I ne hadde spoken, as grace was,
Ye wolde han slayn your-self anoon?' quod she.
'Ye, douteless'; and she answerde, 'allas!
For, by that ilke lord that made me,
I nolde a forlong wey on-lyve han be,
After your deeth, to han be crowned quene
Of all the lond the sonne on shyneth shene.

178. 'But with this selve swerd, which that here is,
My-selve I wolde have slayn!'—quod she tho;
'But ho, for we han right y-now of this,
And late us ryse and streight to bedde go,
And therë lat us speken of our wo.
For, by the morter which that I see brenne,
Knowe I ful wel that day is not fer henne.'

179. Whan they were in hir bedde, in armes folde,
Nought was it lyk tho nightes here-biforn;
For pitously ech other gan biholde,
As they that hadden al hir blisse y-lorn,
Biwaylinge ay the day that they were born.
Til at the last this sorwful wight Criseyde
To Troilus these ilke wordes seyde:—

180. 'Lo, herte myn, wel wot ye this,' quod she,
'That if a wight alwey his wo compleyne,
And seketh nought now holpen for to be,
It nis but folye and encrees of peyne;
And sin that here assembled be we tweyne
To finde bote of wo that we ben inne,
It were al tyme sone to biginne.

181. 'I am a womman, as ful wel ye woot,
And as I am avysed sodeynly,
So wol I telle yow, whyl it is hoot.

Me thinketh thus, that neither ye nor I
Oughte half this wo to make skilfully.
For there is art y-now for to redresse
That yet is mis, and sleen this hevinesse.

182. 'Sooth is, the wo, the whiche that we ben inne,
For ought I woot, for no-thing elles is
But for the cause that we sholden twinne.
Considered al, ther nis no-more amis.
But what is thanne a remede un-to this,
But that we shape us sone for to mete?
This al and som, my dere herte swete.

183. 'Now that I shal wel bringen it aboute
To come ayein, sone after that I go,
Ther-of am I no maner thing in doute.
For dredeles, with-inne a wouke or two,
I shal ben here; and, that it may be so
By alle right, and in a wordes fewe,
I shal yow wel an heep of weyes shewe.

184. 'For which I wol not make long sermoun,
For tyme y-lost may not recovered be;
But I wol gon to my conclusioun,
And to the beste, in ought that I can see.
And, for the love of god, for-yeve it me
If I speke ought ayein your hertes reste;
For trewely, I speke it for the beste;

185. 'Makinge alwey a protestacioun,
That now these wordes, whiche that I shal seye,
Nis but to shewe yow my mocioun,
To finde un-to our helpe the beste weye;
And taketh it non other wyse, I preye.
For in effect what-so ye me comaunde,
That wol I doon, for that is no demaunde.

186. 'Now herkeneth this, ye han wel understonde,
My going graunted is by parlement
So ferforth, that it may not be with-stonde
For al this world, as by my jugement.
And sin ther helpeth noon avysement
To letten it, lat it passe out of minde;
And lat us shape a bettre wey to finde.

187. 'The sothe is, that the twinninge of us tweyne
Wol us disese and cruelliche anoye.
But him bihoveth som-tyme han a peyne,
That serveth love, if that he wol have joye.
And sin I shal no ferthere out of Troye
Than I may ryde ayein on half a morwe,
It oughte lasse causen us to sorwe:

188. 'So as I shal not so ben hid in muwe,
That day by day, myn owene herte dere,
Sin wel ye woot that it is now a truwe,
Ye shul ful wel al myn estat y-here.
And er that truwe is doon, I shal ben here,
And thanne have ye bothe Antenor y-wonne
And me also; beth glad now, if ye conne;

189. 'And thenk right thus, "Criseyde is now agoon,
But what! she shal come hastely ayeyn";
And whanne, allas? by god, lo, right anoon,
Er dayes ten, this dar I saufly seyn.
And thanne at erste shul we been so fayn,
So as we shulle to-gederes ever dwelle,
That al this world ne mighte our blisse telle.

190. 'I see that ofte, ther-as we ben now,
That for the beste, our conseil for to hyde,
Ye speke not with me, nor I with yow
In fourtenight; ne see yow go ne ryde.
May ye not ten dayes thanne abyde,
For myn honour, in swich an aventure?
Y-wis, ye mowen elles lyte endure!

191. 'Ye knowe eek how that al my kin is here,
But-if that onliche it my fader be;
And eek myn othere thinges alle y-fere,
And nameliche, my dere herte, ye,
Whom that I nolde leven for to see
For al this world, as wyd as it hath space;
Or elles, see ich never Joves face!

192. 'Why trowe ye my fader in this wyse
Coveiteth so to see me, but for drede
Lest in this toun that folkes me dispyse

By-cause of him, for his unhappy dede?
What woot my fader what lyf that I lede?
For if he wiste in Troye how wel I fare,
Us neded for my wending nought to care.

193. 'Ye seen that every day eek, more and more,
Men trete of pees; and it supposed is,
That men the quene Eleyne shal restore,
And Grekes us restore that is mis.
So though ther nere comfort noon but this,
That men purposen pees on every syde,
Ye may the bettre at ese of herte abyde.

194. 'For if that it be pees, myn herte dere,
The nature of the pees mot nedes dryve
That men moste entrecomunen y-fere,
And to and fro eek ryde and gon as blyve
Alday as thikke as been flen from an hyve;
And every wight han libertee to bleve
Wher-as him list the bet, with-outen leve.

195. 'And though so be that pees ther may be noon,
Yet hider, though ther never pees ne were,
I moste come; for whider sholde I goon,
Or how mischaunce sholde I dwelle there
Among tho men of armes ever in fere?
For which, as wisly god my soule rede,
I can not seen wher-of ye sholden drede.

196. 'Have here another wey, if it so be
That al this thing ne may yow not suffyse.
My fader, as ye knowen wel, pardee,
Is old, and elde is ful of coveityse.
And I right now have founden al the gyse,
With-oute net, wher-with I shal him hente;
And herkeneth how, if that ye wole assente.

197. 'Lo, Troilus, men seyn that hard it is
The wolf ful, and the wether hool to have;
This is to seyn, that men ful ofte, y-wis,
Mot spenden part, the remenaunt for to save.
For ay with gold men may the herte grave
Of him that set is up-on coveityse;
And how I mene, I shall it yow devyse.

198. 'The moeble which that I have in this toun
Un-to my fader shal I take, and seye,
That right for trust and for savacioun
It sent is from a freend of his or tweye,
The whiche freendes ferventliche him preye
To senden after more, and that in hye,
Whyl that this toun stant thus in jupartye.

199. 'And that shal been an huge quantitee,
Thus shal I seyn, but, lest it folk aspyde,
This may be sent by no wight but by me;
I shal eek shewen him, if pees bityde,
What frendes that ich have on every syde
Toward the court, to doon the wrathe pace
Of Priamus, and doon him stonde in grace.

200. 'So, what for o thing and for other, swete,
I shall him so enchaunten with my sawes,
That right in hevene his sowle is, shal he mete!
For al Appollo, or his clerkes lawes,
Or calculinge avayleth nought three hawes;
Desyr of gold shal so his sowle blende,
That, as me lyst, I shal wel make an ende.

201. 'And if he wolde ought by his sort it preve
If that I lye, in certayn I shal fonde
Distorben him, and plukke him by the sleve,
Makinge his sort, and beren him on honde,
He hath not wel the goddes understonde.
For goddes speken in amphibologyes,
And, for a sooth, they tellen twenty lyes.

202. 'Eek drede fond first goddes, I suppose,
Thus shal I seyn, and that his coward herte
Made him amis the goddes text to glose,
Whan he for ferde out of his Delphos sterte.
And but I make him sone to converte,
And doon my reed with-inne a day or tweye,
I wol to yow oblige me to deye.'

203. And treweliche, as writen wel I finde,
That al this thing was seyd of good entente;
And that hir herte trewe was and kinde

Towardes him, and spak right as she mente,
And that she starf for wo neigh, whan she wente,
And was in purpos ever to be trewe;
Thus writen they that of hir werkes knewe.

204. This Troilus, with herte and eres spradde,
Herde al this thing devysen to and fro;
And verraylich him semed that he hadde
The selve wit; but yet to lete her go
His herte misforyaf him ever-mo.
But fynally, he gan his herte wreste
To trusten hir, and took it for the beste.

205. For which the grete furie of his penaunce
Was queynt with hope, and ther-with hem bitwene
Bigan for joye the amorouse daunce.
And as the briddes, whan the sonne is shene,
Delyten in hir song in leves grene,
Right so the wordes that they spake y-fere
Delyted hem, and made hir hertes clere.

206. But natheles, the wending of Criseyde,
For al this world, may nought out of his minde;
For which ful ofte he pitously hir preyde,
That of hir heste he might hir trewe finde.
And seyde hir, 'certes, if ye be unkinde,
And but ye come at day set in-to Troye,
Ne shal I never have hele, honour, ne joye.

207. 'For al-so sooth as sonne up-rist on morwe,
And, god! so wisly thou me, woful wrecche,
To reste bringe out of this cruel sorwe,
I wol my-selven slee if that ye drecche.
But of my deeth though litel be to recche,
Yet, er that ye me cause so to smerte,
Dwel rather here, myn owene swete herte!

208. 'For trewely, myn owene lady dere,
Tho sleightes yet that I have herd yow stere
Ful shaply been to failen alle y-fere.
For thus men seyn, "that oon thenketh the bere,
But al another thenketh his ledere."
Your sire is wys, and seyd is, out of drede,
"Men may the wyse at-renne, and not at-rede."

209. 'It is ful hard to halten unespyed
Bifore a crepul, for he can the craft;
Your fader is in sleighte as Argus yëd;
For al be that his moeble is him biraft,
His olde sleight is yet so with him laft,
Ye shal not blende him for your woman-hede,
Ne feyne a-right, and that is al my drede.

210. 'I noot if pees shal ever-mo bityde;
But, pees or no, for ernest ne for game,
I woot, sin Calkas on the Grekes syde
Hath ones been, and lost so foule his name,
He dar no more come here ayein for shame;
For which that weye, for ought I can espye,
To trusten on, nis but a fantasye.

211. 'Ye shal eek seen, your fader shal yow glose
To been a wyf, and as he can wel preche,
He shal som Greek so preyse and wel alose,
That ravisshen he shal yow with his speche,
Or do yow doon by force as he shal teche.
And Troilus, of whom ye nil han routhe,
Shal causeles so sterven in his trouthe!

212. 'And over al this, your fader shal despyse
Us alle, and seyn this citee nis but lorn;
And that th' assege never shal aryse,
For-why the Grekes han it alle sworn
Til we be slayn, and doun our walles torn.
And thus he shal you with his wordes fere,
That ay drede I, that ye wol bleve there.

213. 'Ye shul eek seen so many a lusty knight
A-mong the Grekes, ful of worthinesse,
And eche of hem with herte, wit, and might
To plesen yow don al his besinesse,
That ye shul dullen of the rudenesse
Of us sely Trojanes, but-if routhe
Remorde yow, or vertue of your trouthe.

214. 'And this to me so grevous is to thinke,
That fro my brest it wol my soule rende;
Ne dredeles, in me ther may not sinke

A good opinioun, if that ye wende;
For-why your faderes sleighte wol us shende.
And if ye goon, as I have told yow yore,
So thenk I nam but deed, with-oute more.

215. 'For which, with humble, trewe, and pitous herte
A thousand tymes mercy I yow preye;
So reweth on myn aspre peynes smerte,
And doth somwhat, as that I shal yow seye,
And lat us stele away bitwixe us tweye;
And thenk that folye is, whan man may chese,
For accident his substaunce ay to lese.

216. 'I mene this, that sin we mowe er day
Wel stele away, and been to-gider so,
What wit were it to putten in assay,
In cas ye sholden to your fader go,
If that ye mighte come ayein or no?
Thus mene I, that it were a gret folye
To putte that sikernesse in jupartye.

217. 'And vulgarly to speken of substaunce
Of tresour, may we bothe with us lede
Y-nough to live in honour and plesaunce,
Til in-to tyme that we shul ben dede;
And thus we may eschewen al this drede.
For everich other wey ye can recorde,
Myn herte, y-wis, may not ther-with acorde.

218. 'And hardily, ne dredeth no poverte,
For I have kin and freendes elles-where
That, though we comen in our bare sherte,
Us sholde neither lakke gold ne gere,
But been honoured whyl we dwelten there.
And go we anoon, for, as in myn entente,
This is the beste, if that ye wole assente.'

219. Criseyde, with a syk, right in this wyse
Answerde, 'y-wis, my dere herte trewe,
We may wel stele away, as ye devyse,
And finde swiche unthrifty weyes newe;
But afterward, ful sore it wol us rewe.
And help me god so at my moste nede
As causeles ye suffren al this drede!

220. 'For thilke day that I for cherisshinge
Or drede of fader, or of other wight,
Or for estat, delyt, or for weddinge
Be fals to yow, my Troilus, my knight,
Saturnes doughter, Juno, thorugh hir might,
As wood as Athamante do me dwelle
Eternaly in Stix, the put of helle!

221. 'And this on every god celestial
I swere it yow, and eek on eche goddesse,
On every Nymphe and deite infernal,
On Satiry and Fauny more and lesse,
That halve goddes been of wildernesse;
And Attropos my thread of lyf to-breste
If I be fals; now trowe me if thow leste!

222. 'And thou, Simoys, that as an arwe clere
Thorugh Troye rennest ay downward to the see,
Ber witnesse of this word that seyd is here,
That thilke day that ich untrewe be
To Troilus, myn owene herte free,
That thou retorne bakwarde to thy welle,
And I with body and soule sinke in helle!

223. 'But that ye speke, awey thus for to go
And leten alle your freendes, god forbede,
For any womman, that ye sholden so,
And namely, sin Troye hath now swich nede
Of help; and eek of o thing taketh hede,
If this were wist, my lif laye in balaunce,
And your honour; god shilde us fro mischaunce!

224. 'And if so be that pees her-after take,
As alday happeth, after anger, game,
Why, lord! the sorwe and wo ye wolden make,
That ye ne dorste come ayein for shame!
And er that ye juparten so your name,
Beth nought to hasty in this hote fare;
For hasty man ne wanteth never care.

225. 'What trowe ye the peple eek al aboute
Wolde of it seye? It is ful light to arede.
They wolden seye, and swere it, out of doute,

That love ne droof yow nought to doon this dede,
But lust voluptuous and coward drede.
Thus were al lost, y-wis myn herte dere,
Your honour, which that now shyneth so clere.

226. 'And also thenketh on myn honestee,
That floureth yet, how foule I sholde it shende,
And with what filthe it spotted sholde be,
If in this forme I sholde with yow wende.
Ne though I livede un-to the worldes ende,
My name sholde I never ayeinward winne;
Thus were I lost, and that were routhe and sinne.

227. 'And for-thy slee with reson al this hete;
Men seyn, "the suffraunt overcometh," pardee;
Eek "who-so wol han leef, he leef mot lete";
Thus maketh vertue of necessitee
By pacience, and thenk that lord is he
Of Fortune ay, that nought wol of hir recche;
And she ne daunteth no wight but a wrecche.

228. 'And trusteth this, that certes, herte swete,
Er Phebus suster, Lucina the shene,
The Leoun passe out of this Ariete,
I wol ben here, with-outen any wene.
I mene, as helpe me Juno, hevenes quene,
The tenthe day, but-if that deeth me assayle,
I wol yow seen, with-outen any fayle.'

229. 'And now, so this be sooth,' quod Troilus,
'I shal wel suffre un-to the tenthe day,
Sin that I see that nede it moot be thus.
But, for the love of god, if it be may,
So lat us stele prively away;
For ever in oon, as for to live in reste,
Myn herte seyth that it wol been the beste.'

230. 'O mercy, god, what lyf is this?' quod she;
'Allas, ye slee me thus for verray tene!
I see wel now that ye mistrusten me;
For by your wordes it is wel y-sene.
Now, for the love of Cynthia the shene,
Mistrust me not thus causeles, for routhe;
Sin to be trewe I have yow plight my trouthe.

231. 'And thenketh wel, that some tyme it is wit
To spende a tyme, a tyme for to winne;
Ne, pardee, lorn am I nought fro yow yit,
Though that we been a day or two a-twinne.
Dryf out the fantasyes yow with-inne;
And trusteth me, and leveth eek your sorwe,
Or here my trouthe, I wol not live til morwe.

232. 'For if ye wiste how sore it doth me smerte,
Ye wolde cesse of this; for god, thou wost,
The pure spirit wepeth in myn herte,
To see yow wepen that I love most,
And that I moot gon to the Grekes ost.
Ye, nere it that I wiste remedye
To come ayein, right here I wolde dye!

233. 'But certes, I am not so nyce a wight
That I ne can imaginen a way
To come ayein that day that I have hight.
For who may holde thing that wol a-way?
My fader nought, for al his queynte pley.
And by my thrift, my wending out of Troye
Another day shal torne us alle to joye.

234. 'For-thy, with al myn herte I yow beseke,
If that yow list don ought for my preyere,
And for the love which that I love yow eke,
That er that I departe fro yow here,
That of so good a comfort and a chere
I may you seen, that ye may bringe at reste
Myn herte, which that is at point to breste.

235. 'And over al this, I pray yow,' quod she tho,
'Myn owene hertes soothfast suffisaunce,
Sin I am thyn al hool, with-outen mo,
That whyl that I am absent, no plesaunce
Of othere do me fro your remembraunce.
For I am ever a-gast, for-why men rede,
That "love is thing ay ful of bisy drede."

236. 'For in this world ther liveth lady noon,
If that ye were untrewe, as god defende!
That so bitraysed were or wo bigoon

As I, that alle trouthe in yow entende.
And douteles, if that ich other wende,
I nere but deed; and er ye cause finde,
For goddes love, so beth me not unkinde.'

237. To this answerde Troilus and seyde,
'Now god, to whom ther nis no cause y-wrye,
Me glade, as wis I never un-to Criseyde,
Sin thilke day I saw hir first with yë,
Was fals, ne never shal til that I dye.
At shorte wordes, wel ye may me leve;
I can no more, it shal be founde at preve.'

238. 'Graunt mercy, goode myn, y-wis,' quod she,
'And blisful Venus lat me never sterve
Er I may stonde of plesaunce in degree
To quyte him wel, that so wel can deserve;
And whyl that god my wit wol me conserve,
I shal so doon, so trewe I have yow founde,
That ay honour to me-ward shal rebounde.

239. 'For trusteth wel, that your estat royal,
Ne veyn delyt, nor only worthinesse
Of yow in werre, or torney marcial,
Ne pompe, array, nobley, or eek richesse,
Ne made me to rewe on your distresse;
But moral vertue, grounded upon trouthe,
That was the cause I first hadde on yow routhe!

240. 'Eek gentil herte and manhod that ye hadde,
And that ye hadde, as me thoughte, in despyt
Everything that souned in-to badde,
As rudenesse and poeplish appetyt;
And that your reson brydled your delyt,
This made, aboven every creature,
That I was your, and shal, whyl I may dure.

241. 'And this may lengthe of yeres not for-do,
Ne remuable fortune deface;
But Juppiter, that of his might may do
The sorwful to be glad, so yeve us grace,
Er nightes ten, to meten in this place,
So that it may your herte and myn suffyse;
And fareth now wel, for tyme is that ye ryse.'

242. And after that they longe y-pleyned hadde,
And ofte y-kist and streite in armes folde,
The day gan ryse, and Troilus him cladde,
And rewfulliche his lady gan biholde,
As he that felte dethes cares colde.
And to hir grace he gan him recomaunde;
Wher him was wo, this holde I no demaunde.

243. For mannes heed imaginen ne can,
Ne entendement considere, ne tonge telle
The cruel peynes of this sorwful man,
That passen every torment doun in helle.
For whan he saugh that she ne mighte dwelle,
Which that his soule out of his herte rente,
With-outen more, out of the chaumbre he wente.

Explicit Liber Quartus

BOOK V

Incipit Liber Quintus

1. Aprochen gan the fatal destinee
That Joves hath in disposicoun,
And to yow, angry Parcas, sustren three,
Committeth, to don execucioun;
For which Criseyde moste out of the toun,
And Troilus shal dwelle forth in pyne
Til Lachesis his threed no lenger twyne.—

2. The golden-tressed Phebus heighe on-lofte
Thryës hadde alle with his bemes shene
The snowes molte, and Zephirus as ofte
Y-brought ayein the tendre leves grene,
Sin that the sone of Ecuba the quene
Bigan to love hir first, for whom his sorwe
Was al, that she departe sholde a-morwe.

3. Ful redy was at pryme Dyomede,
Criseyde un-to the Grekes ost to lede,
For sorwe of which she felte hir herte blede,
As she that niste what was best to rede.
And trewely, as men in bokes rede,
Men wiste never womman han the care,
Ne was so looth out of a toun to fare.

4. This Troilus, with-outen reed or lore,
As man that hath his joyes eek forlore,
Was waytinge on his lady ever-more
As she that was the soothfast crop and more
Of al his lust, or joyes here-tofore.
But Troilus, now farewel al thy joye,
For shaltow never seen hir eft in Troye!

5. Soth is, that whyl he bood in this manere,
He gan his wo ful manly for to hyde,
That wel unnethe it seen was in his chere;
But at the yate ther she sholde oute ryde
With certeyn folk, he hoved hir t' abyde,
So wo bigoon, al wolde he nought him pleyne,
That on his hors unnethe he sat for peyne.

6. For ire he quook, so gan his herte gnawe,
Whan Diomede on horse gan him dresse,
And seyde un-to him-self this ilke sawe,
'Allas,' quod he, 'thus foul a wrecchednesse
Why suffre ich it, why nil ich it redresse?
Were it not bet at ones for to dye
Than ever-more in langour thus to drye?

7. 'Why nil I make at ones riche and pore
To have y-nough to done, er that she go?
Why nil I bringe al Troye upon a rore?
Why nil I sleen this Diomede also?
Why nil I rather with a man or two
Stele hir a-way?   Why wol I this endure?
Why nil I helpen to myn owene cure?'

8. But why he nolde doon so fel a dede,
That shal I seyn, and why him liste it spare:
He hadde in herte alwey a maner drede,
Leste that Criseyde, in rumour of this fare,
Sholde han ben slayn; lo, this was al his care.
And elles, certeyn, as I seyde yore,
He hadde it doon, with-outen wordes more.

9. Criseyde, whan she redy was to ryde,
Ful sorwfully she sighte, and seyde 'allas!'
But forth she moot, for ought that may bityde,
And forth she rit ful sorwfully a pas.
Ther nis non other remedie in this cas.
What wonder is though that hir sore smerte,
Whan she forgoth hir owene swete herte?

10. This Troilus, in wyse of curteisye,
With hauke on hond, and with an huge route
Of knightes, rood and dide hir companye,
Passinge al the valey fer with-oute.
And ferther wolde han riden, out of doute,
Ful fayn, and wo was him to goon so sone;
But torne he moste, and it was eek to done.

11. And right with that was Antenor y-come
Out of the Grekes ost, and every wight
Was of it glad, and seyde he was welcome.

And Troilus, al nere his herte light,
He peyned him with al his fulle might
Him to with-holde of wepinge at the leste,
And Antenor he kiste, and made feste.

12. And ther-with-al he moste his leve take,
And caste his eye upon hir pitously,
And neer he rood, his cause for to make,
To take hir by the honde al sobrely.
And lord! so she gan wepen tendrely!
And he ful softe and sleighly gan hir seye,
'Now hold your day, and dooth me not to deye.'

13. With that his courser torned he a-boute
With face pale, and un-to Diomede
No word he spak, ne noon of al his route;
Of which the sone of Tydeus took hede,
As he that coude more than the crede
In swich a craft, and by the reyne hir hente;
And Troilus to Troye homwarde he wente.

14. This Diomede, that ladde hir by the brydel,
Whan that he saw the folk of Troye aweye,
Thoughte, 'al my labour shal not been on ydel,
If that I may, for somwhat shal I seye.
For at the worste it may yet shorte our weye.
I have herd seyd, eek tymes twyës twelve,
"He is a fool that wol for-yete himselve."'

15. But natheles this thoughte he wel ynough,
'That certaynly I am aboute nought
If that I speke of love, or make it tough;
For douteles, if she have in hir thought
Him that I gesse, he may not been y-brought
So sone awey; but I shal finde a mene,
That she not wite as yet shal what I mene.'

16. This Diomede, as he that coude his good,
Whan this was doon, gan fallen forth in speche
Of this and that, and asked why she stood
In swich disese, and gan hir eek biseche,
That if that he encrese mighte or eche
With any thing hir ese, that she sholde
Comaunde it him, and seyde he doon it wolde.

17. For trewely he swoor hir, as a knight,
That ther nas thing with whiche he mighte hir plese,
That he nolde doon his peyne and al his might
To doon it, for to doon hir herte an ese.
And preyede hir, she wolde hir sorwe apese,
And seyde, 'y-wis, we Grekes con have joye
To honouren yow, as wel as folk of Troye.'

18. He seyde eek thus, 'I woot, yow thinketh straunge,
No wonder is, for it is to yow newe,
Th' aqueintaunce of these Trojanes to chaunge,
For folk of Grece, that ye never knewe.
But wolde never god but-if as trewe
A Greek ye shulde among us alle finde
As any Trojan is, and eek as kinde.

19. 'And by the cause I swoor yow right, lo, now,
To been your freend, and helply, to my might,
And for that more acqueintaunce eek of yow
Have ich had than another straunger wight,
So fro this forth I pray yow, day and night,
Comaundeth me, how sore that me smerte,
To doon al that may lyke un-to your herte;

20. 'And that ye me wolde as your brother trete,
And taketh not my frendship in despyt;
And though your sorwes be for thinges grete,
Noot I not why, but out of more respyt,
Myn herte hath for to amende it greet delyt.
And if I may your harmes not redresse,
I am right sory for your hevinesse.

21. 'And though ye Trojans with us Grekes wrothe
Han many a day be, alwey yet, pardee,
O god of love in sooth we serven bothe.
And, for the love of god, my lady free,
Whom so ye hate, as beth not wroth with me.
For trewely, ther can no wight yow serve,
That half so looth your wraththe wolde deserve.

22. 'And nere it that we been so neigh the tente
Of Calkas, which that seen us bothe may,
I wolde of this yow telle al myn entente;

But this enseled til another day.
Yeve me your hond, I am, and shal ben ay,
God help me so, whyl that my lyf may dure,
Your owene aboven every creature.

23. 'Thus seyde I never er now to womman born;
For god myn herte as wisly glade so,
I lovede never womman here-biforn
As paramours, ne never shal no mo.
And, for the love of god, beth not my fo;
Al can I not to yow, my lady dere,
Compleyne aright, for I am yet to lere.

24. 'And wondreth not, myn owene lady bright,
Though that I speke of love to you thus blyve;
For I have herd or this of many a wight,
Hath loved thing he never saugh his lyve.
Eek I am not of power for to stryve
Ayens the god of love, but him obeye
I wol alwey, and mercy I yow preye.

25. 'Ther been so worthy knightes in this place,
And ye so fair, that everich of hem alle
Wol peynen him to stonden in your grace.
But mighte me so fair a grace falle,
That ye me for your servaunt wolde calle,
So lowly ne so trewely you serve
Nil noon of hem, as I shal, til I sterve.'

26. Criseide un-to that purpos lyte answerde,
As she that was with sorwe oppressed so
That, in effect, she nought his tales herde,
But here and there, now here a word or two.
Hir thoughte hir sorwful herte brast a-two.
For whan she gan hir fader fer aspye,
Wel neigh doun of hir hors she gan to sye.

27. But natheles she thonked Diomede
Of al his travaile, and his goode chere,
And that him liste his friendship hir to bede;
And she accepteth it in good manere,
And wolde do fayn that is him leef and dere;
And trusten him she wolde, and wel she mighte,
As seyde she, and from hir hors she alighte.

28. Hir fader hath hir in his armes nome,
And tweynty tyme he kiste his doughter swete,
And seyde, 'O dere doughter myn, welcome!'
She seyde eek, she was fayn with him to mete,
And stood forth mewet, mildë, and mansuete.
But here I leve hir with hir fader dwelle,
And forth I wol of Troilus yow telle.

29. To Troye is come this woful Troilus.
In sorwe aboven alle sorwes smerte,
With felon look, and face dispitous.
Tho sodeinly doun from his hors he sterte,
And thorugh his paleys, with a swollen herte,
To chambre he wente; of no-thing took he hede,
Ne noon to him dar speke a word for drede.

30. And there his sorwes that he spared hadde
He yaf an issue large, and 'deeth!' he cryde;
And in his throwes frenetyk and madde
He cursed Jove, Appollo, and eek Cupyde,
He cursed Ceres, Bacus, and Cipryde,
His burthe, him-self, his fate, and eek nature,
And, save his lady, every creature.

31. To bedde he goth, and weyleth there and torneth
In furie, as dooth he, Ixion, in helle;
And in this wyse he neigh til day sojorneth.
But tho bigan his herte a lyte unswelle
Thorugh teres which that gonnen up to welle;
And pitously he cryde up-on Criseyde,
And to him-self right thus he spak, and seyde:—

32. 'Wher is myn owene lady lief and dere,
Wher is hir whyte brest, wher is it, where?
Wher been hir armes and hir eyen clere,
That yesternight this tyme with me were?
Now may I wepe allone many a tere,
And graspe aboute I may, but in this place,
Save a pilowe, I finde nought t' enbrace.

33. 'How shal I do? Whan shal she com ayeyn?
I noot, allas! why leet ich hir to go?
As wolde god, ich hadde as tho be sleyn!

O herte myn, Criseyde, O swete fo!
O lady myn, that I love and no mo!
To whom for ever-mo myn herte I dowe;
See how I deye, ye nil me not rescowe!

34. 'Who seeth yow now, my righte lode-sterre?
Who sit right now or stant in your presence?
Who can conforten now your hertes werre?
Now I am gon, whom yeve ye audience?
Who speketh for me right now in myn absence?
Allas, no wight; and that is al my care;
For wel wot I, as yvel as I ye fare.

35. 'How shulde I thus ten dayes ful endure,
Whan I the firste night have al this tene?
How shal she doon eeke, sorwful creature?
For tendernesse, how shal she this sustene,
Swich wo for me?   O pitous, pale, and grene
Shal been your fresshe wommanliche face
For langour, er ye torne un-to this place.'

36. And whan he fil in any slomeringes,
Anoon biginne he sholde for to grone,
And dremen of the dredfulleste thinges
That mighte been; as, mete he were allone
In place horrible, makinge ay his mone,
Or meten that he was amonges alle
His enemys, and in hir hondes falle.

37. And ther-with-al his body sholde sterte,
And with the stert al sodeinliche awake,
And swich a tremour fele aboute his herte,
That of the feer his body sholde quake;
And there-with-al he sholde a noyse make,
And seme as though he sholde falle depe
From heighe a-lofte; and than he wolde wepe,

38. And rewen on him-self so pitously,
That wonder was to here his fantasye.
Another tyme he sholde mightily
Conforte him-self, and seyn it was folye,
So causeles swich drede for to drye,
And eft biginne his aspre sorwes newe,
That every man mighte on his sorwes rewe.

39. Who coude telle aright or ful discryve
His wo, his pleynte, his langour, and his pyne?
Nought al the men that han or been on-lyve.
Thou, redere, mayst thy-self ful wel devyne
That swich a wo my wit can not defyne.
On ydel for to wryte it sholde I swinke,
Whan that my wit is wery it to thinke.

40. On hevene yet the sterres were sene,
Al-though ful pale y-waxen was the mone;
And whyten gan the orisonte shene
Al estward, as it woned is to done.
And Phebus with his rosy carte sone
Gan after that to dresse him up to fare,
Whan Troilus hath sent after Pandare.

41. This Pandare, that of al the day biforn
Ne mighte have comen Troilus to see,
Al-though he on his heed it hadde y-sworn,
For with the king Pryam alday was he,
So that it lay not in his libertee
No-wher to gon, but on the morwe he wente
To Troilus, whan that he for him sente.

42. For in his herte he coude wel devyne,
That Troilus al night for sorwe wook;
And that he wolde telle him of his pyne,
This knew he wel y-nough, with-oute book.
For which to chaumbre streight the wey he took,
And Troilus tho sobreliche he grette,
And on the bed ful sone he gan him sette.

43. 'My Pandarus,' quod Troilus, 'the sorwe
Which that I drye, I may not longe endure.
I trowe I shal not liven til to-morwe;
For whiche I wolde alwey, on aventure,
To thee devysen of my sepulture
The forme, and of my moeble thou dispone
Right as thee semeth best is for to done.

44. 'But of the fyr and flaumbe funeral
In whiche my body brenne shal to glede,
And of the feste and pleyes palestral

At my vigile, I pray thee take good hede
That al be wel; and offre Mars my stede,
My swerd, myn helm, and, leve brother dere,
My sheld to Pallas yef, that shyneth clere.

45. 'The poudre in which myn herte y-brend shal torne,
That preye I thee thou take and it conserve
In a vessel, that men clepeth an urne,
Of gold, and to my lady that I serve,
For love of whom thus pitously I sterve,
So yeve it hir, and do me this plesaunce,
To preye hir keep it for a remembraunce.

46. 'For wel I fele, by my maladye,
And by my dremes now and yore ago,
Al certeinly, that I mot nedes dye.
The owle eek, which that hight Ascaphilo,
Hath after me shright alle thise nightes two.
And, god Mercurie! of me now, woful wrecche,
The soule gyde, and, whan thee list, it fecche!'

47. Pandare answerde, and seyde, 'Troilus,
My dere freend, as I have told thee yore,
That it is folye for to sorwen thus,
And causeles, for whiche I can no-more.
But who-so wol not trowen reed ne lore,
I can not seen in him no remedye,
But lete him worthen with his fantasye.

48. 'But Troilus, I pray thee tel me now,
If that thou trowe, er this, that any wight
Hath loved paramours as wel as thou?
Ye, god wot, and fro many a worthy knight
Hath his lady goon a fourtenight,
And he not yet made halvendel the fare.
What nede is thee to maken al this care?

49. 'Sin day by day thou mayst thy-selven see
That from his love, or elles from his wyf,
A man mot twinnen of necessitee,
Ye, though he love hir as his owene lyf;
Yet nil he with him-self thus maken stryf.
For wel thow wost, my leve brother dere,
That alwey freendes may nought been y-fere.

50. 'How doon this folk that seen hir loves wedded
By freendes might, as it bi-tit ful ofte,
And seen hem in hir spouses bed y-bedded?
God woot, they take it wysly, faire and softe.
For-why good hope halt up hir herte on-lofte,
And for they can a tyme of sorwe endure;
As tyme hem hurt, a tyme doth hem cure.

51. 'So sholdestow endure, and late slyde
The tyme, and fonde to ben glad and light.
Ten dayes nis so long not t' abyde.
And sin she thee to comen hath bihight,
She nil hir hestes breken for no wight.
For dred thee not that she nil finden weye
To come ayein, my lyf that dorste I leye.

52. 'Thy swevenes eek and al swich fantasye
Dryf out, and lat hem faren to mischaunce;
For they procede of thy malencolye,
That doth thee fele in sleep al this penaunce.
A straw for alle swevenes signifiaunce!
God helpe me so, I counte hem not a bene,
Ther woot no man aright what dremes mene.

53. 'For prestes of the temple tellen this,
That dremes been the revelaciouns
Of goddes, and as wel they telle, y-wis,
That they ben infernals illusiouns;
And leches seyn, that of complexiouns
Proceden they, or fast, or glotonye.
Who woot in sooth thus what they signifye?

54. 'Eek othere seyn that thorugh impressiouns,
As if a wight hath faste a thing in minde,
That ther-of cometh swiche avisiouns;
And othere seyn, as they in bokes finde,
That, after tymes of the yeer by kinde,
Men dreme, and that th' effect goth by the mone;
But leve no dreem, for it is nought to done.

55. 'Wel worth of dremes ay thise olde wyves,
And treweliche eek augurie of thise foules;
For fere of which men wenen lese her lyves,

As ravenes qualm, or shryking of thise oules.
To trowen on it bothe fals and foul is.
Allas, allas, so noble a creature
As is a man, shal drede swich ordure!

56. 'For which with al myn herte I thee beseche,
Un-to thy-self that al this thou foryive;
And rys up now with-oute more speche,
And lat us caste how forth may best be drive
This tyme, and eek how freshly we may live
Whan that she cometh, the which shal be right sone;
God help me so, the beste is thus to done.

57. 'Rys, lat us speke of lusty lyf in Troye
That we han lad, and forth the tyme dryve;
And eek of tyme cominge us rejoye,
That bringen shal our blisse now so blyve;
And langour of these twyës dayes fyve
We shal ther-with so foryete or oppresse,
That wel unnethe it doon shal us duresse.

58. 'This toun is ful of lordes al aboute,
And trewes lasten al this mene whyle.
Go we pleye us in som lusty route
To Sarpedon, not hennes but a myle.
And thus thou shalt the tyme wel bigyle,
And dryve it forth un-to that blisful morwe,
That thou hir see, that cause is of thy sorwe.

59. 'Now rys, my dere brother Troilus;
For certes, it noon honour is to thee
To wepe, and in thy bed to jouken thus.
For trewely, of o thing trust to me,
If thou thus ligge a day, or two, or three,
The folk wol wene that thou, for cowardyse,
Thee feynest syk, and that thou darst not ryse.'

60. This Troilus answerde, 'O brother dere,
This knowen folk that han y-suffred peyne,
That though he wepe and make sorwful chere,
That feleth harm and smert in every veyne,
No wonder is; and though I ever pleyne,
Or alwey wepe, I am no-thing to blame,
Sin I have lost the cause of al my game.

61. 'But sin of fyne I moot force aryse,
I shal aryse, as sone as ever I may;
And god, to whom myn herte I sacrifyse,
So sende us hastely the tenthe day!
For was ther never fowl so fayn of May,
As I shal been, whan that she cometh in Troye,
That cause is of my torment and my joye.

62. 'But whider is thy reed,' quod Troilus,
'That we may pleye us best in al this toun?'
'By god, my conseil is,' quod Pandarus,
'To ryde and pleye us with king Sarpedoun.'
So longe of this they speken up and doun,
Til Troilus gan at the laste assente
To ryse, and forth to Sarpedoun they wente.

63. This Sarpedoun, as he that honourable
Was ever his lyve, and ful of heigh prowesse,
With al that mighte y-served been on table,
That deyntee was, al coste it greet richesse,
He fedde hem day by day, that swich noblesse,
As seyden bothe the moste and eek the leste,
Was never er that day wist at any feste.

64. Nor in this world ther is non instrument
Delicious, through wind, or touche, or corde,
As fer as any wight hath ever y-went,
That tonge telle or herte may recorde,
That at that feste it nas wel herd acorde;
Ne of ladies eek so fayr a companye
On daunce, er tho, was never y-seyn with yë.

65. But what avayleth this to Troilus,
That for his sorwe no-thing of it roughte?
For ever in oon his herte piëtous
Ful bisily Criseyde his lady soughte.
On hir was ever al that his herte thoughte.
Now this, now that, so faste imagininge,
That glade, y-wis, can him no festeyinge.

66. These ladies eek that at this feste been,
Sin that he saw his lady was a-weye,
It was his sorwe upon hem for to seen,

Or for to here on instrumentz so pleye.
For she, that of his herte berth the keye,
Was absent, lo, this was his fantasye,
That no wight sholde make melodye.

67. Nor ther nas houre in al the day or night,
Whan he was ther-as no wight mighte him here,
That he ne seyde, 'O lufsom lady bright,
How have ye faren, sin that ye were here?
Wel-come, y-wis, myn owene lady dere.'
But welaway, al this nas but a mase;
Fortune his howve entended bet to glase.

68. The lettres eek, that she of olde tyme
Hadde him y-sent, he wolde allone rede,
An hundred sythe, a-twixen noon and pryme;
Refiguringe hir shap, hir womanhede,
With-inne his herte, and every word and dede
That passed was, and thus he droof to an ende
The ferthe day, and seyde, he wolde wende.

69. And seyde, 'leve brother Pandarus,
Intendestow that we shul herë bleve
Til Sarpedoun wol forth congeyen us?
Yet were it fairer that we toke our leve.
For goddes love, lat us now sone at eve
Our leve take, and homward lat us torne;
For trewely, I nil not thus sojorne.'

70. Pandare answerde, 'be we comen hider
To fecchen fyr, and rennen hoom ayeyn?
God helpe me so, I can not tellen whider
We mighten goon, if I shal soothly seyn,
Ther any wight is of us more fayn
Than Sarpedoun; and if we hennes hye
Thus sodeinly, I holde it vilanye,

71. 'Sin that we seyden that we wolde bleve
With him a wouke; and now, thus sodeinly,
The ferthe day to take of him our leve,
He wolde wondren on it, trewely!
Lat us holde forth our purpos fermely;
And sin that ye bihighten him to byde,
Hold forward now, and after lat us ryde.'

72. Thus Pandarus, with alle peyne and wo,
Made him to dwelle; and at the woukes ende,
Of Sarpedoun they toke hir leve tho,
And on hir wey they spedden hem to wende.
Quod Troilus, 'now god me grace sende,
That I may finden, at myn hom-cominge,
Criseyde comen!' and ther-with gan he singe.

73. 'Ye, hasel-wode!' thoughte this Pandare,
And to him-self ful softely he seyde,
'God woot, refreyden may this hote fare
Er Calkas sende Troilus Criseyde!'
But natheles, he japed thus, and seyde,
And swor, y-wis, his herte him wel bihighte,
She wolde come as soon as ever she mighte.

74. Whan they un-to the paleys were y-comen
Of Troilus, they doun of hors alighte,
And to the chambre hir wey than han they nomen.
And in-to tyme that it gan to nighte,
They spaken of Criseÿde the brighte.
And after this, whan that hem bothe leste,
They spedde hem fro the soper un-to reste.

75. On morwe, as sone as day bigan to clere,
This Troilus gan of his sleep t' abreyde,
And to Pandare, his owene brother dere,
'For love of god,' ful pitously he seyde,
'As go we seen the paleys of Criseyde;
For sin we yet may have namore feste,
So lat us seen hir paleys at the leste.'

76. And ther-with-al, his meynee for to blende,
A cause he fond in toune for to go,
And to Criseydes hous they gonnen wende.
But lord! this sely Troilus was wo!
Him thoughte his sorweful herte braste a-two.
For whan he saugh hir dores sperred alle,
Wel neigh for sorwe a-doun he gan to falle.

77. Therwith whan he was war and gan biholde
How shet was every windowe of the place,
As frost, him thoughte, his herte gan to colde;

For which with chaunged deedlich pale face,
With-outen word, he forth bigan to pace;
And, as god wolde, he gan so faste ryde,
That no wight of his contenaunce aspyde.

78. Than seyde he thus, 'O paleys desolat,
O hous, of houses whylom best y-hight,
O paleys empty and disconsolat,
O thou lanterne, of which queynt is the light,
O paleys, whylom day, that now art night,
Wel oughtestow to falle, and I to dye,
Sin she is went that wont was us to gye!

79. 'O paleys, whylom croune of houses alle,
Enlumined with sonne of alle blisse!
O ring, fro which the ruby is out-falle,
O cause of wo, that cause hast been of lisse!
Yet, sin I may no bet, fayn wolde I kisse
Thy colde dores, dorste I for this route;
And fare-wel shryne, of whiche the seynt is oute!'

80. Ther-with he caste on Pandarus his yë
With chaunged face, and pitous to biholde;
And whan he mighte his tyme aright aspye,
Ay as he rood, to Pandarus he tolde
His newe sorwe, and eek his joyes olde,
So pitously and with so dede an hewe,
That every wight mighte on his sorwe rewe.

81. Fro thennesforth he rydeth up and doun,
And every thing com him to remembraunce
As he rood forth by places of the toun
In whiche he whylom hadde al his plesaunce.
'Lo, yond saugh I myn owene lady daunce;
And in that temple, with her eyen clere,
Me caughte first my righte lady dere.

82. 'And yonder have I herd ful lustily
My dere herte laugh, and yonder pleye
Saugh I hir ones eek ful blisfully.
And yonder ones to me gan she seye,
"Now goode swete, love me wel, I preye."
And yond so goodly gan she me biholde,
That to the deeth myn herte is to hir holde

83. 'And at that corner, in the yonder hous,
Herde I myn alderlevest lady dere
So wommanly, with voys melodious,
Singen so wel, so goodly, and so clere,
That in my soule yet me thinketh I here
The blisful soun; and, in that yonder place,
My lady first me took un-to hir grace.'

84. Thanne thoughte he thus, 'O blisful lord Cupyde,
Whanne I the proces have in my memorie,
How thou me hast werreyed on every syde,
Men mighte a book make of it, lyk a storie.
What nede is thee to seke on me victorie,
Sin I am thyn, and hoolly at thy wille?
What joye hastow thyn owene folk to spille?

85. 'Wel hastow, lord, y-wroke on me thyne ire,
Thou mighty god, and dredful for to greve!
Now mercy, lord, thou wost wel I desire
Thy grace most, of alle lustes leve.
And live and deye I wol in thy bileve;
For which I n' axe in guerdon but a bone,
That thou Criseyde ayein me sende sone.

86. 'Distreyne hir herte as faste to retorne
As thou dost myn to longen hir to see;
Than woot I wel, that she nil not sojorne.
Now, blisful lord, so cruel thou ne be
Un-to the blood of Troye, I preye thee,
As Juno was un-to the blood Thebane,
For which the folk of Thebes caughte hir bane.'

87. And after this he to the yates wente
Ther-as Criseyde out-rood a ful good paas,
And up and doun ther made he many a wente,
And to him-self ful ofte he seyde 'allas!
From hennes rood my blisse and my solas!
As wolde blisful god now, for his joye,
I mighte hir seen ayein come in-to Troye.

88. 'And to the yonder hille I gan hir gyde,
Allas! and there I took of hir my leve!
And yond I saugh hir to hir fader ryde,

For sorwe of which myn herte shal to-cleve.
And hider hoom I com whan it was eve;
And here I dwelle out-cast from alle joye,
And shal, til I may seen hir eft in Troye.'

89. And of him-self imagined he ofte
To ben defet, and pale, and waxen lesse
Than he was wont, and that men seyde softe,
'What may it be? who can the sothe gesse
Why Troilus hath al this hevinesse?'
And al this nas but his malencolye,
That he hadde of him-self swich fantasye.

90. Another tyme imaginen he wolde
That every wight that wente by the weye
Had of him routhe, and that they seyen sholde,
'I am right sory Troilus wol deye.'
And thus he droof a day yet forth or tweye.
As ye have herd, swich lyf right gan he lede,
As he that stood bitwixen hope and drede.

91. For which him lyked in his songes shewe
Th' encheson of his wo, as he best mighte,
And make a song of wordes but a fewe,
Somwhat his woful herte for to lighte.
And whan he was from every mannes sighte,
With softe voys he, of his lady dere,
That was absent, gan singe as ye may here.

92. 'O sterre, of which I lost have al the light,
With herte soor wel oughte I to bewayle,
That ever derk in torment, night by night,
Toward my deeth with wind in stere I sayle;
For which the tenthe night if that I fayle
The gyding of thy bemes brighte an houre,
My snip and me Caribdis wol devoure.'

93. This song when he thus songen hadde, sone
He fil ayein in-to his sykes olde;
And every night, as was his wone to done,
He stood the brighte mone to beholde,
And al his sorwe he to the mone tolde;
And seyde, 'y-wis, when thou art horned newe,
I shal be glad, if al the world be trewe!

94. 'I saugh thyn hornes olde eek by the morwe,
When hennes rood my righte lady dere,
That cause is of my torment and my sorwe;
For whiche, O brighte Lucina the clere,
For love of god, ren faste aboute thy spere!
For whan thyn hornes newe ginne springe,
Than shal she come, that may my blisse bringe!'

95. The day is more, and lenger every night,
Than they be wont to be, him thoughte tho;
And that the sonne wente his course unright
By lenger wey than it was wont to go;
And seyde, 'y-wis, me dredeth ever-mo,
The sonnes sone, Pheton, be on-lyve,
And that his fadres cart amis he dryve.'

96. Upon the walles faste eek wolde he walke,
And on the Grekes ost he wolde see,
And to him-self right thus he wolde talke,
'Lo, yonder is myn owene lady free,
Or elles yonder, ther tho tentes be!
And thennes comth this eyr, that is so sote,
That in my soule I fele it doth me bote.

97. 'And hardely this wind, that more and more
Thus stoundemele encreseth in my face,
Is of my ladyes depe sykes sore.
I preve it thus, for in non othere place
Of al this toun, save onliche in this space,
Fele I no wind that souneth so lyk peyne;
It seyth, "allas! why twinned be we tweyne?"'

98. This longe tyme he dryveth forth right thus,
Til fully passed was the nynthe night;
And ay bi-syde him was this Pandarus,
That bisily dide alle his fulle might
Him to comforte, and make his herte light;
Yevinge him hope alwey, the tenthe morwe
That she shal come, and stinten al his sorwe.

99. Up-on that other syde eek was Criseyde,
With wommen fewe, among the Grekes stronge;
For which ful ofte a day 'allas!' she seyde,

'That I was born! Wel may myn herte longe
After my deeth; for now live I to longe!
Allas! and I ne may it not amende;
For now is wors than ever yet I wende.

100. 'My fader nil for no-thing do me grace
To goon ayein, for nought I can him queme;
And if so be that I my terme passe,
My Troilus shal in his herte deme
That I am fals, and so it may wel seme.
Thus shal I have unthank on every syde;
That I was born, so weylawey the tyde!

101. 'And if that I me putte in jupartye,
To stele awey by nighte, and it bifalle
That I be caught, I shal be holde a spye;
Or elles, lo, this drede I most of alle,
If in the hondes of som wrecche I falle,
I am but lost, al be myn herte trewe;
Now mighty god, thou on my sorwe rewe!'

102. Ful pale y-waxen was hir brighte face,
Hir limes lene, as she that al the day
Stood whan she dorste, and loked on the place
Ther she was born, and ther she dwelt hadde ay.
And al the nighte wepinge, allas! she lay.
And thus despeired, out of alle cure,
She ladde hir lyf, this woful creature.

103. Ful ofte a day she sighte eek for destresse,
And in hir-self she wente ay portrayinge
Of Troilus the grete worthinesse,
And alle his goodly wordes recordinge
Sin first that day hir love bigan to springe.
And thus she sette hir woful herte a-fyre
Thorugh remembraunce of that she gan desyre.

104. In al this world ther nis so cruel herte
That hir hadde herd compleynen in hir sorwe,
That nolde han wopen for hir peynes smerte,
So tendrely she weep, bothe eve and morwe.
Hir nedede no teres for to borwe.
And this was yet the worste of al hir peyne,
Ther was no wight to whom she dorste hir pleyne.

105. Ful rewfully she loked up-on Troye,
Biheld the toures heighe and eek the halles;
'Allas!' quod she, 'the plesaunce and the joye
The whiche that now al torned in-to galle is,
Have I had ofte with-inne yonder walles!
O Troilus, what dostow now?' she seyde;
'Lord! whether yet thou thenke up-on Criseyde?

106. 'Allas! I ne hadde trowed on your lore,
And went with yow, as ye me radde er this!
Thanne hadde I now not syked half so sore.
Who mighte have seyd, that I had doon a-mis
To stele awey with swich on as he is?
But al to late cometh the letuarie,
Whan men the cors un-to the grave carie.

107. 'To late is now to speke of this matere;
Prudence, allas! oon of thyn eyen three
Me lakked alwey, er that I cam here;
On tyme y-passed, wel remembred me;
And present tyme eek coude I wel y-see.
But futur tyme, er I was in the snare,
Coude I not seen; that causeth now my care.

108. 'But natheles, bityde what bityde,
I shal to-morwe at night, by est or weste,
Out of this ost stele on som maner syde,
And go with Troilus wher-as him leste.
This purpos wol I holde, and this is beste.
No fors of wikked tonges janglerye,
For ever on love han wrecches had envye.

109. 'For who-so wole of every word take hede,
Or rewlen him by every wightes wit,
Ne shal he never thryven, out of drede.
For that that som men blamen ever yit,
Lo, other maner folk commenden it.
And as for me, for al swich variaunce,
Felicitee clepe I my suffisaunce.

110. 'For which, with-outen any wordes mo,
To Troye I wol, as for conclusioun.'
But god it wot, er fully monthes two,

She was ful fer fro that entencioun.
For bothe Troilus and Troye toun
Shal knotteles through-out hir herte slyde;
For she wol take a purpos for t' abyde.

111. This Diomede, of whom yow telle I gan,
Goth now, with-inne him-self ay arguinge
With al the sleighte and al that ever he can,
How he may best, with shortest taryinge,
In-to his net Criseydes herte bringe.
To this entente he coude never fyne;
To fisshen hir, he leyde out hook and lyne.

112. But natheles, wel in his herte he thoughte,
That she nas nat with-oute a love in Troye.
For never, sithen he hir thennes broughte,
Ne coude he seen her laughe or make joye.
He niste how best hir herte for t' acoye.
'But for t' assaye,' he seyde, 'it nought ne greveth;
For he that nought n' assayeth, nought n' acheveth.'

113. Yet seide he to him-self upon a night,
'Now am I not a fool, that woot wel how
Hir wo for love is of another wight,
And here-up-on to goon assaye hir now?
I may wel wite, it nil not been my prow.
For wyse folk in bokes it expresse,
"Men shal not wowe a wight in hevinesse."

114. 'But who-so mighte winnen swich a flour
From him, for whom she morneth night and day,
He mighte seyn, he were a conquerour.'
And right anoon, as he that bold was ay,
Thoughte in his herte, 'happe, how happe may,
Al sholde I deye, I wol hir herte seche;
I shal no more lesen but my speche.'

115. This Diomede, as bokes us declare,
Was in his nedes prest and corageous;
With sterne voys and mighty limes square,
Hardy, testif, strong, and chevalrous
Of dedes, lyk his fader Tideus.
And som men seyn, he was of tunge large;
And heir he was of Calidoine and Arge.

116. Criseyde mene was of hir stature,
Ther-to of shap, of face, and eek of chere,
Ther mighte been no fairer creature.
And ofte tyme this was hir manere,
To gon y-tressed with hir heres clere
Doun by hir coler at hir bak bihinde,
Which with a threde of gold she wolde binde.

117. And, save hir browes joyneden y-fere,
Ther was no lak, in ought I can espyen;
But for to speken of hir eyen clere,
Lo, trewely, they writen that hir syen,
That Paradys stood formed in hir yën.
And with hir riche beautee ever-more
Strof love in hir, ay which of hem was more.

118. She sobre was, eek simple, and wys with-al,
The beste y-norisshed eek that mighte be,
And goodly of hir speche in general,
Charitable, estatliche, lusty, and free;
Ne never-mo ne lakkede hir pitee;
Tendre-herted, slydinge of corage;
But trewely, I can not telle hir age.

119. And Troilus wel waxen was in highte,
And complet formed by proporcioun
So wel, that kinde it not amenden mighte;
Yong, fresshe, strong, and hardy as lyoun;
Trewe as steel in ech condicioun;
On of the beste enteched creature,
That is, or shal, whyl that the world may dure.

120. And certainly in storie it is y-founde,
That Troilus was never un-to no wight,
As in his tyme, in no degree secounde
In durring don that longeth to a knight.
Al mighte a geaunt passen him of might,
His herte ay with the firste and with the beste
Stod paregal, to durre don that him leste.

121. But for to tellen forth of Diomede:—
It fil that after, on the tenthe day,
Sin that Criseyde out of the citee yede,

This Diomede, as fresshe as braunche in May,
Com to the tente ther-as Calkas lay,
And feyned him with Calkas han to done;
But what he mente, I shal yow telle sone.

122. Criseyde, at shorte wordes for to telle,
Welcomed him, and doun by hir him sette;
And he was ethe y-nough to maken dwelle.
And after this, with-outen longe lette,
The spyces and the wyn men forth hem fette;
And forth they speke of this and that y-fere,
As freendes doon, of which som shal ye here.

123. He gan first fallen of the werre in speche
Bitwixe hem and the folk of Troye toun;
And of th' assege he gan hir eek byseche,
To telle him what was hir opinioun.
Fro that demaunde he so descendeth doun
To asken hir, if that hir straunge thoughte
The Grekes gyse, and werkes that they wroughte;

124. And why hir fader tarieth so longe
To wedden hir un-to som worthy wight.
Criseyde, that was in hir peynes stronge
For love of Troilus, hir owene knight,
As fer-forth as she conning hadde or might,
Answerde him tho; but, as of his entente,
It semed not she wiste what he mente.

125. But natheles, this ilke Diomede
Gan in him-self assure, and thus he seyde,
'If ich aright have taken of yow hede,
Me thinketh thus, O lady myn, Criseyde,
That sin I first hond on your brydel leyde,
Whan ye out come of Troye by the morwe,
Ne coude I never seen yow but in sorwe.

126. 'Can I not seyn what may the cause be
But-if for love of som Troyan it were,
The which right sore wolde athinken me
That ye, for any wight that dwelleth there
Sholden spille a quarter of a tere,
Or pitously your-selven so bigyle;
For dredelees, it is nought worth the whyle.

127. 'The folk of Troye, as who seyth, alle and some
In preson been, as ye your-selven see;
For thennes shal not oon on-lyve come
For al the gold bitwixen sonne and see.
Trusteth wel, and understondeth me,
Ther shal not oon to mercy goon on-lyve,
Al were he lord of worldes twyës fyve!

128. 'Swich wreche on hem, for fecching of Eleyne,
Ther shal be take, er that we hennes wende,
That Manes, which that goddes ben of peyne,
Shal been agast that Grekes wol hem shende.
And men shul drede, un-to the worldes ende,
From hennes-forth to ravisshe any quene,
So cruel shal our wreche on hem be sene.

129. 'And but-if Calkas lede us with ambages,
That is to seyn, with double wordes slye,
Swich as men clepe a "word with two visages,"
Ye shul wel knowen that I nought ne lye,
And al this thing right seen it with your yë,
And that anoon; ye nil not trowe how sone;
Now taketh heed, for it is for to done.

130. 'What wene ye your wyse fader wolde
Han yeven Antenor for yow anoon,
If he ne wiste that the citee sholde
Destroyed been?   Why, nay, so mote I goon!
He knew ful wel ther shal not scapen oon
That Troyan is; and for the grete fere,
He dorste not, ye dwelte lenger there.

131. 'What wole ye more, lufsom lady dere?
Lat Troye and Troyan fro your herte pace!
Dryf out that bittre hope, and make good chere
And clepe ayein the beautee of your face,
That ye with salte teres so deface,
For Troye is brought in swich a jupartye,
That, it to save, is now no remedye.

132. 'And thenketh wel, ye shal in Grekes finde
A more parfit love, er it be night,
Than any Troyan is, and more kinde,

And bet to serven yow wol doon his might.
And if ye vouche sauf, my lady bright,
I wol ben he to serven yow my-selve,
Ye, lever than be lord of Greces twelve!'

133. And with that word he gan to waxen reed,
And in his speche a litel wight he quook,
And caste a-syde a litel wight his heed,
And stinte a whyle; and afterwards awook,
And sobreliche on hir he threw his look,
And seyde, 'I am, al be it yow no joye,
As gentil man as any wight in Troye.

134. 'For if my fader Tydeus,' he seyde,
'Y-lived hadde, I hadde been, er this,
Of Calidoine and Arge a king, Criseyde!
And so hope I that I shal yet, y-wis.
But he was slayn, allas! the more harm is,
Unhappily at Thebes al to rathe,
Polymites and many a man to scathe.

135. 'But herte myn, sin that I am your man,
And been the ferste of whom I seche grace,
To serven you as hertely as I can,
And ever shal, whyl I to live have space,
So, er that I departe out of this place,
Ye wol me graunte, that I may to-morwe,
At bettre leyser, telle yow my sorwe.'

136. What shold I telle his wordes that he seyde?
He spak y-now, for o day at the meste;
It preveth wel, he spak so that Criseyde
Graunted, on the morwe, at his requeste,
For to speken with him at the leste,
So that he nolde speke of swich matere;
And thus to him she seyde, as ye may here:

137. As she that hadde hir herte on Troilus
So faste, that ther may it noon arace;
And straungely she spak, and seyde thus:
'O Diomede, I love that ilke place
Ther I was born; and Joves, for his grace,
Delivere it sone of al that doth it care!
God, for thy might, so leve it wel to fare!

138. 'That Grekes wolde hir wraththe on Troye wreke,
If that they mighte, I knowe it wel, y-wis.
But it shal not bifallen as ye speke;
And god to-forn, and ferther over this,
I wot my fader wys and redy is;
And that he me hath bought, as ye me tolde,
So dere, I am the more un-to him holde.

139. 'That Grekes been of heigh condicioun,
I woot eek wel; but certein, men shal finde
As worthy folk with-inne Troye toun,
As conning, and as parfit and as kinde,
As been bitwixen Orcades and Inde.
And that ye coude wel your lady serve,
I trowe eek wel, hir thank for to deserve.

140. 'But as to speke of love, y-wis,' she seyde,
'I hadde a lord, to whom I wedded was,
The whos myn herte al was, til that he deyde;
And other love, as helpe me now Pallas,
There in myn herte nis, ne never was.
And that ye been of noble and heigh kinrede,
I have wel herd it tellen, out of drede.

141. 'And that doth me to han so gret a wonder,
That ye wol scornen any womman so.
Eek, god wot, love and I be fer a-sonder;
I am disposed bet, so mote I go,
Un-to my deeth, to pleyne and maken wo.
What I shal after doon, I can not seye;
But trewely, as yet me list not pleye.

142. 'Myn herte is now in tribulacioun,
And ye in armes bisy, day by day.
Here-after, whan ye wonnen han the toun,
Paraunter, thanne so it happen may,
That whan I see that I never er say,
Than wole I werke that I never wroughte!
This word to yow y-nough suffysen oughte.

143. 'To-morwe eek wol I speke with yow fayn,
So that ye touchen nought of this matere.
And whan yow list, ye may come here ayeyn;

And, er ye gon, thus muche I seye yow here:
As helpe me Pallas with hir heres clere,
If that I sholde of any Greek han routhe,
It sholde be your-selven, by my trouthe!

144. 'I sey not therfore that I wol yow love,
Ne I sey not nay, but in conclusioun,
I mene wel, by god that sit above':—
And ther-with-al she caste hir eyen doun,
And gan to syke, and seyde, 'O Troye toun,
Yet bidde I god, in quiete and in reste
I may yow seen, or do myn herte breste.'

145. But in effect, and shortly for to seye,
This Diomede al freshly newe ayeyn
Gan pressen on, and faste hir mercy preye;
And after this, the sothe for to seyn,
Hir glove he took, of which he was ful fayn.
And fynally, when it was waxen eve,
And al was wel, he roos and took his leve.

146. The brighte Venus folwede and ay taughte
The wey, ther brode Phebus doun alighte;
And Cynthea hir char-hors over-raughte
To whirle out of the Lyon, if she mighte;
And Signifer his candeles shewed brighte,
Whan that Criseyde un-to hir bedde wente
In-with hir fadres faire brighte tente,

147. Retorning in hir soule ay up and doun
The wordes of this sodein Diomede,
His greet estat, and peril of the toun,
And that she was allone and hadde nede
Of freendes help; and thus bigan to brede
The cause why, the sothe for to telle,
That she tok fully purpos for to dwelle.

148. The morwe com, and goostly for to speke,
This Diomede is come un-to Criseyde,
And shortly, lest that ye my tale breke,
So wel he for him-selve spak and seyde,
That alle hir sykes sore adoun he leyde.
And fynally, the sothe for to seyne,
He refte hir of the grete of al hir peyne.

149. And after this the story telleth us,
That she him yaf the faire baye stede,
The which he ones wan of Troilus;
And eek a broche (and that was litel nede)
That Troilus was, she yaf this Diomede.
And eek, the bet from sorwe him to releve,
She made him were a pencel of hir sleve.

150. I finde eek in the stories elles-where,
Whan through the body hurt was Diomede
Of Troilus, tho weep she many a tere,
Whan that she saugh his wyde woundes blede;
And that she took to kepen him good hede,
And for to hele him of his sorwes smerte.
Men seyn, I not, that she yaf him hir herte.

151. But trewely, the story telleth us,
Ther made never womman more wo
Than she, whan that she falsed Troilus.
She seyde, 'allas! for now is clene a-go
My name of trouthe in love, for ever-mo!
For I have falsed oon, the gentileste
That ever was, and oon the worthieste!

152. 'Allas, of me, un-to the worldes ende,
Shal neither been y-written nor y-songe
No good word, for thise bokes wol me shende,
O, rolled shal I been on many a tonge!
Through-out the world my belle shal be ronge;
And wommen most wol hate me of alle.
Allas, that swich a cas me sholde falle!

153. 'They wol seyn, in as muche as in me is,
I have hem doon dishonour, weylawey!
Al be I not the firste that dide amis,
What helpeth that to do my blame awey?
But sin I see there is no bettre way,
And that to late is now for me to rewe,
To Diomede algate I wol be trewe.

154. 'But Troilus, sin I no better may,
And sin that thus departen ye and I,
Yet preye I god, so yeve yow right good day

As for the gentileste, trewely,
That ever I say, to serven feithfully,
And best can ay his lady honour kepe':—
And with that word she brast anon to wepe.

155. 'And certes, yow ne haten shal I never,
And freendes love, that shal ye han of me,
And my good word, al mighte I liven ever.
And, trewely, I wolde sory be
For to seen yow in adversitee.
And giltelees, I woot wel, I yow leve;
But al shal passe; and thus take I my leve.'

156. But trewely, how longe it was bitwene,
That she for-sook him for this Diomede,
Ther is non auctor telleth it, I wene.
Take every man now to his bokes hede;
He shal no terme finden, out of drede.
For though that he bigan to wowe hir sone,
Er he hir wan, yet was ther more to done.

157. Ne me ne list this sely womman chyde
Ferther than the story wol devyse.
Hir name, allas! is publisshed so wyde,
That for hir gilt it oughte y-now suffyse.
And if I mighte excuse hir any wyse,
For she so sory was for hir untrouthe,
Y-wis, I wolde excuse hir yet for routhe.

158. This Troilus, as I biforn have told,
Thus dryveth forth, as wel as he hath might.
But often was his herte hoot and cold,
And namely, that ilke nynthe night,
Which on the morwe she hadde him byhight
To come ayein: god wot, ful litel reste
Hadde he that nighte; no-thing to slepe him leste.

159. The laurer-crouned Phebus, with his hete,
Gan, in his course ay upward as he wente,
To warmen of th' est see the wawes wete;
And Nisus doughter song with fresh entente,
Whan Troilus his Pandare after sente;
And on the walles of the toun they pleyde,
To loke if they can seen ought of Criseyde.

160. Til it was noon, they stoden for to see
Who that ther come; and every maner wight,
That cam fro fer, they seyden it was she,
Til that they coude knowen him a-right,
Now was his herte dul, now was it light;
And thus by-japed stonden for to stare
Aboute nought, this Troilus and Pandare.

161. To Pandarus this Troilus tho seyde,
'For ought I wot, bi-for noon, sikerly,
In-to this toun ne comth nought here Criseyde.
She hath y-now to done, hardily,
To winnen from hir fader, so trowe I;
Hir olde fader wol yet make hir dyne
Er that she go; god yeve his herte pyne!'

162. Pandare answerde, 'it may wel be, certeyn;
And for-thy lat us dyne, I thee biseche;
And after noon than mayst thou come ayeyn.'
And hoom they go, with-oute more speche;
And comen ayein, but longe may they seche
Er that they finde that they after cape;
Fortune hem bothe thenketh for to jape.

163. Quod Troilus, 'I see wel now, that she
Is taried with hir olde fader so,
That er she come, it wol neigh even be.
Com forth, I wol un-to the yate go.
Thise portours been unkonninge ever-mo;
And I wol doon hem holden up the yate
As noughte ne were, al-though she come late.'

164. The day goth faste, and after that comth eve,
And yet com nought to Troilus Criseyde.
He loketh forth by hegge, by tree, by greve,
And fer his heed over the wal he leyde.
And at the laste he torned him, and seyde,
'By god, I woot hir mening now, Pandare!
Al-most, y-wis, al newe was my care.

165. 'Now douteles, this lady can hir good;
I woot, she meneth ryden prively.
I comende hir wysdom, by myn hood!

She wol not maken peple nycely
Gaure on hir, whan she comth; but softely
By nighte in-to the toun she thenketh ryde.
And, dere brother, thenk not longe t' abyde.

166. 'We han nought elles for to doon, y-wis.
And Pandarus, now woltow trowen me?
Have here my trouthe, I see hir! yond she is.
Heve up thyn eyen, man! maystow not see?'
Pandare answerde, 'nay, so mote I thee!
Al wrong, by god; what seystow, man, wher art?
That I see yond nis but a fare-cart.'

167. 'Allas, thou seist right sooth,' quod Troilus;
'But hardely, it is not al for nought
That in myn herte I now rejoyse thus.
It is ayein som good I have a thought.
Noot I not how, but sin that I was wrought,
Ne felte I swich a confort, dar I seye;
She comth to-night, my lyf, that dorste I leye!'

168. Pandare answerde, 'it may be wel, y-nough';
And held with him of al that ever he seyde;
But in his herte he thoughte, and softe lough,
And to him-self ful sobrely he seyde:
'From hasel-wode, ther Joly Robin pleyde,
Shal come al that that thou abydest here;
Ye, fare-wel al the snow of ferne yere!'

169. The wardein of the yates gan to calle
The folk which that with-oute the yates were,
And bad hem dryven in hir bestes alle,
Or al the night they moste bleven there.
And fer with-in the night, with many a tere,
This Troilus gan hoomward for to ryde;
For wel he seeth it helpeth nought t' abyde.

170. But natheles, he gladded him in this;
He thoughte he misacounted hadde his day,
And seyde, 'I understonde have al a-mis.
For thilke night I last Criseyde say,
She seyde, "I shal ben here, if that I may,
Er that the mone, O dere herte swete!
The Lyon passe, out of this Ariete."

171. 'For which she may yet holde al hir biheste.'
And on the morwe un-to the yate he wente,
And up and down, by west and eek by este,
Up-on the walles made he many a wente.
But al for nought; his hope alwey him blente;
For which at night, in sorwe and sykes sore
He wente him hoom, with-outen any more.

172. This hope al clene out of his herte fledde,
He nath wher-on now lenger for to honge;
But for the peyne him thoughte his herte bledde,
So were his throwes sharpe and wonder stronge.
For when he saugh that she abood so longe,
He niste what he juggen of it mighte,
Sin she hath broken that she him bihighte.

173. The thridde, ferthe, fifte, sixte day
After tho dayes ten, of which I tolde,
Bitwixen hope and drede his herte lay,
Yet som-what trustinge on hir hestes olde.
But whan he saugh she nolde hir terme holde,
He can now seen non other remedye,
But for to shape him sone for to dye.

174. Ther-with the wikked spirit, god us blesse,
Which that men clepeth wode jalousye,
Gan in him crepe, in al this hevinesse;
For which, by-cause he wolde sone dye,
He ne eet ne dronk, for his malencolye,
And eek from every companye he fledde;
This was the lyf that al the tyme he ledde.

175. He so defet was, that no maner man
Unnethe mighte him knowe ther he wente;
So was he lene, and ther-to pale and wan,
And feble, that he walketh by potente;
And with his ire he thus him-selven shente.
And who-so axed him where-of him smerte,
He seyde, his harm was al aboute his herte.

176. Pryam ful ofte, and eek his moder dere,
His bretheren and his sustren gonne him freyne
Why he so sorwful was in al his chere,

And what thing was the cause of al his peyne;
But al for nought; he nolde his cause pleyne,
But seyde, he felte a grevous maladye
A-boute his herte, and fayn he wolde dye.

177. So on a day he leyde him doun to slepe,
And so bifel that in his sleep him thoughte,
That in a forest faste he welk to wepe
For love of hir that him these peynes wroughte;
Ane up and doun as he the forest soughte,
He mette he saugh a boor with tuskes grete,
That sleep ayein the bright sonnes hete.

178. And by this boor, faste in his armes folde,
Lay kissing ay his lady bright Criseyde:
For sorwe of which, whan he it gan biholde,
And for despyt, out of his slepe he breyde,
And loude he cryde on Pandarus, and seyde,
'O Pandarus, now knowe I crop and rote!
I nam but deed, ther nis non other bote!

179. 'My lady bright Criseyde hath me bitrayed,
In whom I trusted most of any wight,
She elles-where hath now hir herte apayed;
The blisful goddes, through hir grete might,
Han in my dreem y-shewed it ful right.
Thus in my dreem Criseyde I have biholde'—
And al this thing to Pandarus he tolde.

180. 'O my Criseyde, allas! what subtiltee,
What newe lust, what beautee, what science,
What wraththe of juste cause have ye to me?
What gilt of me, what fel experience
Hath fro me raft, allas! thyn advertence?
O trust, O feyth, O depe aseüraunce,
Who hath me reft Criseyde, al my plesaunce?

181. 'Allas! why leet I you from hennes go,
For which wel neigh out of my wit I breyde?
Who shal now trowe on any othes mo?
God wot I wende, O lady bright, Criseyde,
That every word was gospel that ye seyde!
But who may bet bigylen, if him liste,
Than he on whom men weneth best to triste?

182. 'What shal I doon, my Pandarus, allas!
I fele now so sharpe a newe peyne,
Sin that ther is no remedie in this cas,
That bet were it I with myn hondes tweyne
My-selven slow, than alwey thus to pleyne.
For through my deeth my wo sholde han an ende,
Ther every day with lyf my-self I shende.'

183. Pandare answerde and seyde, 'allas the whyle
That I was born; have I not seyd er this,
That dremes many a maner man bigyle?
And why? for folk expounden hem a-mis.
How darstow seyn that fals thy lady is,
For any dreem, right for thyn owene drede?
Let be this thought, thou canst no dremes rede.

184. 'Paraunter, ther thou dremest of this boor,
It may so be that it may signifye
Hir fader, which that old is and eek hoor,
Ayein the sonne lyth, on poynt to dye,
And she for sorwe ginneth wepe and crye,
And kisseth him, ther he lyth on the grounde;
Thus shuldestow thy dreem a-right expounde.'

185. 'How mighte I thanne do?' quod Troilus,
'To knowe of this, ye, were it never so lyte?'
'Now seystow wysly,' quod this Pandarus.
'My reed is this, sin thou canst wel endyte,
That hastely a lettre thou hir wryte,
Thorugh which thou shalt wel bringen it aboute,
To knowe a sooth of that thou art in doute.

186. 'And see now why; for this I dar wel seyn,
That if so is that she untrewe be,
I can not trowe that she wol wryte ayeyn.
And if she wryte, thou shalt ful sone see,
As whether she hath any libertee
To come ayein, or elles in som clause,
If she be let, she wol assigne a cause.

187. 'Thou hast not writen hir sin that she wente,
Nor she to thee, and this I dorste leye,
Ther may swich cause been in hir entente,

That hardely thou wolt thy-selven seye,
That hir a-bood the beste is for yow tweye.
Now wryte hir thanne, and thou shalt fele sone
A sothe of al; ther is no more to done.'

188. Acorded been to this conclusioun,
And that anoon, these ilke lordes two;
And hastely sit Troilus adoun,
And rolleth in his herte to and fro,
How he may best discryven hir his wo.
And to Criseyde, his owene lady dere,
He wroot right thus, and seyde as ye may here.

189. 'Right fresshe flour, whos I have been and shal,
With-outen part of elles-where servyse,
With herte, body, lyf, lust, thought, and al;
I, woful wight, in every humble wyse
That tonge telle or herte may devyse,
As ofte as matere occupyeth place,
Me recomaunde un-to your noble grace.

190. 'Lyketh it yow to witen, swete herte,
As ye wel knowe how longe tyme agoon
That ye me lafte in aspre peynes smerte,
Whan that ye wente, of which yet bote noon
Have I non had, but ever wers bigoon
Fro day to day am I, and so mot dwelle,
While it yow list, of wele and wo my welle!

191. 'For which to yow, with dredful herte trewe,
I wryte, as he that sorwe dryfth to wryte,
My wo, that every houre encreseth newe,
Compleyninge as I dar or can endyte.
And that defaced is, that may ye wyte
The teres, which that fro myn eyen reyne,
That wolde speke, if that they coude, and pleyne.

192. 'Yow first biseche I, that your eyen clere
To look on this defouled ye not holde;
And over al this, that ye, my lady dere,
Wol vouche-sauf this lettre to biholde.
And by the cause eek of my cares colde,
That sleeth my wit, if ought amis me asterte,
For-yeve it me, myn owene swete herte.

193. 'If any servant dorste or oughte of right
Up-on his lady pitously compleyne,
Than wene, I that ich oughte be that wight,
Considered this, that ye these monthes tweyne
Han taried, ther ye seyden, sooth to seyne,
But dayes ten ye nolde in ost sojourne,
But in two monthes yet ye not retourne.

194. 'But for-as-muche as me mot nedes lyke
Al that yow list, I dar not pleyne more,
But humblely with sorwful sykes syke;
Yow wryte ich myn unresty sorwes sore,
Fro day to day desyring ever-more
To knowen fully, if your wil it were,
How ye han ferd and doon, whyl ye be there.

195. 'The whos wel-fare and hele eek god encresse
In honour swich, that upward in degree
It growe alwey, so that it never cesse;
Right as your herte ay can, my lady free,
Devyse, I prey to god so mote it be.
And graunte it that ye sone up-on me rewe
As wisly as in al I am yow trewe.

196. 'And if yow lyketh knowen of the fare
Of me, whos wo ther may no wight discryve,
I can no more but, cheste of every care,
At wrytinge of this lettre I was on-lyve,
Al redy out my woful gost to dryve;
Which I delaye, and holde him yet in honde,
Upon the sight of matere of your sonde.

197. 'Myn eyen two, in veyn with which I see,
Of sorweful teres salte arn waxen welles;
My song, in pleynte of myn adversitee;
My good, in harm; myn ese eek waxen helle is.
My joye, in wo; I can sey yow nought elles,
But turned is, for which my lyf I warie,
Everich joye or ese in his contrarie.

198. 'Which with your cominge hoom ayein to Troye
Ye may redresse, and more a thousand sythe
Than ever ich hadde, encresen in me joye.

For was there never herte yet so blythe
To han his lyf, as I shal been as swythe
As I yow see; and, though no maner routhe
Commeve yow, yet thinketh on your trouthe.

199. 'And if so be my gilt hath deeth deserved,
Or if you list no more up-on me see,
In guerdon yet of that I have you served,
Biseche I yow, myn hertes lady free,
That here-upon ye wolden wryte me,
For love of god, my righte lode-sterre,
Ther deeth may make an ende of al my werre.

200. 'If other cause aught doth yow for to dwelle,
That with your lettre ye me recomforte;
For though to me your absence is an helle,
With pacience I wol my wo comporte,
And with your lettre of hope I wol desporte.
Now wryteth, swete, and lat me thus not pleyne;
With hope, or deeth, delivereth me fro peyne.

201. 'Y-wis, myn owene dere herte trewe,
I woot that, whan ye next up-on me see,
So lost have I myn hele and eek myn hewe,
Criseyde shal nought conne knowe me!
Y-wis, myn hertes day, my lady free,
So thursteth ay myn herte to biholde
Your beautee, that my lyf unnethe I holde.

202. 'I sey no more, al have I for to seye
To you wel more than I telle may;
But whether that ye do me live or deye,
Yet pray I god, so yeve yow right good day
And fareth wel, goodly fayre fresshe may,
As ye that lyf or deeth me may comaunde;
And to your trouthe ay I me recomaunde

203. 'With hele swich that, but ye yeven me
The same hele, I shal noon hele have.
In you lyth, whan yow list that it so be,
The day in which me clothen shal my grave.
In yow my lyf, in yow might for to save
Me from disese of alle peynes smerte;
And fare now wel, myn owene swete herte!

'LE VOSTRE T.'

204. This lettre forth was sent un-to Criseyde,
Of which hir answere in effect was this:
Ful pitously she wroot ayein, and seyde,
That al-so sone as that she might, y-wis,
She wolde come, and mende al that was mis.
And fynally she wroot and seyde him thanne,
She wolde come, ye, but she niste whanne.

205. But in hir lettre made she swich festes,
That wonder was, and swereth she loveth him best,
Of which he fond but botmelees bihestes.
But Troilus, thou mayst now, est or west,
Pype in an ivy leef, if that thee lest;
Thus gooth the world; god shilde us from mischaunce,
And every wight that meneth trouthe avaunce!

206. Encresen gan the wo fro day to night
Of Troilus, for taryinge of Criseyde;
And lessen gan his hope and eek his might,
For which al doun he in his bed him leyde;
He ne eet, ne dronk, ne sleep, ne word he seyde,
Imagininge ay that she was unkinde;
For which wel neigh he wex out of his minde.

207. This dreem, of which I told have eek biforn,
May never come out of his remembraunce;
He thoughte ay wel he hadde his lady lorn,
And that Joves, of his purveyaunce,
Him shewed hadde in sleep the signifiaunce
Of hir untrouthe and his disaventure,
And that the boor was shewed him in figure.

208. For which he for Sibille his suster sente,
That called was Cassandre eek al aboute;
And al his dreem he tolde hir er he stente,
And hir bisoughte assoilen him the doute
Of the stronge boor, with tuskes stoute;
And fynally, with-inne a litel stounde,
Cassandre him gan right thus his dreem expounde.

209. She gan first smyle, and seyde, 'O brother dere,
If thou a sooth of this desyrest knowe,
Thou most a fewe of olde stories here,

To purpos, how that Fortune over-throwe
Hath lordes olde; through which, with-inne a throwe,
Thou wel this boor shalt knowe, and of what kinde
He comen is, as men in bokes finde.

210. 'Diane, which that wrooth was and in ire
For Grekes nolde doon hir sacrifyse,
Ne encens up-on hir auter sette a-fyre,
She, for that Grekes gonne hir so dispyse,
Wrak hir in a wonder cruel wyse.
For with a boor as greet as oxe in stalle
She made up frete hir corn and vynes alle.

211. 'To slee this boor was al the contree reysed,
A-monges which ther com, this boor to see,
A mayde, oon of this world the best y-preysed;
And Meleagre, lord of that contree,
He lovede so this fresshe mayden free
That with his manhood, er he wolde stente,
This boor he slow, and hir the heed he sente;

212. 'Of which, as olde bokes tellen us,
Ther roos a contek and a greet envye;
And of this lord descended Tydeus
By ligne, or elles olde bokes lye;
But how this Meleagre gan to dye
Thorugh his moder, wol I yow not telle,
For al to long it were for to dwelle.'

[*Argument of the 12 Books of Statius'* Thebais]

Associat profugum Tideo *primus* Polimitem;
Tidea legatum docet insidiasque *secundus*;
Tercius Hemoniden canit et vates latitantes;
Quartus habet reges ineuntes prelia septem;
Mox furie Lenne *quinto* narratur et anguis;
Archimori bustum *sexto* ludique leguntur;
Dat Graios Thebes et vatem *septimus* vmbris;
Octauo cecidit Tideus, spes, vita Pelasgis;
Ypomedon *nono* moritur cum Parthonopeo;
Fulmine percussus, *decimo* Capaneus superatur;
Vndecimo sese perimunt per vulnera fratres;
Argiuam flentem narrat *duodenus* et ignem.

213. She toldë eek how Tydeus, er she stente,
Un-to the stronge citee of Thebes,
To cleyme kingdom of the citee, wente,
For his felawe, daun Polymites,
Of which the brother, daun Ethyocles,
Ful wrongfully of Thebes held the strengthe;
This tolde she by proces, al by lengthe.

214. She tolde eek how Hemonides asterte,
Whan Tydeus slough fifty knightes stoute.
She tolde eek al the prophesyes by herte,
And how that sevene kinges, with hir route,
Bisegeden the citee al aboute;
And of the holy serpent, and the welle,
And of the furies, al she gan him telle.

215. Of Archimoris buryinge and the pleyes,
And how Amphiorax fil through the grounde,
How Tydeus was slayn, lord of Argeyes,
And how Ypomedoun in litel stounde
Was dreynt, and deed Parthonope of wounde;
And also how Cappanëus the proude
With thonder-dint was slayn, that cryde loude.

216. She gan eek telle him how that either brother,
Ethyocles and Polymite also,
At a scarmyche, eche of hem slough other,
And of Argyves wepinge and hir wo;
And how the town was brent she tolde eek tho.
And so descendeth doun from gestes olde
To Diomede, and thus she spak and tolde.

217. 'This ilke boor bitokneth Diomede,
Tydeus sone, that doun descended is
Fro Meleagre, that made the boor to blede.
And thy lady, wher-so she be, y-wis,
This Diomede hir herte hath, and she his.
Weep if thou wolt, or leef; for, out of doute,
This Diomede is inne, and thou art oute.'

218. 'Thou seyst nat sooth,' quod he, 'thou sorcereses,
With al thy false goost of prophesye!
Thou wenest been a greet devyneresse;

Now seestow not this fool of fantasye
Peyneth hir on ladyes for to lye?
Awey,' quod he, 'ther Joves yeve thee sorwe!
Thou shalt be fals, paraunter, yet to-morwe!

219. 'As wel thou mightest lyen on Alceste,
That was of creatures, but men lye,
That ever weren, kindest and the beste.
For whanne hir housbonde was in jupartye
To dye him-self, but-if she wolde dye,
She chees for him to dye and go to helle,
And starf anoon, as us the bokes telle.'

220. Cassandre goth, and he with cruel herte
For-yat his wo, for angre of hir speche;
And from his bed al sodeinly he sterte,
As though al hool him hadde y-mad a leche.
And day by day he gan enquere and seche
A sooth of this, with al his fulle cure;
And thus he dryeth forth his aventure.

221. Fortune, whiche that permutacioun
Of thinges hath, as it is hir committed
Through purveyaunce and disposicioun
Of heighe Jove, as regnes shal ben flitted
Fro folk in folk, or whan they shal ben smitted,
Gan pulle awey the fetheres brighte of Troye
Fro day to day, til they ben bare of joye.

222. Among al this, the fyn of the parodie
Of Ector gan approchen wonder blyve;
The fate wolde his soule sholde unbodie,
And shapen hadde a mene it out to dryve;
Ayeins which fate him helpeth not to stryve;
But on a day to fighten gan he wende,
At which, allas! he caughte his lyves ende.

223. For which me thinketh every maner wight
That haunteth armes oughte to biwayle
The deeth of him that was so noble a knight;
For as he drough a king by th' aventayle,
Unwar of this, Achilles through the mayle
And through the body gan him for to ryve;
And thus this worthy knight was brought of lyve.

224. For whom, as olde bokes tellen us,
Was maad swich wo, that tonge it may not telle;
And namely, the sorwe of Troïlus,
That next him was of worthinesse welle.
And in this wo gan Troïlus to dwelle,
That, what for sorwe, and love, and for unreste,
Ful ofte a day he bad his herte breste.

225. But natheles, though he gan him dispeyre,
And dradde ay that his lady was untrewe,
Yet ay on hir his herte gan repeyre.
And as these loveres doon, he soughte ay newe
To gete ayein Criseyde, bright of hewe.
And in his herte he wente hir excusinge,
That Calkas causede al hir taryinge.

226. And ofte tyme he was in purpos grete
Him-selven lyk a pilgrim to disgyse,
To seen hir; but he may not contrefete
To been unknowen of folk that weren wyse,
Ne finde excuse aright that may suffyse,
If he among the Grekes knowen were;
For which he weep ful ofte many a tere.

227. To hir he wroot yet ofte tyme al newe
Ful pitously, he lefte it nought for slouthe,
Biseching hir that, sin that he was trewe,
She wolde come ayein and holde hir trouthe.
For which Criseyde up-on a day, for routhe,
I take it so, touchinge al this matere,
Wrot him ayein, and seyde as ye may here.

228. 'Cupydes sone, ensample of goodlihede,
O swerd of knighthod, sours of gentilesse!
How mighte a wight in torment and in drede
And helelees, yow sende as yet gladnesse?
I hertelees, I syke, I in distresse;
Sin ye with me, nor I with yow may dele,
Yow neither sende ich herte may nor hele.

229. 'Your lettres ful, the papir al y-pleynted,
Conseyved hath myn hertes piëtee;
I have eek seyn with teres al depeynted

Your lettre, and how that ye requeren me
To come ayein, which yet ne may not be.
But why, lest that this lettre founden were,
No mencioun ne make I now, for fere.

230. 'Grevous to me, god woot, is your unreste,
Your haste, and that, the goddes ordenaunce,
It semeth not ye take it for the beste.
Nor other thing nis in your remembraunce,
As thinketh me, but only your plesaunce.
But beth not wrooth, and that I yow b2seche;
For that I tarie, is all for wikked speche.

231. 'For I have herd wel more than I wende,
Touchinge us two, how thinges han y-stonde;
Which I shal with dissimulinge amende.
And beth nought wrooth, I have eek understonde,
How ye ne doon but holden me in honde.
But now no fors, I can not in yow gesse
But alle trouthe and alle gentilesse.

232. 'Comen I wol, but yet in swich disjoynte
I stonde as now, that what yeer or what day
That this shal be, that can I not apoynte.
But in effect, I prey yow, as I may,
Of your good word and of your friendship ay.
For trewely, whyl that my lyf may dure,
As for a freend, ye may in me assure.

233. 'Yet preye I yow on yvel ye ne take,
That it is short which that I to yow wryte;
I dar not, ther I am, wel lettres make,
Ne never yet ne coude I wel endyte.
Eek greet effect men wryte in place lyte.
Th' entente is al, and nought the lettres space;
And fareth now wel, god have you in his grace!
                                    'LA VOSTRE C.'

234. This Troilus this lettre thoughte al straunge,
Whan he it saugh, and sorwefully he sighte;
Him thoughte it lyk a kalendes of chaunge;
But fynally, he ful ne trowen mighte
That she ne wolde him holden that she highte;
For with ful yvel wil list him to leve
That loveth wel, in swich cas, though him greve.

235. But natheles, men seyn that, at the laste,
For any thing, men shal the sothe see;
And swich a cas bitidde, and that as faste,
That Troilus wel understood that she
Nas not so kinde as that hir oughte be.
And fynally, he woot now, out of doute,
That al is lost that he hath been aboute.

236. Stood on a day in his malencolye
This Troilus, and in suspecioun
Of hir for whom he wende for to dye.
And so bifel, that through-out Troye toun,
As was the gyse, y-bore was up and doun
A maner cote-armure, as seyth the storie,
Biforn Deiphebe, in signe of his victorie.

237. The whiche cote, as telleth Lollius,
Deiphebe it hadde y-rent from Diomede
The same day; and whan this Troilus
It saugh, he gan to taken of it hede,
Avysing of the lengthe and of the brede,
And al the werk; but as he gan biholde,
Ful sodeinly his herte gan to colde.

238. As he that on the coler fond withinne
A broche, that he Criseyde yaf that morwe
That she from Troye moste nedes twinne,
In remembraunce of him and of his sorwe;
And she him leyde ayein hir feyth to borwe
To kepe it ay; but now, ful wel he wiste,
His lady nas no lenger on to triste.

239. He gooth him hoom, and gan ful sone sende
For Pandarus; and al this newe chaunce,
And of this broche, he tolde him word and ende,
Compleyninge of hir hertes variaunce,
His longe love, his trouthe, and his penaunce;
And after deeth, with-outen wordes more,
Ful faste he cryde, his reste him to restore.

240. Than spak he thus, 'O lady myn Criseyde,
Wher is your feyth, and where is your biheste?
Wher is your love, wher is your trouthe?' he seyde;

'Of Diomede have ye now al this feste!
Allas, I wolde have trowed at the leste,
That, sin ye nolde in trouthe to me stonde,
That ye thus nolde han holden me in honde!

241. 'Who shal now trowe on any othes mo?
Allas, I never wolde han wend, er this,
That ye, Criseyde, coude han chaunged so;
Ne, but I hadde a-gilt and doon amis,
So cruel wende I not your herte, y-wis,
To slee me thus; allas, your name of trouthe
Is now for-doon, and that is al my routhe.

242. 'Was ther non other broche yow liste lete
To feffe with your newe love,' quod he,
'But thilke broche that I, with teres wete,
Yow yaf, as for a remembraunce of me?
Non other cause, allas, ne hadde ye
But for despyt, and eek for that ye mente
Al-outrely to shewen your entente!

243. 'Through which I see that clene out of your minde
Ye han me cast, and I ne can nor may,
For al this world, with-in myn herte finde
T' unloven yow a quarter of a day!
In cursed tyme I born was, weylaway!
That ye, that doon me al this wo endure,
Yet love I best of any creature.

244. 'Now god,' quod he, 'me sende yet the grace
That I may meten with this Diomede!
And trewely, if I have might and space,
Yet shal I make, I hope, his sydes blede.
O god,' quod he, 'that oughtest taken hede
To fortheren trouthe, and wronges to punyce,
Why niltow doon a vengeaunce on this vyce?

245. 'O Pandare, that in dremes for to triste
Me blamed hast, and wont art ofte upbreyde,
Now maystow see thy-selve, if that thee liste,
How trewe is now thy nece, bright Criseyde!
In sondry formes, god it woot,' he seyde,
'The goddes shewen bothe joye and tene
In slepe, and by my dreme it is now sene.

246. 'And certaynly, with-oute more speche,
From hennes-forth, as ferforth as I may,
Myn owene deeth in armes wol I seche;
I recche not how sone be the day!
But trewely, Criseyde, swete may,
Whom I have ay with al my might y-served,
That ye thus doon, I have it nought deserved.'

247. This Pandarus, that alle these thinges herde,
And wiste wel he seyde a sooth of this,
He nought a word ayein to him answerde;
For sory of his frendes sorwe he is,
And shamed, for his nece hath doon a-mis;
And stant, astoned of these causes tweye,
As stille as stoon: a word ne coude he seye.

248. But at the laste thus he spak, and seyde,
'My brother dere, I may thee do no-more,
What shulde I seyn? I hate, y-wis, Criseyde!
And god wot, I wol hate hir evermore!
And that thou me bisoughtest doon of yore,
Havinge un-to myn honour ne my reste
Right no reward, I dide al that thee leste.

249. 'If I dide ought that mighte lyken thee,
It is me leef; and of this treson now,
God woot, that it a sorwe is un-to me!
And dredelees, for hertes ese of yow,
Right fayn wolde I amende it, wiste I how.
And fro this world, almighty god I preye,
Delivere hir sone; I can no-more seye.'

250. Gret was the sorwe and pleynt of Troilus;
But forth hir cours Fortune ay gan to holde.
Criseyde loveth the sone of Tydeus,
And Troilus mot wepe in cares colde.
Swich is this world; who-so it can biholde,
In ech estat is litel hertes reste;
God leve us for to take it for the beste!

251. In many cruel batayle, out of drede,
Of Troilus, this ilke noble knight,
As men may in these olde bokes rede,

Was sene his knighthod and his grete might.
And dredelees, his ire, day and night,
Ful cruelly the Grekes ay aboughte;
And alwey most this Diomede he soughte.

252. And ofte tyme, I finde that they mette
With blody strokes and with wordes grete,
Assayinge how hir speres weren whette;
And god it woot, with many a cruel hete
Gan Troilus upon his helm to-bete.
But natheles, fortune it nought ne wolde,
Of otheres hond that either deyen sholde.—

253. And if I hadde y-taken for to wryte
The armes of this ilke worthy man,
Than wolde I of his batailles endyte.
But for that I to wryte first bigan
Of his love, I have seyd as that I can.
His worthy dedes, who-so list hem here,
Reed Dares, he can telle hem alle y-fere.

254. Bisechinge every lady bright of hewe,
And every gentil womman, what she be,
That al be that Criseyde was untrewe,
That for that gilt she be not wrooth with me.
Ye may hir gilt in othere bokes see;
And gladlier I wol wryten, if yow leste,
Penelopeës trouthe and good Alceste.

255. Ne I sey not this al-only for these men,
But most for wommen that bitraysed be
Through false folk; god yeve hem sorwe, amen!
That with hir grete wit and subtiltee
Bitrayse yow! and this commeveth me
To speke, and in effect yow alle I preye,
Beth war of men, and herkeneth what I seye!—

256. Go, litel book, go litel myn tregedie,
Ther god thy maker yet, er that he dye,
So sende might to make in som comedie!
But litel book, no making thou n' envye,
But subgit be to alle poesye;
And kis the steppes, wher-as thou seest pace
Virgile, Ovyde, Omer, Lucan, and Stace.

257. And for ther is so greet diversitee
In English and in wryting of our tonge,
So preye I god that noon miswryte thee,
Ne thee mismetre for defaute of tonge.
And red wher-so thou be, or elles songe,
That thou be understonde I god beseche!
But yet to purpos of my rather speche.—

258. The wraththe, as I began yow for to seye,
Of Troilus, the Grekes boughten dere;
For thousandes his hondes maden deye,
As he that was with-outen any pere,
Save Ector, in his tyme, as I can here.
But weylaway, save only goddes wille,
Dispitously him slough the fiers Achille.

259. And whan that he was slayn in this manere,
His lighte goost ful blisfully is went
Up to the holownesse of the seventh spere,
In convers letinge every element;
And there he saugh, with ful avysement,
The erratik sterres, herkeninge armonye
With sownes fulle of hevenish melodye.

260. And doun from thennes faste he gan avyse
This litel spot of erthe, that with the see
Enbraced is, and fully gan despyse
This wrecched world, and held al vanitee
To respect of the pleyn felicitee
That is in hevene above; and at the laste,
Ther he was slayn, his loking doun he caste;

261. And in him-self he lough right at the wo
Of hem that wepten for his deeth so faste;
And dampned al our werk that folweth so
The blinde lust, the which that may not laste,
And sholden al our herte on hevene caste.
And forth he wente, shortly for to telle,
Ther as Mercurie sorted him to dwelle.—

262. Swich fyn hath, lo, this Troilus for love,
Swich fyn hath al his grete worthinesse;
Swich fyn hath his estat real above,

Swich fyn his lust, swich fyn hath his noblesse;
Swich fyn hath false worldes brotelnesse.
And thus bigan his lovinge of Criseyde,
As I have told, and in this wyse he deyde.

263. O yonge fresshe folkes, he or she,
In which that love up groweth with your age,
Repeyreth hoom from worldly vanitee,
And of your herte up-casteth the visage
To thilke god that after his image
Yow made, and thinketh al nis but a fayre
This world, that passeth sone as floures fayre.

264. And loveth him, the which that right for love
Upon a cros, our soules for to beye,
First starf, and roos, and sit in hevene a-bove;
For he nil falsen no wight, dar I seye,
That wol his herte al hoolly on him leye.
And sin he best to love is, and most meke,
What nedeth feyned loves for to seke?

265. Lo here, of Payens corsed olde rytes,
Lo here, what alle hir goddes may availle;
Lo here, these wrecched worldes appetytes;
Lo here, the fyn and guerdon for travaille
Of Jove, Appollo, of Mars, of swich rascaille!
Lo here, the forme of olde clerkes speche
In poetrye, if ye hir bokes seche.—

266. O moral Gower, this book I directe
To thee, and to the philosophical Strode,
To vouchen sauf, ther nede is, to corecte,
Of your benignitees and zeles gode.
And to that sothfast Crist, that starf on rode,
With al myn herte of mercy ever I preye;
And to the lord right thus I speke and seye:

267. Thou oon, and two, and three, eterne on-lyve,
That regnest ay in three and two and oon,
Uncircumscript, and al mayst circumscryve,
Us from visible and invisible foon
Defende; and to thy mercy, everychoon,
So make us, Jesus, for thy grace, digne,
For love of mayde and moder thyn benigne! Amen.

Explicit Liber Troili et Criseydis

ROBERT HENRYSON
THE TESTAMENT OF CRESSEID

THE TESTAMENT OF CRESSEID

Ane dooly sesoun to ane cairfull dyte
Suld correspond, and be equivalent.
Richt sa it wes quhen I began to wryte
This tragedy; the wedder richt fervent,
Quhen Aries, in middis of the Lent,
Shouris of haill can fra the north discend;
That scantly fra the cauld I micht defend.

Yit nevertheles, within myn orature
I stude, quhen Tytan had his bemis bricht
Withdrawin doun and sylit under cure;
And fair Venus, the bewty of the nicht,
Uprais, and set unto the west full richt
Hir goldin face, in oppositioun
Of god Phebus direct discending doun.

Throwout the glas hir bemis brast sa fair
That I micht see, on every syde me by,
The northin wind had purifyit the air,
And shed the misty cloudis fra the sky.
The froist freisit, the blastis bitterly
Fra pole Artyk come quhisling loud and shill,
And causit me remuf aganis my will.

For I traistit that Venus, luifis quene,
To quhom sum-tyme I hecht obedience,
My faidit hart of luf sho wald mak grene;
And therupon, with humbil reverence,
I thocht to pray hir hy magnificence;
But for greit cald as than I lattit was,
And in my chalmer to the fyr can pas.

Thocht luf be hait, yit in ane man of age
It kendillis nocht sa sone as in youthheid,
Of quhom the blude is flowing in ane rage;
And in the auld the curage douf and deid,
Of quhilk the fyr outward is best remeid,
To help be phisik quhair that nature failit;
I am expert, for baith I have assailit.

351

I mend the fyr, and beikit me about,
Than tuik ane drink my spreitis to comfort,
And armit me weill fra the cauld thairout.
To cut the winter-nicht, and mak it short,
I tuik ane quair, and left all uther sport,
Writtin be worthy Chaucer glorious,
Of fair Cresseid and lusty Troilus.

And thair I fand, efter that Diomeid
Ressavit had that lady bricht of hew,
How Troilus neir out of wit abraid,
And weipit soir, with visage paill of hew;
For quhilk wanhope his teiris can renew,
Quhill esperans rejoisit him agane:
Thus quhyl in joy he levit, quhyl in pane.

Of hir behest he had greit comforting,
Traisting to Troy that sho suld mak retour,
Quhilk he desyrit maist of eirdly thing,
For-quhy sho was his only paramour.
Bot quhen he saw passit baith day and hour
Of hir gaincome, than sorrow can oppres
His woful hart in cair and hevines.

Of his distres me neidis nocht reheirs,
For worthy Chaucer, in the samin buik,
In guidly termis and in joly veirs
Compylit hes his cairis, quha will luik.
To brek my sleip ane uther quair I tuik,
In quilk I fand the fatall desteny
Of fair Cresseid, that endit wretchitly.

Quha wait gif all that Chauceir wrait was trew?
Nor I wait nocht gif this narratioun
Be authoreist, or fenyeit of the new
Be sum poeit, throw his inventioun,
Maid to report the lamentatioun
And woful end of this lusty Cresseid,
And quhat distres sho thoillit, and quhat deid.

Quhen Diomed had all his appetyt,
And mair, fulfillit of this fair lady,
Upon ane uther he set his haill delyt,

And send to hir ane lybel of répudy,
And hir excludit fra his company.
Than desolait sho walkit up and doun,
And, sum men sayis, into the court commoun.

O fair Cresseid! the flour and *A-per-se*
Of Troy and Grece, how was thou fortunait,
To change in filth all thy feminitee,
And be with fleshly lust sa maculait,
And go amang the Greikis air and lait
Sa giglot-lyk, takand thy foull plesance!
I have pity thee suld fall sic mischance!

Yit nevertheles, quhat-ever men deme or say
In scornful langage of thy brukilnes,
I sall excuse, als far-furth as I may,
Thy womanheid, thy wisdom, and fairnes,
The quilk Fortoun hes put to sic distres
As hir pleisit, and na-thing throw the gilt
Of thee, throw wikkit langage to be spilt.

This fair lady, in this wys destitut
Of all comfort and consolatioun,
Richt prively, but fellowship, on fut
Disgysit passit far out of the toun
Ane myle or twa, unto ane mansioun
Beildit full gay, quhair hir father Calchas,
Quhilk than amang the Greikis dwelland was.

Quhan he hir saw, the caus he can inquyr
Of hir cuming; sho said, syching full soir,
'Fra Diomeid had gottin his desyr
He wox wery, and wald of me nö moir!'
Quod Calchas, 'Douchter, weip thow not thairfor;
Peraventure all cummis for the best;
Welcum to me; thow art full deir ane gest.'

This auld Calchas, efter the law was tho,
Wes keeper of the tempill, as ane preist,
In quhilk Venus and hir son Cupido
War honourit; and his chalmer was thaim neist;
To quhilk Cresseid, with baill aneuch in breist,
Usit to pas, hir prayeris for to say,
Quhill at the last, upon ane solempne day,

As custom was, the pepill far and neir,
Befoir the none, unto the tempill went
With sacrifys devoit in thair maneir.
But still Cresseid, hevy in hir intent,
In-to the kirk wald not hir-self present,
For giving of the pepil ony deming
Of hir expuls fra Diomeid the king;

But past into ane secreit orature
Quhair sho micht weip hir wofull desteny.
Behind hir bak sho cloisit fast the dure,
And on hir knëis bair fell down in hy.
Upon Venus and Cupid angerly
Sho cryit out, and said on this same wys,
'Allas! that ever I maid yow sacrifys!

'Ye gave me anis ane devyn responsaill
That I suld be the flour of luif in Troy;
Now am I maid an unworthy outwaill,
And all in cair translatit is my joy.
Quha sall me gyde? quha sall me now convoy,
Sen I fra Diomeid and nobill Troilus
Am clene excludit, as abject odious?

'O fals Cupide, is nane to wyte bot thow
And thy mother, of luf the blind goddes!
Ye causit me alwayis understand and trow
The seid of luf was sawin in my face,
And ay grew grene throw your supply and grace.
But now, allas! that seid with froist is slane,
And I fra luifferis left, and all forlane!'

Quhen this was said, doun in ane extasy,
Ravisht in spreit, intill ane dream sho fell;
And, be apperance, hard, quhair sho did ly,
Cupid the king ringand ane silver bell,
Quhilk men micht heir fra hevin unto hell;
At quhais sound befoir Cupide appeiris
The sevin planetis, discending fra thair spheiris,

Quhilk hes powèr of all thing generábill
To reull and steir, be thair greit influence,
Wedder and wind and coursis variábill.

And first of all Saturn gave his sentence,
Quhilk gave to Cupid litill reverence,
But as ane busteous churl, on his maneir,
Com crabbitly, with auster luik and cheir.

His face fronsit, his lyr was lyk the leid,
His teith chatterit and cheverit with the chin,
His ene drowpit, how, sonkin in his heid,
Out of his nois the meldrop fast can rin,
With lippis bla, and cheikis leine and thin,
The yse-shoklis that fra his hair doun hang
Was wonder greit, and as ane speir als lang.

Atour his belt his lyart lokkis lay
Felterit unfair, ourfret with froistis hoir;
His garmound and his gyte full gay of gray;
His widderit weid fra him the wind out woir.
Ane busteous bow within his hand he boir;
Under his gyrdil ane flash of felloun flanis
Fedderit with yse, and heidit with hail-stanis.

Than Juppiter richt fair and amiábill,
God of the starnis in the firmament,
And nureis to all thing[is] generábill,
Fra his father Saturn far different,
With burely face, and browis bricht and brent;
Upon his heid ane garland wonder gay
Of flouris fair, as it had been in May.

His voice was cleir, as cristal wer his ene;
As goldin wyr sa glitterand was his hair;
His garmound and his gyte full gay of grene,
With goldin listis gilt on every gair;
Ane burely brand about his middill bair,
In his right hand he had ane groundin speir,
Of his father the wraith fra us to weir.

Nixt efter him com Mars, the god of ire,
Of stryf, debait, and all dissensioun;
To chyde and fecht, als feirs as ony fyr;
In hard harnes, hewmound and habirgeoun,
And on his hanche ane rousty fell fachioun:
And in his hand he had ane rousty sword,
Wrything his face with mony angry word.

Shaikand his sword, befoir Cupide he com
With reid visage and grisly glowrand ene;
And at his mouth ane bullar stude of fome,
Lyk to ane bair quhetting his tuskis kene
Richt tuilyour-lyk, but temperance in tene;
Ane horn he blew, with mony busteous brag,
Quhilk all this warld with weir hes maid to wag.

Than fair Phebus, lanterne and lamp of licht
Of man and beist, baith frute and flourishing,
Tender nuréis, and banisher of nicht,
And of the warld causing, be his moving
And influence, lyf in all eirdly thing;
Without comfort of quhom, of forse to nocht
Must all ga dy, that in this warld is wrocht.

As king royáll he raid upon his chair,
The quhilk Phaeton gydit sum-tyme unricht;
The brichtnes of his face, quhen it was bair,
Nane micht behald for peirsing of his sicht.
This goldin cart with fyry bemes bricht
Four yokkit steidis, full different of hew,
But bait or tyring throw the spheiris drew.

The first was soyr, with mane als reid as rois,
Callit Eöy, in-to the orient;
The secund steid to name hecht Ethiös,
Quhytly and paill, and sum-deill ascendent;
The thrid Peros, richt hait and richt fervent;
The feird was blak, callit Philegoney,
Quhilk rollis Phebus down in-to the sey.

Venus was thair present, that goddes gay,
Hir sonnis querrel for to defend, and mak
Hir awin complaint, cled in ane nyce array,
The ane half grene, the uther half sabill-blak;
Quhyte hair as gold, kemmit and shed abak;
But in hir face semit greit variance,
Quhyles perfit treuth, and quhylës inconstance.

Under smyling sho was dissimulait,
Provocative with blenkis amorous;
And suddanly changit and alterait,

Angry as ony serpent venemous,
Richt pungitive with wordis odious.
Thus variant sho was, quha list tak keip,
With ane eye lauch, and with the uther weip:

In taikning that all fleshly paramour,
Quhilk Venus hes in reull and governance,
Is sum-tyme sweit, sum-tyme bitter and sour,
Richt unstabill, and full of variance,
Mingit with cairfull joy, and fals plesance;
Now hait, now cauld; now blyth, now full of wo;
Now grene as leif, now widderit and ago.

With buik in hand than com Mercurius,
Richt eloquent and full of rethory;
With pólite termis and delicious;
With pen and ink to réport all redy;
Setting sangis, and singand merily.
His hude was reid, heklit atour his croun,
Lyk to ane poeit of the auld fassoun.

Boxis he bair with fine electuairis,
And sugerit syropis for digestioun;
Spycis belangand to the pothecairis,
With mony hailsum sweit confectioun;
Doctour in phisik, cled in scarlot goun,
And furrit weill, as sic ane aucht to be,
Honest and gude, and not ane word coud le.

Nixt efter him com lady Cynthia,
The last of all, and swiftest in hir spheir,
Of colour blak, buskit with hornis twa,
And in the nicht sho listis best appeir;
Haw as the leid, of colour na-thing cleir.
For all hir licht sho borrowis at hir brothir
Titan; for of hir-self sho hes nane uther.

Hir gyte was gray, and full of spottis blak;
And on hir breist ane churl paintit ful evin,
Beirand ane bunch of thornis on his bak,
Quhilk for his thift micht clim na nar the hevin.
Thus quhen they gadderit war, thir goddis sevin,
Mercurius they cheisit with ane assent
To be foir-speikar in the parliament.

Quha had ben thair, and lyking for to heir
His facound toung and termis exquisyte,
Of rhetorik the praktik he micht leir,
In breif sermone ane pregnant sentence wryte.
Befoir Cupide vailing his cap a lyte,
Speiris the caus of that vocacioun;
And he anon shew his intencioun.

'Lo!' quod Cupide, 'quha will blaspheme the name
Of his awin god, outhir in word or deid,
To all goddis he dois baith lak and shame,
And suld have bitter panis to his meid.
I say this by yonder wretchit Cresseid,
The quhilk throw me was sum-tyme flour of lufe,
Me and my mother starkly can reprufe.

'Saying, of hir greit infelicitè
I was the caus; and my mother Venus,
Ane blind goddes hir cald, that micht not see,
With slander and defame injurious.
Thus hir leving unclene and lecherous
Sho wald returne on me and [on] my mother,
To quhom I shew my grace abone all uther.

'And sen ye ar all sevin deificait,
Participant of dévyn sapience,
This greit injúry don to our hy estait
Me-think with pane we suld mak recompence;
Was never to goddis don sic violence.
As weill for yow as for myself I say;
Thairfoir ga help to révenge, I yow pray.'

Mercurius to Cupid gave answeir,
And said, 'Shir king, my counsall is that ye
Refer yow to the hyest planeit heir,
And tak to him the lawest of degrè,
The pane of Cresseid for to modify;
As god Saturn, with him tak Cynthia.'
'I am content,' quod he, 'to tak thay twa.'

Than thus proceidit Saturn and the Mone,
Quhen thay the mater rypely had degest;
For the dispyt to Cupid sho had done,

And to Venus oppin and manifest,
In all hir lyf with pane to be opprest
And torment sair, with seiknes incurábill,
And to all lovers be abominábill.

This dulefull sentence Saturn tuik on hand,
And passit doun quhair cairfull Cresseid lay;
And on hir heid he laid ane frosty wand,
Than lawfully on this wyse can he say:
'Thy greit fairnes, and al thy bewty gay,
Thy wantoun blude, and eik thy goldin hair,
Heir I exclude fra thee for evermair.

'I change thy mirth into melancholy,
Quhilk is the mother of all pensivenes;
Thy moisture and thy heit in cald and dry;
Thyne insolence, thy play and wantones
To greit diseis: thy pomp and thy riches
In mortall neid; and greit penuritie
Thow suffer sall, and as ane beggar die.'

O cruel Saturn, fraward and angry,
Hard is thy dome, and to malicious!
On fair Cresseid quhy hes thow na mercy,
Quhilk was sa sweit, gentill, and amorous?
Withdraw thy sentence, and be gracious
As thow was never; so shawis thow thy deid,
Ane wraikfull sentence gevin on fair Cresseid.

Than Cynthia, quhen Saturn past away,
Out of hir sait discendit down belyve,
And red ane bill on Cresseid quhair sho lay,
Contening this sentence diffinityve:
'Fra heil of body I thee now depryve,
And to thy seiknes sal be na recure,
But in dolour thy dayis to indure.

'Thy cristall ene minglit with blude I mak,
Thy voice sa cleir unplesand, hoir, and hace;
Thy lusty lyre ourspred with spottis blak,
And lumpis haw appeirand in thy face.
Quhair thow cummis, ilk man flee the place;
Thus sall thou go begging fra hous to hous,
With cop and clapper, lyk ane lazarous.'

This dooly dream, this ugly visioun,
Brocht to ane end, Cresseid fra it awoik,
And all that court and convocatioun
Vanischit away. Than rais sho up and tuik
Ane poleist glas, and hir shaddow coud luik;
And quhen sho saw hir face sa déformait,
Gif sho in hart was wa aneuch, god wait!

Weiping full sair, 'Lo! quhat it is,' quod she,
'With fraward langage for to mufe and steir
Our crabbit goddis, and sa is sene on me!
My blaspheming now have I bocht full deir;
All eirdly joy and mirth I set areir.
Allas, this day! Allas, this woful tyde,
Quhen I began with my goddis to chyde!'

Be this was said, ane child com fra the hall
To warn Cresseid the supper was redy;
First knokkit at the dure, and syne coud call—
'Madame, your father biddis you cum in hy;
He has mervell sa lang on grouf ye ly,
And sayis, "Your prayërs been to lang sum-deill;
The goddis wait all your intent full weill."'

Quod sho, 'Fair child, ga to my father deir,
And pray him cum to speik with me anon.'
And sa he did, and said, 'Douchter, quhat cheir?'
'Allas!' quod she, 'father, my mirth is gon!'
'How sa?' quod he; and sho can all expone,
As I have tauld, the vengeance and the wrak,
For hir trespas, Cupide, on hir coud tak.

He luikit on hir ugly lipper face,
The quhilk befor was quhyte as lilly-flour;
Wringand his handis, oftymes he said, Allas!
That he had levit to see that wofull hour!
For he knew weill that thair was na succour
To hir seiknes; and that dowblit his pane;
Thus was thair cair aneuch betwix tham twane.

Quhen thay togidder murnit had full lang,
Quod Cresseid, 'Father, I wald not be kend;
Thairfor in secreit wyse ye let me gang

To yon hospítall at the tounis end;
And thidder sum meit, for cheritie, me send
To leif upon; for all mirth in this eird
Is fra me gane; sik is my wikkit weird.'

Than in ane mantill and ane bevar hat,
With cop and clapper, wonder prively,
He opnit ane secreit yet, and out thairat
Convoyit hir, that na man suld espy,
Unto ane village half ane myle thairby;
Deliverit hir in at the spittail-hous,
And dayly sent hir part of his almous.

Sum knew hir weill, and sum had na knawlege
Of hir, becaus sho was sa déformait
With bylis blak, ourspred in hir visage,
And hir fair colour faidit and alterait.
Yit thay presumit, for hir hy regrait
And still murning, sho was of nobill kin;
With better will thairfor they tuik hir in.

The day passit, and Phebus wènt to rest,
The cloudis blak ourquhelmit all the sky;
God wait gif Cresseid was ane sorrowful gest,
Seeing that uncouth fair and herbery.
But meit or drink sho dressit hir to ly
In ane dark corner of the hous allone;
And on this wyse, weiping, sho maid hir mone.

THE COMPLAINT OF CRESSEID

'O sop of sorrow sonken into cair!
O caytive Cresseid! now and ever-mair
Gane is thy joy and all thy mirth in eird;
Of all blyithnes now art thow blaiknit bair;
Thair is na salve may saif thee of thy sair!
Fell is thy fortoun, wikkit is thy weird;
Thy blis is baneist, and thy baill on breird!
Under the eirth god gif I gravin wer,
Quhar nane of Grece nor yit of Troy micht heird!

'Quhair is thy chalmer, wantounly besene
With burely bed, and bankouris browderit bene,
Spycis and wynis to thy collatioun;
The cowpis all of gold and silver shene,
The swete meitis servit in plaittis clene,
With saipheron sals of ane gude seessoun;
The gay garmentis, with mony gudely goun,
Thy plesand lawn pinnit with goldin prene?
All is areir thy greit royáll renoun!

'Quhair is thy garding, with thir greissis gay
And fresshe flouris, quhilk the quene Floray
Had paintit plesandly in every pane,
Quhair thou was wont full merily in May
To walk, and tak the dew be it was day,
And heir the merle and mavis mony ane;
With ladyis fair in carrolling to gane,
And see the royal rinkis in thair array
In garmentis gay, garnischit on every grane?

'Thy greit triumphand fame and hy honour,
Quhair thou was callit of eirdly wichtis flour,
All is decayit; thy weird is welterit so,
Thy hy estait is turnit in darknes dour!
This lipper ludge tak for thy burelie bour,
And for thy bed tak now ane bunch of stro.
For waillit wyne and meitis thou had tho,
Tak mowlit breid, peirry, and syder sour;
But cop and clapper, now is all ago.

'My cleir voice and my courtly carrolling,
Quhair I was wont with ladyis for to sing,
Is rawk as ruik, full hiddeous, hoir, and hace;
My plesand port all utheris precelling,
Of lustines I was held maist conding;
Now is deformit the figour of my face;
To luik on it na leid now lyking hes.
Sowpit in syte, I say with sair siching—
Lugeit amang the lipper-leid—"Alas!"

'O ladyis fair of Troy and Grece, attend
My misery, quhilk nane may comprehend,

My frivoll fortoun, my infelicitie,
My greit mischief, quhilk na man can amend.
Be war in tyme, approchis neir the end,
And in your mynd ane mirrour mak of me.
As I am now, peradventure that ye,
For all your micht, may cum to that same end,
Or ellis war, gif ony war may be.

'Nocht is your fairnes bot ane faiding flour,
Nocht is your famous laud and hy honour
Bot wind inflat in uther mennis eiris;
Your roising reid to rotting sall retour.
Exempill mak of me in your memour,
Quhilk of sic thingis wofull witnes beiris.
All welth in eird away as wind it weiris;
Be war thairfor; approchis neir the hour;
Fortoun is fikkil quhen sho beginnis and steiris.'

Thus chydand with her drery desteny,
Weiping, sho woik the nicht fra end to end,
But all in vane; hir dule, hir cairfull cry
Micht nocht remeid, nor yit hir murning mend.
Ane lipper-lady rais, and till hir wend,
And said, 'Quhy spurnis thou aganis the wall,
To sla thyself, and mend na-thing at all?

'Sen that thy weiping dowbillis bot thy wo,
I counsall thee mak vertew of ane neid,
To leir to clap thy clapper to and fro,
And live efter the law of lipper-leid.'
Thair was na buit, bot forth with thame sho yeid
Fra place to place, quhill cauld and hounger sair
Compellit hir to be ane rank beggair.

That samin tyme, of Troy the garnisoun,
Quhilk had to chiftane worthy Troilus,
Throw jeopardy of weir had strikkin doun
Knichtis of Grece in number mervellous.
With greit triúmph and laud victorious
Agane to Troy richt royally thay raid
The way quhair Cresseid with the lipper baid.

Seing that company cum, all with ane stevin
They gaif ane cry and shuik coppis gude speid;
Said, 'Worthy lordis, for goddis lufe of hevin,
To us lipper part of your almous-deid.'
Than to thair cry nobill Troilus tuik heid;
Having pity, neir by the place can pas
Quhair Cresseid sat, nat witting quhat sho was.

Than upon him sho kest up baith her ene,
And with ane blenk it com in-to his thocht
That he sum-tyme hir face befoir had sene;
But sho was in sic ply he knew hir nocht.
Yit than hir luik in-to his mind it brocht
The sweit visage and amorous blenking
Of fair Cresseid, sumtyme his awin darling.

Na wonder was, suppois in mynd that he
Tuik hir figure sa sone, and lo! now, quhy;
The idole of ane thing in cace may be
Sa deip imprentit in the fantasy,
That it deludis the wittis outwardly,
And sa appeiris in forme and lyke estait
Within the mynd as it was figurait.

Ane spark of lufe than till his hart coud spring,
And kendlit all his body in ane fyre;
With hait fevir ane sweit and trimbilling
Him tuik, quhill he was ready to expyre;
To beir his sheild his breist began to tyre;
Within ane whyle he changit mony hew,
And nevertheles not ane ane-uther knew.

For knichtly pity and memoriall
Of fair Cresseid, ane girdill can he tak,
Ane purs of gold and mony gay jowáll,
And in the skirt of Cresseid doun can swak;
Than raid away, and not ane word he spak,
Pensive in hart, quhill he com to the toun,
And for greit cair oft-syis almaist fell doun.

The lipper-folk to Cresseid than can draw,
To see the equall distribucioun
Of the almous; but quhan the gold they saw,

Ilk ane to uther prevely can roun,
And said, 'Yon lord hes mair affectioun,
However it be, unto yon lazarous
Than to us all; we knaw be his almous.'

'Quhat lord is yon?' quod sho, 'have ye na feill,
Hes don to us so greit humanitie?'
'Yes,' quod a lipper-man, 'I knaw him weill;
Shir Troilus it is, gentill and free.'
Quhen Cresseid understude that it was he,
Stiffer than steill thair stert ane bitter stound
Throwout hir hart, and fell doun to the ground.

Quhen sho, ourcom, with syching sair and sad,
With mony cairfull cry and cald—'Ochane!
Now is my breist with stormy stoundis stad,
Wrappit in wo, ane wretch full will of wane';
Than swounit sho oft or sho coud refrane,
And ever in hir swouning cryit sho thus:
'O fals Cresseid, and trew knicht Troilus!

'Thy luf, thy lawtee, and thy gentilnes
I countit small in my prosperitie;
Sa elevait I was in wantones,
And clam upon the fickill quheill sa hie;
All faith and lufe, I promissit to thee,
Was in the self fickill and frivolous;
O fals Cresseid, and trew knicht Troilus!

'For lufe of me thou keipt gude countinence,
Honest and chaist in conversatioun;
Of all wemen protectour and defence
Thou was, and helpit thair opinioun.
My mynd, in fleshly foull affectioun,
Was inclynit to lustis lecherous;
Fy! fals Cresseid! O, trew knicht Troilus!

'Lovers, be war, and tak gude heid about
Quhom that ye lufe, for quhom ye suffer paine;
I lat yow wit, thair is richt few thairout
Quhom ye may traist, to have trew lufe againe;
Preif quhen ye will, your labour is in vaine
Thairfor I reid ye tak thame as ye find;
For they ar sad as widdercock in wind.

'Becaus I knaw the greit unstabilnes
Brukkil as glas, into my-self I say,
Traisting in uther als greit unfaithfulnes,
Als unconstant, and als untrew of fay.
Thocht sum be trew, I wait richt few ar they.
Quha findis treuth, lat him his lady ruse;
Nane but my-self, as now, I will accuse.'

Quhen this was said, with paper sho sat doun,
And on this maneir maid hir testament:
'Heir I beteich my corps and carioun
With wormis and with taidis to be rent;
My cop and clapper, and myne ornament,
And all my gold, the lipper-folk sall have,
Quhen I am deid, to bury me in grave.

'This royall ring, set with this ruby reid,
Quhilk Troilus in drowry to me send,
To him agane I leif it quhan I am deid,
To mak my cairfull deid unto him kend.
Thus I conclude shortly, and mak ane end.
My spreit I leif to Diane, quhair sho dwellis,
To walk with hir in waist woddis and wellis.

'O Diomeid! thow hes baith broche and belt
Quhilk Troilus gave me in takinning
Of his trew lufe!'—And with that word sho swelt.
And sone ane lipper-man tuik of the ring.
Syne buryit hir withoutin tarying,
To Troilus furthwith the ring he bair,
And of Cresseid the deith he can declair.

Quhen he had hard hir greit infirmitè,
Hir legacy and lamentatioun,
And how sho endit in sik povertè,
He swelt for wo, and fell doun in ane swoun;
For greit sorrow his hart to birst was boun.
Syching full sadly, said, 'I can no moir;
Sho was untrew, and wo is me thairfor!'

Sum said he maid ane tomb of merbell gray,
And wrait hir name and superscriptioun,
And laid it on hir grave, quhair that sho lay,

In goldin letteris, conteining this ressoun:
'Lo! fair ladyis, Cresseid of Troyis toun,
Sumtyme countit the flour of womanheid,
Under this stane, late lipper, lyis deid!'

Now, worthy wemen, in this ballet short,
Made for your worship and instructioun,
Of cheritè I monish and exhort,
Ming not your luf with fals deceptioun.
Beir in your mynd this short conclusioun
Of fair Cresseid, as I have said befoir;
Sen sho is deid, I speik of hir no moir.

GLOSSARY

GLOSSARY

TROILUS AND CRISEYDE

Abet: abetting, aid
Abood: delay, tarrying
Abregge: abridge, shorten
Abreyde: awake
Abusion: abuse, absurdity, a shameful thing
Abyden: abide, await, dwell
Accesse: feverish attack
Accident: that which is accidental, incident
Accusement: accusation
Acurse: curse
Adawe: awake, recover
Adrad: afraid
Advertence: attention
Advocacyes: pleas
Afere: on fire
Affectis: desires
Affyle: file, render smooth
Aforyeyn: over against
Agame: in play
Agilten: do wrong, offend, sin
Agree: please
Agreef: in dudgeon, sadly
Agrysen: shudder, tremble
Al: all; *al and som:* the whole matter
Al: although
Alambyk: alembic
Alday: continually
Alderbeste: best of all
Alderfirst: first of all
Alderlest: least of all
Alderlevest: dearest of all
Aldermost: most of all
Alderwysest: wisest of all
Algate: in any case
Along on: owing to
Alose: commend
Amayed: dismayed
Ambages: ambiguous words
Amorwe: on the morrow, in the morning

Amphibologyes: ambiguities
Anonright: immediately
Apaye: satisfy, please
Apeiren: injure, perish
Arace: eradicate, uproot
Arede: explain, disclose, divine
Arten: constrain, urge
Ascaunces: as if to say
Ascry: outcry
Ashamed: put to shame; *for pure ashamed:* for very shame
Aspact: astrological aspect
Aspre: sharp, bitter
Assoilen: discharge
Assure: feel secure, trust
Asterte: escape
Atempre: temperate, moderate
Athinken: displease
Atrede: surpass in counsel
Atrenne: surpass in running
Atwinne: apart
Avale: fall down
Avaunt: boast
Avauntour: boaster
Aventayle: ventail
Aventure: chance, circumstance; *on aventure:* in case of mishap; *in aventure:* in the hands of fortune
Avyse: consider
Avysement: consideration
Await: waiting, watchfulness
Awepe: a-weeping
Ayein: opposite to
Ayein: again
Ayeinward: back again

Baite: feed
Balaunce: balance; *in balaunce:* in jeopardy
Bane: cause of death, slayer
Barbe: barb, part of woman's headdress

Bauderye: bawdry
Bede: offer, command
Been: bees
Belle: bell; *bere the belle:* be the first
Berd: beard; *in the berd:* face to face
Bere: bear
Bere: bier
Bere: bear, carry; *beren him on hand:* assure him
Bet: better
Bete: remedy, heal
Bidde: ask, pray
Bigoon: provided; *wel bigoon* fortunate, contented; *sorw-fully bigoon:* distressed
Biheste: promise, command
Bihete: promise
Bihighte: promised
Bihovely: helpful
Bileve: faith, creed
Bilinne: cease
Biseyn: provided; *goodly biseyn:* fair to see
Bishitte: shut up
Bithinke: think of
Bitraise: betray
Bitrenden: encircle, twine round
Biware: spend
Biwepe: bemoan
Biwryen: disclose, reveal
Blende: blind, deceive
Bleve: remain, dwell
Bleynte: turned aside
Blyve: quickly, soon; *as blyve:* very soon, as soon as possible
Bonde: bondman
Bone: petition, boon
Bore: hole
Borne: smooth, burnish
Borwe: pledge; *to borwe:* in pledge; *Venus here to borwe:* Venus being your pledge
Bote: good, benefit, advantage, healing
Botelees: without remedy
Bothe: both; *your bother:* of you both
Botmelees: bottomless, unreal
Brede: breadth, space; *on brede:* abroad

Breme: furious
Brenne: burn
Brenningly: ardently
Breste: burst
Breyde: start
Brotel: brittle, frail
Byjaped: tricked, made a jest of

Calendes: beginning
Calle: caul; *maken him a howve above a calle:* befool him
Cankedort: state of suspense, critical position
Cape: gape
Cas: accident, chance; *upon cas:* by chance
Caste: throw, contrive, calculate astrologically, consider
Cause: cause; *cause causinge:* first cause
Char: chariot
Charge: be of importance
Cheep: market, price; *as good cheep:* as cheaply
Chere: face, countenance
Cherl: churl, man
Chimenee: fireplace
Chiteringe: chattering, chirping
Clepen: call, name
Clippe: embrace
Closet: small room
Combre-world: one who encumbers the world
Combust: quenched (as being too near the sun)
Comeve: instigate, induce, influence
Complexioun: temperament
Comprende: comprehend, contain
Comune: general, common to all
Congeyen: dismiss
Conne: be able, have experience, know how
Conning: skill, knowledge
Consistorie: council
Contek: strife, contest
Contenance: appearance; *fond his contenance:* pretended
Cordeth: agrees
Cote-armure: coat-armour, coat showing coat of arms
Covenable: fit, proper

Coye: calm, cajole
Craftily: artfully, in a studied manner
Crepul: cripple
Crop: top; *crop and rote:* top and root, everything
Curacioun: cure, healing
Cure: cure, remedy, diligence, attention

Dan, daun: lord, sir
Daunger: disdain
Debaat: strife, quarrelling
Declamed: discussed
Deel: part; *eche a del:* every whit; *no del:* no whit
Dees: dice
Defence: resistance, prohibition
Defende: defend, forbid
Defet: exhausted, disfigured
Defyne: pronounce, declare
Deliberen: deliberate, consider
Deliverly: quickly
Departe: separate, sever, distinguish
Dere: injure
Derre: more dearly
Despeired: sunk in despair
Desponeth: disposes
Desporte: rejoice
Destreyne: distress, constrain, mislead
Determyne: come to an end
Devyn: astrologer
Devyne: guess, prophesy, suspect
Devyse: relate, tell, recommend
Deynous: scornful
Deyntee: worth, value, dainty
Dighte: ordain, place, array; *him dighte:* betook himself
Digne: worthy
Dignely: scornfully
Directe: address
Disclaundre: reproach
Discryve: describe
Disese: discomfort, grief, misery
Disese: trouble, vex, distress
Disjoynt: difficult, position, peril
Dispitous: spiteful, grievous, pitiless
Disturne: turn aside
Dokke: dock (plant)

Doom: judgment, opinion
Doutance: doubt, perplexity
Doute: doubt, lack
Doutous: doubtful
Dowe: grant, give
Drecche: be tedious, vex
Drecchinge: delay
Drede: dread; *out of drede:* without doubt
Dredeles: without doubt
Drenchen: drown
Dresse: dispose, get ready, prepare
Drye: endure
Dulcarnon: inexplicable dilemma, one's wit's end
Dulle: feel dull
Duresse: hardship
Durring: daring; *durring don:* daring to do
Dyverseth: varies.

Eche: increase, add to
Eem: uncle
Eft: again
Egal: equal, equally
Emforth: as far as extends
Empryse: enterprise, undertaking
Enchesoun: cause
Endyte: write, tell
Engyn: contrivance, skill
Enhabit: devoted
Enseled: sealed up, fully granted
Enteched: endued with good qualities
Entende: attend, incline to, perceive
Ententifly: attentively
Entrecomunen: intercommunicate
Entremette: take part in, meddle with
Ernest: seriousness
Erst: first, at first
Ethe: easy
Everichoon: every one

Fare: behaviour, business, company; *in rumour of this fare:* when this conduct was heard of
Faren: behave, go, travel
Fare-cart: travelling cart

Faste: closely, fast; *as faste*: very quickly
Fawe: anxiously
Fayr: a fair thing
Fecches: vetches
Feffe: present
Fel: skin
Feldefare: field-fare; *farewel feldefare*: all is lost
Fele: many
Felen: feel, experience, try to find out
Felon: angry
Ferd: fear
Fere: companion
Fere: frighten
Ferne yere: last year
Feste: feast, encouragement, merriment, token of pleasure
Festeyinge: feasting, entertainment
Fette: fetched
Flaumbe: flame
Fleigh: fled
Flemen: banish
Fleminge: banishment, flight
Flete: float, bathe
Flitte: remove
Fonde: endeavour, test
Forby: past
Forbyse: instruct by examples
Fordo: destroy
Fors: force; *no fors*: no matter
Forshapen: metamorphosed
Forshright: exhausted with shrieking
Forthinke: seem amiss, seem serious
Forthy: therefore
Fortuna maior: a name for the auspicious planet Jupiter
Forward: agreement
Foryede: gave up
Founes: fawns, young desires
Frape: company, troop
Fremede: foreign; *fremed and tame*: every one
Frete: eat
Freyne: ask
Frote: rub
Fyn: end, death; *for fyn*: finally

Fyn: fine; *of fyne force*: of very need
Fyne: finish, cease

Gabbe: boast, prate, lie
Gamen: game, sport
Gaude: gaud, toy, pretence
Gaure: stare
Gerful: fitful, wayward
Geste: romance, tale, exploit; *in geste*: in romance form
Ginne: begin
Glase: glaze, furnish with glass; *glase his howve*: give him a glass cap, a useless defence
Glede: glowing coal or ashes
Glente: glanced
Glose: interpret, explain, persuade cunningly
Goodly: patiently, reasonably, rightly
Goostly: truly
Grace: favour; *harde grace*: displeasure, disfavour
Grame: anger, grief, harm
Grant mercy: best thanks
Graven: engrave, bury
Gree: favour, good part; *in gree*: favourably
Greet: great; *the grete*: the chief part
Greve: grove
Grisly: horrible, very serious
Groyn: murmur
Gruf: in a grovelling posture
Gye: guide
Gyle: trick

Half: behalf, side, part
Halt: holds
Halvendel: the half part
Hameled: cut off
Hard: hard; *of hard*: with difficulty
Hardely: unhesitatingly, certainly
Hardiment: boldness
Hay: hedge
Hele: health
Heleless: out of health
Helply: helpful
Henne: hence

Hente: catch, seize

Here and howne: meaning uncertain, but seems to signify people of all sorts

Herie: praise

Heroner: falcon for herons

Heryinge: praising, glory

Heste: command

Hierdes: protectress

Ho: stop

Holde: keep, preserve, esteem

Holt: plantation

Hond: hand; *beren him on hond*: make him believe; *holden in hond*: retain, cajole

Hoor: hoary, white-haired

Hote: promise, be called

Hove: hover, dwell, wait about

Howve: hood

Hye: haste

Hyre: payment, ransom

Infortune: misfortune, ill fortune

Inhelde: pour in, infuse

Inknette: drew in

Jangle: chatter, prate

Janglerye: gossip

Jo: take effect, come about

Jompre: jumble

Jouken: slumber

Juparte: imperil, endanger

Juste: joust, tourney, tilt

Kalendes: beginning

Kecche: catch, clutch

Kepe: take care, intend

Kevere: recover

Kinde: nature

Kinde: natural

Knowe: knee

Kythe: show

Labbe: tell-tale

Lak: want, defect

Lakken: find fault with, disparage

Lappe: fold, lappet, edge of a garment

Lasse: less

Lay: law

Layser: leisure

Leef: lief, pleasing, loved one, lover

Lere: teach, learn

Lese: pasture

Lese: lose

Lest: pleasure

Lest: pleases

Lete: let, let go, forsake, let alone, consider

Lette: hindrance, delay

Lette: hinder

Lette-game: kill-joy

Letuarie: remedy

Leve: leave

Leve: believe

Leve: allow, grant

Leveful: allowable

Lewed: ignorant

Ley: lied

Leye: lay, cause to lie, lay a wager, pledge

Lighte: make light, rejoice, render cheerful, alleviate

Lightly: easily

Lisse: comfort, joy

Lissen: alleviate

List: it pleases

Lofte, on: aloft, in the air

Lore: teaching, advice, lesson

Lyf: life; *on lyve*: alive; *of lyve*: out of life; *my lyve*: in my life; *lyves*: living

Lyke: please

Lyne: line; *as lyne right*: straight as a line

Lyte: small, little; *into litel*: very nearly

Lythe: alleviate, cheer

Makelees: peerless

Making: poetry

Malt: melted

Mansuete: courteous

Martyre: martyrdom

Mase: bewilderment

Mat: exhausted

Medle: mingle

Meed: reward; *to medes*: for a reward

Mene: middle, of middle size

Message: message, messenger

Mesure: moderation

Mete: dream

Meve: move, stir
Mewet: mute
Meynee: household followers
Mis: wrong, amiss
Misaunter: misadventure, misfortune
Mischaunce: ill luck
Misledden: misconducted
Mislyved: of ill life, treacherous
Misse: fail
Moeble: moveable goods
Mokre: hoard up
Mone: lament
Moot: must
Morter: metal bowl for holding wax, with wick
Mote: atom
Mountance: amount, length
Mowe: grimace
Mowen: be able
Muable: changeable
Muse: consider
Muwe: mew
Muwe: change
Myne: undermine

Namely: especially
Nas: was not
Nath: hath not
Nedely: of necessity
Nere: wast not, were not, should not
Nerf: nerve, sinew
Nevene: name
Nighte: grow dark
Nil: will not
Niste: knew not
Nobley: nobility, noble rank
Nolde: would not
Nomen: taken
Nones, for the: for the nonce, for the time
Noot, not: know not
Nost: knowest not
Note: note (in music), tune; *by note:* in concord
Notifie: take note of
Nouncerteyn: uncertainty
Nouthe: now
Novelrye: novelty
Nyce: foolish
Nycetee: folly, scrupulousness

Oon: one, united, agreed; *ever in oon:* ever alike; *that oon ·* one thing; *felle at oon:* came to agreement
Ordal: ordeal
Ordenee: well-ordered
Ordeyne: regulated
Ordure: rubbish
Ost: host, army
Ounded: wavy
Overal: everywhere, in all directions
Overcome: come to pass

Pace: pass, go
Palestral: athletic
Paramours: passionately
Paraunter: perhaps
Paregal: fully equal
Parfit: perfect
Parodie: period
Payd: pleased
Pencel: small banner, sleeve worn as token
Perseveraunce: endurance, constancy.
Peyne: pain of torture; *in the peyne:* under torture
Peyne: take pains, endeavour
Piëtee: pity
Piëtous: piteous, sorrowful
Plat, platly: plainly
Plesaunce: pleasure
Plete: plead
Pleyne: complain
Plighte: plucked, drew
Plighte: pledged
Plyt: plight
Plyte: fold, turn backwards and forwards
Poeplish: popular
Pose: put the case
Possed: pushed
Potente: crutch
Pous: pulse
Prees: crowd
Prenten: imprint
Press: throng; *in press:* under a press, in a suppressed state
Prest: prompt

Preve: proof; *at preve:* to the proof; *armes preve:* proof of fighting power
Proces: argument, matter
Propretee: peculiar possession
Prow: profit
Pryme: prime (of day), usually 9 a.m.
Prys: price, worth, praise
Pulle: pluck
Purchacen: procure, acquire
Pure: very
Purveyaunce: providence, prearrangement
Purveyen: provide, foresee
Purveyinge: providence
Put: pit
Pye: magpie
Pyk: pike (fish)
Pyke: peep, pick at
Pyne: pain, lament

Qualm: foreboding of death
Quappe: palpitate
Quelle: strike
Queme: please, subserve
Quenche: put a stop to, extinguish
Quiken: quicken, revive, grow
Quisshin: cushion

Rakel: rash, hasty
Raket: game of rackets
Rakle: behave rashly
Rathe: soon
Rather: earlier
Ravisshe: snatch away
Rëal: royal
Recche: reck, care
Reche: proceed
Recorde: remember
Rede: read, advise, interpret
Rede: red, i.e. gold
Reed: counsel
Rees: great haste
Refere: return
Refreyden: grow cold
Refus: refused, rejected
Refut: place of refuge
Regne: kingdom, realm
Rejoye: rejoice
Remorde: cause remorse
Remuable: changeable

Rente: revenue, tribute
Repreve: shame
Repreve: reproach
Requeren: entreat, seek
Rescous: rescue, help
Resport: regard
Respyt: delay; *out of more respyt:* without any delay
Reward: regard, attention
Reyse: build up
Risshe: rush
Rivere, for: for the sport of hawking
Ron: rained
Rote: root; *on rote:* firmly rooted
Roune, rowne: whisper
Route: company
Route: roar
Rowe: roughly, angrily

Save-garde: safe-conduct
Sawe: saying, speech
Say: saw
Scripture: writing, inscription
Scrivenish: like a scrivener
See: seat
Selde: seldom
Selinesse: happiness
Sentement: feeling, fancy, susceptibility
Sentence: meaning
Sepulture: mode of burial, tomb
Sette: set, place, esteem
Shal: owe
Shapen: plan, devise, befall, cut out
Shaply: likely
Shawe: wood
Shende: disgrace, ruin, render contemptible, reproach
Shene: bright, fair
Shene: brightly
Shette: shut, enclose
Shorte: shorten
Shour: shower, onset, conflict
Shrewednesse: wickedness
Siker: sure
Siker: surely, uninterruptedly
Sikernesse: security
Sithen: since
Sitte: befit, suit
Skile: reason

Skilful: reasonable
Skilfully: reasonably
Slake: grow slack, wane
Slee: slay
Sleighly: cunningly
Sleighte: trickery; (pl.) plans
Slomeringe: slumber
Smitted: besmirched, dishonoured
Somdel: somewhat
Sonde: message, sending
Soor: sore, wound
Soor: grieved
Sort: lot, destiny, divination
Sorted: allotted
Sote: sweet
Sothe: truth
Soune: sound, utter, tend, relate to
Sowe: sew up
Span-newe: span-new, bran-new
Spare: spare, refrain
Sperred: barred
Spete: spit
Spore: spur
Spyr: spire, shoot
Stenten: leave off
Stere: helm, guide; *in stere:* upon my rudder
Stere: steer, rule
Stere: stir, move, excite, propose
Sterelees: rudderless
Sterte: start, go quickly, move away
Sterve: die
Stewe: small room
Stokked: fastened in the stocks
Stounde: time, hour, season
Stoundemele: at various times, from time to time
Straungely: distantly
Strecche: extend; *long streight:* stretched at full length
Stree: straw
Streite: closely
Substaunce: majority
Sucred: sugared
Suffisaunce: sufficiency
Suffraunt: patient
Surquidrie: arrogance
Suwe: follow
Swappe: strike, dash
Sweigh: motion, sway

Swelte: die
Swinke: toil
Swogh: swoon
Swote: sweetly
Swythe: quickly
Sye: sink down
Syke: sigh
Sythe: time

Take: take, give, come to pass
Tale: talk, speak
Talent: inclination, wish
Tecches: evil qualities, defects
Testif: headstrong
Thar: is necessary
Thee: thrive
Therto: besides
Thewes: habits, natural qualities
Thirlen: pierce
Tho: those
Tho: then
Thourgh-girt: struck through
To-sterte: start asunder
To-tere: rend, tear in pieces, deface
Tough: troublesome, pertinacious
Transmuwe: transform
Traunce: tramp about
Traysen: betray
Trete: treat, treat of, speak
Trewe: truce
Trist: trust
Triste: tryst, station
Triste: trust
Trowen: believe
Twinne: sever, part
Tyden: befall, happen

Unbroyden: unbraided
Ungiltif: guiltless
Unkindely: unnaturally
Unkouth: strange, wonderful
Unmighty: unable
Unneste: leave the nest
Unnethe: scarcely
Unnethes: scarcely
Unsely: unhappy
Unsittinge: unfit
Unskilful: foolish
Unthrift: nonsense
Unthrifty: profitless

Unwist: unknown; *unwist of:* uninformed of, unknown by

Unwrye: reveal

Ver: the spring

Verre: glass

Viage: voyage, expedition, attempt

Voyde: voidee, light dessert with wine and spices

Voyden: get rid of, expel

Voys: commendation, report

Waden: enter into

Wantrust: distrust

Warien: curse

Wayten: observe, expect

Wede: robe, garment

Weldy: active

Welken: heaven, sky

Wel-willy: benevolent

Wene: supposition, doubt

Wenen: suppose

Wente: turn, path, passage

Werbul: tune

Werne: refuse

Werre: war, trouble

Wey: way

Weymentinge: lament

Weyven: turn aside, waive, neglect

Wher: whether

Whylom: once, formerly

Whyt: white, i.e. silver

Wierdes: fates

Wight: person, man

Wikke: evil, wicked

Winde: turn, revolve, ply, bend

Winke: remain awake

Winne: win, gain, conquer; *winne fro:* get away from

Wis, wisly: certainly

Wisse: instruct

Wit: reason, judgment

Witen: know

Wivere: snake, wyvern

Wodnesse: madness

Wone: custom

Wone: dwell

Wood: mad

Woon: resource

Worthen: be, dwell; *worth up:* mount

Wouke, wyke: week

Wrathen: make angry

Wreche: vengeance, punishment

Wreke: avenge

Wrye: hide, disguise

Wryen: turn, go

Wrythe: turn aside, wriggle out, wreathe

Wyse: way, manner

Wyte: blame

Y-beten: beaten

Y-blowe: blown

Y-brend: burnt

Y-cleped: called, invoked

Ydel: idle, empty, vain

Y-drad: dreaded

Yë: eye

Yede: walked, went

Yelden: yield to, requite

Yelpe: boast, prate

Yerde: rod, stick

Yerne: soon; *as yerne:* very soon

Yerne: yearn for, be longed for, desire

Y-fere: together

Y-founde: found

Y-heried: praised

Y-japed: jested

Y-knet: knotted, tightly bound

Y-knowe: know, known

Y-lered: educated

Y-lissed: eased

Y-medled: mingled

Y-nogh, y-now: enough

Y-nome: caught, overcome

Y-norisshed: educated

Y-pleynted: full of complaint

Y-red: read

Y-ronne: run

Y-sene: seen

Y-shore: shorn

Y-sounded: sunk

Y-sworn: sworn

Y-thee: thrive

Y-wis: certainly

Y-wonne: gained, won

Y-wryen: hidden

Y-yeve: given

Abject: thing cast off
Abone: above
Abreyde: to start up, awake
Ago: gone away
Almous-deid: charity
Als: as
Aneuch: enough
Anis: once
A-per-se: A by itself, the chief letter, prime thing
Areir: away, gone
Aries: the constellation of the Ram, the first sign of the Zodiac
Atour: beyond
Auster: stern
Authoreist: authorized

Baid: abode
Baill: bale, sorrow
Bair: boar
Bait: food (for horses)
Bankouris: benches
Be: by the time that, when
Behest: promise
Beikit: warmed
Belyve: at once
Bene: excellently
Besene: arrayed
Beteich: bequeath
Bevar: made of beaver
Bill: proclamation
Bla: livid
Blaiknit: made bleak, deprived
Blenk: glance, look
Boun: ready
Brast: penetrated
Breird: the first shoots of grass, corn, or other crops; *on breird:* sprouting, growing
Breist: breast
Brent: high, smooth
Brukilnes: frailty
Brukkil: brittle

Buit: advantage, profit
Bullar: bubble
Burely: goodly, handsome
Buskit: adorned
Busteous: boisterous, rough, huge
But: without
By: with reference to
Bylis: boils, tumours

Cace: case; *in cace:* perchance
Cairful: full of care, mournful
Can: know; *can pas:* did pass; *can discend:* caused to descend
Caytive: wretched
Chair: chariot, car
Chalmer: chamber
Chese: choose
Cheverit: shivered
Clam: climbed
Clapper: clap-dish, as carried by lepers
Clim: climb
Conding: excellent
Convoy: escort
Cop: cup
Curage: heart
Cure: guard

Deformait: deformed, ugly
Degest: digested, considered
Deid: death
Deid: dead
Deificait: accounted as gods
Deming: suspicion
Diffinityve: definite
Dissimulait: full of dissimulation
Dooly: mournful
Douf: benumbed
Dour: stern, severe
Dressit: prepared
Drowpit: drooped
Drowry: love-token
Duleful: grievous
Dyte: ditty, song, poem

Efter: according as
Eird: earth
Eirdly: earthly
Electuairis: electuaries
Ene: eyes
Eöy: Eous
Esperaunce: hope
Ethios: Aethan
Evin: exactly
Expert: experienced
Expone: recount
Expuls: expulsion, repulse
Extasy: excited state of feeling

Fachioun: falchion
Facound: eloquent
Fair: fare
Fassoun: fashion
Fay: faith
Federed: feathered
Feill: experience, knowledge
Feird: fourth
Felloun: destructive
Felterit: matted
Feminitee: womanliness
Fenyeit: feigned
Fervent: severe
Flanis: arrows
Flash: sheaf, quiver
Foir-speikar: first speaker
For: for fear of
Force: of force, of necessity
Forlane: forlorn
For-quhy: because
Fortunait: afflicted by fortune
Fra: from, from the time
Frivoll: frivolous, poor, base
Fronsit: wrinkled

Gair: gore, strip
Garmound: garment
Garnisoun: garrison
Generabill: created
Gif: if
Giglot-lyk: wantonly
Grane: grain, minute particular
Gravin: buried
Greissis: grasses
Grouf: flat on the ground; *on grouf*: grovelling
Groundin: sharp
Gyte: mantle

Habirgeoun: coat of mail
Hace: hoarse
Hait: hot
Hanche: haunch, hip
Hard: heard
Haw: wan, dull of colour
Hecht: promised, was named
Heil: health
Heird: prob. for *heir it*, hear it
Heklit: drawn forward over
Herbery: shelter
Hewmound: helmet
Hoir: hoary, old, feeble
How: hollow
Hude: hood
Hy: haste

Inflat: inflated, blown
Intill: into

Kemmit: combed
Keip: heed

Lak: reproof, blame, reproach
Lattit: hindered
Lawfully: according to law
Lawtee: loyalty
Lazarous: leper
Le: lie
Leid: lead
Leid: person
Leir: learn
Lipper: belonging to lepers, leprous
Lipper-leid: leper-folk
Listis: borders
Ludge: lodging house
Luifis: of love
Lyart: grey
Lybel: bill (of divorce)
Lyre: complexion
Lyte: little

Maculait: stained
Mavis: thrush
Meid: reward, recompense
Meldrop: hanging drop of mucus
Merle: blackbird
Ming: mingle, mix
Modify: adjudge, appoint, specify
Mowlit: mouldy
Mufe: move, provoke

Nar: nearer
Neist: nearest
New, of the new: newly
None: noon
Nureis: nurse
Nyce: elaborate

Oftsyis: oftentimes
Orature: oratory
Ourfret: covered over
Ourspred: overspread
Outhir: either
Outwaill: outcast

Pane: plot of ground, bed for flowers
Part: give
Peirry: perry
Peirsing: piercing
Pensivenes: sadness
Peros: Pyroeis
Philegoney: Phlegon
Ply: plight
Poleist: polished
Precelling: excelling
Preif: prove, make trial
Prene: brooch
Pungitive: stinging

Quair: book
Quhair: where
Quhais: whose, of which
Quheill: wheel
Quhill: until
Quhisling: whistling
Quhyl: sometimes
Quhytly: whitish

Rawk: hoarse
Recure: recovery
Regrait: complaint
Remeid: remedy
Remuf: move away, change
Responsaill: response
Ressoun: declaration
Rethory: rhetoric
Retour: return
Returne: throw back
Reull: rule, order
Rin: run; *can rin:* did run
Rinkis: men

Rois: rose
Roising: growing rosy
Roun: whisper
Rousty: rusty
Ruik: rook
Ruse: praise

Sa, so.
Sad: settled, constant, steadfast
Saipheron: made with saffron
Sait: seat
Sals: sauce
Sawin: sown
Scantly: scarcely
Seid: seed
Sermone: discourse
Sessoun: seasoning
Sey: sea
Shaddow: reflection, image
Shed: dispersed
Shill: shrilly
Sho: she
Sowpit: drenched
Soyr: sorrel
Speid: speed; *good speid:* eagerly, quickly
Speiris: asks
Spille: destroy
Spreit: spirit
Spurnis: kickest
Stad: beset
Starkly: strongly, severely
Starnis: stars
Steir: govern
Steir: stir
Stevin: voice
Stounde: sudden pain
Stro: straw
Suld: should
Sum-deill: somewhat
Suppois: though
Swak: throw; *can swak:* threw
Sweit: sweat
Swelt: fainted
Syching: sighing
Sylit: ceiled, covered
Syte: sorrow

Taidis: toads
Taikning: token
Tene: anger
Tho: then

Thocht: though
Thoillit: suffered
Traistit: trusted
Tuilyour: quarreller; *tuilyour-lyk:* quarrelsome
Tytan: the sun

Unfair: horribly
Unricht: wrongly

Vailing: lowering
Variance: change
Vocacioun: calling of an assembly

Wa: sad
Waillit: chosen
Wait: knows
Wanhope: despair
War: worse

Weid: dress
Weir: guard, ward off
Weird: destiny
Weiris: wears, wastes away
Wellis: streams, rills
Welterit: overturned
Wicht: wight, man
Widderit: withered, faded
Will of wane: at a loss what to do
Woir: carried, wafted away
Wonder: very
Wraikful: vengeful
Wrait: wrote
Wrak: vengeance
Wyr: wire
Wyte: blame

Yeid: went
Yet: gate
Yse-shoklis: icicles